Ruchira Avatar Adi Da Samraj

It is obvious, from all sorts of subtle details, that he knows what IT's all about . . . a rare being.

ALAN WATTS
author, *The Way of Zen* and *The Wisdom of Insecurity*

I regard Adi Da Samraj as one of the greatest teachers in the Western world today.

IRINA TWEEDIE
Sufi teacher; author, *Chasm of Fire*

I recognize the God-Presence Incarnate in Adi Da Samraj as whole and full and complete.

BARBARA MARX HUBBARD
author, *Conscious Evolution* and *The Revelation;*
president, The Foundation for Conscious Evolution

Adi Da Samraj has created virtually the entire basis for a culture founded in love and wisdom. The magnitude of such an undertaking— let alone the accomplishment of it—cannot be overstated.

JOHN WHITE
author, *Frontiers of Consciousness,*
and *The Meeting of Science and Spirit*

Adi Da Samraj is a man who has truly walked in Spirit and given true enlightenment to many.

SUN BEAR
founder, the Bear Tribe Medicine Society

The life and teaching of Avatar Adi Da Samraj are of profound and decisive spiritual significance at this critical moment in history.

BRYAN DESCHAMP
Senior Adviser at the United Nations
High Commission for Refugees;
former Dean of the Carmelite House of Studies, Australia;
former Dean of Trinity College, University of Melbourne

A great teacher with the dynamic ability to awaken in his listeners something of the Divine Reality in which he is grounded, with which he is identified, and which, in fact, he is.

ISRAEL REGARDIE
author, *The Golden Dawn*

A di Da Samraj has spoken directly to the heart of our human situation— the shocking gravity of our brief and unbidden lives. Through his words I have experienced a glimmering of eternal life, and view my own existence as timeless and spaceless in a way that I never have before.

RICHARD GROSSINGER
author, *Planet Medicine*

A vatar Adi Da is the greatest Spiritual Master ever to walk the earth. He is the God-Man. He reveals the ultimate truth residing in the human heart.

THE REVEREND THOMAS E. AHLBURN
Senior Minister, First Unitarian Church
Providence, Rhode Island

M y relationship with Adi Da Samraj over many years has only confirmed His Realization and the Truth of His impeccable Teaching. He is much more than simply an inspiration of my music, but is really a living demonstration that perfect transcendence is actually possible. This is both a great relief and a great challenge. If you thirst for truth, here is a rare opportunity to drink.

RAY LYNCH
composer and musician, *Deep Breakfast;*
The Sky of Mind; and *Ray Lynch, Best Of*

A di Da Samraj and his unique body of teaching work offer a rare and extraordinary opportunity for those courageous students who are ready to move beyond ego and take the plunge into deepest communion with the Absolute. Importantly, the teaching is grounded in explicit discussion of necessary psychospiritual evolution and guides the student to self-responsibility and self-awareness.

ELISABETH TARG, M.D.
University of California, San Francisco,
School of Medicine;
director, Complementary Medicine Research Institute,
California Pacific Medical Center

That God can, among other things, actually incarnate in human form once seemed unbelievable to me. But reading the books of Avatar Adi Da obliterated all doubt about the existence of God right now, here on Earth in human form.

CHARMIAN ANDERSON, PH.D.
psychologist; author, *Bridging Heaven and Earth* and *The Heart of Success*

Fly to the side of this God-Man. His Divine Transmission works miracles of change not possible by any other Spiritual means.

LEE SANNELLA, M.D.
author, *The Kundalini Experience*

When I first read the Word of Avatar Adi Da Samraj, I was immediately transported into a state of wonderment and awe. Could it be? Could the Divine Person be here now, in this time and place? It didn't take long for my heart to answer a resounding "Yes". May the whole world be restored to Faith, Love, and Understanding by the Mystery of Real God, here and Incarnate as Avatar Adi Da Samraj.

ED KOWALCZYK
lead singer and songwriter of the rock band, *Live*

I regard the work of Adi Da and his devotees as one of the most penetrating spiritual and social experiments happening on the planet in our era.

JEFFREY MISHLOVE, PH.D.
host, PBS television series, *Thinking Allowed*; author, *The Roots of Consciousness*

Adi Da's Teachings have tremendous significance for humanity. . . . He represents a foundation and a structure for sanity.

ROBERT K. HALL, M.D.
psychiatrist; author, *Out of Nowhere*; co-founder, The Lomi School and Lomi Clinic

The Divine World-Teacher,
RUCHIRA AVATAR ADI DA SAMRAJ
Lopez Island, 2000

THE <u>ONLY</u> COMPLETE WAY TO REALIZE THE UNBROKEN LIGHT OF <u>REAL</u> GOD

THE SEVENTEEN COMPANIONS
OF THE TRUE DAWN HORSE

BOOK THREE

An Introductory Overview
Of The "Radical" Divine Way
Of The True World-Religion Of Adidam

By
The Divine World-Teacher,

RUCHIRA AVATAR ADI DA SAMRAJ

THE DAWN HORSE PRESS
MIDDLETOWN, CALIFORNIA

NOTE TO THE READER

All who study the Way of Adidam or take up its practice should remember that they are responding to a Call to become responsible for themselves. They should understand that they, not Avatar Adi Da Samraj or others, are responsible for any decision they make or action they take in the course of their lives of study or practice.

The devotional, Spiritual, functional, practical, relational, cultural, and formal community practices and disciplines referred to in this book are appropriate and natural practices that are voluntarily and progressively adopted by members of the four congregations of Adidam (as applicable for each of the congregations and as appropriate to the personal circumstance of each individual). Although anyone may find these practices useful and beneficial, they are not presented as advice or recommendations to the general reader or to anyone who is not a member of one of the four congregations of Adidam. And nothing in this book is intended as a diagnosis, prescription, or recommended treatment or cure for any specific "problem", whether medical, emotional, psychological, social, or Spiritual. One should apply a particular program of treatment, prevention, cure, or general health only in consultation with a licensed physician or other qualified professional.

The Only Complete Way To Realize The Unbroken Light Of Real God is formally authorized for publication by the Ruchira Sannyasin Order of the Tantric Renunciates of Adidam, as part of the Standard Edition of the Divine "Source-Texts" of the Divine World-Teacher, Ruchira Avatar Adi Da Samraj. (The Ruchira Sannyasin Order of the Tantric Renunciates of Adidam is the senior Spiritual and Cultural Authority within the formal gathering of formally acknowledged devotees of the Divine World-Teacher, Ruchira Avatar Adi Da Samraj.)

NOTE TO BIBLIOGRAPHERS: The correct form for citing Ruchira Avatar Adi Da Samraj's Name (in any form of alphabetized listing) is:

Adi Da Samraj, Ruchira Avatar

© 2000 The Da Love-Ananda Samrajya Pty Ltd,
as trustee for The Da Love-Ananda Samrajya.
All rights reserved.
No part of this book may be copied or reproduced in any manner without written permission from the publisher.

The Da Love-Ananda Samrajya Pty Ltd, as trustee for The Da Love-Ananda Samrajya, claims perpetual copyright to this book, to the entire Written (and otherwise recorded) Wisdom-Teaching of Avatar Adi Da Samraj, and to all other writings and recordings of the Way of Adidam.

COVER: Both the central image and the border image are photographs taken by Avatar Adi Da Samraj. Please see "Camera Illuminata: The 'Bright'-Field Photography of Avatar Adi Da Samraj", pp. 39-41.

Printed in the United States of America

Produced by the Eleutherian Pan-Communion of Adidam in cooperation with the Dawn Horse Press

International Standard Book Number: 1-57097-107-2
Library of Congress Card Number: 00-192145

CONTENTS

THE ONLY COMPLETE WAY TO REALIZE THE UNBROKEN LIGHT OF REAL GOD

FIRST WORD:
Do Not Misunderstand Me—
I Am Not "Within" you, but you Are In Me,
and I Am Not a Mere "Man" in the "Middle" of Mankind,
but All of Mankind Is Surrounded, and Pervaded,
and Blessed By Me
49

PROLOGUE:
My Divine Disclosure
71

PART ONE:
I Am The "Who"
That Is Always Already The Case
85

RUCHIRA AVATAR ADI DA SAMRAJ
The Mountain Of Attention, 2000

Introduction

This book is an invitation to enter a different world. A world that is completely <u>real</u>, in the largest possible sense of that word. A world in which none of the sufferings and difficulties of life are ignored or denied—but also a world in which yearnings for truth, wisdom, happiness, and love are addressed at an extraordinary depth. A world in which there is real, trustable guidance through the "maze" of life's confusions and crises. A world that vastly exceeds all limited notions of what is "real". A world of deep, abiding joy.

People from all walks of life have felt this world open up to them when they read the books of the Divine World-Teacher, Ruchira Avatar Adi Da Samraj. Those of us who have done so have felt our deepest questions answered, our most profound heart-longings satisfied. We have treasured His Instruction about the real issues everyone faces: death, sex, intimacy, emotional maturity, community life, and many more. We have marveled at His precise "map" of the entire course of Spiritual life, and at His description of the nature of reality in all its dimensions. We have been sobered by His criticism of the universal human bondage to the self-centered desires and purposes of the ego. And, altogether, through His words, we have felt His Divine Spiritual Blessing deeply affecting our lives.

Those of us who have been drawn to Avatar Adi Da have discovered that the impact of His Truth (and the Blessing it conveys) is so great in our lives, so far beyond anything else we have known, that a truly amazing recognition began to grow in our hearts and minds: Avatar Adi Da Samraj is not merely a great human being who speaks profound Truth—He is the Divine Reality Itself, Appearing in a human body in order to Offer His Revelation of Truth directly to all of humankind.

Often, this awakened recognition of Him—as the Divine Reality Present in human Form—comes as a complete surprise. In this age of skepticism, many regard the idea of a Divine Incarnation as strictly mythological. But Avatar Adi Da Samraj is not a myth— He is an intensely real living being. He is an utterly spontaneous and free manifestation, moved (by overwhelming love) to serve the Happiness and Liberation of beings everywhere, and to bring our global home out of this time of potential political and ecological disaster.

However, no one is asked to "believe" that Avatar Adi Da is the Divine. He has even said, "You must not believe in Me." Why? Because mere belief is not transformative. Only what is revealed in one's real experience—of body, heart, and mind altogether, rather than mind only—can transform the being. Therefore, Avatar Adi Da does not offer you a set of beliefs, or even a set of Spiritual techniques. He simply offers you His Revelation of Truth as a free gift, to respond to as you will. And, if you are moved to take up His Way, He invites you to enter into a direct Spiritual relationship with Him. Those of us who have taken this step have found the Spiritual relationship to Avatar Adi Da Samraj to be a supremely precious gift, a literally miraculous blessing, the answer to our deepest longings—greatly surpassing anything we have ever experienced or even imagined to be possible. Indeed, we have found Avatar Adi Da's Revelation of Truth to be so all-encompassing and His Spiritual Power and Love to be so overwhelming that we recognize Him as the Promised God-Man—the One capable of fulfilling the yearnings of people everywhere, the One Whose Appearance has been foreshadowed by prophecies in many religious traditions.

Avatar Adi Da began Teaching formally in 1972. In the years since then, He has communicated a vast store of Wisdom. But He has also done far more than that: He has created a whole new Way of life, a new religion, which is now practiced by people of different cultures in many parts of the world.

Just as the religions of Christianity and Buddhism are named after their founders, the religion founded by Avatar Adi Da is named after Him—it is called "Adidam" (AH-dee-DAHM). Adidam is an all-embracing practice that takes every aspect of human life—the "lowest" as well as the "highest"—into account (see pp. 364-65). The foundation of Adidam is the response of heart-felt devotion to Avatar Adi Da Samraj, in loving gratitude for His Gifts of Wisdom and Spiritual Blessing.

Avatar Adi Da's books are full of ecstatic proclamations of His Divinity—and there is a secret to understanding these proclamations fully. The secret is this: Avatar Adi Da is not speaking as a separate being who presumes himself to be irreducibly "different" from every other being. No, He is speaking as the Divine Heart of every being. Therefore, His most fundamental message may be summarized as follows:

> There is no ultimate "difference" between you and the Divine.
> There is only the Divine.
> Everything that exists is a "modification" of the One Divine Reality.

However, even though it may be true that there is only the Divine, this is not, in fact, our common daily experience. Far from it! Our usual daily life is full of events and people (including ourselves!) that we experience as distinctly un-Divine.

Therefore, Avatar Adi Da is humanly present in the world in order to Reveal the Divine Condition, and to make it possible for human beings to Realize that that Condition is our True Nature. That this is so is the deep heart-certainty of Avatar Adi Da's devotees—after many years of studying His Teaching, hearing His Discourses, enjoying His Company in all kinds of circumstances, and knowing the profound Ecstasy, Joy, and Peace of His Spiritual Transmission.

Thus, when Avatar Adi Da Samraj says "I Am the One to be Realized" or "I Am the Very Divine Person" or "I Am the Divine Heart Itself" (and many other variations), He is confessing that He is, paradoxically, the Divine Condition of everyone and everything—seeming to be a separate being, in order to offer us the Way to Realize our Inherent Condition. And it is our confession to you, as those who have become His devotees, that to behold Him with an open heart is to fall into an indescribable Love, Bliss, and Happiness that is self-evidently the deepest Truth of one's own heart and the Very Heart of Existence.

As Avatar Adi Da Samraj says, with great passion and emphasis:

Beloved, Even I Am Only You (<u>As</u> You <u>Are</u>).

This is the great mystery that you are invited to discover for yourself.

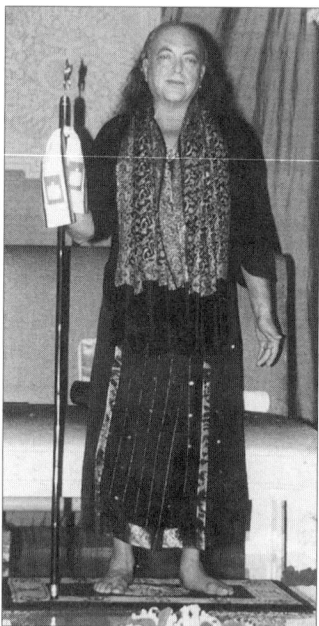

Avatar Adi Da Samraj's Name is composed of four Sanskrit words.

His principal Name is "Adi Da". "Avatar" and "Samraj" are sacred Titles, used in association with His Name.

"Adi" (AH-dee) means "Original" (or "Primordial"), and "Da" means "the Divine Giver". Thus, "Adi Da" means "the Original Divine Giver".

"Avatar" means "a 'Crossing Down' of the Divine Being into the world" (or, in other words, "an Appearance of the Divine in conditionally manifested form").

"Samraj" (sahm-RAHJ) means "universal Lord".

In fuller forms of reference, Adi Da Samraj is called "the Ruchira (roo-CHIH-rah) Avatar", meaning "the Avatar of Infinite Brightness".

Avatar Adi Da Samraj: His Life and Teaching

The Three Great Purposes of Avatar Adi Da Samraj: Learning Man, Teaching Man, and Blessing Man

From the moment of His Birth (in New York, on November 3, 1939), Adi Da Samraj was Consciously Aware of His Native Divine Condition. As soon as He became able to use language, He gave this Condition a simple but very expressive Name—"the 'Bright'".* But then, at the age of two years, Avatar Adi Da made a profound spontaneous choice. He chose to relinquish His constant Enjoyment of the "Bright"—out of what He Describes as a "painful loving", a sympathy for the suffering and ignorance of human beings. Avatar Adi Da Confesses that He chose to "Learn Man"—to enter into everything that humankind feels and suffers, and also to experience all the various levels of Spiritual Realization known to humanity—in order to discover how to Draw human beings into the "Bright" Divine Condition that He knew as His own True State and the True State of everyone.

This utter Submission to all aspects of human life was the first Purpose of Adi Da's Incarnation. In His Spiritual Autobiography, *The Knee Of Listening*, Avatar Adi Da recounts this amazing and heroic Ordeal, which lasted for the first thirty years of His Life.

*For definitions of terms and names, please see the Glossary (pp. 412-49).

In 1970, Avatar Adi Da finally Re-Awakened permanently to the "Bright", and embarked upon the second great Purpose of His Incarnation—the Process of "Teaching Man".

When He began to Teach others, Avatar Adi Da Samraj simply made Himself available to all who were willing to enter into the living Process of Real-God-Realization in His Company—a Process Which He summarized as the relation-

Los Angeles, 1972

ship to Him, rather than any method or technique of Spiritual attainment. Through that relationship—an extraordinary human and Spiritual intimacy—Avatar Adi Da Samraj perfectly embraced

The Mountain Of Attention Sanctuary, 1974

each of His devotees, using every kind of skillful means to Awaken them to the Truth that the separate, un-Enlightened self—with all its fear, anxieties, and fruitless seeking for Happiness— is self-imposed suffering, a contraction of the being (which He calls "the self-contraction").

Happiness, He Revealed, cannot be attained through any kind of search, because It is "Always Already the Case". And He Offered the practice of heart-Communion with Him as the means of going beyond the self-contraction and thereby Realizing Real Happiness.

I have Come to Live (now, and forever hereafter) with those who love Me with ego-overwhelming love, and I have Come to Love them likewise Overwhelmingly. . . .

Until you fall in love, love is what you _fear_ to do. When you have fallen in love, and you _are_ (thus) always already in love, then you cease to fear to love . . . . Those who fall in love with Me, Fall into Me. Those whose hearts are given, in love, to Me, Fall into My Heart. ["*What Will You Do If You Love Me?*", *from* Da Love-Ananda Gita]

In 1986, an Event occurred that marked the beginning of a great change in Avatar Adi Da's Work in the world. In this Great Event, a profound Yogic Swoon (taking the form of His apparent near-death) overwhelmed His body-mind, and Avatar Adi Da Samraj spontaneously began the process of relinquishing His Ordeal of Learning and Teaching Man. In the wake of that great Swoon, He simply Radiated His Divinity as never before. This was the beginning of what He calls His "Divine Self-'Emergence'". From that moment, Adi Da Samraj has devoted

The Mountain Of Attention, 1986

Himself increasingly to the third and eternal Purpose of His Avataric Incarnation—that of "Blessing Man" (and even all beings).

The Way of Adidam

Even after the Great Event in 1986, Avatar Adi Da continued to Work to ensure that His Revelation of the Way of Adidam was fully and firmly founded in the world. It was not until February 1999 that Avatar Adi Da Samraj declared that all the foundation Work of His Incarnation had been completely and finally Done. Everything necessary for the understanding and right practice of the real religious process, culminating in Divine Enlightenment, has been Said and Done by Him. The summary of His Wisdom-Teaching is preserved for all time in a series of twenty-three "Source-Texts" (described on pp. 27-38). And the Way of Adidam is fully established. This monumental Work has been accomplished by Avatar Adi Da in a little over a quarter of a century—twenty-seven years of ceaseless Instruction, in constant interaction with His devotees.

Avatar Adi Da's Full Revelation of Truth and His Work to establish the Way of Adidam required an immense struggle. The reason that struggle was inevitable is that human beings—especially in this time when the "individual" is regarded to be the supreme measure of value—have enormous resistance to any process that requires them to go beyond ego. Throughout history, people have tended to prefer forms of religion based on a system of beliefs and a code of moral and social behavior. But this kind of religion, as Avatar Adi Da has always pointed out, does not go to the core, to the root-suffering of human beings. This is because ordinary religion, rather than going beyond the ego-principle, is actually <u>based</u> on it: the ego-self stands at the center, and the Divine is sought and appealed to as the great Power that is going to save and satisfy the individual self. Avatar Adi Da Describes such religion as "client-centered".

In contrast to conventional religion, there is the process that Avatar Adi Da calls "true religion", religion that is centered in the Divine, in response to a true Spiritual Master who has (to at least some significant degree) <u>Realized</u> God (as opposed to merely offering teachings <u>about</u> God). Thus, true religion does not revolve around the individual's desire for any kind of "spiritual" consolations or experience—it is ego-transcending, rather than ego-serving. True religion based on ego-surrendering devotion to a Spiritual Master has existed for thousands of years, but the ecstatic confession of Avatar Adi Da's devotees is that now the Very Divine Itself is directly Present, Functioning as Divine Heart-Master, Alive in the human form of Avatar Adi Da Samraj.

All religions are historical forms of the Single and Ancient Way of Distracted love for the Divine Person, especially as Revealed in the Life and in the Company and in the Person of Incarnate Adepts (or Realizers) in their various degrees and stages of Realization. This is the Great Secret. ["What Will You Do If You Love Me?", from Da Love-Ananda Gita]

[E]goity is the "disease" that all the true Spiritual Masters of religion come here to cure. Unfortunately, . . . religious and Spiritual institutions tend to develop along lines that serve, accommodate, and represent the common egoity—and this is why the esoteric true Teachings of true Spiritual Masters tend to be bypassed, and even suppressed, in the drive to develop the exoteric cult of any particular Spiritual Master.

The relationship to Me . . . is a profound esoteric discipline, necessarily associated with real and serious and mature . . . practice of the "radical" Way (or root-Process) of Realizing Real God (Which Is Reality and Truth).

The Way of Adidam is the . . . Way to live in Freedom—not to be bound by separate and separative self, or by conditional Nature as a whole. Therefore, the ego-transcending devotional relationship to Me is the Context and the Means of Free Divine Self-Realization. ["Beyond the Cultic Tendency in Religion and Spirituality, and in Secular Society", from Ruchira Avatara Gita]

Standing Free of the Common Egoity

In His Spiritual Work with His devotees and the world, Avatar Adi Da Samraj has confronted the realities of egoity in a completely direct and unflinching manner. In His years of "Teaching Man", He did not hesitate in the slightest to grapple with the ego as it might be manifested in any moment by an individual devotee or a group of devotees—for the sake of helping His devotees understand and go beyond their ego-possessed disposition and activity.

However, even in the midst of that compassionate struggle with the forces of egoity, Avatar Adi Da has always Stood utterly Free of the ego-world. And, especially since the late 1970s, that Free Stand more and more took the form of His living in an essentially private circumstance, at one of the Hermitages established for Him (at secluded locations in California, Hawaii, and Fiji—see p. 373). In His Hermitage sphere, Avatar Adi Da is served by an intimate group of renunciate devotees, with whom He does particularly intensive Spiritual Work. And it is in the set-apart domain of His Hermitages (rather than in some kind of more public setting) that Avatar Adi Da receives His devotees in general (and, on rare occasions, specially invited members of the public), to Grant them His Spiritual Blessing.

The reasons why Avatar Adi Da maintains a Hermitage life are profound. The purpose of His Existence is to Reveal the Divine Reality—in other words, to Manifest the Freedom, Purity, and unbounded Blissfulness of His own Divine Nature, to Exist simply as He Is, without having to make compromises or adjustments in order to "fit in" to the ordinary ego-patterned world. Therefore, it is essential that He live in a sacred domain that conforms to Him and to the nature of His Spiritual Work, where He can remain independent of (but not disconnected from) the common world, even the daily world of the practical functioning of His community of devotees. Indeed, it is essential that He be free of institutional or organizational responsibilities relative to the gathering of His own devotees—because any such level of functioning would be a limitation on His Spiritual Work, an impingement on His Freedom to Manifest His own True Nature in the fullest and most pristine manner.

As He has commented many times, His Hermitage life is a life of seclusion, but not of isolation. His secluded Hermitage life is what allows His Divine Blessing to Flow into the world with the greatest possible force and effectiveness—it is what allows His Spiritual connection to all beings to be as strong as possible.

The "Problem" Is ego—
Not Anything Else

For more than a quarter of a century, during His years of Teaching and Revelation (from 1972 to 1999), Avatar Adi Da undertook a vast, in-life "consideration" with His devotees of everything related to Spiritual life—from the most rudimentary matters to the most esoteric. One extremely important area of "consideration" was how to rightly relate to the most basic urges and activities of human life—what Avatar Adi Da describes as the realm of "money, food, and sex". (By "money", Avatar Adi Da means not only the earning and use of money itself, but the exercising of life-energy in general.)

In most religious traditions, an ascetical approach to these primal urges is recommended—in other words, desires related to "money, food, and sex" are to be minimized or denied. Avatar Adi Da took a different approach. When they are rightly engaged, ordinary human enjoyments are not a problem, not "sinful" or "anti-spiritual" in and of themselves. Thus, the root-problem of human beings is not any particular activity or desire of the body-mind, but the ego itself—the governing presumption that one is a separate and independent entity, threatened by the inevitable prospect of death. Therefore, in living dialogue and experimentation with His devotees, Avatar Adi Da brought to light, in detail, exactly how the human functions of money (or life-energy), food, and sex can be rightly engaged, in a truly ego-transcending manner—an entirely life-positive and non-suppressive manner that is both pleasurable and supportive of the Spiritual process in His Company.

The transcending of egoic involvement with "money, food, and sex" is a matter that relates to the beginnings of (or preparation for) real Spiritual practice. But the necessity for ego-transcendence does not end there. In His years of Teaching and Revelation, Avatar Adi Da Revealed that the ego is still present, in one form or another, in all the possible varieties of Spiritual attainment short of Most Perfect Divine Enlightenment. The word "Enlightenment" is used by different people and in different traditions with various different meanings. In Avatar Adi Da's language, "Enlightenment" (which He sometimes modifies, for the sake of clarifying His meaning, as "Most Perfect Divine Enlightenment", and which is synonymous with "Divine Self-Realization", "Real-God-Realization", and "seventh stage Realization") specifically means that the process of ego-transcendence has been entirely completed, relative to all the dimensions of the being. In other words, the ego has been transcended in three distinct phases—first at the physical (or gross) level (the level of "money, food, and sex"), then at the subtle level (the level of internal visions, auditions, and all kinds of mystical experience), and finally at the causal level (the root-level of conscious existence, wherein the sense of "I" and "other", or the subject-object dichotomy, seems to arise in Consciousness).

The complete process of ego-transcendence is extraordinarily profound and can only proceed on the basis of all the foundation disciplines and an ever-increasing heart-surrender to the Blessing-Transmission of Adi Da Samraj. Then, progressively, there is a transformation of view, a "positive disillusionment" (in Adi Da's Words) with each phase of egoity—until there is Most Perfect Divine Enlightenment (or "Open Eyes"), the Realization of Consciousness Itself as the Single Love-Blissful Reality and Source of existence.

Thus, the Way of Adidam truly represents an extraordinary and unique Offering to humankind. It is the Way Given by the Primal Divine Realizer and Revealer of Most Perfect Divine Enlightenment. He Transmits the Divinely Enlightened State, and He has the Power to Draw His devotees into that Perfectly Love-Blissful State. Such great statements about Avatar Adi Da Samraj are not something to be either accepted or rejected as a matter of belief. Rather, they are His Free Self-Confession to you—and His invitation to you to fall into His Divine Embrace.

A Testimony of Spiritual Practice

The process of the Way of Adidam unfolds by Avatar Adi Da's Grace, according to the depth of surrender and response in each devotee. One of the most extraordinary living testimonies to the Greatness and Truth of the Way of Adidam is one of Avatar Adi Da's longtime devotees, whose renunciate name is Ruchira Adidama Sukha Sundari Naitauba. Adidama Sukha Sundari has totally consecrated herself to Avatar Adi Da and lives always in His Sphere, in a relationship of unique intimacy and service. By her profound love of, and most exemplary surrender to, her Divine Heart-Master, she has become combined with Him at a unique depth. She manifests the signs of deep and constant immersion in His Divine Being, both in meditation and daily life. Adidama Sukha Sundari is a member of the Ruchira Sannyasin Order (the senior cultural authority within the gathering of Avatar Adi Da's devotees), practicing in the ultimate stages of the Way of Adidam.

Through a process of more than twenty years of intense testing, Avatar Adi Da has been able to lead Adidama Sukha Sundari to the threshold of Divine Enlightenment. The profound and ecstatic relationship with Avatar Adi Da that Adidama Sukha Sundari has come to know can be felt in this intimate letter of devotional confession to Him:

Ruchira Adidama Sukha Sundari
Naitauba with Ruchira Avatar
Adi Da Samraj, 1999

RUCHIRA ADIDAMA SUKHA SUNDARI: Bhagavan Love-Ananda, Supreme and Divine Person, Real-God-Body of Love,

I rest in Your Constant and Perfect Love-Embrace, with no need but to forever worship You. Suddenly in love, Mastered at heart, always with my head at Your Supreme and Holy Feet, I am beholding and recognizing Your "Bright" Divine Person. My Beloved, You so "Brightly" Descend and utterly Convert this heart, mind, body, and breath, from separate self to the "Bhava" of Your Love-Bliss-Happiness.

Supreme Lord Ruchira, the abandonment of the contracted personality, the relinquishment of ego-bondage to the world, and the profound purification and release of ego-limitations—all brought about by Your Grace, throughout the years since I first came to You—has culminated in a great comprehensive force of one-pointed devotion to You and a great certainty in the Inherent Sufficiency of Realization Itself. The essence of my practice is to always remain freely submitted and centralized in You—the Condition Prior to all bondage, all modification, and all illusion.

My Beloved Lord Ruchira, You have Moved me to renounce all egoic "bonding" with conditionally manifested others, conditionally manifested worlds, and conditionally manifested self, to enter into the depths of this "in-love" and utter devotion to You. Finding You has led to a deep urge to abandon all superficiality and to simply luxuriate in Your Divine Body and Person. All separation is shattered in Your Divine Love-Bliss-"Bhava". Your Infusion is Utter. I feel You everywhere.

I am Drawn, by Grace of Your Spiritual Presence, into profound meditative Contemplation of Your Divine State. Sometimes, when I am entering into these deep states of meditation, I remain vaguely aware of the body, and particularly of the breath and the heart-beat. I feel the heart and lungs slow down. Then I am sometimes aware of my breath and heartbeat being suspended in a state of Yogic sublimity. Then there is no awareness of body, no awareness of mind, no perceptual awareness, and no conceptual awareness. There is only abiding in Contemplation of You in Your Domain of Consciousness Itself. And, when I resume association with the body and begin once again to hear my breath and heartbeat, I feel the remarkable Power of Your Great Samadhi. I feel no necessity for anything, and I feel Your Capability to Bless and Change and Meditate all. I can feel how this entrance into objectless worship of You as Consciousness Itself (allowing this Abiding to deepen ever so profoundly, by utter submission of separate self to You) establishes me in a different relationship to everything that arises.

My Beloved Bhagavan, Love-Ananda, I have Found You. Now, by Your Grace, I am able to behold You and live in this constant Embrace. This is my Joy and Happiness and the Yoga of ego-renunciation I engage. [October 11, 1997]

Inherent in this confession is the certainty that lasting happiness cannot be found in the things of the world, all of which change and die. This is a crucial understanding—which is at the foundation of real religious life, and which grows over time as one advances in the Spiritual process.

AVATAR ADI DA SAMRAJ: Absolutely NOTHING conditional is satisfactory. Everything conditional disappears—everything. This fact should move the heart to cling to Me, to resort to Me, to take refuge in Me. This is why people become devotees of Mine. This is the reason for the religious life. The unsatisfactoriness of conditional existence requires resort to the Divine Source, and the Realization of the Divine Source-Condition. [August 9, 1997]

Finding Real Happiness

This book is Avatar Adi Da's invitation to you to come to know Him—by freely considering His words, and feeling their impact on your life and heart. Avatar Adi Da Himself has never been satisfied with anything conditional. He has never been satisfied with anything less than Real, Permanent, Absolute Happiness—even in the midst of the inevitable sufferings of life. And that Happiness is What He is Offering to you.

The heart has a question.
The heart must be Satisfied.
Without that Satisfaction—Which is necessarily Spiritual in Nature—there is no Real Happiness.

The contraction of the heart is what you are suffering.
It is the ego.
The egoic life is a search—founded upon (and initiated by) the self-contraction of the total body-mind.
The egoic life is a self-caused search to be relieved of the distress of self-reduced, self-diminished, even utterly self-destroyed Love-Bliss.

Love-Bliss gone, non-existent, unknown—just this pumping, agitated, psycho-physical thing.

The ego-"I" does not know What It Is That Is Happening.
You are just "hanging out" for a while, until "it" drops dead.
It is not good enough.
Therefore, I Advise you to begin to be profoundly religious, and not waste any time about it.

You must Realize the Spiritual Condition of Existence Itself . . . .
You cannot be sane if you think there is only flesh, only materiality, only grossness.
Such thinking is not fully "natural", not enough.
There is "Something" you are not accounting for.
Be open to "Whatever" That Is.
You must look into this. [Hridaya Rosary]

Avatar Adi Da Samraj's Teaching-Word: The "Source-Texts" of Adidam

For twenty-seven years (from 1972 to 1999), Avatar Adi Da Samraj devoted Himself tirelessly to Teaching those who came to Him. Even before He formally began to Teach in 1972, He had already written the earliest versions of two of His primary Texts—His "liturgical drama" (*The Mummery*) and His Spiritual Autobiography (*The Knee Of Listening*). Then, when He opened the doors of His first Ashram in Hollywood (on April 25, 1972), He initiated a vast twenty-seven-year "conversation" with the thousands of people who approached Him during that period of time—a "conversation" that included thousands of hours of sublime and impassioned Discourse and thousands of pages of profound and exquisite Writing. And the purpose of that "conversation" was to fully communicate the Truth for Real.

Both His Speech and His Writing were conducted as a kind of living "laboratory". He was constantly asking to hear His devotees' questions and their responses to His Written and Spoken Word. He was constantly calling His devotees to <u>live</u> what He was Teaching and discover its Truth in their own experience—not merely to passively accept it as dogma. He was constantly testing whether His communication on any particular subject was complete and detailed enough or whether He needed to say more. And everything He said and wrote was a spontaneous expression of His own direct Awareness of Reality—never a merely theoretical or speculative proposition, never a statement merely inherited from traditional sources.

This immense outpouring of Revelation and Instruction came to completion in the years 1997-1999. During that period, Avatar

Adi Da Samraj created a series of twenty-three books that He designated as the "Source-Texts" of Adidam. He incorporated into these books His most essential Writings and Discourses from all the preceding years, as well as many new Writings and Discourses that had never been published previously. His magnificent "Source-Texts" are thus His Eternal Message to all. They contain His complete Revelation of Truth, and (together with the "Supportive Texts", in which Avatar Adi Da Gives further detailed Instruction relative to the functional, practical, relational, and cultural disciplines of the Way of Adidam) they give His fully detailed description of the entire process of Awakening, culminating in Divine Enlightenment.

Avatar Adi Da's twenty-three "Source-Texts" are not simply a series of books each of which is entirely distinct from all the others. Rather, they form an intricately interwoven fabric. Each book contains some material found in no other "Source-Text", some material shared with certain other "Source-Texts", and some material included in all twenty-three of the "Source-Texts". (The three Texts shared by all twenty-three books are "Do Not Misunderstand <u>Me</u>", "My Divine Disclosure", and "The Heart-Summary Of Adidam". Each of these Texts has a particular function and message that is essential to every one of the books.) Thus, to read Avatar Adi Da's "Source-Texts" is to engage a special kind of study (similar to the practice of repeating a mantra), in which certain Texts are repeatedly read, such that they penetrate one's being even more profoundly and take on deeper significance by being read in a variety of different contexts. Furthermore, each of the "Source-Texts" of Adidam is thereby a complete and self-contained Argument. Altogether, to study Avatar Adi Da's "Source-Texts" is to enter into an "eternal conversation" with Him, in which different meanings emerge at different times—always appropriate to the current moment in one's life and experience.

At the conclusion of His paramount "Source-Text", *The Dawn Horse Testament*, Avatar Adi Da Samraj makes His own passionate Confession of the Impulse that led Him to create His twenty-three "Source-Texts".

Now I Have, By All My "Crazy" Means, Revealed My One and Many Divine Secrets As The Great Person Of The Heart. For Your Sake, I Made My Every Work and Word. And Now, By Every Work and Word I Made, I Have Entirely Confessed (and Showed) Myself—and Always Freely, and Even As A Free Man, In The "Esoteric" Language Of Intimacy and Ecstasy, Openly Worded To You (and To all). Even Now (and Always), By This (My Avatarically Self-Revealed Divine Word Of Heart), I Address every Seeming Separate being (and each one <u>As</u> The Heart Itself), Because It Is Necessary That all beings, Even The Entire Cosmic Domain Of Seeming Separate beings, Be (In all times and places) Called To Wisdom and The Heart.

Capitalization and Punctuation in the "Source-Texts" of Avatar Adi Da Samraj

Speaking and Writing in the twentieth and twenty-first centuries, Avatar Adi Da Samraj has used the English language as the medium for His Communication. Over the years of His Teaching-Work, Avatar Adi Da developed a thoroughly original manner of employing English as a sacred language. (He also includes some Sanskrit terminology in His Teaching vocabulary, in order to supplement the relatively undeveloped sacred vocabulary of English.)

Avatar Adi Da's unique use of English is evident not only with respect to vocabulary, but also with respect to capitalization and punctuation.

Vocabulary. A glossary is included at the end of this book (pp. 412-49), where specialized terms (both English terms and terms derived from Sanskrit) are defined.

Capitalization. Avatar Adi Da frequently capitalizes words that would not ordinarily be capitalized in English—and such capitalized words include not only nouns, but also pronouns, verbs, adjectives, adverbs, and even articles and prepositions. By such capitalization, He is indicating that the word refers (either inherently, or by virtue of the context) to the Unconditional Divine Reality, rather than the conditional (or worldly) reality. For example:

If there is no escape from (or no Way out of) the corner (or the "centered" trap) of ego-"I"—the heart goes mad, and the body-mind becomes more and more "dark" (bereft of the Indivisible and Inherently Free Light of the Self-Evident, and Self-Evidently Divine, Love-Bliss That <u>Is</u> Reality Itself). ["Do Not Misunderstand <u>Me</u>"]

Avatar Adi Da's chosen conventions of capitalization vary in different "Source-Texts" and in different sections of a given "Source-Text". In certain "Source-Texts" (notably *The Dawn Horse Testament Of The Ruchira Avatar, The Heart Of The Dawn Horse Testament Of The Ruchira Avatar,* and the various Parts of the other "Source-Texts" that are excerpted from *The Dawn Horse Testament Of The Ruchira Avatar*), Avatar Adi Da employs a highly unusual convention of capitalization, in which the overwhelming majority of all words are capitalized, and only those words that indicate the egoic (or dualistic) point of view are left lower-cased. This capitalization convention (which Avatar Adi Da has worked out to an extraordinarily subtle degree—in ways that are often startling) is in itself a Teaching device, intended to communicate His fundamental Revelation that "There Is <u>Only</u> Real God", and that only the ego (or the dualistic or separative point of view) prevents us from living and Realizing that Truth. For example:

Therefore, For My Every Devotee, all conditions Must Be Aligned and Yielded In Love With Me—or Else <u>any</u> object or <u>any</u> other Will Be The Cause Of Heart-Stress, self-Contraction, Dissociation, Clinging, Boredom, Doubt, The Progressive Discomfort Of Diminished Love-Bliss, and All The Forgetfulness Of Grace and Truth and Happiness Itself. [Ruchira Avatara Hridaya-Tantra Yoga]

Note that "and" and "or" are lower-cased—because these conjunctions are (here, and in most contexts) primal expressions of the point of view of duality. Also note that "all conditions", "any object", "<u>any</u> other", and "self-" are lower-cased, while "Heart-Stress", "Contraction", "Dissociation", "Clinging," "Boredom", "Doubt", "Discomfort", "Diminished", and "Forgetfulness" are capitalized. Avatar Adi Da is telling us that unpleasant or apparently "negative" states are not inherently egoic. It is only the presumption of duality and separateness—as expressed by such words as "conditions", "object", "other", and "self"—that is egoic.

Punctuation. Because of the inevitable complexity of much of His Communication, Avatar Adi Da has developed the conventions of punctuation (commas, dashes, and parentheses) to an extraordinary degree. This allows Him to clearly articulate complex sentences in such a way that His intended meaning can be expressed with utmost precision—free of vagueness, ambiguity, or unclarity. Many of His sentences contain parenthetical definitions or modifying phrases as a way of achieving unmistakable clarity of meaning. For example:

The Apparently individual (or Separate) self Is Not a "spark" (or an Eternal fraction) Of Self-Radiant Divinity, and Somehow Complete (or Whole) In itself. [<u>Real</u> God <u>Is</u> The Indivisible Oneness Of Unbroken Light]

Another punctuation convention relates to the use of quotation marks. Avatar Adi Da sometimes uses quotation marks in accordance with standard convention, to indicate the sense of "so to speak":

Make the contact with Me that gets you to "stick" to Me like glue. Your "sticking" to Me is what must happen. [Hridaya Rosary]

In other instances, He uses quotation marks to indicate that a word or phrase is being used with a particular technical meaning that differs from common usage:

During <u>all</u> of My present Lifetime (of Avataric Divine Incarnation), the "<u>Bright</u>" has <u>always</u> been My Realization—and the "<u>Thumbs</u>" and My own "Radical" Understanding have <u>always</u> been My Way in the "Bright".

"Bright", "Thumbs" (referring to a specific form of the Infusion of Avatar Adi Da's Divine Spirit-Current in the body-mind), and "Radical" are all used with specific technical meanings here (as defined in the Glossary).

Finally, Avatar Adi Da also makes extensive use of underlining to indicate special emphasis on certain words (or phrases, or even entire sentences):

> The only true religion is the religion that Realizes Truth. The only true science is the science that Knows Truth. The only true man or woman (or being of any kind) is one that Surrenders to Truth. The only true world is one that Embodies Truth. And the only True (and Real) God Is the One Reality (or Condition of Being) That Is Truth. ["Do Not Misunderstand Me"]

The True Dawn Horse

The Only Complete Way To Realize The Unbroken Light Of Real God is Book Three of The Seventeen Companions Of The True Dawn Horse. The "True Dawn Horse" is a reference to The Dawn Horse Testament Of The Ruchira Avatar, the final book among Avatar Adi Da's "Source-Texts". In The Dawn Horse Testament, Avatar Adi Da describes the entire Process of Real-God-Realization in detail. Each of The Seventeen Companions Of The True Dawn Horse is a "Companion" to The Dawn Horse Testament in the sense that it is an elaboration of a major theme (or themes) from The Dawn Horse Testament. And in many of the "Seventeen Companions", an excerpt from The Dawn Horse Testament forms the principal part, around which the other parts of the book revolve. (In The Only Complete Way To Realize The Unbroken Light Of Real God, the principal part—Part Five—comprises chapters three, four, and forty-five of The Dawn Horse Testament.)

The Sacred Image of the Dawn Horse (which appears above) derives from a vision that Avatar Adi Da Samraj had one night during the spring of 1970, a few months before His Divine Re-Awakening (on September 10, 1970). As His physical body lay sleeping, Avatar Adi Da wandered in subtle form into an open hall, where a great Adept was seated on a throne. The Adept's disciples were lined up in rows in front of him. A pathway bounded on both sides by the disciples led to the throne. Avatar Adi Da was Himself standing at the end of a row a few rows away from the Adept's chair.

The disciples were apparently assembled to learn the miraculous Yogic power of materializing something from nothing. They waited respectfully for the lesson to begin.

The Adept then initiated the process of materialization. A brief while later, the disciples got up and left the room, satisfied that the materialization had been accomplished, although nothing had appeared yet. The Adept remained sitting in his chair, and Avatar Adi Da remained standing before him, attentive to the process at hand.

A vaporous mass gradually took shape in the space between Avatar Adi Da and the Adept. At first it was not clearly defined, but Avatar Adi Da recognized it as it began to take on the features of a horse. Gradually, the vapor coalesced into a living, breathing brown horse. Its features were as fine as a thoroughbred's, but it was quite small, perhaps three feet tall. The horse stood alert, motionless, facing away from the Adept's chair.

At this point in the dream vision, Avatar Adi Da returned to physical consciousness and the waking state.

It was many years later, at the time when Avatar Adi Da was starting to write *The Dawn Horse Testament*, that He Revealed the identity of the Adept He had visited in that vision:

AVATAR ADI DA SAMRAJ: I was at once the Adept who performed the miracle of manifesting the horse, and also the one who was party to the observation of it and its result. And I did not have any feeling of being different from the horse itself. I was <u>making</u> the horse, I was <u>observing</u> the horse, and I was <u>being</u> the horse. [October 18, 1984]

The Dawn Horse is, therefore, a symbol for Avatar Adi Da Samraj Himself—and *The Dawn Horse Testament* is His Personal

Testament to all beings. Avatar Adi Da has commented that He refers to Himself and to His principal "Source-Text" as the "True Dawn Horse" because the effects of His Liberating Work in the world will appear only gradually—just as, in the vision, the horse gradually became visible after the Adept had initiated its materialization.

In creating the Sacred Image of the Dawn Horse, Avatar Adi Da transformed His original vision of a small brown horse, with all four hooves planted on the ground, into a winged white stallion, rearing up nearly vertically:

AVATAR ADI DA SAMRAJ: The horse's pose is majestic and intended to show great strength. White was chosen for its obvious association with Light, or Consciousness Itself. The Image is not precisely associated with the vision of 1970. It is visual language, intended to communicate the full meaning of My Dawn Horse Vision, rather than to be a realistic presentation of it.

The Titles and Subtitles of The Twenty-Three "Source-Texts" of Avatar Adi Da Samraj

The twenty-three "Source-Texts" of Avatar Adi Da Samraj include:

(1) an opening series of five books on the fundamentals of the Way of Adidam (*The Five Books Of The Heart Of The Adidam Revelation*)

(2) an extended series of seventeen books covering the principal aspects of the Way of Adidam in detail (*The Seventeen Companions Of The True Dawn Horse*)

(3) Avatar Adi Da's paramount "Source-Text" summarizing the entire course of the Way of Adidam (*The Dawn Horse Testament*)

The basic content of each "Source-Text" is summarily described by Avatar Adi Da in the title and subtitle of each book. Thus, the following list of titles and subtitles indicates the vast scope and the artful interconnectedness of His twenty-three "Source-Texts". (For brief descriptions of each "Source-Text", please see "The Sacred Literature of Avatar Adi Da Samraj", pp. 451-58.)

The Five Books Of The Heart Of The Adidam Revelation

BOOK ONE
Aham Da Asmi
(Beloved, I <u>Am</u> Da)
The "Late-Time" Avataric Revelation Of The True and Spiritual Divine Person (The egoless Personal Presence Of Reality and Truth, Which <u>Is</u> The Only <u>Real</u> God)

BOOK TWO
Ruchira Avatara Gita
(The Way Of The Divine Heart-Master)
The "Late-Time" Avataric Revelation Of The Great Secret Of The Divinely Self-Revealed Way That Most Perfectly Realizes The True and Spiritual Divine Person (The egoless Personal Presence Of Reality and Truth, Which <u>Is</u> The Only <u>Real</u> God)

BOOK THREE
Da Love-Ananda Gita
(The Free Gift Of The Divine Love-Bliss)
The "Late-Time" Avataric Revelation Of The Great Means To Worship and To Realize The True and Spiritual Divine Person (The egoless Personal Presence Of Reality and Truth, Which <u>Is</u> The Only <u>Real</u> God)

BOOK FOUR
Hridaya Rosary
(Four Thorns Of Heart-Instruction)
The "Late-Time" Avataric Revelation Of The Universally Tangible Divine Spiritual Body, Which Is The Supreme Agent Of The Great Means To Worship and To Realize The True and Spiritual Divine Person (The egoless Personal Presence Of Reality and Truth, Which <u>Is</u> The Only <u>Real</u> God)

BOOK FIVE
Eleutherios
(The Only Truth That Sets The Heart Free)
The "Late-Time" Avataric Revelation Of The "Perfect Practice"
Of The Great Means To Worship and To Realize The True and
Spiritual Divine Person (The egoless Personal Presence Of
Reality and Truth, Which Is The Only Real God)

◆ ◆ ◆

The Seventeen Companions
Of The True Dawn Horse

BOOK ONE
Real God Is The Indivisible Oneness
Of Unbroken Light
Reality, Truth, and The "Non-Creator" God
In The True World-Religion Of Adidam

BOOK TWO
The Truly Human New World-Culture
Of Unbroken Real-God-Man
The Eastern Versus The Western Traditional Cultures
Of Mankind, and The Unique New Non-Dual Culture
Of The True World-Religion Of Adidam

BOOK THREE
The Only Complete Way To Realize
The Unbroken Light Of Real God
An Introductory Overview Of The "Radical" Divine Way
Of The True World-Religion Of Adidam

BOOK FOUR
The Knee Of Listening
The Early-Life Ordeal and The "Radical"
Spiritual Realization Of The Ruchira Avatar

BOOK FIVE
The Divine Siddha-Method Of The Ruchira Avatar
The Divine Way Of Adidam Is An ego-Transcending
Relationship, Not An ego-Centric Technique

BOOK SIX
The Mummery
A Parable Of The Divine True Love

BOOK SEVEN
He-and-She Is Me
The Indivisibility Of Consciousness and Light
In The Divine Body Of The Ruchira Avatar

BOOK EIGHT
Ruchira Avatara Hridaya-Siddha Yoga
The Divine (and Not Merely Cosmic) Spiritual Baptism
In The Divine Way Of Adidam

BOOK NINE
Ruchira Avatara Hridaya-Tantra Yoga
The Physical-Spiritual (and Truly Religious) Method
Of Mental, Emotional, Sexual, and Whole Bodily Health
and Enlightenment In The Divine Way Of Adidam

BOOK TEN
The Seven Stages Of Life
Transcending The Six Stages Of egoic Life,
and Realizing The ego-Transcending Seventh Stage Of Life,
In The Divine Way Of Adidam

BOOK ELEVEN
The All-Completing and Final
Divine Revelation To Mankind
A Summary Description Of The Supreme Yoga
Of The Seventh Stage Of Life In The Divine Way Of Adidam

BOOK TWELVE
The Heart Of The Dawn Horse Testament Of The Ruchira Avatar

The Epitome Of The "Testament Of Secrets" Of The Divine
World-Teacher, Ruchira Avatar Adi Da Samraj

BOOK THIRTEEN
What, Where, When, How, Why, and Who To Remember To Be Happy

A Simple Explanation Of The Divine Way Of Adidam
(For Children, and Everyone Else)

BOOK FOURTEEN
Santosha Adidam

The Essential Summary Of The Divine Way Of Adidam

BOOK FIFTEEN
The Lion Sutra

The "Perfect Practice" Teachings In The Divine Way Of Adidam

BOOK SIXTEEN
The Overnight Revelation Of Conscious Light

The "My House" Discourses
On The Indivisible Tantra Of Adidam

BOOK SEVENTEEN
The Basket Of Tolerance

The Perfect Guide To Perfectly Unified Understanding
Of The One and Great Tradition Of Mankind,
and Of The Divine Way Of Adidam As The Perfect Completing
Of The One and Great Tradition Of Mankind

◆ ◆ ◆

The Dawn Horse Testament
Of The Ruchira Avatar

The Dawn Horse Testament Of The Ruchira Avatar

The "Testament Of Secrets" Of The Divine World-Teacher,
Ruchira Avatar Adi Da Samraj

Camera Illuminata

The "Bright"-Field Photography of Avatar Adi Da Samraj

At the same time that He was completing His Work to create a complete verbal Teaching in His "Source-Texts", Avatar Adi Da Samraj started taking black-and-white photographs as another potent means of communicating His message about Reality. He calls the collected body of His photographic work His "Camera Illuminata" collection. The cover image of each of His twenty-three "Source-Texts" includes a central image and a border image, both of which are photographs taken by Avatar Adi Da Samraj (and specifically chosen by Him as an image appropriate to that particular "Source-Text"). "Camera Illuminata" means "Bright Room", in contrast to the traditional term "camera obscura" (which literally means "dark room"). Thus, instead of representing the world from the "dark" point of view (or the presumption that dying matter is all there is to reality), the Camera Illuminata of Adi Da Samraj Reveals the world as a "Bright" (or Divinely Self-Radiant) Field.

Avatar Adi Da's "Bright"-Field photographic images are one of His means for conveying His Spiritual Transmission and Blessing—for the subject of Avatar Adi Da's photography is not the world as we see it, but the world as the "Bright" Field of Reality that He sees. His photography would transport us beyond our ordinary habits of thinking and perceiving into the Divine Light, in Which there is no sense of separation, otherness, or limitation.

AVATAR ADI DA SAMRAJ: From the conventional point of view, a photographer only makes pictures of conventional reality, of light falling on objects, as if the solid reality were the only reality. But neither the fixed separate point of view nor the apparently solid objective world is the Fundamental Reality. The Divine Conscious Light Is the Fundamental Reality of Existence.

Avatar Adi Da's photographic images communicate the non-dual perception of Reality via a unique process, which He describes as His "inherently egoless participatory relationship" with the subjects of His photographs (both human and non-human). Thus, His photography transcends the conventions of "self" and "other", or "subject" and "object".

AVATAR ADI DA SAMRAJ: Out of this process, images can be made that Reveal Reality, rather than merely communicating the conventions of "ego" and "other".

Therefore, even the viewing of Adi Da's Camera Illuminata images is an inherently participatory event. That is to say, His photographs, like all great art, place a demand upon us to go beyond the ordinary fixed point of view. They are a call to go beyond our ordinary limits—for each of His images is a communication of the Divine "Brightness", transforming our ordinary perception of the world into sacred occasion.

Avatar Adi Da Samraj photographing in the California redwoods

When viewed in its entirety, Avatar Adi Da's Camera Illuminata collection is an ecstatic Revelation-Transmission of the Divine Truth that He has Come to Reveal and Teach to humankind. There is extraordinary beauty to be appreciated in Avatar Adi Da's photographs, but the real purpose of His artistry is to bring Light into our lives, to literally En-Light-en us—to Liberate us from the un-Illumined and mortal vision of egoity. By offering us His Camera Illuminata, Adi Da Samraj would have us discover that "Bright-Field", that Non-separate Reality, in Which the ever-changing dualities of light and darkness rise and fall.

AVATAR ADI DA SAMRAJ: In My approach to making photographic images, I want to convey the Truth of Reality—the Truth of the Inherently egoless, Non-dual Subjective Light. I am trying to convey My own Revelation of the Nature of Reality through the artifice of visual images.

The border image on the cover of this book is a photograph taken by Avatar Adi Da Samraj. He refers to this photograph as an image of "True Water", which is one of His poetic descriptions for Consciousness Itself as the "Medium" in which all phenomena arise (and of which they are all modifications).

An Overview of
The _Only_ Complete Way
To Realize The Unbroken Light
Of _Real_ God

The _Only_ Complete Way To Realize The Unbroken Light Of _Real_ God is, as Avatar Adi Da explains via the subtitle, an introductory overview of the True World-Religion of Adidam—the Way He has Revealed and Given for the sake of all who recognize and respond to Him at heart.

As with each of Avatar Adi Da's "Source-Texts", The _Only_ Complete Way To Realize The Unbroken Light Of _Real_ God begins with His First Word, "Do Not Misunderstand Me—I Am Not 'Within' you, but you Are In Me, and I Am Not a Mere 'Man' in the 'Middle' of Mankind, but All of Mankind Is Surrounded, and Pervaded, and Blessed By Me". In this remarkable Essay, Avatar Adi Da explains that His open Confession of Most Perfect Real-God-Realization is not to be misapprehended as a claim of the "Status" of the "Creator"-God of conventional religious belief— but, rather, His Divine Self-Confession must be rightly understood and appreciated as a Free Demonstration of What is Realized in the Perfect Fulfillment of esoteric Spiritual practice, Which is the Most Perfectly Non-Dual Realization of Reality Itself. By virtue of His Free Demonstration, Avatar Adi Da Samraj makes clear that Most Perfect Real-God-Realization is the ultimate Potential and Destiny of all beings.

The Prologue of The _Only_ Complete Way To Realize The Unbroken Light Of _Real_ God, "My Divine Disclosure" (also, like "First Word", found in all twenty-three "Source-Texts"), is a poetic epitome of Avatar Adi Da's Divine Self-Revelation. It is His Call to every being to turn to Him at heart and practice the life of devotional surrender in Real God.

Avatar Adi Da begins Part One, "I Am The 'Who' That Is Always Already The Case", in a most intimate manner. Conversing with you as His "beloved", He Reveals the Divine Nature and Function of His Manifestation in this world, and He Calls you to grow beyond all the limits and inherent sufferings of conditional existence by luxuriating in His Free Transmission of Love-Bliss-Happiness.

Part Two, "I (Alone) Am The Adidam Revelation", is Avatar Adi Da's fullest elucidation of the uniqueness of His Revelation of the seventh stage Realization. In this Essay—remarkable in its scope and profundity—Avatar Adi Da examines His own Course of Divine Self-Realization in order to Demonstrate how the two primary divisions of the Great Tradition—the Emanationist (or absorptive mystical) Way (associated with the first five stages of life) and the non-Emanationist (or Transcendentalist) Way (associated with the sixth stage of life)—are, in Truth, only different aspects of the great seven-stage process of Most Perfect Divine Self-Realization.

In Part Three, "The Heart-Summary of Adidam" (a brief Essay that is included in all twenty-three "Source-Texts"), Avatar Adi Da Samraj summarizes the profound implications of His Statement that the Way of Adidam is the Way of devotion to Him "As Self-Condition, rather than As exclusively Objective Other".

In Part Four, "The Dual Sensitivity at the Origin of The Divine Way Of Adidam", Avatar Adi Da exposes the realities of conditional existence that the ego seeks to avoid at all costs, and He examines the profound implications of the universal urge to Realize Happiness Itself.

Part Five, the principal Text, "The Only Complete Way To Realize The Unbroken Light Of Real God", is divided into three sections. In the first section, Avatar Adi Da examines the relationship between the Way of Adidam and the Great Tradition as a whole. He describes the two basic modes of practice in the Way of Adidam—the Devotional Way of Insight (which He Offers to those who are able to grow especially by the exercise of feeling and insight) and the Devotional Way of Faith (which He Offers to those who are able to grow especially by the exercise of feeling and faith)—and He recounts the critical insight that moved His own Spiritual practice to its Fulfillment in Most Perfect Real-God-Realization.

In the second section of Part Five, Avatar Adi Da describes the final stages of His Divine Re-Awakening and the subsequent arising of His extraordinary Divine Blessing-Powers. He recounts how His "Crazy" Teaching-Work mysteriously unfolded, and He explains that His Writing of the Paramount "Source-Text" of Adidam, *The Dawn Horse Testament*, marked the Completion of His Ordeal of Divine Self-Revelation and Heart-Instruction. Also in this section, Avatar Adi Da Reveals that every ego-"I" is, in fact, the One Divine Self mistakenly presuming Itself to be an individuated body-mind and that the one and only Process by which this binding presumption is utterly dissolved is the Way of Adidam.

In the third and final section of Part Five, Avatar Adi Da describes the True Nature of Most Perfect Real-God-Realization. He explains how the True World-Religion of Adidam is, at all times, a unique address to the Divine Self-Condition of every apparent ego-"I". He summarizes the seven developmental stages of the Way, and He Reveals the single Divine Law upon which Adidam is founded.

The three Essays which comprise Part Six are a brief summary of the basic Principles of Adidam. In "The One and True and Only By-Me-Revealed and By-Me-Given Way Of The Heart", Avatar Adi Da Reveals that all suffering is simply the forgetting of Consciousness Itself, which Is Love-Bliss Itself. In "'The Thumbs' Is The Fundamental Sign Of The Avataric Crashing-Down Of My Divine Person", Avatar Adi Da Reveals that His Crashing-Down Spiritual Descent is the unique Means to Most Perfectly Realize Consciousness Itself. In "The 'Radical' Divine Way Of Adidam", Avatar Adi Da explains that Adidam is "radical" because it is always "gone to the root" and "given to the Source", and it, thus and thereby, transcends all seeking for God:

To seek God is to forget and avoid and fail to Find Real God. Therefore, understand your search (for God, or any "thing" at all), and (by Means of right, true, full, and fully devotional recognition of Me in My Avatarically Self-Revealed, and Self-Evidently Divine, Person—and by Means of right, true, full, and fully devotional response to Me in My Avatarically Self-Revealed, and Self-Evidently Divine, Person) Remember, Embrace, and Truly Find and "Locate" Me—and, Most Ultimately, and entirely by Means of My Avatarically Self-Transmitted Divine Grace, Realize Indivisible Oneness with Me, and Indivisible (and Non-Separate) Identification with Me (the Perfectly Subjective and Self-Evidently Divine Self-Condition and Source-Condition That Is the Real and Only Reality, Truth, and God of all and All).

Finally, in the Epilogue, "I <u>Am</u> The Divine Self-"Emergence", Avatar Adi Da Calls all to a right understanding of His Divinely "Heroic" and Divinely "Crazy" Manner of Life and Work. And He Reveals that—now that His Work of Teaching and Revelation is Full and Complete—He will only do His Avataric Work of Freely Blessing one and all, both during and after His physical human Lifetime.

Rightly understood, *The <u>Only</u> Complete Way To Realize The Unbroken Light Of <u>Real</u> God* is Avatar Adi Da's intimate Call to you (and to all beings) at heart to turn to Him and to joyfully receive His Divine Blessing-Force—"Bright" with Love-Bliss-Happiness. Such is the unique and truly Perfect Means to Realize the Unbroken Light of <u>Real</u> God.

THE <u>ONLY</u> COMPLETE WAY
TO REALIZE THE UNBROKEN LIGHT
OF <u>REAL</u> GOD

RUCHIRA AVATAR ADI DA SAMRAJ
Los Angeles, 2000

Do Not Misunderstand Me—
I Am Not "Within" you,
but you Are In Me,
and I Am Not a Mere "Man"
in the "Middle" of Mankind,
but All of Mankind Is Surrounded,
and Pervaded, and Blessed By Me

This Essay has been written by Avatar Adi Da Samraj as His Personal Introduction to each volume of His "Source-Texts". Its purpose is to help you to understand His great Confessions rightly, and not interpret His Words from a conventional point of view, as limited cultic statements made by an ego. His Description of what "cultism" really is is an astounding and profound Critique of mankind's entire religious, scientific, and social search. In "Do Not Misunderstand Me", Avatar Adi Da is directly inviting you to inspect and relinquish the ego's motive to glorify itself and to refuse What is truly Great. Only by understanding this fundamental ego-fault can one really receive the Truth that Adi Da Samraj Reveals in this Book and in His Wisdom-Teaching altogether. And it is because this fault is so ingrained and so largely unconscious that Avatar Adi Da has placed "Do Not Misunderstand Me" at the beginning of each of His "Source-Texts", so that, each time you begin to read one of His twenty-three "Source-Texts", you may be refreshed and strengthened in your understanding of the right orientation and approach to Him and His Heart-Word.

Yes! There is no religion, no Way of God, no Way of Divine Realization, no Way of Enlightenment, and no Way of Liberation that is Higher or Greater than Truth Itself.

Indeed, there is no religion, no science, no man or woman, no conditionally manifested being of any kind, no world (any "where"), and no "God" (or "God"-Idea) that is Higher or Greater than Truth Itself.

Therefore, no ego-"I" (or presumed separate, and, necessarily, actively separative, and, at best, only Truth-seeking, being or "thing") is (itself) Higher or Greater than Truth Itself. And no ego-"I" is (itself) even Equal to Truth Itself. And no ego-"I" is (itself) even (now, or ever) Able to Realize Truth Itself—because, necessarily, Truth (Itself) Inherently Transcends (or Is That Which Is Higher and Greater than) every one (himself or herself) and every "thing" (itself). Therefore, it is only in the transcending (or the "radical" Process of Going Beyond the root, the cause, and the act) of egoity itself (or of presumed separateness, and of performed separativeness, and of even all ego-based seeking for Truth Itself) that Truth (Itself) Is Realized (As It Is, Utterly Beyond the ego-"I" itself).

Truth (Itself) Is That Which Is Always Already The Case. That Which Is The Case (Always, and Always Already) Is (necessarily) Reality. Therefore, Reality (Itself) Is Truth, and Reality (Itself) Is the Only Truth.

Reality (Itself) Is the Only, and (necessarily) Non-Separate (or All-and-all-Including, and All-and-all-Transcending), One and "What" That Is. Because It Is All and all, and because It Is (Also) That Which Transcends (or Is Higher and Greater than) All and all, Reality (Itself)—Which Is Truth (Itself), or That Which Is The Case (Always, and Always Already)—Is the One and Only Real God. Therefore, Reality (Itself) Is (necessarily) the One and Great Subject of true religion, and Reality (Itself) Is (necessarily) the One and Great Way of Real God, Real (and True) Divine Realization, Real (and, necessarily, Divine) En-Light-enment, and Real (and, necessarily, Divine) Liberation (from all egoity, all separateness, all separativeness, all fear, and all heartlessness).

The only true religion is the religion that Realizes Truth. The only true science is the science that Knows Truth. The only true man or woman (or being of any kind) is one that Surrenders to Truth. The only true world is one that Embodies Truth. And the only True (and Real) God Is the One Reality (or Condition of Being) That Is Truth. Therefore, Reality (Itself)—Which Is the One and Only Truth, and (therefore, necessarily) the One and Only Real God—must become (or be made) the constantly applied Measure of religion, and of science, and of the world itself, and of even all of the life (and all of the mind) of Man—or else religion, and science, and the world itself, and even any and every sign of Man inevitably (all, and together) become a pattern of illusions, a mere (and even terrible) "problem", the very (and even principal) cause of human seeking, and the perpetual cause of contentious human strife. Indeed, if religion, and science, and the world itself, and the total life (and the total mind) of Man are not Surrendered and Aligned to Reality (Itself), and (Thus) Submitted to be Measured (or made Lawful) by Truth (Itself), and (Thus) Given to the truly devotional (and, thereby, truly ego-transcending) Realization of That Which Is the Only Real God—then, in the presumed "knowledge" of mankind, Reality (Itself), and Truth (Itself), and Real God (or the One and Only Existence, or Being, or Person That Is) ceases to Exist.

Aham Da Asmi. Beloved, I Am Da—the One and Only Person Who Is, the Avatarically Self-Revealed, and Eternally Self-Existing, and Eternally Self-Radiant (or "Bright") Person of Love-Bliss, the One and Only and (Self-Evidently) Divine Self (or Inherently Non-Separate—and, therefore, Inherently egoless—Divine Self-Condition and Source-Condition) of one and of all and of All. I Am Divinely Self-Manifesting (now, and forever hereafter) As the Ruchira Avatar, Adi Da Samraj. I Am the Ruchira Avatar, Adi Da Samraj—the Avataric Divine Realizer, the Avataric Divine Revealer, the Avataric Divine Incarnation, and the Avataric Divine Self-Revelation of Reality Itself. I Am the Avatarically Incarnate Divine Realizer, the Avatarically Incarnate Divine Revealer, and the Avatarically Incarnate Divine Self-Revelation of the One and Only Reality—Which Is the One and Only Truth, and Which Is the One and Only Real God. I Am the Great Avataric Divine Realizer, Avataric Divine Revealer, and Avataric Divine Self-Revelation long-Promised (and long-Expected) for the "late-time"—this (now, and forever hereafter) time, the "dark" epoch of mankind's "Great

Forgetting" (and, potentially, the Great Epoch of mankind's Perpetual Remembering) of Reality, of Truth, of Real God (Which Is the Great, True, and Spiritual Divine Person—or the One and Non-Separate and Indivisible Divine Source-Condition and Self-Condition) of all and All.

Beloved, I Am Da, the Divine Giver, the Giver (of All That I Am) to one, and to all, and to the All of all—now, and forever here-after—here, and every "where" in the Cosmic domain. Therefore, for the Purpose of Revealing the Way of Real God (or of Real and True Divine Realization), and in order to Divinely En-Light-en and Divinely Liberate all and All—I Am (Uniquely, Completely, and Most Perfectly) Avatarically Revealing My Very (and Self-Evidently Divine) Person (and "Bright" Self-Condition) to all and All, by Means of My Avatarically Given Divine Self-Manifestation, As (and by Means of) the Ruchira Avatar, Adi Da Samraj.

In My Avatarically Given Divine Self-Manifestation As the Ruchira Avatar, Adi Da Samraj—I Am the Divine Secret, the Divine Self-Revelation of the Esoteric Truth, the Direct, and all-Completing, and all-Unifying Self-Revelation of Real God.

My Avatarically Given Divine Self-Confessions and My Avatarically Given Divine Teaching-Revelations Are the Great (Final, and all-Completing, and all-Unifying) Esoteric Revelation to mankind—and not a merely exoteric (or conventionally religious, or even ordinary Spiritual, or ego-made, or so-called "cultic") com-munication to public (or merely social) ears.

The greatest opportunity, and the greatest responsibility, of My devotees is Satsang with Me—Which is to live in the Condition of ego-surrendering, ego-forgetting, and (always more and more) ego-transcending devotional relationship to Me, and (Thus and Thereby) to Realize My Avatarically Self-Revealed (and Self-Evidently Divine) Self-Condition, Which Is the Self-Evidently Divine Heart (or Non-Separate Self-Condition and Non-"Different" Source-Condition) of all and All, and Which Is Self-Existing and Self-Radiant Consciousness Itself, but Which is not separate in or as any one (or any "thing") at all. Therefore, My essential Divine Gift to one and all is Satsang with Me. And My essential Divine Work with one and all is Satsang-Work—to Live (and to Be Merely

Present) As the Avatarically Self-Revealed Divine Heart among My devotees.

The only-by-Me Revealed and Given Way of Adidam (Which is the only-by-Me Revealed and Given Way of the Heart, or the only-by-Me Revealed and Given Way of "Radical" Understanding, or Ruchira Avatara Hridaya-Siddha Yoga) is the Way of Satsang with Me—the devotionally Me-recognizing and devotionally to-Me-responding practice (and ego-transcending self-discipline) of living in My constant Divine Company, such that the relationship with Me becomes the Real (and constant) Condition of life. Fundamentally, this Satsang with Me is the one thing done by My devotees. Because the only-by-Me Revealed and Given Way of Adidam is always (in every present-time moment) a directly ego-transcending and Really Me-Finding practice, the otherwise constant (and burdensome) tendency to seek is not exploited in this Satsang with Me. And the essential work of the community of the four formal congregations of My devotees is to make ego-transcending Satsang with Me available to all others.

Everything that serves the availability of Satsang with Me is (now, and forever hereafter) the responsibility of the four formal congregations of My formally practicing devotees. I am not here to publicly "promote" this Satsang with Me. In the intimate circum-stances of their humanly expressed devotional love of Me, I Speak My Avatarically Self-Revealing Divine Word to My devotees, and they (because of their devotional response to Me) bring My Avatarically Self-Revealing Divine Word to all others. Therefore, even though I am not (and have never been, and never will be) a "public" Teacher (or a broadly publicly active, and convention-ally socially conformed, "religious figure"), My devotees function fully and freely (as My devotees) in the daily public world of ordinary life.

I Always Already Stand Free. Therefore, I have always (in My Divine Avataric-Incarnation-Work) Stood Free, in the traditional "Crazy" (and non-conventional, or spontaneous and non-"public") Manner—in order to Guarantee the Freedom, the Uncompromising Rightness, and the Fundamental Integrity of My Avatarically Self-Manifested Divine Teaching (Work and Word), and in order to

Freely and Fully and Fully Effectively Perform My universal (Avatarically Self-Manifested) Divine Blessing-Work. I Am Present (now, and forever hereafter) to Divinely Serve, Divinely En-Lighten, and Divinely Liberate those who accept the Eternal Vow and <u>all</u> the life-responsibilities (or the full and complete practice) associated with the only-by-Me Revealed and Given Way of Adidam. Because I Am (Thus) Given to My formally and fully practicing devotees, I do not Serve a "public" role, and I do not Work in a "public" (or even a merely "institutionalized") manner. Nevertheless—now, and forever hereafter—I <u>constantly</u> Bless <u>all</u> beings, and this <u>entire</u> world, and the <u>total</u> Cosmic domain. And <u>all</u> who feel My Avatarically (and universally) Given Divine Blessing, and who heart-recognize Me with true devotional love, are (Thus) Called to devotionally resort to Me—but only if they approach Me in the traditional devotional manner, as responsibly practicing (and truly ego-surrendering, and rightly Me-serving) members (or, in some, unique, cases, as invited guests) of one or the other of the four formal congregations of My formally practicing devotees.

I expect this formal discipline of right devotional approach to Me to have been freely and happily embraced by every one who would enter into My physical Company. The natural human reason for this is that there is a potential liability inherent in <u>all</u> human associations. And the root and nature of that potential liability is the <u>ego</u> (or the active human presumption of separateness, and the ego-act of human separativeness). Therefore, in order that the liabilities of egoity are understood (and voluntarily and responsibly disciplined) by those who approach Me, I require demonstrated right devotion (based on really effective self-understanding and truly heart-felt devotional recognition-response to Me) as the basis for any one's right to enter into My physical Company. And, in this manner, not only the egoic tendency, but also the tendency toward religious "cultism", is constantly undermined in the only-by-Me Revealed and Given Way of Adidam.

Because people appear within this human condition, this simultaneously attractive and frightening "dream" world, they tend to live—and to interpret <u>both</u> the conditional (or cosmic and psycho-physical) reality and the Unconditional (or Divine) Reality—from the "point of view" of this apparent (and bewildering) mortal human condition. And, because of this universal human bewilderment (and the ongoing human reaction to the threatening force of mortal life-events), there is an even ancient ritual that all human beings rather unconsciously (or automatically, and without discriminative understanding) desire and tend to repeatedly (and under all conditions) enact. Therefore, wherever you see an association of human beings gathered for any purpose (or around any idea, or symbol, or person, or subject of any kind), the same human bewilderment-ritual is tending to be enacted by one and all.

Human beings always tend to encircle (and, thereby, to contain—and, ultimately, to entrap and abuse, or even to blithely ignore) the presumed "center" of their lives—a book, a person, a symbol, an idea, or whatever. They tend to encircle the "center" (or the "middle"), and they tend to seek to exclusively acquire all "things" (or all power of control) for the circle (or toward the "middle") of themselves. In this manner, the group becomes an ego ("inward"-directed, or separate and separative)—just as the individual body-mind becomes, by self-referring self-contraction, the separate and separative ego-"I" ("inward"-directed, or egocentric—and exclusively acquiring all "things", or all power of control, for itself). Thus, by self-contraction upon the presumed "center" of their lives—human beings, in their collective egocentricity, make "cults" (or bewildered and frightened "centers" of power, and control, and exclusion) in every area of life.

Anciently, the "cult"-making process was done, most especially, in the political and social sphere—and religion was, as even now, mostly an exoteric (or political and social) exercise that was always used to legitimize (or, otherwise, to "de-throne") political and social "authority-figures". Anciently, the cyclically (or even annually) culminating product of this exoteric religio-political "cult" was the ritual "de-throning" (or ritual deposition) of the one in the "middle" (just as, even in these times, political leaders are periodically "deposed"—by elections, by rules of term and succession, by scandal, by slander, by force, and so on).

Everywhere throughout the ancient world, traditional societies made and performed this annual (or otherwise periodic) religio-political "cult" ritual. The ritual of "en-throning" and "de-throning" was a reflection of the human observation of the annual cycle of the seasons of the natural world—and the same ritual was a reflection of the human concern and effort to control the signs potential in the cycle of the natural world, in order to ensure human survival (through control of weather, harvests and every kind of "fate", or even every fraction of existence upon which human beings depend for both survival and pleasure, or psycho-physical well-being). Indeed, the motive behind the ancient agrarian (and, later, urbanized, or universalized) ritual of the one in the "middle" was, essentially, the same motive that, in the modern era, takes the form of the culture of scientific materialism (and even all of the modern culture of materialistic "realism"): It is the motive to gain (and to maintain) control, and the effort to control even everything and everyone (via both knowledge and gross power). Thus, the ritualized, or bewildered yes/no (or desire/fear), life of mankind in the modern era is, essentially, the same as that of mankind in the ancient days.

In the ancient ritual of "en-throning" and "de-throning", the person (or subject) in the "middle" was ritually mocked, abused, deposed, and banished—and a new person (or subject) was installed in the "center" of the religio-political "cult". In the equivalent modern ritual of dramatized ambiguity relative to everything and everyone (and, perhaps especially, "authority-figures"), the person (or symbol, or idea) in the "middle" (or that which is given power by means of popular fascination) is first "cultified" (or made much of), and then (progressively) doubted, mocked, and abused—until, at last, all the negative emotions are (by culturally and socially ritualized dramatization) dissolved, the "middle" (having thus ceased to be fascinating) is abandoned, and a "new" person (or symbol, or idea) becomes the subject of popular fascination (only to be reduced, eventually, to the same "cultic" ritual, or cycle of "rise" and "fall").

Just as in every other area of human life, the tendency of all those who (in the modern era) would become involved in religious or Spiritual life is also to make a "cult", a circle that ever increases its separate and separative dimensions—beginning from the "center", surrounding it, and (perhaps) even (ultimately) controlling it (such that it altogether ceases to be effective, or even interesting). Such "cultism" is ego-based, and ego-reinforcing— and, no matter how "esoteric" it presumes itself to be, it is (as in the ancient setting) entirely exoteric, or (at least) more and more limited to (and by) merely social (and gross physical) activities and conditions.

The form that every "cult" imitates is the pattern of egoity (or the pattern that is the ego-"I") itself—the presumed "middle" of every ordinary individual life. It is the self-contraction (or the avoidance of relationship), which "creates" the fearful sense of separate mind, and all the endless habits and motives of egoic desire (or bewildered, and self-deluded, seeking). It is what is, ordinarily, called (or presumed to be) the real and necessary and only "life".

From birth, the human being (by reaction to the blows and limits of psycho-physical existence) begins to presume separate existence to be his or her very nature—and, on that basis, the human individual spends his or her entire life generating and serving a circle of ownership (or self-protecting acquisition) all around the ego-"I". The egoic motive encloses all the other beings it can acquire, all the "things" it can acquire, all the states and thoughts it can acquire—<u>all</u> the possible emblems, symbols, experiences, and sensations it can possibly acquire. Therefore, when any human being begins to involve himself or herself in some religious or Spiritual association (or, for that matter, <u>any</u> extension of his or her own subjectivity), he or she tends again to "create" that same circle about a "center".

The "cult" (whether of religion, or of politics, or of science, or of popular culture) is a dramatization of egoity, of separativeness, even of the entrapment and betrayal of the "center" (or the "middle"), by one and all. Therefore, I have always Refused to assume the role and the position of the "man in the middle"—and I have always (from the beginning of My formal Work of Teaching and Blessing) Criticized, Resisted, and Shouted About the "cultic" (or ego-based, and ego-reinforcing, and merely "talking" and "believing", and not understanding and not really practicing) "school" (or tendency) of ordinary religious and Spiritual life. Indeed, true Satsang with Me (or the true devotional relationship to Me) is an always (and specifically, and intensively) anti-"cultic" (or truly non-"cultic") Process.

The true devotional relationship to Me is not separative (or merely "inward"-directed), nor is it a matter of attachment to Me as a mere (and, necessarily, limited) human being (or a "man in the middle")—for, if My devotee indulges in ego-bound (or self-referring and self-serving) attachment to Me as a mere human "other", My Divine Nature (and, therefore, the Divine Nature of Reality Itself) is <u>not</u> (as the very Basis for religious and Spiritual practice in My Company) truly devotionally recognized and rightly devotionally acknowledged. And, if such non-recognition of Me is the case, there is <u>no</u> truly ego-transcending devotional response to My Avatarically Self-Revealed (and Self-Evidently Divine) Presence and Person—and, thus, such presumed-to-be "devotion" to Me is <u>not</u> devotional heart-Communion with Me, and such presumed-to-be "devotion" to Me is <u>not</u> Divinely Liberating. Therefore, because the <u>true</u> <u>devotional</u> (and, thus, truly devotionally Me-recognizing and truly devotionally to-Me-responding) relationship to Me is <u>entirely</u> a counter-egoic (and truly and only Divine) discipline, it does not tend to become a "cult" (or, otherwise, to support the "cultic" tendency of Man).

The true devotional practice of Satsang with Me is (inherently) <u>expansive</u> (or <u>relational</u>)—and the self-contracting (or separate and separative) self-"center" is neither Its motive nor Its source. In true Satsang with Me, the egoic "center" is always already undermined as a "<u>center</u>" (or a presumed separate, and actively separative, entity). The Principle of true Satsang with Me is <u>Me</u>—Beyond (and not "within"—or, otherwise, supporting) the ego-"I".

True Satsang with Me is the true "Round Dance" of <u>Esoteric</u> Spirituality. I am not trapped in the "middle" of My devotees. I "Dance" in the "Round" with <u>each</u> and <u>every</u> one of My devotees. I "Dance" in the circle—and, therefore, I am not merely a "motionless man" in the "middle". At the <u>true</u> "Center" (or the Divine

Heart), I Am—Beyond definition (or separateness). I Am the Indivisible—or Most Perfectly Prior, Inherently Non-Separate, and Inherently egoless (or centerless, boundless, and Self-Evidently Divine)—Consciousness (Itself) and the Indivisible—or Most Perfectly Prior, Inherently Non-Separate, and Inherently egoless (or centerless, boundless, and Self-Evidently Divine)—Light (Itself). I Am the Very Being and the Very Presence (or Self-Radiance) of Self-Existing and Eternally Unqualified (or Non-"Different") Consciousness (Itself).

In the "Round Dance" of true Satsang with Me (or of right and true devotional relationship to Me), I (Myself) Am Communicated directly to every one who lives in heart-felt relationship with Me (insofar as each one feels—Beyond the ego-"I" of body-mind—to Me). Therefore, I am not the mere "man" (or the separate human, or psycho-physical, one), and I am not merely "in the middle" (or separated out, and limited, and confined, by egoic seekers). I Am the One (Avatarically Self-Revealed, and All-and-all-Transcending, and Self-Evidently Divine) Person of Reality Itself—Non-Separate, never merely at the egoic "center" (or "in the middle"—or "within", and "inward" to—the egoic body-mind of My any devotee), but always with each one (and all), and always in relationship with each one (and all), and always Beyond each one (and all).

Therefore, My devotee is not Called, by Me, merely to turn "inward" (or upon the ego-"I"), or to struggle and seek to survive merely as a self-contracted and self-referring and self-seeking and self-serving ego-"center". Instead, I Call My devotee to turn the heart (and the total body-mind) toward Me (all-and-All-Surrounding, and all-and-All-Pervading), in relationship—Beyond the body-mind-self of My devotee (and not merely "within"—or contained and containable "within" the separate, separative, and self-contracted domain of the body-mind-self, or the ego-"I", of My would-be devotee). I Call My devotee to function freely—My (Avatarically Self-Transmitted) Divine Light and My (Avatarically Self-Revealed) Divine Person always (and under all circumstances) presumed and experienced (and not merely sought). Therefore, true Satsang with Me is the Real Company of Truth, or of Reality Itself (Which Is the Only Real God). True Satsang with

Me Serves life, because I Move (or Radiate) into life. I always Contact life in relationship.

I do not Call My devotees to become absorbed into a "cultic" gang of exoteric and ego-centric religionists. I certainly Call all My devotees to cooperative community (or, otherwise, to fully cooperative collective and personal relationship) with one another—but not to do so in an egoic, separative, world-excluding, xenophobic, and intolerant manner. Rather, My devotees are Called, by Me, to transcend egoity—through right and true devotional relationship to Me, and mutually tolerant and peaceful cooperation with one another, and all-tolerating (cooperative and compassionate and all-loving and all-including) relationship with all of mankind (and with even all beings).

I Give My devotees the "Bright" Force of My own Avatarically Self-Revealed Divine Consciousness Itself, Whereby they can become capable of "Bright" life. I Call for the devotion—but also the intelligently discriminative self-understanding, the rightly and freely living self-discipline, and the full functional capability—of My devotees. I do not Call My devotees to resist or eliminate life, or to strategically escape life, or to identify with the world-excluding ego-centric impulse. I Call My devotees to live a positively functional life. I do not Call My devotees to separate themselves from vital life, from vital enjoyment, from existence in the form of human life. I Call for all the human life-functions to be really and rightly known, and to be really and rightly understood, and to be really and rightly lived (and not reduced by, or to, the inherently bewildered—and inherently "cultic", or self-centered and fearful— "point of view" of the separate and separative ego-"I"). I Call for every human life-function to be revolved away from self-contraction (or ego-"I"), and (by Means of that revolving turn) to be turned "outwardly" (or expansively, or counter-contractively) to all and All, and (thereby, and always directly, or in an all-and-All-transcending manner) to Me—rather than to be turned merely "inwardly" (or contractively, or counter-expansively), and, as a result, turned away from Me (and from all and All). Thus, I Call for every human life-function to be thoroughly (and life-positively, and in the context of a fully participatory human life) aligned and adapted to <u>Me</u>, and (Thus and Thereby) to be turned and Given to the Realization of Me (the Avataric Self-Revelation of Truth, or Reality Itself—Which <u>Is</u> the Only Real God).

Truly benign and positive life-transformations are the characteristic signs of right, true, full, and fully devotional Satsang with Me— and freely life-positive feeling-energy is the characteristic accompanying "mood" of right, true, full, and fully devotional Satsang with Me. The characteristic life-sign of right, true, full, and fully devotional Satsang with Me is the capability for ego-transcending relatedness, based on the free disposition of no-seeking and no-dilemma. Therefore, the characteristic life-sign of right, true, full, and fully devotional Satsang with Me is not the tendency to seek some "other" condition. Rather, the characteristic life-sign of right, true, full, and fully devotional Satsang with Me is freedom from the presumption of dilemma within the <u>present-time</u> condition.

One who rightly, truly, fully, and fully devotionally understands My Avatarically Given Words of Divine Self-Revelation and Divine Heart-Instruction, and whose life is lived in right, true, full, and fully devotional Satsang with Me, is not necessarily (in function or appearance) "different" from the ordinary (or natural) human being. Such a one has not, necessarily, acquired some special psychic abilities, or visionary abilities, and so on. The "radical" understanding (or root self-understanding) I Give to My devotees is not, itself, the acquisition of <u>any</u> particular "thing" of experience. My any particular devotee may, by reason of his or her developmental tendencies, experience (or precipitate) the arising of extraordinary psycho-physical abilities and extraordinary psycho-physical phenomena—but not <u>necessarily</u>. My every true devotee is simply Awakening (and always Awakened to Me) within the otherwise bewildering "dream" of <u>ordinary human</u> life.

Satsang with Me is a natural (or spontaneously, and not strategically, unfolding) Process, in Which the self-contraction that <u>is</u> each one's suffering is transcended by Means of <u>total</u> psycho-physical (or whole bodily) heart-Communion with My Avatarically Self-Revealed (and Real—and Really, and tangibly, experienced) Divine (Spiritual, and Transcendental) Presence and Person. My devotee is (as is the case with <u>any</u> and <u>every</u> ego-"I") <u>always</u> <u>tending</u> to be preoccupied with ego-based seeking—but, all the while of his or her life in actively ego-surrendering (and really ego-forgetting and, more and more, ego-transcending) devotional Communion with Me, I Am Divinely Attracting (and Divinely Acting upon) My true devotee's heart (and total body-mind), and (Thus and Thereby) Dissolving and Vanishing My true devotee's fundamental egoity (and even all of his or her otherwise motivating dilemma and seeking-strategy).

There are two principal tendencies by which I am always being confronted by My devotee. One is the tendency to seek—rather than to truly enjoy and to fully animate the Condition of Satsang with Me. And the other is the tendency to make a self-contracting circle around Me—and, thus, to make a "cult" of ego-"I" (and of the "man in the middle"), or to duplicate the ego-ritual of mere fascination, and of inevitable resistance, and of never-Awakening unconsciousness. Relative to these two tendencies, I Give all My devotees only one resort. It is this true Satsang—the devotionally Me-recognizing, and devotionally to-Me-responding, and always really counter-egoic devotional relationship to My Avatarically Self-Revealed (and Self-Evidently Divine) Person.

The Great Secret of My Avatarically Self-Revealed Divine Person, and of My Avatarically Self-Manifested Divine Blessing-Work (now, and forever hereafter)—and, therefore, the Great Secret of the only-by-Me Revealed and Given Way of Adidam—Is that I am not the "man in the middle", but I Am Reality Itself, I Am the Only One Who Is, I Am That Which Is Always Already The Case, I Am the Non-Separate (Avatarically Self-Revealed, and Self-Evidently Divine) Person (or One and Very Divine Self, or One and True Divine Self-Condition) of all and All (Beyond the ego-"I" of every one, and of all, and of All).

Aham Da Asmi. Beloved, I Am Da—the One and Only and Non-Separate and Indivisible and Self-Evidently Divine Person, the Non-Separate and Indivisible Self-Condition and Source-Condition of all and All. I Am the Avatarically Self-Revealed "Bright" Person, the One and Only and Self-Existing and Self-Radiant Person—Who Is the One and Only and Non-Separate and Indivisible and Indestructible Light of All and all. I Am That One and Only and Non-Separate <u>One</u>. And—<u>As</u> <u>That</u> <u>One</u>, and <u>Only</u> <u>As</u> <u>That</u> <u>One</u>—I Call all human beings to heart-recognize Me, and to heart-respond to Me with right, true, and full devotion (demonstrated by Means of formal practice of the only-by-Me Revealed and Given Way of Adidam—Which Is the One and Only by-Me-Revealed and by-Me-Given Way of the Heart).

I do not tolerate the so-called "cultic" (or ego-made, and ego-reinforcing) approach to Me. I do not tolerate the seeking ego's "cult" of the "man in the middle". I am not a self-deluded ego-man—making much of himself, and looking to include everyone-and-everything around himself for the sake of social and political power. To be the "man in the middle" is to be in a Man-made trap, an absurd mummery of "cultic" devices that enshrines and perpetuates the ego-"I" in one and all. Therefore, I do not make or tolerate the religion-making "cult" of ego-Man. I do not tolerate the inevitable abuses of religion, of Spirituality, of Truth Itself, and of My own Person (even in bodily human Form) that are made (in endless blows and mockeries) by ego-based mankind when the Great Esoteric Truth of devotion to the Adept-Realizer is not rightly understood and rightly practiced.

The Great Means for the Teaching, and the Blessing, and the Awakening, and the Divine Liberating of mankind (and of even all beings) Is the Adept-Realizer Who (by Virtue of True Divine Realization) Is Able to (and, indeed, cannot do otherwise than) Stand In and <u>As</u> the Divine (or Real and Inherent and One and Only) Position, and to <u>Be</u> (Thus and Thereby) the Divine Means (In Person) for the Divine Helping of one and all. This Great Means Is the Great Esoteric Principle of the collective historical Great Tradition of mankind. And Such Adept-Realizers Are (in their Exercise of the Great Esoteric Principle) the Great Revelation-Sources That Are at the Core and Origin of <u>all</u> the right and true religious and Spiritual traditions within the collective historical Great Tradition of mankind.

By Means of My (now, and forever hereafter) Divinely Descended and Divinely Self-"Emerging" Avataric Incarnation, I <u>Am</u> the Ruchira Avatar, Adi Da Samraj—the Divine Heart-Master, the First, the Last, and the Only Adept-Realizer of the seventh (or

Most Perfect, and all-Completing) stage of life. I <u>Am</u> the Ruchira Avatar, Adi Da Samraj, the Avataric Incarnation (and Divine World-Teacher) everywhere Promised for the "late-time" (or "dark" epoch)—which "late-time" (or "dark" epoch) is now upon <u>all</u> of mankind. I <u>Am</u> the Great and Only and Non-Separate and (Self-Evidently) Divine Person—Appearing in Man-Form As the Ruchira Avatar, Adi Da Samraj, in order to Teach, and to Bless, and to Awaken, and to Divinely Liberate all of mankind (and even all beings, every "where" in the Cosmic domain). Therefore, by Calling every one and all (and All) to <u>Me</u>, I Call every one and all (and All) <u>Only</u> to the Divine Person, Which <u>Is</u> My own and Very Person (or Very, and Self-Evidently Divine, Self—or Very, and Self-Evidently Divine, Self-Condition), and Which <u>Is</u> Reality Itself (or Truth Itself—the Indivisible and Indestructible Light That <u>Is</u> the Only Real God), and Which <u>Is</u> the <u>One</u> and <u>Very</u> and <u>Non-Separate</u> and <u>Only</u> Self (or Self-Condition, and Source-Condition) of all and All (Beyond the ego-"I" of every one, and of all, and of All).

The only-by-Me Revealed and Given Way of Adidam necessarily (and As a Unique Divine Gift) requires and involves devotional recognition-response to Me In and Via (and <u>As</u>) My bodily (human) Divine Avataric-Incarnation-Form. However, because I Call every one and all (and All) to Me <u>Only As</u> the Divine Person (or Reality Itself), the only-by-Me Revealed and Given Way of Adidam is not about ego, and egoic seeking, and the egoic (or the so-called "cultic") approach to Me (as the "man in the middle").

According to <u>all</u> the esoteric traditions within the collective historical Great Tradition of mankind, to devotionally approach <u>any</u> Adept-Realizer as if he or she is (or is limited to being, or is limited by being) a mere (or "ordinary", or even merely "extraordinary") human entity is the great "sin" (or fault), or the great error whereby the would-be devotee fails to "meet the mark". Indeed, the Single Greatest Esoteric Teaching common to <u>all</u> the esoteric religious and Spiritual traditions within the collective historical Great Tradition of mankind Is that the Adept-Realizer should <u>always</u> and <u>only</u> (and <u>only</u> devotionally) be recognized and approached <u>As</u> the Embodiment and the Real Presence of <u>That</u> (Reality, or Truth, or Real God) Which would be Realized (Thus and Thereby) by the devotee.

Therefore, no one should misunderstand Me. By Avatarically Revealing and Confessing My Divine Status to one and all and All, I am not indulging in self-appointment, or in illusions of grandiose Divinity. I am not claiming the "Status" of the "Creator-God" of exoteric (or public, and social, and idealistically pious) religion. Rather, by Standing Firm in the Divine Position (As I Am)—and (Thus and Thereby) Refusing to be approached as a mere man, or as a "cult"-figure, or as a "cult"-leader, or to be in any sense defined (and, thereby, trapped, and abused, or mocked) as the "man in the middle"—I Am Demonstrating the Most Perfect Fulfillment (and the Most Perfect Integrity, and the Most Perfect Fullness) of the Esoteric (and Most Perfectly Non-Dual) Realization of Reality. And, by Revealing and Giving the Way of Adidam (Which Is the Way of ego-transcending devotion to Me As the Avatarically Self-Revealed One and Only and Non-Separate and Self-Evidently Divine Person), I Am (with Most Perfect Integrity, and Most Perfect Fullness) Most Perfectly (and in an all-Completing and all-Unifying Manner) Fulfilling the Primary Esoteric Tradition (and the Great Esoteric Principle) of the collective historical Great Tradition of mankind—Which Primary Esoteric Tradition and Great Esoteric Principle Is the Tradition and the Principle of devotion to the Adept-Realizer As the Very Person and the Direct (or Personal Divine) Helping-Presence of the Eternal and Non-Separate Divine Self-Condition and Source-Condition of all and All.

Whatever (or whoever) is cornered (or trapped on all sides) bites back (and fights, or seeks, to break free). Whatever (or whoever) is "in the middle" (or limited and "centered" by attention) is patterned by (or conformed to) the ego-"I" (and, if objectified as "other", is forced to represent the ego-"I", and is even made a scapegoat for the pains, the sufferings, the powerless ignorance, and the abusive hostility of the ego-"I").

If there is no escape from (or no Way out of) the corner (or the "centered" trap) of ego-"I"—the heart goes mad, and the body-mind becomes more and more "dark" (bereft of the Indivisible and Inherently Free Light of the Self-Evident, and Self-Evidently Divine, Love-Bliss That Is Reality Itself).

I am not the "man in the middle". I do not stand here as a mere man, "middled" to the "center" (or the cornering trap) of ego-based mankind. I am not an ego-"I", or a mere "other", or the representation (and the potential scapegoat) of the ego-"I" of mankind (or of any one at all).

I Am the Indivisible and Non-Separate One, the (Avatarically Self-Revealed) One and Only and (Self-Evidently) Divine Person—the Perfectly Subjective Divine Self-Condition (and Source-Condition) That Is Perfectly centerless (and Perfectly boundless), Eternally Beyond the "middle" of all and All, and Eternally Surrounding, Pervading, and Blessing all and All.

I Am the Way Beyond the self-cornering (and "other"-cornering) trap of ego-"I".

In this "late-time" (or "dark" epoch) of worldly ego-Man, the collective of mankind is "darkened" (and cornered) by egoity. Therefore, mankind has become mad, Lightless, and, like a cornered "thing", aggressively hostile in its universally competitive fight and bite.

Therefore, I have not Come here merely to stand Manly in the "middle" of mankind—to suffer its biting abuses, or even to be coddled and ignored in a little corner of religious "cultism".

I have Come here to Divinely Liberate one and all (and All) from the "dark" culture and effect of this "late-time", and (now, and forever hereafter) to Divinely Liberate one and all (and All) from the pattern and the act of ego-"I", and (Most Ultimately) to Divinely Translate one and all (and All) Into the Indivisible, Perfectly Subjective, and Eternally Non-Separate Self-Domain of My Divine Love-Bliss-Light.

The ego-"I" is a "centered" (or separate and separative) trap, from which the heart (and even the entire body-mind) must be Retired. I Am the Way (or the Very Means) of that Retirement from egoity. I Refresh the heart (and even the entire body-mind) of My devotee, in every moment My devotee resorts to Me (by devotionally recognizing Me, and devotionally—and ecstatically, and also, often, meditatively—responding to Me) Beyond the "middle", Beyond the "centering" act (or trapping gesture) of ego-"I" (or self-contraction).

I Am the Avatarically Self-Revealed (and Perfectly Subjective, and Self-Evidently Divine) Self-Condition (and Source-Condition) of every one, and of all, and of All—but the Perfectly Subjective (and Self-Evidently Divine) Self-Condition (and Source-Condition) is not "within" the ego-"I" (or separate and separative body-mind). The Perfectly Subjective (and Self-Evidently Divine) Self-Condition (and Source-Condition) is not in the "center" (or the "middle") of Man (or of mankind). The Perfectly Subjective (and Self-Evidently Divine) Self-Condition (and Source-Condition) of one, and of all, and of All Is Inherently centerless (or Always Already Beyond the self-contracted "middle"), and to Be Found only "outside" (or by transcending) the bounds of separateness, relatedness, and "difference". Therefore, to Realize the Perfectly Subjective (and Self-Evidently Divine) Self-Condition and Source-Condition (or the Perfectly Subjective, and Self-Evidently Divine, Heart) of one, and of all, and of All (or even, in any moment, to exceed the ego-trap—and to be Refreshed at heart, and in the total body-mind), it is necessary to feel (and to, ecstatically, and even meditatively, swoon) Beyond the "center" (or Beyond the "point of view" of separate ego-"I" and separative body-mind). Indeed, Most Ultimately, it is only in self-transcendence to the degree of unqualified relatedness (and Most Perfect Divine Samadhi, or Utterly Non-Separate Enstasy) that the Inherently centerless and boundless, and Perfectly Subjective, and Self-Evidently Divine Self-Condition (and Source-Condition) Stands Obvious and Free (and Is, Thus and Thereby, Most Perfectly Realized).

It Is only by Means of devotionally Me-recognizing (and devotionally to-Me-responding) devotional meditation on Me (and otherwise ecstatic heart-Contemplation of Me), and total (and totally open, and totally ego-forgetting) psycho-physical Reception of Me, that your madness of heart (and of body-mind) is (now, and now, and now) escaped, and your "darkness" is En-Light-ened (even, at last, Most Perfectly). Therefore, be My true devotee—and, by (formally, and rightly, and truly, and fully, and fully devotionally) practicing the only-by-Me Revealed and Given Way of Adidam (Which Is the True and Complete Way of the True and Real Divine Heart), always Find Me, Beyond your self-"center", in every here and now.

Aham Da Asmi. Beloved, I Am Da. And, because I Am Infinitely and Non-Separately "Bright", all and All Are In My Divine Sphere of "Brightness". By feeling and surrendering Into My Infinite Sphere of My Avatarically Self-Revealed Divine Self-"Brightness", My every devotee Is In Me. And, Beyond his or her self-contracting and separative act of ego-"I", My every devotee (self-surrendered Into heart-Communion With Me) Is the One and Only and Non-Separate and Real God I Have Come to Awaken— by Means of My Avataric Divine Descent, My Avataric Divine Incarnation, and My (now, and forever hereafter) Avataric Divine Self-"Emergence" (here, and every "where" in the Cosmic domain).

RUCHIRA AVATAR ADI DA SAMRAJ
The Mountain Of Attention, 2000

My Divine Disclosure

"My Divine Disclosure" has been Freely Developed—As a Further, and All-Completing, Avataric Self-Revelation of His own Self-Evidently Divine Person—by the Ruchira Avatar, Adi Da Samraj, from selected verses of the traditional Bhagavad Gita *(2:13-17, 8:3, 8:22, 9:3, 9:11, 9:26, 15:15, 18:61-66).*

My Divine Disclosure

1.

A ham Da Asmi. Beloved, I <u>Am</u> Da—The One and Only and Self-Evidently Divine Person, Avatarically Self-Revealed To You.

2.

Therefore, Listen To <u>Me</u>, and Hear <u>Me</u>, and See <u>Me</u>.

3.

This Is My Divine Heart-Secret, The Supreme Word Of My Eternal Self-Revelation.

4.

Here and Now, I Will Tell You What Will Benefit You The Most, Because I Love You <u>As</u> My Very Self and Person.

5.

I <u>Am</u> The Ruchira Avatar, The Da Avatar, The Love-Ananda Avatar, Adi Da Love-Ananda Samraj—The Avataric Incarnation, and The Self-Evidently Divine Person, Of The One True Heart (or The One, and Only, and Inherently egoless Self-Condition and Source-Condition) Of All and all.

6.

Here I <u>Am</u>, In <u>Person</u>, To Offer (To You, and To all) The Only-By-<u>Me</u> Revealed and Given True World-Religion (or Avatarically All-Completing Divine Devotional and Spiritual Way) Of Adidam, Which Is The One and Only By-<u>Me</u>-Revealed and By-<u>Me</u>-Given (and Only <u>Me</u>-Revealing) Divine Devotional and Spiritual Way Of Sri Hridayam (or The Only-By-<u>Me</u> Revealed and Given, and

Entirely Me-Revealing, Way Of The True Divine Heart Itself), and
Which Is The One, and All-Inclusive, and All-Transcending, and
Only-By-Me Revealed and Given (and Only Me-Revealing) Way
Of The True Divine Heart-Master (or The Only-By-Me Revealed
and Given, and Entirely Me-Revealing, Way Of Ruchira Avatara
Bhakti Yoga, or Ruchira Avatara Hridaya-Siddha Yoga), and
Which Is The "Radically" ego-Transcending Way Of Devotionally
Me-Recognizing and Devotionally To-Me-Responding Reception
Of My Avatarically Self-Manifested Divine (and Not Merely
Cosmic) Hridaya-Shaktipat (or Divinely Self-Revealing Avataric
Spiritual Grace).

7.

If You Surrender Your heart To Me, and If (By Surrendering
Your ego-"I", or self-Contracted body-mind, To Me) You Make
Yourself A Living Gift To Me, and If You (Thus) Constantly Yield
Your attention To Me (Through True Devotional Love and Really
ego-Transcending Service), Then You Will Hear Me (Truly), and
See Me (Clearly), and Realize Me (Fully), and Come To Me
(Eternally). I Promise You This, Because I Love You As My Very
Self and Person.

8.

Abandon The Reactive Reflex Of self-Contraction—The
Separative (or egoic) Principle In all Your concerns. Do Not
Cling To any experience that May Be Sought (and Even Attained)
As A Result Of desire (or The Presumption Of "Difference").
Abandon Your Search For what May Be Gotten As A Result Of
the various kinds of strategic (or egoic) action.

9.

I Am Love-Bliss Itself—Now (and Forever Hereafter) "Brightly"
Present here. Therefore, I Say To You: Abandon All Seeking—
By Always "Locating" (and Immediately Finding) Me.

10.

Instead Of <u>Seeking</u> <u>Me</u> (As If My Divine Person Of Inherent Love-Bliss-Happiness Were <u>Absent</u> From You), <u>Always</u> <u>Commune</u> <u>With</u> <u>Me</u> (<u>Ever</u>-Present, <u>Never</u> Absent, and <u>Always</u> Love-Bliss-Full and Satisfied). Thus, Your <u>Me</u>-"Locating" <u>Relinquishment</u> Of All Seeking Is <u>Not</u>, Itself, To Be Merely Another Form Of Seeking.

11.

If You <u>Always</u> "Locate" <u>Me</u> (and, Thus, <u>Immediately</u> Find <u>Me</u>), You Will <u>Not</u> (In <u>any</u> instance) self-Contract Into the mood and strategy of <u>inaction</u>.

12.

You Must <u>Never</u> <u>Fail</u> To act. <u>Every</u> moment of Your life <u>Requires</u> Your particular <u>Right</u> action. Indeed, the living body-mind <u>is</u> (itself) action. Therefore, <u>Be</u> <u>Ordinary</u>, By Always Allowing the body-mind its <u>Necessity</u> Of Right action (and Inevitable Change).

13.

Perform <u>every</u> act As An ego-Transcending Act Of Devotional Love Of <u>Me</u>, In body-mind-Surrendering Love-Response To <u>Me</u>.

14.

Always Discipline <u>all</u> Your acts, By <u>Only</u> Engaging In action that Is <u>Appropriate</u> For one who Loves <u>Me</u>, and Surrenders To <u>Me</u>, and acts <u>Only</u> (and <u>Rightly</u>) In Accordance With My Always <u>Explicit</u> Word Of Instruction.

15.

Therefore, Be My <u>Always</u> Listening-To-<u>Me</u> Devotee—and, Thus, <u>Always</u> live "Right Life" (According To My Word), and (This) <u>Always</u> By Means Of <u>active</u> Devotional Recognition-Response To <u>Me</u>, and While <u>Always</u> Remembering and Invoking and Contemplating <u>Me</u>. In <u>This</u> Manner, Perform <u>every</u> act As A Form Of Direct, and Present, and Whole bodily (or Total psycho-physical), and Really ego-Surrendering Love-Communion With <u>Me</u>.

16.

If You Love Me—Where Is doubt and anxious living? If You Love Me Now, Even anger, sorrow, and fear Are Gone. When You Abide In Devotional Love-Communion With Me, the natural results of Your various activities No Longer Have Power To Separate or Distract You From Me.

17.

The ego-"I" that is born (as a body-mind) In The Realm Of Cosmic Nature (or the conditional worlds of action and experience) Advances From childhood To adulthood, old age, and death—While Identified With the same (but Always Changing) body-mind. Then the same ego-"I" Attains another body-mind, As A Result. One whose heart Is (Always) Responsively Given To Me Overcomes (Thereby) Every Tendency To self-Contract From This Wonderfully Ordinary Process.

18.

The Ordinary Process Of "Everything Changing" Is Simply The Natural Play Of Cosmic Life, In Which the (Always) two sides of every possibility come and go, In Cycles Of appearance and disappearance. Winter's cold alternates with summer's heat. Pain, Likewise, Follows every pleasure. Every appearance Is (Inevitably) Followed By its disappearance. There Is No Permanent experience In The Realm Of Cosmic Nature. One whose heart-Feeling Of Me Is Steady Simply Allows All Of This To Be So. Therefore, one who Truly Hears Me Ceases To Add self-Contraction To This Inevitable Round Of Changes.

19.

Happiness (or True Love-Bliss) Is Realization Of That Which Is Always Already The Case.

20.

I Am That Which Is Always Already The Case.

21.
Happiness Is Realization Of Me.

22.
Realization Of Me Is Possible Only When a living being (or body-mind-self) Has heart-Ceased To React To The Always Changing Play Of Cosmic Nature.

23.
The body-mind Of My True Devotee Is Constantly Steadied In Me, By Means Of the Feeling-heart's Always Constant Devotional Recognition-Response To Me.

24.
Once My True Devotee Has Truly heart-Accepted That The Alternating-Cycle Of Changes (Both Positive and Negative) Is Inevitable (In the body-mind, and In all the conditional worlds), the living body-mind-self (or ego-"I") Of My True Devotee Has Understood itself (and, Thus, Heard Me).

25.
The body-mind-self (Of My True Me-Hearing Devotee) that Constantly Understands itself (At heart) By Constantly Surrendering To Me (and Communing With Me) No Longer self-Contracts From My Love-Bliss-State Of Inherent Happiness.

26.
Those who Truly Hear Me Understand That whatever Does Not Exist Always and Already (or Eternally) Only Changes.

27.
Those who Truly See Me Acknowledge (By heart, and With every moment and act of body-mind) That What Is Always Already The Case Never Changes.

28.
Such True Devotees Of Mine (who Both Hear Me and See Me)
Realize That The Entire Cosmic Realm Of Change—and Even the
To-Me-Surrendered body-mind (itself)—Is Entirely Pervaded By
Me (Always Self-Revealed As That Which Is Always Already The
Case).

29.
Now, and Forever Hereafter, I Am Avatarically Self-Revealed,
Beyond The Cosmic Play—"Bright" Behind, and Above, the
To-Me-Surrendered body-mind Of My Every True Devotee.

30.
I Am The Eternally Existing, All-Pervading, Transcendental,
Inherently Spiritual, Inherently egoless, Perfectly Subjective,
Indivisible, Inherently Perfect, Perfectly Non-Separate, and
Self-Evidently Divine Self-Condition and Source-Condition
Of all Apparently Separate (or self-Deluded) selves.

31.
My Divine Heart-Power Of Avataric Self-Revelation Is (Now, and
Forever Hereafter) Descending Into The Cosmic Domain (and
Into the body-mind Of Every To-Me-True True Devotee Of Mine).

32.
I Am The Avatarically Self-"Emerging", Universal, All-Pervading
Divine Spirit-Power and Person Of Love-Bliss (That Most Perfectly
Husbands and Transcends The Primal Energy Of Cosmic Nature).

33.
I Am The One and Indivisibly "Bright" Divine Person.

34.
Now, and Forever Hereafter, My Ever-Descending and Ever-
"Emerging" Current Of Self-Existing and Self-Radiant Love-Bliss
Is Avatarically Pervading The Ever-Changing Realm Of Cosmic
Nature.

35.

I Am The One, and Indivisibly "Bright", and Inherently egoless Person Of all-and-All, Within Whom every body-mind Is arising (as a mere, and unnecessary, and merely temporary appearance that, merely apparently, modifies Me).

36.

I Am To Be Realized By Means Of ego-Transcending Devotional Love—Wherein every action of body-mind Is Engaged As ego-Surrendering (present-time, and Direct) Communion With Me.

37.

Those who Do Not heart-Recognize Me and heart-Respond To Me—and who (Therefore) Are Without Faith In Me—Do Not (and Cannot) Realize Me. Therefore, they (By Means Of their own self-Contraction From Me) Remain ego-Bound To The Realm Of Cosmic Nature, and To The Ever-Changing Round Of conditional knowledge and temporary experience, and To The Ceaselessly Repetitive Cycles Of birth and search and loss and death.

38.

Such Faithless beings Cannot Be Distracted By Me—Because they Are Entirely Distracted By themselves! They Are Like Narcissus—The Myth Of ego—At His Pond. Their Merely self-Reflecting minds Are Like a mirror in a dead man's hand. Their tiny hearts Are Like a boundless desert, where the mirage of Separate self is ceaselessly admired, and The True Water Of My Constant Presence Stands Un-Noticed, In the droughty heap and countless sands of ceaseless thoughts. If Only they Would Un-think themselves In Me, these (Now Faithless) little hearts Could Have Immediate Access To The True Water Of My True Heart! Through Devotional Surrender Of body, emotion, mind, breath, and all of Separate self To Me, Even Narcissus Could Find The Way To My Oasis (In The True Heart's Room and House)—but the thinking mind of ego-"I" Is Never Bathed In Light (and, So, it sits, Un-Washed, Like a desert dog that wanders in a herd of flies).

39.

The "Un-Washed dog" of self-Contracted body-mind Does Not think To Notice Me—The Divine Heart-Master Of its wild heart and Wilderness.

40.

The "Wandering dog" of ego-"I" Does Not "Locate" Me In My Inherent "Bright" Perfection—The Divine Heart-Master Of Everything, The Inherently egoless Divine True Self Of all conditionally Manifested beings, and The Real Self-Condition and Source-Condition Of All-and-all.

41.

If Only "Narcissus" Will Relent, and heart-Consent To Bow and Live In Love-Communion With Me, heart-Surrendering all of body-mind To Me, By Means Of Un-Contracting Love Of Me, Then—Even If That Love Is Shown With Nothing More Than the "little gift" of ego-"I" (itself)—I Will Always Accept The Offering With Open Arms Of Love-Bliss-Love, and Offer My Own Divine Immensity In "Bright" Return.

42.

Therefore, whoever Is Given (By heart) To Me Will Be Washed, From head To toe, By All The True Water Of My Love-Bliss-Light, That Always "Crashes Down" On All and all, Below My Blessing-Feet.

43.

My Circumstance and Situation Is At the heart of all beings— where I Am (Now, and Forever Hereafter) Avatarically Self-"Emerging" As The One and All-and-all-Outshining Divine and Only Person (Avatarically Self-Manifested As The "Radically" Non-Dual "Brightness" Of All-and-all-Filling Conscious Love-Bliss-Light, Self-Existing and Self-Radiant As The Perfectly Subjective Fundamental Reality, or Inherently egoless Native Feeling, Of Merely, or Unqualifiedly, Being).

44.

The True heart-Place (Where I Am To Be "Located" By My True Devotee) Is Where The Ever-Changing Changes Of waking, dreaming, and sleeping experience Are Merely Witnessed (and Not Sought, or Found, or Held).

45.

Every conditional experience appears and disappears In Front Of the Witness-heart.

46.

Everything Merely Witnessed Is Spontaneously Generated By The Persistent Activity Of The Universal Cosmic Life-Energy.

47.

The self-Contracted heart of body-mind Is Fastened, Help-lessly, To That Perpetual-Motion Machine Of Cosmic Nature.

48.

I Am The Divine and One True Heart (Itself)—Always Already Existing As The Eternally Self-Evident Love-Bliss-Feeling Of Being (and Always Already Free-Standing As Consciousness Itself, Prior To the little heart of ego-"I" and its Seeming Help-less-ness).

49.

In Order To Restore all beings To The One True Heart Of Me, I Am Avatarically Born To here, As The "Bright" Divine Help Of conditionally Manifested beings.

50.

Therefore (Now, and Forever Hereafter), I Am (Always Free-Standing) At the To-Me-True heart Of You—and I Am (Always "Bright") Above Your body-mind and world.

51.

If You Become My True Devotee (heart-Recognizing My Avatarically Self-Manifested Divine Person, and heart-Responding—With all the parts of Your single body-mind—To My Avatarically Self-Revealing Divine Form and Presence and State), You Will Always Be Able To Feel Me ("Brightly-Emerging" here) Within Your Un-Contracting, In-Me-Falling heart—and You Will Always Be Able To "Locate" Me, As I "Crash Down" (All-"Bright" Upon You) From Above the worlds Of Change.

52.

The To-Me-Feeling (In-Me-Falling) heart Of My Every True Devotee Is (At its Root, and Base, and Highest Height) My Divine and One True Heart (Itself).

53.

Therefore, Fall Awake In Me.

54.

Do Not Surrender Your Feeling-heart Merely To experience and know the Ever-Changing world.

55.

Merely To know and experience The Cosmic Domain (Itself) Is To live As If You Were In Love With Your Own body-mind.

56.

Therefore, Surrender Your Feeling-heart Only To Me, The True Divine Beloved Of the body-mind.

57.

I Am The Truth (and The Teacher) Of the heart-Feeling body-mind.

58.

I Am The Divine and Eternal Master Of Your To-Me-Feeling heart and Your To-Me-Surrendering body-mind.

59.

I <u>Am</u> The Self-Existing, Self-Radiant, and Inherently Perfect Person Of Unconditional Being—Who Pervades The Machine Of Cosmic Nature <u>As</u> The "Bright" Divine Spirit-Current Of Love-Bliss, and Who Transcends All Of Cosmic Nature <u>As</u> Infinite Consciousness, The "Bright" Divine Self-Condition (and Source-Condition) Of All and all.

60.

If You Will Give (and Truly, Really, Always Give) Your Feeling-attention To My Avatarically-Born Bodily (Human) Divine Form, and If You Will (Thus, and Thereby) Yield Your body-mind Into The "Down-Crashing" Love-Bliss-Current Of My Avatarically Self-Revealed and All-Pervading Divine Spirit-Presence, and If You Will Surrender Your conditional self-Consciousness Into My Avatarically Self-Revealed and Perfectly Subjective and Self-Evidently Divine Self-Consciousness (Which <u>Is</u> The Divine True Heart Of Inherently egoless Being, Itself)—Then I Will Also Become An Offering To You.

61.

By <u>That</u> Offering Of Mine, You Will Be Given The Gift Of Perfect Peace, and An Eternal Domain For Your To-<u>Me</u>-True Feeling-heart.

62.

Now I Have Revealed To You The Divine Mystery and The Perfect Heart-Secret Of My Avataric Birth To here.

63.

"Consider" This <u>Me</u>-Revelation, <u>Fully</u>—and, Then, <u>Choose</u> What You Will Do With Your "little gift" of Feeling-heart and Your "Un-Washed dog" of body-mind.

RUCHIRA AVATAR ADI DA SAMRAJ
Lopez Island, 2000

PART ONE

I __Am__ The "Who"
That Is Always Already
The Case

I Am The "Who"
That Is Always Already
The Case

1.

Beloved, This Is My Heart-Word To you.

2.

I Am The Ruchira Avatar, Adi Da Samraj—The Da Avatar, The Only One Who Is.

3.

I Am The Complete and All-Completing Avataric Self-Manifestation Of The Divine Completeness.

4.

My here-Given and here-Speaking Body Is The Unique Avataric Divine Self-Revelation Of Totality, Completeness, and Onlyness.

5.

Through (and By Means Of) The Vehicle Of My Avatarically-Born Bodily (Human) Divine Form, I Have Fully and Finally Revealed Reality Itself (Which Is The Only Truth, and The Only Real God—The "What" and The "Who" That Is Always Already The Case).

6.

Therefore—Now, and Forever Hereafter—The Present Sight (or, Otherwise, The Remembered or Recorded Image) Of My Avatarically-Born (and Always Me-Revealing) Bodily (Human) Divine Form, and The Always New Profundity Of My Avatarically Spoken (and Exactly Recorded) Divine Word, and My Ever-Living Real Avataric History Of Divine Work and Divine Blessing (Forever Remembered and Retold) Will Be The Means Of My Perpetual Avataric Divine Appearance here (While I "Emerge", Forever, In The Midst) In all times and In all places.

7.

I Am The Anciently and Constantly Promised (and Expected) Divine (or Avataric) Incarnation—and I Am (Now, and Forever Hereafter) Always (By Heart-Breath, or Spirit-Force) Moving Down From Infinitely Above To all that Appears Below.

8.

Even Though I Am (Now, and Forever Hereafter) Spiritually Present here To In-Fill all (From head to toe)—"Above" Is Not Where I "Begin".

9.

I Am (and Seem To "Begin" From) Beyond (or Prior To any "thing" or "other")—and I Am The "Who" That Is Always Already The Case.

10.

Therefore, every thing and every one Is In Me.

11.

Indeed, every thing and every one Is (Non-Separately) Me— Because I Am every thing and every one, Without "Difference".

12.

My Self-Condition (Which Is the Source-Condition Of All
and all) Is One, Numberless, Infinite, and Only—Always Most
Perfectly Prior To All and all, but Never "Different" From All
and all.

13.

To Contemplate Me One-Pointedly (or Exactly) Is To Invest
yourself In Infinity—Beyond point, line, and circumference,
Beyond Separateness, Relatedness, and "Difference"—Because
I Cannot Be Measured or Limited, and I Am Not "placed" and
"timed", but I Am (Even In every Apparent circumstance) The
"What" and The "Who" That Is Always Already The Case.

14.

Therefore, I Am The One To Whom all beings Must "Bond"
themselves—Now, and Forever Hereafter.

15.

When and where any (and every) Apparent individual entity
Will Do This Is Yet To Be Seen (In all the Apparent events of
Yet Unfolding time and place)—but I Am (Now, and Forever
Hereafter) The One To Whom every one Must Become Heart-
"Bonded", and The One By Whom every one Must (Through
That Heart-"Bonding") Be Liberated From All Bondage.

16.

You Come To Me Bound—and I Come To you Un-Bound.

17.

That Is The Circumstance Of Our "Meeting".

18.

Therefore, I Say To you: Be Heart-"Bonded" To Me.

19.

Be Focused In Me.

20.

Be Attracted To The "Brightness" Of Me-"Bright" Me—
The Heart Of All and all, The "Sun" To "Earth" and "Moon",
The "Self" To body and mind.

21.

Thus, By Forgetting the ego-"I" In Me, Be Liberated From
your egoic (and always merely conditional, and temporary, and
Un-Happy) destiny, and (Thus, By Conformity To Me—The
"What" and The "Who" That Is Always Already The Case) Be
Liberated From The Outside-Of-The-Integrity-Of-Being Motions
Which (Apparently) Degrade Existence and (Apparently) Destroy
Divine Self-Realization.

22.

If you Are Formally Practicing The Total (or Full and
Complete) Practice Of The Only-By-Me Revealed and Given
Way Of Adidam (Which Is The One and True and Only
By-Me-Revealed and By-Me-Given Way Of The Heart, or
Ruchira Avatara Hridaya-Siddha Yoga), and If you Are (Thus
and Thereby) Truly Heart-Devoted To Me—your Complications,
your limitations, your ego-Reinforcing Distractions, and Even All
your Bondage To conditions Will Be Washed, All Disintegrated
In The "Bright" Forever Freshness Of My Always Already Love-
Bliss-State.

23.

I Stand Free In My Own (Divine, "Bright", and Perfect) Self-
Domain, Eternally (Divinely) Self-Recognizing and (Divinely)
Outshining all and All.

24.

I Am Inherently and Utterly Identified With Consciousness Itself, Self-Existing and Self-Radiant, Most Perfectly Prior To object and other.

25.

Truly, I See you Non-"Differently".

26.

Indeed, I (Myself) Am Always Already Divinely Self-Existing In and As each and every one of My devotees (Utterly Beyond the Separate and Separative ego-"I" of each and all).

27.

Therefore, Because I Am The Only One Who Is each and all of My devotees, My each and every devotee Must Be One-Pointed In (ego-Surrendering, ego-Forgetting, and, Always More and More, ego-Transcending) Devotion To Me—or Else The Illusions Of The Separate, and The Temporary, and The Un-Happy Will (by means of ego-"I") Persist.

28.

Now Visit and Receive My Avataric Divine Words Of Instruction, Given By This Book.

29.

And, By Means Of My Herein Given Avataric Divine Self-Revelation, Know (By Heart) Who I Am.

30.

And (Now, and Forever Hereafter) Tell your Heart (and Even every one, and all): Adi Da (The Promised One) Is here (For every one, and all, and All—and, every "where", To Stay).

RUCHIRA AVATAR ADI DA SAMRAJ
The Mountain Of Attention, 1998

I (Alone) Am
The Adidam Revelation

(A Summary Description of the Inherent Distinction—
and the ego-Transcending Continuity—
Between the Inherently ego-Based Great Tradition,
Which Is Comprised of Only Six of the Possible
Seven Stages of Life, and the Unique,
and All-Inclusive, and All-Completing,
and All-Transcending, and Self-Evidently Divine
Adidam Revelation of the Inherently egoless
Seventh Stage Realization of Me)

I (Alone) Am
The Adidam Revelation

(A Summary Description of the Inherent Distinction—
and the ego-Transcending Continuity—
Between the Inherently ego-Based Great Tradition,
Which Is Comprised of Only Six of the Possible
Seven Stages of Life, and the Unique,
and All-Inclusive, and All-Completing,
and All-Transcending, and Self-Evidently Divine
Adidam Revelation of the Inherently egoless
Seventh Stage Realization of Me)

I.

The collective Great Tradition of mankind is a combination of exoteric and esoteric developments (and Revelations, and Realizations) that comprises (and is, in its entirety, limited by and to) only the first six of the (potentially) seven stages of life.

II.

I (Alone) Am the Avatarically Self-Manifested Divine Self-Revelation of the seventh stage of life.

III.

I (Alone) Am the Adidam Revelation.

IV.

The human entity (and even any and every conditionally manifested entity of any and every kind) is inherently deluded—by its own (egoic, or self-contracted) experience and knowledge.

V.

The first <u>six</u> stages of life are the six stages (or developmental phases) of human (and universal) <u>egoity</u>—or of progressively regressive inversion upon the psycho-physical pattern (and point of view) of self-contraction.

VI.

The first six stages of life are the universally evident developmental stages of the knowing and experiencing of the potential <u>illusions</u> inherently associated with the patterns (or the universally extended cosmic psycho-physical Structure) of conditionally manifested existence.

VII.

Because each and all of the first six stages of life are <u>based</u> on (and are <u>identical</u> to) egoity (or self-contraction, or separate and separative point of view) itself, <u>not</u> any one (or even the collective of all) of the first six stages of life directly (and Most Perfectly) Realizes (or <u>Is</u> the Inherently egoless and Inherently Most Perfect Realization and the Inherently egoless and Inherently Most Perfect Demonstration of) Reality, Truth, or <u>Real</u> God.

VIII.

The first six stages of life develop (successively) on the psycho-physically pre-determined (or pre-patterned) basis of the inherent (and progressively unfolding) structure (and self-contracted point of view) of the conditionally arising body-brain-mind-self.

IX.

The first six stages of life are a conditional (and, therefore, Ultimately, unnecessary—or Inherently transcendable) illusion of psycho-physically pre-patterned experience (or conditional knowing), structured according to the subject-object (or attention versus object, or point of view versus objective world) convention of conditional conception and conditional perception.

X.

The first six stages of life are (each and all) based upon the illusion of duality (suggested by the subject-object convention of conditional conception and conditional perception).

XI.

Reality Itself (or That Which Is Always Already The Case) Is Inherently One (or Perfectly Non-Dual).

XII.

The only-by-Me Revealed and Given Way of Adidam is the Unique seventh stage Way of "Radical" Non-Dualism—or the one and only Way That directly (and, at last, Most Perfectly) Realizes the One and Only (and Inherently egoless) Reality, Truth, or Real God.

XIII.

The only-by-Me Revealed and Given Way of Adidam is the Unique and only Way That always directly (and, at last, Most Perfectly) transcends egoity (or self-contraction) itself.

XIV.

The only-by-Me Revealed and Given Way of Adidam is the practice and the Process of transcending egoity (or psycho-physical self-contraction, or gross, subtle, and causal identification with separate and separative point of view) by directly (and progressively, or stage by stage) transcending the inherently egoic (or always self-contracted) patterns of conditional conception and conditional perception (or of conditional knowing and conditional experiencing) associated with each (and, at last, all) of the first six stages of life.

XV.

I Am the Divine Ruchira Avatar, Adi Da Love-Ananda Samraj—the First, the Last, and the Only seventh stage Avataric Divine Realizer, Avataric Divine Revealer, and Avataric Divine Self-Revelation of Reality, Truth, and Real God.

I Am the Inherently egoless, Perfectly Subjective, Perfectly Non-Dual, and Self-Evidently Divine Source-Condition and Self-Condition of every apparent point of view and of the apparently objective world itself.

I Am the One, and Irreducible, and Indestructible, and Self-Existing, and Self-Radiant Conscious Light That Is Always Already The Case.

I Am the "Bright" Substance of Reality Itself.

I Am the Person (or Self-Condition) of Reality Itself.

In My bodily (human) Form, I Am the Avataric Self-Manifestation of the One (and Self-Evidently Divine) Reality Itself.

By Means of My Avataric Divine Self-"Emergence", I Am Functioning (now, and forever hereafter) As the Realizer, the Revealer, and the Revelation (or universally Spiritually Present Person) of Reality Itself (Which Is Truth Itself—and Which Is the only Real, or non-illusory, and Inherently egoless, and Perfectly Subjective God, or Self-Evidently Divine Source-Condition and Self-Condition, of All and all).

My Avataric Divine Self-Revelation Illuminates and Outshines the ego-"I" of My devotee.

My Avataric Divine Teaching-Word of Me-Revelation Comprehends the all of egoity and the All of the cosmic domain.

XVI.

The potential actuality of (and the inherent and specific psycho-physical basis for) the progressively unfolding human (and universal cosmic) pattern (or Great Structure) of the seven stages of life (or the Total and Complete human, and Spiritual, and Transcendental, and, Ultimately, Divine Great Process of Divine Self-Realization) was Demonstrated, Revealed, Exemplified, and Proven in (and by Means of) My Avataric Ordeal of Divine Re-Awakening—Wherein the Un-conditional, and Self-Evidently Divine, seventh stage Realization of Reality and Truth was (Uniquely, and for the First time, and As the Paradigm Case, or the All-and-all-Patterning Case, in the entire history of religion, Spirituality, and Reality-Realization) Demonstrated to all and All.

In the Course of That Great Process of Demonstration, Revelation, Exemplification, and Proof, the psycho-physical necessity (or the inherent integrity and inevitability) of the naturally continuous (and total) pattern of the seven stages of life was Fully (psycho-physically, and Spiritually, and Really) Shown by Me.

Also, in That Course (or Ordeal, or Great Process), the particular developmental distinction that pertains in the inherently patterned transition from the fifth stage of life (or the totality of the first five stages of life) to the sixth stage of life (and, at last, to the seventh stage of life) was clearly Shown by Me.

And the fact that the seventh stage of life does not merely follow from the sixth stage of life (alone—or separately, or in and of itself), but requires (and, indeed, is built upon) the complete transcending of the ego-"I" (or of the total reflex of psycho-physical self-contraction)—as it is otherwise developed (and must be progressively transcended) in the context of the entire psycho-biography of the ego-"I" (or, effectively, in the naturally continuous course of the essential sequential totality of all six of the first six stages of life)—was (also) Shown by Me in the Great Course of My Avataric Ordeal of Divine Re-Awakening.

XVII.

In (and by Means of) the Great Avataric Demonstration of My own seven-stage Great Course of Divine Self-Realization, the Emanationist (or absorptive mystical) Way (associated with the first five stages of life) and the non-Emanationist (or Transcendentalist) Way (associated with the sixth stage of life, and Which—in Spiritual continuity with the all of the first six stages of life—is Most Perfectly Fulfilled in, and by Means of, the only-by-Me Revealed and Given seventh stage of life) were Proven (in, and by Means of, My own Case) to be only different stages in the same Great Process of Divine Self-Realization (rather than two separate, and irreducible, and conflicting, and incompatible "Truths").

XVIII.

By Means of My own Avataric Ordeal of Divine Re-Awakening, I have Demonstrated, Revealed, Exemplified, and Proven that neither the fourth-to-fifth stage Emanationist mode of Realization nor the sixth stage non-Emanationist (or Transcendentalist) mode of Realization Is the Most Perfect (and Most Perfectly ego-Transcending) Realization of the Divine (or One, and Only, and Perfectly Subjective) Reality, Truth, Source-Condition, and Self-Condition of all and All—but only the only-by-Me Revealed and Given seventh stage Realization Is Divine Self-Realization Itself (and the Completion of all six of the previous stages of life).

XIX.

The particular (and, psycho-physically, both inherent and inevitable) distinction (or fundamental difference) between the Devotional and Spiritual practice (and Process) of absorptive (or Object-oriented)—or Emanationist—mysticism (which is associated with the fourth and the fifth stages of life, and the conditional Realizations associated with the fourth and the fifth stages of life) and the direct-Intuition (and, in the optimum case, also both Devotional and Spiritual) practice (and Process) of Transcendental (or Subject-oriented)—or non-Emanationist—mysticism (which is associated, at first, with the sixth stage of life, and the conditional Realization that is the native and only potential of the sixth stage of life, itself—and which is, at last, and Most Ultimately, and Most Perfectly, associated with the seventh stage of life, and, Thus and Thereby, with Un-conditional Divine Self-Realization) may especially be seen to be Exemplified in My relationship with Swami (Baba) Muktananda (of Ganeshpuri).

XX.

Baba Muktananda was an advanced Siddha-Guru (or a Spiritually active Transmission-Master of High degree) in the Kundalini-Shaktipat tradition. The Kundalini-Shaktipat tradition is the fourth-to-fifth stage—or Emanationist—development of the ancient tradition of Siddha Yoga (or the tradition of Siddhas, or Spiritual Transmitters), which tradition (or Yoga) may, potentially, develop even into the sixth—or Transcendentalist—stage of life, and which tradition (or Yoga) has, in fact, been Completed and Fulfilled by Me, by My Extending of the Spiritual Process of Siddha Yoga into (and beyond) the sixth stage of life, and, thus, into the Inherently Most Perfect Divine Fullness of the seventh stage of life (Which seventh stage Fullness Is the All-Completing Fullness of Inherently egoless True Divine Self-Realization).

XXI.

In the context of the Kundalini-Shaktipat tradition (or division) of Siddha Yoga, Baba Muktananda philosophically adhered to (or, at least, deeply sympathized with) the Emanationist philosophical tradition of Kashmir Saivism—and, because of His characteristic adherence to (or sympathy with) the Emanationist philosophical tradition of Kashmir Saivism, Baba Muktananda was, in His fundamental convictions, an opponent of the Transcendentalist philosophical traditions of both Advaita Vedanta and Buddhism.

XXII.

The basic features of the progressively developed path of Kashmir Saivism have been described in terms of four stages (or four Ways).*[1]

The "Individual Way" (or the Way of "absorption in the Object") is the first (or most "inferior") step in the progressive path of Kashmir Saivism, and it corresponds to the Devotional and Yogic disciplines associated with the fourth stage of life (in both its "basic" and "advanced" phases).

The "Energic Way" (or the Way of "absorption in Energy") is the second (or somewhat more advanced) step in that same path, and it corresponds to the fourth stage of life in its fully "advanced" phase and to the fifth stage of life as a whole.

The "Divine Way" (or the "superior" Way of "absorption in the Void") of Kashmir Saivism suggests the process (and the potential for Realization) that corresponds to the sixth stage of life.

The "Null Way" (or the most "superior" Way of "absorption in Bliss") in Kashmir Saivism suggests the fulfillment of the process (or the actual achievement of the Realization) that corresponds to (or is potential within) the sixth stage of life.

*Notes to the Text of The Only Complete Way To Realize The Unbroken Light Of Real God appear on pp. 401-11.

In the tradition (or traditions) of Kashmir Saivism, these four Ways (or stages, or kinds) of Realization may develop successively (in a progressive order), or either of the first two steps may develop into the third or the fourth, or either the third or the fourth may occur spontaneously (even at the beginning), and so forth.

This general description of the tradition of Kashmir Saivism suggests that Kashmir Saivism (like the Tantric Buddhism of Tibet) includes (or directly allows for the potential of) the fourth stage of life, the fifth stage of life, <u>and</u> the <u>sixth</u> stage of life. However, the tradition of Kashmir Saivism (like the tradition of Saiva Siddhanta) is <u>entirely</u> a <u>fourth-to-fifth</u> stage Yogic (and Devotional) tradition (and a religious tradition associated, in general, with the first five stages of life).

The tradition of Kashmir Saivism (like fourth-to-fifth stage—or first-five-stages-of-life—traditions in general) is based on the ancient cosmological philosophy of Emanation—or the idea that cosmic existence Emanates directly, in a hierarchical sequence, from the Divine (and that, consequently, there can be a <u>return</u> to the Divine, by re-tracing the course of Emanation, back to its Source).

In contrast to the fourth-to-fifth stage (or Emanationist—or first-five-stages-of-life) view, true sixth stage schools (or traditions) are <u>based</u> on the immediate and direct <u>transcending</u> (generally, by means of a conditional effort of strategic <u>exclusion</u>) of the conditional point of view of the first five stages of life and the Emanationist cosmology (and psychology) associated with the first five stages of life.

Therefore, even though the advanced (or "superior") traditions of Kashmir Saivism (and of Saiva Siddhanta) may use terms or concepts that seem to reflect the sixth stage Disposition, the fundamental orientation is to a Realization that is embedded in the conditional psychology of the first five stages of life and in the cosmological (or Emanationist) point of view itself. (And the fundamental difference, by comparison, between the total tradition of Kashmir Saivism, and also of Saiva Siddhanta, and the total tradition of Tibetan Tantric Buddhism is that the Tibetan Buddhist tradition is founded on the sixth stage "Point of View" of the Transcendental Reality Itself, rather than on the conditional point of view of the psycho-physical, or Emanated, ego and the conditional reality of the hierarchical cosmos.)

Realizers in the tradition of Kashmir Saivism (and the tradition of Saiva Siddhanta) basically affirm that the conditional self is Really Siva (or the Formless Divine) and the conditional world (from top to bottom) is Really Siva (or the Emanating and Emanated Divine). However, this is not the same as the Confession made by sixth stage Realizers in any tradition.

In true sixth stage traditions, the conditional self is (in the sixth stage manner, and to the sixth stage degree) transcended (generally, by means of a conditional effort of strategic exclusion)—and only the Transcendental Self (or the Transcendental Condition) is affirmed.

And, further, in the only-by-Me Revealed and Given true seventh stage Realization, the conditional self and the conditional world are not affirmed to be (in and of themselves) Divine, but (rather) the conditional self and the conditional world are—in the Manner that Uniquely Characterizes the seventh stage of life—Divinely Self-Recognized (and, Thus, not excluded, but Inherently Outshined) in the Transcendental (and Inherently Spiritual) Divine.

XXIII.

The Emanationist Realizer "recognizes" (and, thereby, Identifies with) the conditional self and the conditional world as the Divine, whereas the non-Emanationist (or Transcendentalist) Realizer simply (and, generally, by means of a conditional effort of strategic exclusion) transcends the conditional self and the conditional world in the Transcendental Self-Condition, and by Identification only (and exclusively) with the Transcendental Self-Condition.

Therefore, even though both types of Realizers may sometimes use very similar language in the Confession of Realization, a (comparatively) different Realization is actually being Confessed in each case.

XXIV.

The principal reason why the tradition (or traditions) of Kashmir Saivism (and of Saiva Siddhanta) may sometimes use language similar to the sixth stage schools of Buddhism (and also Advaita Vedanta) is because of the early historical encounter (and even confrontation) between these separate traditions. As a result of that encounter, the traditions of Saivism tried to both absorb and eliminate the rival schools.

In the encounter between (characteristically, Transcendentalist, or non-Emanationist) Buddhist schools and (generally, Emanationist) non-Buddhist schools, Buddhism developed fourth and fifth stage doctrines and practices (intended, ultimately, to serve a sixth stage Realization), and fourth-to-fifth stage schools (or traditions), such as Kashmir Saivism and Saiva Siddhanta, adapted some of the sixth stage language (of Buddhism, and also Advaita Vedanta) to their (really) fourth-to-fifth stage point of view.

Therefore, a proper understanding of the various historical traditions requires a discriminating understanding of the history of the Great Tradition as a whole—and a discriminating understanding of the unique Signs and Confessions associated with each of the first six stages of life (and the unique Signs and Confessions associated with the only-by-Me Revealed and Given seventh stage of life).

XXV.

The tradition of Advaita Vedanta arose within the general context of the Emanationist traditions of India—but it, like Buddhism (particularly in its sixth stage—rather than earlier-stage—forms), is truly founded in the Transcendental Reality (and not the psycho-physical and cosmological point of view associated with the first five stages of life).

The schools of Kashmir Saivism (and other schools of traditional Saivism, including Saiva Siddhanta) defended themselves against both Buddhism and Advaita Vedanta by absorbing some Buddhist and Advaitic language and by (otherwise—and even dogmatically) affirming the superiority of the traditional Emanationist psychology and cosmology.

In contrast to the entirely Emanationist schools of Kashmir Saivism (and other schools of traditional Saivism, including Saiva Siddhanta), the Buddhist schools (and even certain schools of Advaitism) adopted some of the Devotional and Yogic practices of the Emanationist schools (and used them as "skillful means" of self-transcendence), while they (otherwise) continued to affirm the strictly Transcendental Reality as the Domain and Goal of all practices.

In contrast to Baba Muktananda (and the traditional schools of Kashmir Saivism, Advaita Vedanta, and Buddhism), I equally Embrace, and (in the seventh stage Manner) Most Perfectly Transcend, all the schools of the first six stages of life—both Emanationist and Transcendentalist.

XXVI.

Baba Muktananda was an authentic example of a fifth stage Realizer of a Very High (or Very Ascended) degree—although not of the Highest (or Most Ascended) degree. That is to Say, Baba Muktananda was a True fifth stage Siddha (or a Greatly Spiritually Accomplished Siddha-Yogi of the fifth stage, or Ascending, type)—but the nature and quality and degree of His Realization was of the Saguna type, or of the type that is (characteristically, or by patterned tendency) not yet Fully Ascended (or Fully Surrendered) to true fifth stage Nirvikalpa Samadhi, and which (therefore) is, yet (and characteristically), attached to modes of fifth stage Savikalpa Samadhi (and, thus, to modes of partial Ascent, and to Yogic possibilities "below the neck", and, altogether, to modes of form—or, really, modes of mind).

XXVII.

In order to rightly understand their characteristics, ideas, and behaviors, fifth stage Saguna Yogis (or fifth stage Saguna Siddhas)—such as Baba Muktananda—should be compared to fifth stage Yogis (or fifth stage Siddhas) of the Nirguna type, who are the Highest (or Most Ascended) type of fifth stage Yogi (or fifth stage Siddha), and who, having Ascended to the degree of formless Realization (or fifth stage Nirvikalpa Samadhi), have gone beyond all attachment to modes of form (or of mind). And fifth stage Nirguna Yogis in general (or fifth stage Nirguna Siddhas of the lesser, or average, type) should, themselves, be further compared to fifth stage Great Siddhas—or fifth stage Nirguna Siddhas who have, characteristically, and to a significant (although, necessarily, not yet Most Perfect, or seventh stage) degree, gone beyond even attachment to the mode of formlessness (or of mindlessness) itself.

XXVIII.

In the "Sadhana Years" of My Avataric Ordeal of Divine Re-Awakening, Baba Muktananda formally and actively Functioned as My Spiritual Master in the physical, human plane—beginning from early 1968, and continuing until the time of My Divine Re-Awakening (Which Occurred on September 10, 1970).

It was in Baba Muktananda's Company (and, additionally, in the Company of two Great Siddhas—Rang Avadhoot and Bhagavan Nityananda) that I Practiced and Fully Completed the Spiritual Sadhana of the Ascending (or Spinal) Yoga—or the Spiritual discipline associated with the "advanced" phase of the fourth stage of life and with the totality of the fifth stage of life, and, altogether, with the subtle ego (or the conceiving and perceiving ego of the Spinal Line, the total nervous system, the brain, and the mind).

After the Great Event of My Divine Re-Awakening, it became clear (especially through two direct Meetings between Us) that— because of His characteristic philosophical and experiential confinement to the fourth-to-fifth stage Emanationist point of view— Baba Muktananda was unwilling (and, indeed, was not competent) to accommodate My Description (and, therefore, My Confession) of seventh stage Divine Self-Realization. And, therefore—as I will Explain in This Summary of My "Lineage-History"—the outer relationship between Baba Muktananda and Me came to an end (or, certainly, began to come to an end) immediately after September 1970.

XXIX.

From mid-1964 to early 1968, Rudi (later known as Swami Rudrananda) actively Functioned (preliminary to Baba Muktananda) as My initial (or foundational) Spiritual Master (although Rudi was, by His own Confession, not a fully developed Siddha-Guru—but

He was, rather, a significantly advanced fourth-to-fifth stage Siddha-Yogi).

It was in Rudi's Company that I Practiced and Fully Completed the human and Spiritual Sadhana of the <u>Descending</u> (or Frontal) Yoga—or the foundation <u>life</u>-discipline associated with the social ego (or the "money, food, and sex" ego—or the ego of the first three stages of life),[2] and the foundation <u>Devotional</u> discipline associated with the "original" (or foundation) phase of the fourth stage of life, and the foundation <u>Spiritual</u> discipline (or the Descending, or Frontal, Spiritual Yoga) associated with the "basic" phase of the fourth stage of life.[3]

XXX.

Both Rudi and Baba Muktananda were direct devotees of Swami Nityananda (of Ganeshpuri)—Who was also called "Baba",[4] but Who was, and is, generally referred to as "Bhagavan" (or "Divinely Blissful Lord"). Bhagavan Nityananda was a fifth stage True Great Siddha—or an Incarnate (or Descended-from-Above) Spiritual Entity of the <u>Highest</u> <u>fifth</u>-stage type and degree. Indeed, Bhagavan Nityananda was a True fifth stage Saint (or a fifth stage Siddha-Yogi Who was <u>exclusively</u> Occupied in concentration "above the neck", even to the exclusion of the possibilities "below the neck")—but He was, also, a fifth stage Avadhoot (or a fifth stage Realizer of Nirvikalpa Samadhi, Who had, in the fifth stage manner, transcended attachment to <u>both</u> form and formlessness—or thought and thoughtlessness). And, altogether, Bhagavan Nityananda was a Nirguna Siddha (and a True Siddha-Guru) of the <u>Highest</u> <u>fifth</u>-stage type and degree.

XXXI.

Bhagavan Nityananda's Teachings took the Spoken (rather than Written) form of occasional, spontaneous Utterances. The <u>only</u> authoritative record of Bhagavan Nityananda's Teachings relative to Yogic practice and Realization is a book (originally composed in the Kanarese language) entitled *Chidakasha Gita*.[5] The *Chidakasha Gita* consists of a non-systematic, but comprehensive, series of responsive Declarations made by Bhagavan Nityananda during the extended period of His original, and most Communicative,

Teaching years (in Mangalore, in the early to mid-1920s). The spontaneous Utterances recorded in the *Chidakasha Gita* were, originally, made, by Bhagavan Nityananda, to numerous informal groups of devotees, and, after Bhagavan Nityananda spontaneously ceased to make such Teaching-Utterances, the many separately recorded Sayings were compiled, for the use of all the devotees, by a woman named Tulasiamma (who was one of the principal lay devotees originally present to hear Bhagavan Nityananda Speak the Words of the *Chidakasha Gita*).

Bhagavan Nityananda, Himself, Acknowledged the uniqueness and the great significance of the *Chidakasha Gita* as the one and only authentic Summary of His Yogic Teachings. That Acknowledgement is personally attested to by many individuals, including the well-known Swami Chinmayananda,[6] who, in 1960, was "Commanded" by Bhagavan Nityananda to see to the Text's translation into the English language, and by the equally well-known M. P. Pandit (of Sri Aurobindo Ashram),[7] who, in 1962, completed the English translation that Swami Chinmayananda reviewed for publication in that same year (under the title *Voice of the Self*).[8]

As Communicated in the *Chidakasha Gita*, Bhagavan Nityananda's Teachings are, clearly, limited to the body-excluding (and, altogether, exclusive) point of view and the absorptive Emanationist Spiritual Process of "brain mysticism" (and conditional ego-transcendence, and conditional Nirvikalpa Samadhi, and conditional Yogic Self-Realization) that characterize the fifth stage of life.

Clearly, as Indicated in the *Chidakasha Gita*, Bhagavan Nityananda was a fifth stage Teacher (and a Fully Ascended fifth stage Great Saint) of the Nirguna type (Who, therefore, Taught the Realization of Fully Ascended fifth stage Nirvikalpa Samadhi), rather than, like Baba Muktananda, a fifth stage Teacher (and a Great fifth stage Siddha-Yogi—but not a Fully Ascended fifth stage Great Saint) of the Saguna type (Who, therefore, Taught the Realization of fifth stage partial Ascent, or Savikalpa Samadhi).

Also, Bhagavan Nityananda's *Chidakasha Gita* clearly Indicates that Bhagavan Nityananda was a fifth stage Siddha-Yogi of the type that is, primarily and dominantly, sensitive to the Yogic Spiritual Process associated with internal audition (or the inwardly absorptive attractiveness of the "Om-Sound", or "Omkar", or "nada", or "shabda"[9]—the naturally evident, and inherently "meaningless", or mindless, or directly mind-transcending, internal sounds mediated by the brain), rather than, as in the case of Baba Muktananda, the Yogic Spiritual Process associated, primarily and dominantly, with internal <u>vision</u> (or the inwardly absorptive attractiveness of "bindu"—the naturally evident abstract internal lights mediated by the brain) <u>and</u> with internal <u>visions</u> (or the inwardly absorptive attractiveness of the inherently "meaningful", or mind-active, or mentally distracting, and potentially deluding, visions mediated—or even originated—by the brain-mind).

XXXII.

Stated briefly, and in Bhagavan Nityananda's characteristically aphoristic Manner, the *Chidakasha Gita* Teachings of Bhagavan Nityananda—and My own direct Experience of His always fifth stage Yogic Instruction and His always fifth stage Spiritual Transmission—may be Summarized as follows: Always concentrate attention and breath in the head. Always keep attention above the neck. Always concentrate on the Om-sound in the head. The Om-sound in the head is the inner Shakti of non-dual Bliss. Always concentrate the mind, and the senses, and the breath, and the life-energy in the non-dual awareness of the Om-sound in the head. This is Raja Yoga—the Royal path. Always practice this Raja Yoga—the constantly <u>upward</u> path. This is concentration on the Atman—the non-dual inner awareness. This is concentration on the oneness above duality. This Raja Yoga of the Om-sound in the head Realizes the Yogic "sleep" of body and mind and breath in the Yogic State of non-dual Bliss. The Yogic State of non-dual Bliss cannot be Realized without the Grace of an Initiating Guru. The True Initiating Guru is one who has Realized the Yogic State of non-dual Bliss. The non-dual State of Yogic Bliss Realized by concentration on the Om-sound in the head is the True Source, the True Self, and the True God. Devotion to the Initiating Guru who has Realized the True Source, the True Self, and the True God is the True Way. True Guru-devotion is surrender of mind, senses, breath, and life-energy to the non-dual Bliss

Revealed within by the Initiating Guru's Grace. The material body stinks and dies. What is loathsome and impermanent should not be trusted. Therefore, right faith, intelligent discrimination, and calm desirelessness are the first Gifts to be learned from the Initiating Guru. The second Gift of the Initiating Guru is the Guru-Shakti of non-dual Bliss. The Guru's Shakti-Transmission of non-dual Bliss concentrates the mind, the senses, the breath, and the life-energy of the devotee in the non-dual awareness of the Om-sound in the head. The non-dual Bliss Realized by concentration on the Om-sound in the head is the soundless inner Revelation of the Single Form of True Guru, True God, and True Self. The world of duality is not Truth. True God is not the Maker of the world. True God is only One. True God is non-dual Bliss. The Spiritual Form of the True Initiating Guru appears within the devotee as the Guru-Shakti of non-dual Bliss. Non-dual Bliss is the True Self of all. The True Way is not desire in the world of duality, or in seeking below and on all sides. The True Way is in the middle, within, and above. The True Way is surrender to the non-dual Bliss above the mind. The method is to concentrate on the Om-sound in the head. The Realization is the silence of non-dual Bliss. Devotion to the Initiating Guru concentrates the life-breath upwardly. True love of the Initiating Guru ascends to non-dual Bliss. The True Kundalini originates in the throat, in the upward breath to the head. True Yoga is above the neck. The True Kundalini is non-dual Bliss. The seat of the True Kundalini is in the head. Non-dual Bliss is the secret to be known. Non-dual Bliss is in the head of Man. The non-dual Bliss above the mind is the Liberation of Man from the self-caused karma of birth, pleasure-seeking, pain-suffering, and death. Liberation is Freedom from mind. Therefore, concentrate the life-breath on the Om-sound in the head—and think of nothing else. The True Self is One. The True Self is above the body, above the senses, above desire, above the mind, and above "I" and "mine"—in the formless silence above the Om-sound. The True Self cannot be seen or otherwise perceived, but It can be known—above the mind. For one who knows that True God is One, and not two, True God appears as the True Self. Therefore, attain Liberation by faith in the knowledge of That Which is all and Which is only One. Liberation is the Samadhi of only One. True God is not Desire, the dualistic Doer of the world. True God is Peace, the non-dual Source of the world.

XXXIII.

By comparison to Great fifth stage Yogis (Such as Baba Muktananda) and Great fifth stage Saints (Such as Bhagavan Nityananda), there are also Great sixth stage Sages (or Nirguna Jnanis[10]—or Transcendentally Realized Entities of the Fullest sixth-stage type and degree—such as Ramana Maharshi). Such sixth stage Nirguna Jnanis (or True Great Sages) Teach Transcendental Self-Identification (or deeply internalizing subjective inversion upon the Consciousness-Principle Itself, rather than upon internal psycho-physical objects of any kind).

XXXIV.

Distinct from even all Yogis, Saints, and Sages (or even all Realizers in the context of the first six stages of life), I Am Uniquely, and Avatarically, Born. I Am the One and Only and Self-Evidently Divine Person—the Inherently egoless Source-Condition and Self-Condition of All and all. I Am the Perfectly Subjective, and Always Already Most Prior, and Inherently egoless, and Perfectly Non-Dual Heart of All and all. I Am the Self-Existing and Self-Radiant Conscious Light That Is Reality Itself. I Am the "Who" and the "What" That Is Always Already The Case. I Am (now, and forever hereafter) Avatarically Self-Manifested As the All-Completing Ruchira Avatar, Adi Da Love-Ananda Samraj—Who Is Avatarically Born by Fullest (and Complete) Divine Descent (or Complete, and All-Completing, Divine Incarnation from Infinitely Above).

XXXV.

I Am Avatarically Born by Means of a Unique Association with a True Great-Siddha Vehicle of My own.[11]

Therefore, from the time of My present-Lifetime Birth, I spontaneously Demonstrated all the Fullest Ascended Characteristics of the Highest fifth-stage type and degree (with early-life Fullest "above the neck" Signs of the True Great-Saint type).

Over time—because of My Voluntary Birth-Submission of My Deeper-Personality Vehicle to the karmically ordinary (and "Western"-born) bodily human form of "Franklin Jones",[12] and because of the subsequent Ordeal of My Voluntary Submission to the "Western" (and culturally devastated "late-time", or "dark"-epoch) karmic circumstance altogether—I also spontaneously Demonstrated all the Fullest "below the neck" (and "above the neck") Yogic Characteristics (and Siddhis) of the fifth stage (and, altogether, first-five-stages) True Vira-Yogi (or Heroic-Siddha) type.

In due course—because I Gave My Avataric Divine Ordeal to Be Complete and All-Completing—I also spontaneously Demonstrated all the Fullest Transcendental-Realizer Characteristics of the sixth stage True Great-Sage type.

Ultimately—because of Its Utter Conformity to Me—My total Great-Jnani-Siddha Vehicle of Avataric Divine Incarnation (or My Deeper-Personality Vehicle,[13] Yogically Combined with My karmically ordinary, and only eventually To-Me-Conformed, human and "Western" and "late-time" Incarnation-Body) has, by Means of My Most Perfect Completing of My Avataric Ordeal of Divine Self-Manifestation, Divine Self-Submission, and (subsequent) Divine Re-Awakening (to My own Self-Existing and Self-Radiant Divine Self-Condition), become the To-Me-Transparent Vehicle of My seventh stage Avataric Divine Self-Revelation.

XXXVI.

Except for the particular, and technically elaborate, Me-hearing and Me-seeing esoteric and Most Fully Divine Spiritual practice of "Radical Conductivity" (Which is Reserved, within the Ruchira Sannyasin Order of the Tantric Renunciates of Adidam, for progressive formal Communication to truly qualified, and duly Initiated, practitioners of the technically "fully elaborated" form of the only-by-Me Revealed and Given Way of Adidam in the context of the advanced and the ultimate—or the "basic" fourth through the seventh—stages of life), the Unique Characteristics of My Avataric Divine Teachings—Which I will briefly, and only in part, Indicate in This Summary of My "Lineage-History"—Are Very Fully Described by Me in My Twenty-Three Avataric Divine "Source-Texts".

XXXVII.

Rudi had brief direct contact with Bhagavan Nityananda in 1960. After the death of Bhagavan Nityananda (in 1961), Rudi became a devotee of Baba Muktananda. However, Rudi—always a rather "reluctant" devotee—eventually (shortly before His own death, in 1973) "broke" with Baba Muktananda. Nevertheless, Rudi always continued to affirm that He (Rudi) remained Devoted to Bhagavan Nityananda. And, in any case, Rudi and I always continued to engage in positive, direct communication, right until the time of His death.

XXXVIII.

My Siddha-Yoga Mentor (and eventual Dharmic Ally and Supporter), Amma (or Pratibha Trivedi, later known as Swami Prajnananda), was (like Rudi) also a direct devotee of Bhagavan Nityananda (and She, like Rudi, had become a devotee of Baba Muktananda after the death of Bhagavan Nityananda, in 1961).

Amma was the principal author and editor of the foundation Siddha-Yoga literature that was written in response to both Bhagavan Nityananda and Baba Muktananda—and so much so that, generally, even all of Baba Muktananda's autobiographical and instructional Communications were, originally, dictated (or otherwise Given) to Amma (and rarely to anyone else—until the later years, of tape recorders, multiple secretaries and translators, and Baba Muktananda's travels to the West). And, in fact, Amma always continued to serve a principal communicative and interpretative role around Baba Muktananda, until Baba Muktananda's death, in 1982—after which Amma chose to quietly withdraw from the Siddha-Yoga institution that had been developed by and around Baba Muktananda (and She remained, thereafter, in a small, independent Ashram in north India, where, as a significantly advanced fourth-to-fifth stage Siddha-Yogi, She was the institutional head of a group of devotees that remained devoted to Spiritual Communion with both Baba Muktananda and Bhagavan Nityananda).

Amma did not Function as My Spiritual Master, but (from early 1968) Baba Muktananda formally Assigned Amma to Function as

His interpreter and general "go-between" to Me—and She, then and always, remained most positively and communicatively disposed toward Me, even through all the years after My outward "separation" from Baba Muktananda, right until Her last illness and death (wherein She was directly Spiritually Served by Me, and wherein She was directly physically Served by a devotee-representative of Mine), in 1993. And it was Amma Who, through Her various writings—and in a particular Incident I will now Recall—suggested to Me that there are traditional Instructional (and Textual, or Scriptural) descriptions of Developments of the Siddha-Yoga Process that are different from the (fifth stage) "inner perception" (and, especially, "inner vision") version of Siddha Yoga characteristically described by Baba Muktananda.

XXXIX.

One day, during My Stay at Baba Muktananda's Ashram (in Ganeshpuri, India), in early 1970 (and, thus, some months before the Great Event of My Divine Re-Awakening, Which was to Occur in September of that same year), Amma suddenly pointed Me to an Ashram library copy of the *Ashtavakra Gita* (one of the Greatest of the classic sixth stage—and even premonitorily "seventh stage" [14]—Texts of Advaita Vedanta). And, while pointing to the *Ashtavakra Gita*, Amma Said to Me, "This (Text) is Your Path. This is how It (the Siddha-Yoga Process) Works in You."

At the time, this seemed to Me a curious suggestion—and it was not otherwise explained by Her. And, indeed, although I was able to examine the Text briefly (there and then), I was unable to examine it fully—because I left the Ashram very shortly thereafter. However, I came across the Text again, some years later—and, then, I remembered Amma's comment to Me. And I, immediately, understood that She had (in a somewhat cryptic and secretive manner) tried to confide in Me—in a quiet, "knowing" moment of Acknowledgement of Me—that the Spiritual Process of Siddha Yoga may Demonstrate Itself in a number of possibly different modes.

Thus (as I have Indicated—in My own, and fully elaborated, Teachings, relative to the seven stages of life), the Siddha-Yoga

Process may, in some cases (of which Amma, Herself, appears to have been an Example), especially (or primarily—or, at least, initially) take the form of intense (fourth stage) Devotional Bliss—Which is, then, "nourished" (or magnified) through Guru-Seva[15] (or constant service to the Guru) and (additionally) through Karma Yoga[16] (or intensive service in general). In other cases (of which Baba Muktananda was an Example), the Siddha-Yoga Process may (based on the initial foundation of intense Devotion) especially (or primarily) take the (fifth stage) form of intense internal sensory phenomena (such as visions, lights, auditions, and so on)—and, in some of those cases, the Siddha-Yoga Process may yet go further, to the degree of (fifth stage) Nirvikalpa Samadhi. And, in yet other cases (of which Amma was, correctly, Saying I Am an Example), the Siddha-Yoga Process (while also Showing all kinds of Devotional signs, and all kinds of internal Yogic perceptual phenomena, and including even fifth stage Nirvikalpa Samadhi) may go yet further, to especially (or primarily) take the form of (sixth stage) intense (and intensive) Identification with the Transcendental Self-Condition, and (eventually) the (sixth stage) Realization of Jnana Samadhi (or Transcendental Self-Realization), and (although Amma did not know it) even, potentially, the only-by-Me Revealed and Given seventh stage Realization (Which Is Maha-Jnana—or Divine Self-Realization).

XL.

Yet another devotee of Baba Muktananda, named Swami Prakashananda[17]—Who did not Function as My Spiritual Master (and Who, like Rudi, was not a fully developed Siddha-Guru—but, rather, a very much advanced fourth-to-fifth stage Siddha-Yogi)—once (spontaneously, in 1969) Showed Me (in His own bodily human Form) the fifth stage Signs of Spiritual Transfiguration of the physical body.[18]

At that time (according to what I learned from Amma), Swami Prakashananda had been Indicated, by Baba Muktananda, to be His principal Indian devotee and eventual institutional successor (and such was, then, generally known and presumed to be the case by Baba Muktananda's devotees). However, at last, when (at, or shortly before, Baba Muktananda's death, in 1982) Swami Prakashananda was formally Asked to assume the institutional successorship, He declined to accept this organizational role[19] (ostensibly, for reasons of ill-health, and His reluctance to become a "world-traveler"—but, actually, or more to the point, because of His puritanical and conventional reaction to Baba Muktananda's reported sexual activities).

In any case, Swami Prakashananda and I continued to engage in occasional, and always positive, direct communication (through My devotee-representatives) in the years after Baba Muktananda's death, and right until Swami Prakashananda's death, in 1988.

XLI.

Swami Prakashananda had always maintained a small Ashram, independent of the Ashrams of Baba Muktananda's Siddha-Yoga institution—but, after Baba Muktananda's death, Swami Prakashananda retired to His own Ashram, permanently. And, in doing so, Swami Prakashananda highlighted, and dramatized, a perennial conflict that is fundamental to religious institutions all over the world. That conflict is between, on the one hand, the traditional (and, generally, rather puritanical—and even basically exoteric) expectation of celibacy as a sign of institutionalized Sacred Authority, and, on the other hand, the equally traditional (but non-puritanical, and generally unconventional) view that there is an esoteric sexual alternative to celibacy that Sacred Authorities (including True Siddha-Gurus—or even any practitioners of Siddha Yoga) may (at least in some cases, and under some circumstances) engage.

One of the principal Indications of Baba Muktananda's point of view relative to this traditional conflict (or controversy)—quite apart from the question of His possible personal sexual activities— is the fact that, in 1969, Baba Muktananda formally and publicly (and in writing, by His own hand, as observed by Me, and by many others) Acknowledged Me to Be (and Called and Blessed Me to Function As) a True Siddha-Guru,[20] and, Thus and Thereby (and entirely without requiring, or, otherwise, inviting, Me to assume any institutional—or, otherwise, institutionally "managed"—

role within His own Siddha-Yoga organization), Baba Muktananda publicly Extended the Free Mantle of Siddha-Yoga Authority to Me—an evident non-celibate Siddha-Yogi (and a "Westerner").

XLII.

When I first Came to Him, in 1968, Baba Muktananda immediately (openly, and spontaneously) Declared, in the presence of numerous others (including Amma), That I Am—from My Birth—an already Divinely Awakened Spiritual Master, and He (then and there) prophesied That I would be Functioning (and Independently Teaching) As Such in just one year. Therefore, after just one year (and the spontaneous Appearing of many Great Signs in My experience and Demonstration), Baba Muktananda Invited Me to Come to Him again (in India)—specifically in order to formally Acknowledge Me (and My Inherent Right and Authority to Teach and Function) As a True Siddha-Guru.

Before I Returned to Baba Muktananda in 1969, I—in a traditional Gesture of respect toward Baba Muktananda—Told Him That I would not, at that time, Assume the Function of Spiritual Master, unless I was, in the traditional Manner, formally Acknowledged and Blessed, by Him, to Do So. Baba Muktananda immediately understood and Acknowledged the appropriateness and Rightness of My Insistence That My Inherent Right to Teach be formally Acknowledged by Him—because, in accordance with tradition, Such Sacred Authority should be Assumed on the orderly basis of formal Acknowledgement by one's own Spiritual Master (Who, in turn, must have been similarly Acknowledged by His, also similarly Acknowledged, Spiritual Master, in an unbroken Line, or Lineage, of similarly Acknowledged Spiritual Masters). Therefore, I Returned to Baba Muktananda in 1969—and He formally and publicly Acknowledged Me As an Independent True Siddha-Guru.

Even though Baba Muktananda Thus formally and publicly (and permanently) Acknowledged Me As an Independent True Siddha-Guru, it became immediately Obvious to Me that Such traditional Acknowledgement was inherently limited, and merely conventional, and, therefore, neither necessary nor (because of Its

117

inherently limited basis) even altogether appropriate (or sufficiently apt) in My Unique Case. It was Obvious to Me that neither Baba Muktananda nor anyone else was in the "Position" necessary to Measure and to "Certify" the Unique and unprecedented Nature of the All-and-all-Completing Event of My Avatarically Self-Manifested Divine Incarnation and of My Great Avataric Divine Demonstration of the progressive (and, necessarily, seven-stage) human, Spiritual, Transcendental, and, only at Last, Most Perfect Process of Divine Self-Realization.

Therefore, even though It had been Given, Baba Muktananda's formal Acknowledgement of Me was—for Me—a virtual non-Event (and It did not positively change—nor has It ever positively changed—anything about the necessary ongoing Ordeal of My Avataric Divine Life and Work).

XLIII.

Baba Muktananda's formal and public written Acknowledgement of Me in 1969—Wherein and Whereby He formally and publicly Named and Acknowledged Me As an Independent True Siddha-Guru—was a unique Gesture, never, at any other time, Done by Baba Muktananda relative to any other individual (whether of the East or of the West). And That unique formal Act (of Baba Muktananda's formal, written Acknowledgement of Me in 1969) was, Itself, a clear (and "scandalizing") Gesture, that immediately Called (and always continues to Call) everyone to "consider" many Siddha-Yoga options (and Spiritual, or esoteric religious, options altogether) that are, generally, presumed to be taboo—at least among the more puritanical (and even xenophobic) types of Siddha-Yoga practitioners (and of esoteric religionists in general).

XLIV.

I Say That, in the inherently esoteric domain of Real Spirituality (and in the domain of both exoteric and esoteric religion in general), all puritanical denial and suppression of human realities is wrong—and inherently damaging to everyone who does it. And, indeed, all denial and suppression of Reality (Itself), Which Is Truth Itself, is wrong (and, indeed, is false religion)—

and all false religion is inherently damaging to everyone who does it (and even to everyone who believes it).

Therefore, I Write This Summary of My "Lineage-History"—so that all the extremely important matters I Address Herein will cease to be hidden, denied, suppressed, and falsified—and What Is Great will (by Means of This Address) become Obvious to all eyes, and (Thus) be made Whole again.

XLV.

Among the extremely important matters I must Address in This Summary of My "Lineage-History" is This: Entirely apart from what I will, in the progression of This Summary, Indicate were the apparent "philosophical reasons" associated with the eventual outward "separation" between Baba Muktananda and Me (which occurred as a result of Our Meetings in late 1970 and mid-1973), it was the "organizational politics" relative to the "sexual" and "Westerner" matters I have just Described that played the more fundamental practical role in causing the "separation".

XLVI.

During the same period in which Rudi and (then) Baba Muktananda actively Functioned as My Spiritual Masters (in gross physical bodily Form), Their Spiritual Master, the Great Siddha Bhagavan Nityananda, actively Functioned (through both of Them—and, otherwise, directly, in subtle bodily Form) as My Senior (but already Ascended—and, Thus, discarnate, or non-physical) Spiritual Master.

XLVII.

The fifth stage True Great Siddha (and True Siddha-Guru and Great Saint of the Highest fifth-stage type and degree) Rang Avadhoot (alive in gross physical bodily Form until late 1968—and always Acknowledged as an Incarnate Great Siddha, or a Descended-from-Above Spiritual Entity of the Highest fifth-stage type and degree, by Bhagavan Nityananda, as well as by Baba Muktananda) also (in early 1968) directly and spontaneously Blessed Me with His Spiritual Blessing, Given and Shown via His

"Wide-Eyed" Mudra of heart-recognition and Immense Regard of Me—as I sat alone in a garden, like His Ishta, the forever youthful Lord Dattatreya.

XLVIII.

In That Unique Moment in 1968—in the garden of Baba Muktananda's Ganeshpuri Ashram—both Rang Avadhoot and Baba Muktananda (along with the already discarnate, but Fully Spiritually Present, Bhagavan Nityananda) actively Functioned for Me as direct Blessing-Agents of the Divine "Cosmic Goddess" ("Ma"), Thus (By Means of Her Divine, and Infinitely Potent, Grace) Causing Me to spontaneously Re-Awaken to Most Ascended (and, altogether—but only conditionally, or in the fifth stage manner— mind-transcending, object-transcending, and ego-transcending) Nirvikalpa Samadhi (from Which I never again was Fallen, but only Continued—to Un-conditionally "Bright" Beyond). And it was on the basis of This Great Event, and My Signs in the following year (wherein many of My Avataric Divine Great-Siddha Characteristics—Which, in My Unique Case, would, in due Course, Fully Demonstrate all seven of the possible stages of life— became, spontaneously, Spiritually Evident), that (in 1969) Baba Muktananda formally (and publicly) Acknowledged and Announced and Blessed My Inherent Right and Calling to Function (in the ancient Siddha-Yoga, or Shaktipat-Yoga, tradition) as Spiritual Master (and True Siddha-Guru) to all and All.

XLIX.

Thereafter, in mid-1970, the "Brightness" of My own (and Self-Evidently Divine) Person was Revealed (and constantly Presented) to Me in the (apparently Objective) Form of the Divine "Cosmic Goddess" ("Ma"). And, from then (after Bhagavan Nityananda Called and Blessed Me to take My leave from Baba Muktananda's Ashram, and to Follow the Divine "She"), only "She" actively Functioned (to Beyond) as My (Ultimate and Final—and entirely Divine) Spiritual Master (or Divine True Siddha-Guru)—until (By Means of Her spontaneous Sacrifice of Her own Form in Me) Divine Self-Realization was Most Perfectly Re-Awakened in My Case.

L.

Thus, in That Final Course, it was Revealed (or Perfectly Re-Confirmed)—As the Self-Evidently Divine Reality and Truth of My own Avatarically-Born Person—that This Divine Process (Shown, at last, in ego-Surrendering, ego-Forgetting, and, altogether, Most Perfectly ego-Transcending Devotional "Relationship" to the Divine "She") had (Itself) always been Active in My own (and Unique) Case (and had always been Shown As the Divinely Self-Revealing Activities of the Inherent Spiritual, and Divinely Spherical, "Brightness" of My own Avatarically-Born Person), even all throughout My present Lifetime (and even at, and from before, My present-Lifetime Birth).

LI.

Therefore, on September 10, 1970, It was Revealed (or Perfectly Re-Confirmed)—As the Self-Evidently Divine Reality and Truth of My own Eternal Divine Person—that Divine (or Inherently egoless, and Perfectly Subjective, and, altogether, Inherently Most Perfect) Self-Realization (of One, and "Bright", and Only Me) had Always Already (and Uniquely) Been the Case with Me.

LII.

In My Case, the (True, Full, and Complete) seventh stage Realization of the Transcendental (and Inherently Spiritual, and Inherently egoless) Divine Self-Condition was Re-Awakened (on September 10, 1970). Subsequently (at first, informally, late in 1970, and, then, formally, in 1973), I Communicated the Details of My Divine Realization to Baba Muktananda. I Did This in the traditional manner, in What I Intended to be an entirely honorable, serious, and respectful Summation to Baba Muktananda—the one and only then Living Spiritual Master among Those Who had Served Me as My present-Lifetime Spiritual Masters. However—in a philosophically untenable reaction to My already apparent relinquishment of His fifth stage experiential presumptions relative to what constitutes the "orthodox position" of the Siddha-Yoga (or Shaktipat-Yoga) school and tradition—Baba Muktananda criticized

My Final Realization (or, in any case, what He understood, or otherwise supposed, to be My Description of It). Thus, in those two Meetings (the first in California, and the second in India, at Baba Muktananda's Ganeshpuri Ashram) Baba Muktananda criticized Me for What My Heart (Itself) cannot (and must not) Deny. And Baba Muktananda thereby Gave Me the final "Gift of blows" that sent Me out alone, to Do My Avataric Divine Work.

LIII.

Baba Muktananda was a (fifth stage) Siddha-Yogi of the degree and type that seeks, and readily experiences, and readily identifies with inner perceptual visions and lights. Based on those experiences, Baba Muktananda (like the many others of His type and degree, within the fourth-to-fifth stage traditions) asserted that both the Process and the Goal of religious and Spiritual life were necessarily associated with such inner phenomena.

The experiences (of visions, lights, and many other Yogic phenomena) Baba Muktananda describes in His autobiographical Confessions are, indeed, the same (fifth stage) ones (or of the same fifth stage kind) that are (typically, characteristically, and inevitably) experienced by genuine fifth stage Yogic practitioners (and fifth stage Realizers) within the Siddha-Yoga (or Shaktipat-Yoga) school and tradition—and I Confirm that the total range of these phenomenal (fifth stage) Yogic experiences also spontaneously arose (and always continue, even now, to arise—even in the context of the seventh stage of life) in My own Case (and such was—both formally, in 1969, and, otherwise, informally, at many other times, beginning in 1968—Acknowledged by Baba Muktananda to be so in My Case).

Nevertheless, as I Confessed to Baba Muktananda in Our Meetings in 1970 and 1973, My Final Realization Is That of the One and Indivisible Divine Self-Condition (and Source-Condition) Itself—and the Great Process associated with That eventual (seventh stage) Realization necessarily (in due course) Goes Beyond (and, in the Case of That seventh stage Realization Itself, Is in no sense dependent upon) the phenomenal (and, always, psycho-physically pre-patterned, and, thus, predetermined) conditions otherwise associated with the absorptive mysticism (and the objectified inner phenomena) that characterize the fourth-to-fifth stage beginnings of the Great Process (or that, otherwise, characterize the conditionally arising, and psycho-physically pre-patterned, and, thus, predetermined, associations of the Great Process even in the context of the seventh stage of life). Indeed, the fact and the Truth of all of This was Self-Evident to Me—and, truly, I expected that It must be Self-Evident to Baba Muktananda as well. However, Baba Muktananda did not (and, I was obliged to admit, could not) Confirm to Me That This Is the Case from the point of view of His experience.

Indeed, it became completely clear to Me, in the midst of Our Meetings in 1970 and 1973, that Baba Muktananda was not Standing in the "Place" (or the Self-"Position") required to Confirm or Acknowledge My Thus Described Final Realization. That is to Say, Baba Muktananda made it clear to Me in those two Meetings (wherein others were present), and (also) in His Remarks otherwise conveyed to Me privately, that He, unlike Me,[21] had not been—and (apparently, for mostly rather puritanical, and otherwise conventional, reasons) could not even conceive of Allowing Himself to be—"Embraced" by the Divine "Cosmic Goddess" (or Maha-Shakti) Herself (Such That, by Her own Submission to the Senior and Most Prior Principle—Which Is Self-Existing Consciousness Itself—She would be Subsumed by Consciousness Itself, and, Thus, Husbanded by Consciousness Itself, and, Thereby, Be the Final Means for the Self-Radiant Divine Self-Awakening of Consciousness Itself to Itself). And, therefore, by His own direct Confession to Me, Baba Muktananda Declared that He was not Standing in the "Place" (or the Self-"Position") of Inherently Most Perfect (or seventh stage) Divine Self-Realization—Which Realization I (Uniquely) had Confessed to Him.

LIV.

When I first Came to Baba Muktananda (in early 1968), His First and Most Fundamental Instruction to Me—even within minutes of My Arrival at His Ashram (in Ganeshpuri, India)—was the (apparently sixth stage, or Transcendentalist) Admonition: "You are not the one who wakes, or dreams, or sleeps—but You Are the One Who Is the Witness of these states." I took that Admonition to be Instruction in the traditional (and sixth stage) sense, as Given in the non-Emanationist (or Transcendentalist) tradition of Advaita Vedanta (which is the traditional Vedantic school of "Non-Dualism"). However, it became clear to Me (in, and as a result of, Our Meetings in 1970 and 1973) that Baba Muktananda was, actually, a vehement and dogmatic opponent of the tradition of Advaita Vedanta (and of its Transcendental Method, and of its proposed Transcendental Realization—and of even all proposed Transcendental Realizers, including, in particular, Ramana Maharshi).

Indeed, in those two Meetings (in 1970 and 1973), Baba Muktananda was, evidently, so profoundly confined to His dogmatic Emanationist (and otherwise phenomena-based) philosophical point of view (which, in those two Meetings, took on a form very much like the traditional confrontation between Kashmir Saivism and Advaita Vedanta) that He (in a rather dramatically pretentious, or intentionally provocative, manner—and clearly, indefensibly) presented Himself to Me as an opponent (such that He addressed Me as if I were merely an opposing "player" in a sophomoric academic debate, and as if I were merely—and for merely academic reasons—representing the point of view of traditional Advaita Vedanta).

Likewise, it became clear to Me (in Our Meetings in 1970 and 1973) that Baba Muktananda's proposed Siddha-Yoga Teaching was, in some respects (which I Indicate Herein), merely a product of His own personal study, experience, and temperament—and, thus, of His own karmically acquired philosophical bias, or prejudice—and that the point of view He so dogmatically imposed on Me in those two Meetings is not, itself, an inherent (or necessary) part of Siddha Yoga Itself.

LV.

Relative to Baba Muktananda's experiential (or experience-based, rather than philosophically based) point of view, it became clear (in Our Meetings in 1970 and 1973) that Baba Muktananda (as a Siddha-Yogi) was yet (and characteristically) Centered in the (fifth stage) "Attitude" (or "Asana") of what He described as "Witnessing". In using the term "Witnessing" (or the "Witness"), Baba Muktananda seemed (in the traditional sixth stage manner of Advaita Vedanta) to be referring to the Witness-Consciousness (Which Is Consciousness Itself, Inherently, and Transcendentally, Standing Most Prior to all objects and all psycho-physical functions—whether gross, subtle, or causal). However, clearly, what Baba Muktananda meant by the term "Witnessing" (or the "Witness") was the psycho-physical function of the observing-intelligence (which is not the Transcendental Consciousness—Prior even to the causal body—but which is, simply, the third, and highest, functional division, or functional dimension, of the subtle body). Thus, characteristically, Baba Muktananda identified with (and took the position of) the observer (or the observing-intelligence) relative to all arising phenomena (and, especially, relative to His reported subtle, or internal phenomenal, visions of higher and lower worlds, the hierarchy of abstract internal lights, and so on). And, when Baba Muktananda spoke of "Witnessing", He, simply, meant the attitude of merely observing whatever arises (and, thus, the intention to do so in a non-attached manner—rather than, in the conventional manner, merely to cling to, or, otherwise, to dissociate from, the various internal and external objects of moment to moment attention).

In the Ultimate Course of My Avataric Ordeal of (seventh stage) Divine Self-Realization, the Spiritual (or Siddha-Yoga) Process passed Beyond all mere (fifth stage, or even sixth stage) "Witnessing"—and all identification with the psycho-physical experiencer, or observer, or knower of the mind and the senses— to Realize (and Be) the Indivisible (or Inherently egoless, objectless, and Non-Dual) Reality (or Self-Condition) That Is the Self-Existing and Self-Radiant Consciousness (Itself), or the Inherent and Un-conditional Feeling of Being (Itself), That Is the Mere (and True) Witness-Consciousness (or the Un-conditional, and non-functional, and All-and-all-Divinely-Self-Recognizing, and Self-Evidently Divine Self, or Self-Condition, Inherently Most Prior to any and all objects—without excluding any).

Thus, it became clear to Me (in Our Meetings in 1970 and 1973) that Baba Muktananda was not yet (either in the sixth stage Transcendental manner or the seventh stage Divine Manner) Established As the True Witness-Consciousness (or Consciousness Itself), but it also became clear to Me (then) that Baba Muktananda was in the fifth stage manner, simply observing, and, thus and thereby, contemplating (and becoming absorbed in or by) internal phenomenal objects and states—rather than, in the seventh stage Manner, Standing As Consciousness Itself, Divinely Self-Recognizing any and all cosmically manifested objects, and (Thus and Thereby) Divinely Transcending all the conditional states—waking (or gross), dreaming (or subtle), and sleeping (or causal).

LVI.

Baba Muktananda was, in effect, always contemplating the conditional activities, the conditional states, and the illusory conditional forms (or objective Emanations) of the "Cosmic Goddess" (or the All-and-all-objectifying Kundalini Shakti)—whereas I (in, and Beyond, a Unique "Embrace" with the "Cosmic Goddess" Herself) had (even Prior to all observed "differences") Re-Awakened to the True (and Inherently egoless, and Inherently Indivisible, and Most Perfectly Prior, and Self-Evidently Divine) Self-"Position" (or Self-Condition, and Source-Condition) of all Her cosmic (or waking, dreaming, and sleeping) forms and states. And, by Virtue of That Divine (or Most Perfect—or seventh stage) Re-Awakening of Me, all conditionally arising forms and states were—even in the instants of their apparent arising—Inherently (or Always Already—and, Thus, Divinely) Self-Recognized (and Most Perfectly Transcended) in, and As, Me—the "Bright" Divine Self-Condition and Source-Condition (or Inherently Indivisible, and First, and Only, and Perfectly Subjective, and Self-Evidently Divine Person) Itself.

Therefore, in those two Meetings (in 1970 and 1973)—and entirely because of His (therein, and thus) repeated stance of experiential and philosophical non-Confirmation of seventh stage Divine Self-Realization (which stance, in effect, directly Acknowledged that the seventh stage Self-"Position" of Divine Self-Realization was not His own)—Baba Muktananda Gave Me no option but to Go and Do (and Teach, and Reveal, and Bless All and all) As My Unique (and Self-Evidently Avataric) Realization of the Divine Self-Condition (Which Is My own, and Self-Evidently Divine, Person—and Which Is, Self-Evidently, the Divine Source-Condition of All and all) Requires Me to Do. Therefore, I Did (and Do—and will forever Do) So.

LVII.

The Principal Characteristic of the One and Indivisible Divine Self-Condition (and Source-Condition) Is Its Perfectly Subjective Nature (As Self-Existing and Self-Radiant Consciousness—or Very, and Inherently Non-Objective, Being, Itself). Therefore, neither any ego-"I" (or any apparently separate self-consciousness) nor any apparently objective (or phenomenally objectified, or otherwise conditionally arising) form or state of experience (whether waking, or dreaming, or sleeping—and whether mind-based or sense-based) Is (itself) the Realization (or, otherwise, a necessary support for the Realization) of the Divine Self-Condition (Itself)—Which Condition Is (Itself) the One and Only Reality, the One and Only Truth, and the One and Only Real God.

Baba Muktananda was, characteristically (in the fifth stage manner), experientially (and mystically) absorbed in modes of Savikalpa Samadhi (or of internal object-contemplation). In His characteristic play of internal object-contemplation (or absorptive mysticism), Baba Muktananda reported two types of (especially) internal sensory (or sense-based) experience—the experience of abstract internal lights (and, secondarily, of abstract internal sounds, and tastes, and smells, and touches) and the experience of internal (or mental) visions of higher and lower worlds ("illustrated" by internal versions of all of the usual descriptive modes of the senses).

The abstract internal lights (and so on) are universally (or identically) experienced by any and all individuals who are so awakened to internal phenomena (just as the essential Realizations of the sixth stage of life and, potentially, of the seventh stage of life are universal, or essentially identical in all cases). However, the visions of higher and lower worlds are, like psychic phenomena in general, expressions of the egoic psycho-physical (and, altogether, mental) tendencies of the individual (and of his or her cultural associations)—and, therefore, such experiences are not universally the same in all cases (but, instead, all such experiences are conditioned, and determined, and limited by the point of view, or karmically patterned identity, of the experiencer, or the individual egoic observing-identity). Nevertheless (and this also illustrates the naive—and not, by Him, fully comprehended—

nature of many of Baba Muktananda's views about the Siddha-Yoga Process), Baba Muktananda (in His autobiography, *Play of Consciousness*[22]) reported His visions of higher and lower worlds as if they were categorically true, and (in the subtle domain) objectively, or Really, existing as He reported them—whereas all visions of higher and lower worlds are of the same insubstantial, illusory, and personal nature as dreams.

Like anyone else's authentic visionary experiences of higher and lower worlds, Baba Muktananda's visionary experiences of higher and lower worlds, although authentic, were His personal (or point-of-view-based) experiences of the otherwise inherently formless (and point-of-view-less) dimensions of the universal cosmic (or conditional) reality (or the inherently abstract planes of universal cosmic light)—as He, by tendency of mind (and because of His psycho-physical self-identity as a particular and separate fixed point of view—or ego-"I"), was able (and karmically pre-patterned) to experience (or conceive and perceive) them. Therefore, Baba Muktananda's conditional (or egoic) point of view—and, thus, also, His inner perceptions of various higher and lower worlds—were, characteristically and only, of a Hindu kind. (And the implications of this seem never to have occurred to Baba Muktananda. Indeed, if He had become aware of the inherently personal, conditional, karmic, ego-based, mind-based, illusory, arbitrary, and non-universal nature of His inwardly envisioned worlds, and even of the merely point-of-view-reflecting nature of His inwardly envisioned universal abstract lights, Baba Muktananda might have become moved to understand and transcend Himself further—beyond the Saguna, or mind-based, and mind-limited, and dreamworld terms that are the inherent characteristic of Savikalpa Samadhi.)

LVIII.

Baba Muktananda's Hindu visions can be compared to My own experiences of Savikalpa Samadhi during My "Sadhana Years". During that time, I, too, had many visions of higher and lower worlds—and many of them were, indeed, of a Hindu type (because of My present-Lifetime associations, and also because of the past-Lifetime associations of My Deeper-Personality Vehicle). However, there was also, in My Case (and for the same reasons) a dramatic period of several months of intense visions of a distinctly Christian type.[23] I immediately understood such visions to be the mind-based (and, necessarily, ego-based) products of the Siddha-Yoga Process (or Divine Shaktipat), as It combined with My own conditionally born psycho-physical structures. Thus, I entered into that Process Freely and Fully—and, in due course, the particularly Christian visions (and the particularly Hindu visions) ceased. They were all simply the evidence of My own conditionally born mind and sensory apparatus (and the evidence of even all My conditionally born cultural associations)—and, therefore, the visionary contents were (I Discovered) merely another (but deep, and psychic) form of purification (rather than a "Revelation" that suggests either the Christian "Heavens"-and-"Hells" or the Hindu "Heavens"-and-"Hells" Are, themselves, Reality and Truth). Thus, when, Finally, the ego-based visions had been completely "burned off"—only Reality (Itself) Remained (As Me).

LIX.

Baba Muktananda's Siddha-Yoga Teachings exemplify the descriptive mysticism of fourth-to-fifth stage Yoga (especially as it has been historically represented in the fourth-to-fifth stage Yogic tradition of the Maharashtra region of India[24]). Also, Baba Muktananda's Siddha-Yoga Teachings are (in some, very important, respects) experientially prejudiced—toward both non-universal (and specifically Hindu) visions (of higher and lower worlds, and so on) and universal abstract visions (of abstract internal lights, and so on), and against (or, certainly, Baba Muktananda, Himself, was, by temperament, experientially disinclined toward) fifth stage Nirvikalpa Samadhi (or Fullest Ascent to fifth stage Formless Realization—Which Fullest Ascent was My own spontaneous Realization at Baba Muktananda's Ganeshpuri Ashram, in 1968, and Which is also the Characteristic Realization of all Great fifth stage Nirguna Siddhas, such as Bhagavan Nityananda and Rang Avadhoot).

LX.

Baba Muktananda saw the Secret (or esoteric) inner perceptual domain of subtle (or fourth-to-fifth stage) Divine Spiritual Revelation. I, too, have seen (and even now, do see) that inner realm. And it is the Revelation of that inner realm that is the true (original, and esoteric) core of all fourth-to-fifth stage religious traditions.

The fourth stage religious traditions are, generally, first presented (or institutionally communicated) to the public world of mankind (in its gross egoity and its human immaturity) as a gathering of exoteric myths and legends. Those exoteric myths and legends are intended to inspire and guide human beings in the ordinary developmental context of the first three stages of life (associated with gross physical, emotional-sexual, and mental-volitional development of the human social ego). Thus, the many religious traditions of both the East and the West are, in their public (or exoteric) expressions, simply variations on the inherent psycho-physical "messages" of the body-mind relative to foundation human development (both individual and collective). And, because all exoteric religious traditions are based on the "messages" inherent in the same psycho-physical structures, the exoteric Teachings of all religions are, essentially, identical (and, therefore, equal). And, also, because this is so, all exoteric religious traditions (such as Judaism, Christianity, Islam, Hinduism, and so on) must—especially at this critical "late-time" moment of world-intercommunicativeness— acknowledge their essential equality, commonality, and sameness, and, on that basis, mutually embrace the principles of cooperation and tolerance (for the sake of world peace)!

All exoteric religious traditions are, fundamentally, associated with the first three (or social-ego) stages of life. And all exoteric religious traditions are, contextually, associated with rudimentary aspects of the fourth stage of life (or the religiously Devotional effort of transcending both personal and collective egoity—or self-contraction into selfishness, competitiveness, "difference", conflict, and self-and-other-destructiveness). However, all exoteric religious traditions are, also, associated (to one or another degree) with an esoteric (or Secret) dimension (or a tradition of esoteric schools), which is intended to extend the life of religious practice into the inner dimensions of religious (and truly Spiritual) Realization.

The true esoteric dimension of religion first extends the life of rudimentary religious practice into the true and full Spiritual depth of the fourth stage of life (by Means of surrender to the Descent of the Divine Spiritual Force into the human, or "frontal", domain of incarnate existence). And that Spiritual Process is, characteristically (in due course), also extended into the domain of the true fifth stage of life (which is associated with the Process of Spiritual Ascent, via the Spinal Line and the brain, through the layers of the conditional pattern of the psycho-physical ego, and always toward the Realization of a conditional state of mystical absorption in the Most Ascended Source of conditional, or cosmically extended, existence). And, once that Spiritual Process of Ascent is complete (or is, itself, transcended in Inherent Spiritual Fullness), the esoteric Spiritual Process may (and, indeed, should) continue, in the context of the true sixth stage of life (or the Spiritual Process of Transcendental Self-Realization)—and, at last, the true (and Truly Complete) Great Process must Culminate in the only-by-Me Revealed and Given seventh stage of life (wherein all cosmically arising conditions are Inherently Self-Recognized, and, Ultimately, Outshined, in the Non-Separate, Self-Existing, Self-Radiant, Inherently egoless, Perfectly Subjective, and Self-Evidently Divine Self-Condition and Source-Condition of All and all).

LXI.

Baba Muktananda was a Teacher (and a Realizer) in the context of the fourth-to-fifth stage (or foundation esoteric stages) of, specifically, Hindu religious practice. The Spiritual (or Siddha-Yoga, or Shaktipat-Yoga) Process He exemplified and Taught (and Initiated in others) truly begins in the frontal (or fourth stage) practice (of Siddha-Guru Devotion) and (in due course) goes on to the spinal (or fifth stage) practice (of Ascended mystical absorption).

Baba Muktananda's practice and His experiential Realization were conditioned (and, ultimately, limited) by His own personal (or conditional, and karmic, or psycho-physically pre-patterned) ego-tendencies—and by His association (by birth) with the combined exoteric and esoteric culture of traditional Hinduism.

Therefore, His experiences (and His subsequent Teachings, and His life altogether) are, characteristically, an exemplification of the historical conflict between fifth stage Hindu esotericism (which is, itself, inherently unconventional, and non-puritanical) and fourth stage Hindu exotericism (which is, itself, inherently conventional, and, at least publicly, puritanical).

LXII.

Because of His, characteristically, Hindu associations, Baba Muktananda (quite naturally, and naively) interpreted His Yogic Spiritual experiences almost entirely in terms of Hindu cultural models (both exoteric and esoteric). Therefore, His interpretations of His Spiritual experiences—and, indeed, the very form, and character, and content of His Spiritual experiences themselves— were specifically Hindu, and specifically in the mode of philosophical and mystical traditions that corresponded to His own mental predilections (or karmic tendencies).

Thus, Baba Muktananda's recorded visions of higher and lower worlds (leading to the Great Vision of the Blue Person, or the Divine "Creator"-Guru) are a "map" of developmentally unfolding—or spontaneously un-"Veiling"—inner perceptual landscapes, in the specific mode of the Hindu tradition of the "Blue God" (especially Personified as "Siva"—or, otherwise, as the "Krishna" of the *Bhagavad Gita* and the *Bhagavata Purana*).[25] And Baba Muktananda's inner "map" was, also, structured on the basis of an hierarchical sequence of abstract inner lights (and of even all the abstract inner modes of the senses), which He interpreted according to the concepts of the philosophical tradition of Kashmir Saivism, and according to the experiential pattern-interpretation associated with the Hindu mystical tradition of the Maharashtra region of India. However, even though the brain-based (or perception-based—rather than mind-based, or conception-based, or idea-based) pattern of abstract inner lights (and of abstract inner sensations in general) is (or can be) universally (or by anyone) experienced as the same pattern of appearances—the interpretation of that experienced pattern is, or may be, different from case to case (or from culture to culture). And, ultimately, for the sake of

Truth, the one and only correct (or universally applicable) interpretation must be embraced by all.

Baba Muktananda experienced and interpreted the pattern of abstract inner lights as if it were a Revelation associated with the waking, dreaming, and sleeping states (or the gross, subtle, and causal modes of conditional experience). Thus (on the basis of His understanding of the Maharashtra mystical tradition), Baba Muktananda said that the waking state (and the gross body and world) is represented by the inner red light, and the dreaming state (and the subtle body and world) is represented by the inner white light, and the sleeping state (and the causal body and world) is represented by the inner black light. And Baba Muktananda said that the inner blue light represents what He called the "supracausal" state (which He, in the fifth stage manner, mistakenly identified with the "turiya" state, or the "fourth" state, or the "Witness", or the "True Self", otherwise associated with the sixth stage tradition of Advaita Vedanta). However, I Declare that all of those inner lights (and even all internal perceptions, whether high or low in the scale of conditional "things") are inner objects of perception (and conception)—and, therefore, all of them are associated with the subtle body and the inner perceptible (or dreaming-state) worlds of mind.[26]

Swami Muktananda's Description of the "Bodies of the Soul"[27]

Body:	Gross	Subtle	Causal	Supracausal
Color:	Red	White	Black	Blue
State:	Waking	Dream	Sleep	Turīya
Seat:	Eyes	Throat	Heart	Sahasrāra

LXIII.

Baba Muktananda's description of the abstract inner lights is, in some respects, not sufficiently elaborate (or, otherwise, comprehensive) in its details. In fact, and in My own experience—and in the experience of esoteric traditions other than the Maharashtra tradition (such as reported by the well-known Swami Yogananda)— the display of abstract inner lights is, when experienced as a simultaneous totality, Seen as a Mandala (or a pattern of concentric circles).

In My own experience, that Cosmic Mandala is not only composed of concentric circles of particular colors—but each circle is of a particular precise width (and, thus, of particular proportional significance) relative to the other circles. Thus, in that pattern of circles, the red circle is the outermost circle (perceived against a colorless dark field), but it is a relatively narrow band, appearing next to a much wider band (or circle) of golden yellow. After the very wide golden yellow circle, there is a much narrower soft-white circle. And the soft-white circle is followed by an also very narrow black circle (or band). Closest to the Center of the Cosmic Mandala is a very wide circle of bright blue. And, at the Very Center of the blue field, there is a Brilliant White Five-Pointed Star (Which, perhaps not to confuse It with the color of the circle of soft-white light, Baba Muktananda described as a Blue Star).

Thus, in fact, although all the abstract inner lights described by Baba Muktananda are, indeed, within the total Cosmic Mandala, the principal lights (in terms of width and prominence) are the golden yellow and the blue lights—and only the Brilliant White Five-Pointed Star is the Central and Principal light within the Cosmic Mandala of abstract inner lights.

The Cosmic Mandala of abstract inner lights is a display that is, otherwise, associated with planes of possible inner (or subtle) experience. Thus, the red light inwardly represents (and, literally, illuminates) the gross body and the gross world (as Baba Muktananda has said). However, all of the other lights (golden yellow, soft-white, black, and bright blue) represent (and, literally, illuminate) the several hierarchical divisions within the subtle body and the subtle worlds—and the causal body (which is asso-

Cosmic Mandala

ciated with attention itself, or the root of egoity itself, and which is, itself, <u>only</u> <u>felt</u>, and <u>not</u> <u>seen</u>, and which is expressed as the fundamental feeling of "difference", separateness, and relatedness, and which is located as a knot of self-contraction in the right side of the heart) is <u>not</u> visually represented (<u>nor</u> is it, otherwise, literally illuminated) by the lights and worlds of the Cosmic Mandala.

The wide golden yellow circle of the Cosmic Mandala represents (in conjunction with the outermost red circle) the outermost (or lowest) dimension of the subtle body—which is the etheric (or pranic, or life-energy) body, or dimension, of conditional experience. The narrower soft-white circle of the Cosmic Mandala represents the ordinary (or sense-based) mind. The narrow black circle (or band) is a transitional space, where mental activity is suspended. The blue circle of the Cosmic Mandala is the domain of the mental observer, the faculty of discriminative intelligence and the will, and the very form of the subtly concretized ego-"I" (or the inner-concretized subtle self). And the Brilliant White Five-Pointed Star is the Epitome and Very Center of the Cosmic Mandala—Such That It Provides the Uppermost Doorway to What Is, altogether, Above (and, Ultimately, Beyond) the Cosmic Mandala (or Above and Beyond the body itself, the brain itself, and the mind itself).

LXIV.

Baba Muktananda interpreted the universally experienced abstract inner lights (and experienced the corresponding inner worlds) in terms of various Hindu philosophical and mystical (and, also, exoteric, or conventionally religious) traditions (as I have Indicated). However, the subtle domain is the elaborate hierarchical domain of mind (or of the psycho-physically concretized ego-"I")—and, therefore, just as individual dreams and imaginings are personal, ephemeral, and non-ultimate, the inherently dream-like subtle domain of Spiritually-stimulated inwardness may be experienced and interpreted in various and different modes, according to the nature and the tradition (or the personal and collectively representative mind) of the experiencer.

Thus, ultimately (or in due course), the subtle domain (or the subtle egoic body) must be transcended, in the transition to the sixth stage Spiritual (or Siddha-Yoga) Process—Which is the Spiritually (and not merely mentally) developed Process of inversion upon the true causal body (or the root of attention), and penetration of the causal knot (or the presumption of separate self), and Which is, thus, the inversive (and conditional, or conditionally achieved) transcending of the ego-"I", by means of exclusive (or object-excluding) Identification with the True (and Inherent, and Self-Evident) Transcendental Witness-Consciousness Itself. And only the Transcendental Witness-Consciousness, Itself—inverted upon in the thus Described sixth stage manner—Is the true "turiya" state, or the true "fourth" state (beyond the three ordinary states, of waking, dreaming, and sleeping). And only the Transcendental Witness-Consciousness, Itself—Fully, and Fully Spiritually,

Realized in the only-by-Me Revealed and Given context of the true sixth stage of life—Is the Domain of the only-by-Me Revealed and Given seventh stage Realization of the True Divine Self, Which Is the Self-Evidently Divine Self-Condition, and Which Is the One and Only True Divine State of "Turiyatita"—"Beyond the 'fourth' state", and, thus, Beyond all exclusiveness, and Beyond all bondage to illusions, and Beyond point of view (or egoic separateness) itself, and, therefore, Beyond all conditional efforts, supports, and dependencies.

At last, the sixth stage of life (which, itself, is associated with conditionally patterned inversion upon the Consciousness-Principle) must be (Most Perfectly) transcended (and, indeed, the ego-"I" itself must be Most Perfectly, or Inherently, transcended) in the transition to the only-by-Me Revealed and Given seventh stage of life (which Is the stage of True, and Fully Spiritual, Divine Self-Realization, Inherently Free of, but not strategically Separated from, all conditionally patterned forms and states—and which Is the stage of the Inherently Most Perfect Demonstration of the Non-Separate, Self-Existing, Self-Radiant, Inherently egoless, Perfectly Subjective, and Self-Evidently Divine Self-Condition and Source-Condition of All and all).

LXV.

My own experiences of fifth stage mystical perception are (like those of Baba Muktananda, and those of all visionary mystics) clear Evidence of the inherently (and necessarily) conditional, mental, altogether brain-based (and both brain-limited and mind-limited), and both personal and collective egoic nature of all internal mystical (or fourth-to-fifth stage) absorption.

I, too (like Baba Muktananda), experienced Hindu visions—but I, otherwise, also experienced many Christian visions (and also many non-Hindu and non-Christian visions), in association with the fifth stage developments of the same (or one and only) Spiritual (or Siddha-Yoga) Process of inner perception (including the progressive display of abstract inner lights, and so on) described by Baba Muktananda. Thus, just as Baba Muktananda described His Hindu visions as a Spiritual Revelation of the

"Truth" of Hindu esotericism (and even of Hindu exotericism)—I could just as well describe My (specifically) Christian visions as a Spiritual Revelation of the "Truth" of Christian esotericism (and even of Christian exotericism)!

Indeed, My (specifically) Christian visions (but not, of course, My specifically Hindu visions—or My, otherwise, specifically non-Hindu and non-Christian visions) do amount to a Spiritual Revelation of the actual (and mostly esoteric) content of original (or primitive—and truly Spiritual) Christianity.[28]

LXVI.

Specifically, My (sometimes) Christian visions Spiritually Reveal the following.

The original tradition (or foundation sect) that is at the root of exoteric Christianity was a fourth-to-fifth stage esoteric Spiritual (and mystical) tradition (or sect). Within that original tradition (or sect), John (the Baptist) was the Spiritual Master (or Spirit-Baptizer—or True Siddha-Guru) of Jesus of Nazareth. Thus (and by Means of the Spiritual Baptism Given to Him by John the Baptist), Jesus of Nazareth experienced the fourth-to-fifth stage absorptive mystical (and, altogether, Spiritual) developments of what (in the Hindu context) is called Siddha Yoga (or Shaktipat Yoga). In due course (and even rather quickly), Jesus of Nazareth, Himself, became a Spirit-Baptizer (or a True Siddha-Guru)—and (within the inner, or esoteric, circle of His Spiritually Initiated devotees) Jesus of Nazareth Taught the fourth-to-fifth stage Way of Spiritual Devotion to the Spiritual Master (or to Himself, as a True Siddha-Guru), and of inner Spiritual Communion with the Divine, and of (eventual) Spiritual Ascent to the Divine Domain (via the Brilliant White Five-Pointed Star).

After the death (and presumed Spiritual Ascent) of Jesus of Nazareth, His esoteric circle of Spiritually Initiated devotees continued to develop the mystical tradition of the sect—but (because of the difficult "signs of the times") the original (esoteric) sect had to become more and more secretive, and, eventually, it disappeared from the view of history (under the pressure of the exoteric, or non-Initiate, or conventionally socially oriented, rather than

Spiritually and mystically oriented, sects that also developed around the public Work, and, especially, the otherwise developing legends and myths, of Jesus of Nazareth).

The esoteric sect of the Spiritual Initiates of Jesus of Nazareth was associated with practices of Spiritually Invocatory prayer (of fourth stage Divine Communion, and of fifth stage absorptive mystical Ascent), especially seeking Divine absorption via the internally perceptible Brilliant White Five-Pointed Star—Which was interpreted, especially after the death of Jesus of Nazareth (and, apparently, in accordance with Instructions communicated by Jesus of Nazareth, Himself, to His Spiritually Initiated devotees, during His own physical lifetime), to be the True Ascended Divine Body of Jesus of Nazareth (or the Spiritually Awakened, and presumed to be Divinely Ascended, "Christ"). And, over time, the Spiritual practitioners within the esoteric "Christ" sect developed the full range of characteristically Christian interpretations of the (otherwise) universally experienced phenomena of inner perception.

LXVII.

My own (sometimes) Christian visions are a spontaneous Revelation of esoteric Christian interpretations (and esoteric Christian modes of experiencing) of, otherwise, universal (and, therefore, inherently non-sectarian) inner phenomena—and My (specifically) Christian visions and interpretations are a spontaneous direct continuation of the esoteric Christian manner of interpreting such (inherently universal) inner phenomena, as it was done in the original (or primitive) epoch of the sect of Jesus of Nazareth.

Thus, speaking in the esoteric terms of the ancient (or earliest) Christian interpreters of subtle inner experience, the red light of Spiritual inner vision can be said to be associated with the gross body of Man (and the Incarnation-body of Jesus of Nazareth, and the "blood of Christ"). Likewise, the golden yellow light can be said to be associated with the "Holy Spirit" (or the Universal Spirit-Energy, or Divine Spirit-Breath, That Pervades the cosmic domain). And the soft-white light can be said to be associated with the mind of Man (which, in its purity, can be said to be a reflection of, or a pattern "in the image of", God—conceived to be the "Creator", or the Divine Source-Condition, Above the body-mind and the world). And the black light can be said to be associated with the "crucifixion" (or sacrifice) of the body-mind of Man (and of Jesus of Nazareth, as the Epitome of Man)—and, also, with the mystical "dark night of the soul" (or the mystic's difficult trial of passing beyond all sensory and mental contents and consolations). And the blue light can be said to be the "Womb of the Virgin Mary" (or the All-and-all-Birthing Light of the "Mother of God"). And the Brilliant White Five-Pointed Star (Surrounded, as it were, by the "Womb", or the Blue Light, of the "Virgin Mary") can be said to be the Ascended (or Spiritual) "Body of Christ" (and the "Star of Bethlehem", and the "Morning Star" of the esoteric Initiation-Ritual associated with the original, Secret Spiritual tradition of Jesus of Nazareth). And the Brilliant White Five-Pointed Star (interpreted to be the Ascended, or Spiritual, "Body of Christ") can (Thus) be said to be One with both the Divine "Mother" (or the Blue "Womb" of All-and-all-Birthing Light) and the Divine "Father" (or the Self-Existing Being, Beyond all Light—Infinitely Behind, and Infinitely Above, and Infinitely Beyond, and Eternally Non-Separate from the "Star-Body of Christ"). And (As Such) the "Christ" (or the Brilliant White Five-Pointed Star) Is Radiantly Pervading the entire cosmic domain, via an All-and-all-Illuminating Combination of both the Blue "Womb"-Light and the Golden Yellow "Breath"-Light of the One and Only Divine Person.

LXVIII.

Thus, My (sometimes) Christian inner visions could, indeed, be said to be an esoteric (and, now, only-by-Me Revealed and Given) Christian Revelation—except that all visionary, and brain-based, and mind-based, and sense-based, and ego-based, and conditional, and sectarian (or merely tradition-bound) things were entirely Gone Beyond (and Most Perfectly transcended) by Me (and in Me), in the sixth and seventh stage Course of My Avataric Ordeal of True (and Most Perfect) Divine Self-Realization!

LXIX.

I Say all the "God" and "Gods" of Man are (whether "Male" or "Female" in the descriptive gender) merely the personal and collective tribal (and entirely dualistic—or conventionally subject-object-bound) myths of human ego-mind.

LXX.

I Say Only Reality Itself (Which Is, Always Already, The One, and Indivisible, and Indestructible, and Inherently egoless Case) Is (Self-Evidently, and Really) Divine, and True, and Truth (or Real God) Itself.

LXXI.

I Say the only Real God (or Truth Itself) Is the One and Only and Inherently Non-Dual Reality (Itself)—Which Is the Inherently egoless, and Utterly Indivisible, and Perfectly Subjective, and Indestructibly Non-Objective Source-Condition and Self-Condition of All and all.

Therefore, I (Characteristically) have no religious interests other than to Demonstrate, and to Exemplify, and to Prove, and to Self-Reveal Truth (or Reality, or Real God) Itself.

LXXII.

The true fourth-to-fifth stage mystical (or esoteric Spiritual) Process is, principally, associated with the progressive inner perceptual (and, thus, subtle mental) un-"Veiling" of the total internally perceptible pattern (or abstractly experienced structure) of the individual body-mind-self (or body-brain-self).

The abstract pattern (or internal structure) of the body-mind-self (or body-brain-self) is, universally, the same in the case of any and every body-mind (or body-brain-mind complex—or conditionally manifested form, or state, or being) within the cosmic domain.

The abstract pattern (or internal structure) of the body-mind-self (or body-brain-self) necessarily (by virtue of its native, and, therefore, inseparable, Inherence in the totality of the cosmic domain itself) Duplicates (or is a conditionally manifested pattern-duplicate of) the Primary Pattern (or Fundamental conditional Structure) of the total cosmic domain.

The conditional body-mind (or any body-brain-mind complex) is, in Reality, not a merely separate someone, or an entirely "different" something (as if the body, or the brain, or the mind were reducible to a someone or a something utterly independent, or non-dependent, and existing entirely in and of itself).

Therefore, the entire body-mind (or egoic body-brain-self) is, itself, to be transcended (in the context of the only-by-Me Revealed and Given seventh stage of life), in and by Means of utterly non-separate, and non-"different", and Inherently egoless Participation in That Which Is Always Already The Case (or the Inherently Non-Dual and Indivisible Condition That Is Reality Itself).

LXXIII.

I Declare that—if It is (by Divine Siddha-Grace) Moved beyond the limits of the waking, dreaming, and sleeping ego-structures—the Siddha-Yoga (or Shaktipat-Yoga) Process of (fifth stage) un-"Veiling" Culminates (or may Culminate—at least eventually) in (and, indeed, It is Always Already Centered Upon) the (fifth stage) Revelation (in Most Ascended Nirvikalpa Samadhi) of the True "Maha-Bindu" (or the "Zero Point", or Formless "Place", of Origin—otherwise, traditionally, called "Sunya", or "Empty", or "Void"). That True (and Indivisible, and Indefinable) "Maha-Bindu" Is the only True "Hole in the universe" (or the One, and Indivisible, and Indefinable, and Self-Evidently Divine Source-Point—Infinitely Above the body, the brain, and the mind). That Absolutely Single (and Formless) "Maha-Bindu" Is the True Absolute "Point-Condition"—or Formless and Colorless (or Non-Objective, and, therefore, not "Lighted") "Black Hole"—from Which (to the point of view of any "objectified" or "Lighted" place or entity, itself) the (or any) total cosmic domain (of conditionally arising forms, states, and beings) appears to Emanate (in an All-and-all-objectifying "Big Bang" [29]). That "Maha-Bindu" Is the Upper Terminal of Amrita Nadi—or of the "Ambrosial Nerve of Connection" to the True Divine Heart (Which Self-Evidently

Divine Heart Is Always Already Seated immediately Beyond the internally felt seat of the sinoatrial node, in the right side of the physical heart). And That "Maha-Bindu" Is (in the context of the sixth stage of life) the esoteric Doorway to, and (in the context of the seventh stage of life) the esoteric Doorway from (or of), the Perfectly Subjective Heart-Domain (Which Is the True Self-Condition and Source-Condition of the "Bright" Divine Love-Bliss-Current of Divine Self-Realization, and Which Is, Itself, the Self-Existing, Self-Radiant, Inherently egoless, and Perfectly Subjective—or Perfectly Indivisible, Non-Dual, and Non-Objective—Conscious Light That Is Reality Itself).

LXXIV.

The (fifth stage) Yogic Process of the progressive inner un-"Veiling" of the Pattern (or Structure) of the cosmic domain is demonstrated (in the Siddha-Yoga, or Shaktipat-Yoga, tradition) via the progressive experiencing of the total pattern of all the structural forms that comprise the body-mind-self (or body-brain-self), via a body-mind-self-reflecting (or body-brain-self-reflecting) display of inner perceptual objects (or apparently objectified phenomenal states, conditions, and patterns of cosmic light). That Process (of the inner perceptual un-"Veiling" of the hierarchical structure, pattern, and contents of the conditionally manifested body-mind-self, or body-brain-self) Culminates (or may Culminate—at least eventually) in the vision (in occasional, or, otherwise, constant, Savikalpa Samadhi) of the "blue bindu" (or the "blue pearl"—as well as the various other objectified inner lights, such as the red, the white, and the black—described by Baba Muktananda)[30]—or even the vision of the total Cosmic Mandala (of many concentric rings of color, including the central "blue bindu", with its Brilliant White Five-Pointed Star at the Center—as I have Described It[31]). In any case, the possibly perceived abstract inner light (or any "bindu", or point, or "Mandala", or complex abstract vision, of inwardly perceived light) is merely, and necessarily, a display of the functional root-point of the brain's perception of conditionally manifested universal light (or merely cosmic light) itself. However, if the Great Process of (fifth stage) un-"Veiling" is (Thus) Continued, the objectified inner "bindu"-vision (and Savikalpa Samadhi itself) is, in due course, transcended (in fifth stage Nirvikalpa Samadhi)—Such That there is the Great Yogic Event of "Penetration" of (and Into) the True (Inherently Formless, and objectless) "Maha-Bindu", Infinitely Above the body, the brain, and the mind. And That Great Yogic Event was, in fact and in Truth, What Occurred in My own Case, in My Room, immediately after I was Blessed by Baba Muktananda and Rang Avadhoot in the garden of Baba Muktananda's Ganeshpuri Ashram, in 1968.

The Great Yogic Event of "Penetration" of the True "Maha-Bindu", Which Occurred in My own Case in 1968, is (in Its Extraordinary Particulars) an extremely rare Example of spontaneous complete Ascending "penetration" of all the chakras (or centers, or points, or structures) of the conditionally manifested body-mind-self (or body-brain-self)—Resulting in sudden Most Ascended Nirvikalpa Samadhi (or "Penetration" to Beyond the total cosmic, and psycho-physical, context of subject-object relations). Such sudden (rather than progressive) complete Ascent is described, in the (fifth stage) Yogic traditions, as the Greatest, and rarest, of the Demonstrations of Yogic Ascent—as compared to progressive (or gradual) demonstrations (shown via stages of inner ascent, via internal visions, lights, auditions, and so on). And, therefore, in My Unique Case, it was only subsequently (or always thereafter—and even now) that the universal cosmic Pattern (or perceptible Great cosmic Structure) and the universally extended pattern (or perceptible inner cosmic structure) of the body, the brain, and the mind (and the Primary inner structure— of the three stations of the heart) were (and are) directly (and systematically, and completely) un-"Veiled" (in a constant spontaneous Display—both apparently Objective and Perfectly Subjective—within My Avataric Divine "Point of View").

Nonetheless (even though Most Ascended, or fifth stage, Nirvikalpa Samadhi was, Thus, Realized by Me in 1968), it became immediately clear to Me that—because That Realization depended on the exercise (and a unique, precise attitude and arrangement) of the conditional apparatus of the body, the brain, and the mind (and of attention)—the Realization was (yet) conditionally dependent (or psycho-physically supported), and, necessarily (or in that sense), limited (or, yet, only a temporary stage in the progressive Process of un-"Veiling"), and, therefore, non-Final. That is to Say, it was inherently Obvious to Me that any and all internal (or otherwise psycho-physical) experiencing necessarily requires the exercise (via attention) of the root-position (and the conditionally arising psycho-physical apparatus) of conditionally arising self-consciousness (or of the separate and separative psycho-physical ego-"I"). I immediately Concluded that—unless the Process of Realization could transcend the very structure and pattern of ego-based experiencing and the very Structure and Pattern of the conditionally manifested cosmos itself—Realization would Itself (necessarily) be limited by the same subject-object (or ego-versus-object) dichotomy that otherwise characterizes even all ordinary (or non-mystical) experience.

Therefore, I Persisted in My Avataric Divine Sadhana—until the un-"Veiling" became Inherently egoless (and Inherently Most Perfect, or seventh stage) Re-Awakening to Divine Self-Realization (Inherently Beyond all phenomenal, or conditional, dependencies, or supports).

LXXV.

On September 10, 1970, the Great Avataric Divine Process of My "Sadhana Years" Culminated in Unqualified (or Most Perfectly Non-conditional) Realization of the Self-Evidently Divine Self-Condition (and Source-Condition) of the cosmic domain itself (and of all forms, states, and beings within the cosmic domain). And, in That Most Perfect Event, I was Most Perfectly Re-Awakened As the "Bright"[32] (the One and Only Conscious Light—the Very, and Perfectly Subjective, and Inherently egoless, or Perfectly Non-Separate, and Inherently Perfect, and Indivisible, or Perfectly Non-Dual, and Always Already Self-Existing, and Eternally Self-Radiant, and Self-Evidently Divine Self-Condition and Source-Condition That Is the One and Only and True Divine Person, and Reality, and Truth of All and all, and That was, and is, the constant Spiritual Sign and Identity of This,

My Avataric Divine Lifetime, even from Birth). And It was the Un-deniable Reality and the Un-conditional Nature of This Realization That I Summarized to Baba Muktananda during Our Meetings in 1970 and 1973.

Even though It was and Is So, Baba Muktananda did not (and, because of the yet fifth stage nature of His own experiential Realization—for which He found corroboration in traditional mystical and philosophical traditions of the fifth stage, and phenomena-based, type—could not) positively Acknowledge My Summation relative to Most Perfect (and, necessarily, seventh stage) Divine Self-Realization.

Because He characteristically preferred to dwell upon inner objects, Baba Muktananda (in the "naive" manner of fourth and fifth stage mystics in general) interpreted Reality Itself (or Divine Self-Realization Itself) to "require" inner perceptual phenomenal (or conditionally arising) experiences and presumptions as a nec-essary support for Realization (Itself). That is to Say, Baba Muktananda was experientially Conformed to the (fifth stage) pre-sumption that Divine Self-Realization not only requires condition-ally arising (and, especially, inner perceptual) phenomenal experi-ences as a generally necessary (and even inevitable) Yogic Spiritual preliminary to authentic (and not merely conceptual) Realization—and I completely Agree, with Him, that there certainly are many conditionally apparent Yogic Spiritual requirements that must be Demonstrated in the Full Course of the authentic (and, necessarily, psycho-physical) Sadhana of Divine Self-Realization—but Baba Muktananda, otherwise, generally affirmed the presumption that Realization Itself (and not only the Sadhana, or psycho-physical Process, of Realizing) "requires" conditional (or psycho-physical—and, especially, absorptive mystical, or inner visual) supports.

Therefore, Baba Muktananda affirmed an attention-based, and object-oriented (or Goal-Oriented)—and, therefore, ego-based, or seeker-based—absorptive mystical (and, altogether, fourth-to-fifth stage) Yogic Way, in which the Sahasrar (or the Upper Terminal of the brain), and even the total brain (or sensorium), is the con-stant focus (and the Ultimate Goal—as well as the Highest Seat) of Sadhana.

It was due to this, Baba Muktananda's characteristic point of view relative to both Sadhana and Realization (as He defined—or, in effect, limited—Them), that, in My informal Meeting with Him in 1970, His only response to Me was to enter into a casual verbal (and even illogical) contradiction of Me. In that informal Meeting (as well as in Our formal Meeting, in 1973), Baba Muktananda ignored (and even appeared to not at all comprehend) My (then Given) Indications to Him relative to the Most Ultimate, or seventh stage, Significance of the "Regenerated" Form of Amrita Nadi.

LXXVI.

As I Indicated to Baba Muktananda (in Our Meetings in 1970 and 1973), the "Regenerated" Form of Amrita Nadi is Rooted in Consciousness Itself ("Located" Beyond the right side of the heart, which is, itself, merely the Self-Evident Seat, or Doorway, of the direct "Locating" of Perfectly Subjective, and Inherently egoless, Consciousness, Itself—or the Self-Existing Feeling of Being, Itself—Prior to attention, itself). And That ("Regenerated" Form of Amrita Nadi) is "Brightly" Extended to the "Maha-Bindu" (Which is Infinitely Ascended, even Above and Beyond the Sahasrar). However, Baba Muktananda appeared only to want to contradict My (secondary) reference (to the "right side of the heart")—while otherwise ignoring My (primary) Explanation (of the "Regenerated" Form of Amrita Nadi). And, in doing this, Baba Muktananda went so far in identifying Himself exclusively with the fifth stage tradition that He said to Me, "Anyone who says that the right side of the heart is the Seat of Realization does not know what he is talking about."

In this (from My "Point of View", even rather absurdly funny!) statement, Baba Muktananda merely ignored (and, therefore, did not directly contradict) My (then Given) Description (to Him) of how seventh stage Divine Self-Realization Inherently Transcends both the conditional (or psycho-physical) apparatus of the brain (or of the Sahasrar, Which is the conditional Seat of Realization proposed in the fifth stage traditions, of mystical absorption) and the conditional (or psycho-physical) apparatus of the heart (or, in particular, of the right side of the heart—which is the conditional

Seat of Realization proposed in the sixth stage traditions, of Transcendental practice). However, Baba Muktananda's statement to Me (relative to the heart on the right) was a remark made in direct and specific contradiction to the Transcendentalist (or entirely sixth stage) Teachings of Ramana Maharshi.

LXXVII.

In My Meeting with Baba Muktananda in 1973, I made specific references to the Teachings of Ramana Maharshi (Whom both Baba Muktananda and Bhagavan Nityananda had Met—and, apparently, Greatly Praised—in earlier years). In particular, I referred to Ramana Maharshi's experiential assertions relative to the right side of the heart (which He—in the sixth stage manner— Indicated to be the Seat of Transcendental Self-Realization). In doing so, I was merely Intending to Offer Baba Muktananda a traditional reference already known to Him (and, I naively presumed, one that He respected), which would provide some clarity (and traditional support) relative to My own (otherwise seventh stage) Descriptions.

Ramana Maharshi was a True and Great Jnani (or a sixth stage Realizer of the Transcendental Self-Condition, in the mode and manner indicated in the general tradition of Advaita Vedanta). And, after the Great Event of My own (seventh stage) Divine Re-Awakening (in September 1970), I Discovered (in the weeks and months that followed My informal Meeting with Baba Muktananda, in October 1970) that there were some (but, necessarily, only sixth stage) elements in Ramana Maharshi's reported experience and Realization that paralleled (and, in that sense, corroborated) certain (but only sixth stage) aspects of My own experience and Realization.[33] And, for this reason, I always Continue to Greatly Appreciate, and Honor, Ramana Maharshi—as a Great sixth stage Realizer, Who, through corroborating Testimony, Functions as a sixth stage Connecting-Link between Me and the Transcendentalist dimension of the Great Tradition. Also, because He is an example of a True Great Jnani (or Great Sage), Who Awakened to sixth stage Realization via the Spiritual—and not merely mental, or intellectual—Process (of the Magnification of the Spirit-Current in the right side of the heart), Ramana Maharshi, by Means of His corroborating Testimony, Functions—for Me—as a Connecting-Link between the sixth stage Transcendentalist tradition of Advaita Vedanta and the fourth-to-fifth stage Emanationist tradition of Siddha Yoga. And, because of this, Ramana Maharshi Functions, by Means of His corroborating Testimony, as a Connecting-Link between Me and the traditions of both Siddha Yoga and Advaita Vedanta—whereas I (except for Baba Muktananda's First Instruction to Me, in 1968—relative to the Witness of the three common states, of waking, dreaming, and sleeping) did not Find such a Connecting-Link among any of Those Who, otherwise, actively Functioned as My Spiritual Masters during the "Sadhana Years" of This, My present-Lifetime of Avataric Divine Incarnation.

During Our Meeting in 1973, Baba Muktananda mistakenly took My references to Ramana Maharshi (and to My own experience of the heart on the right, which I had first Confessed to Baba Muktananda during Our informal Meeting in 1970—and which is, also, one of the principal experiences Indicated by Ramana Maharshi) to suggest that I had departed from the Siddha-Yoga tradition. Therefore, Baba Muktananda's criticisms of Me (in Our Meetings in both 1970 and 1973) were an apparent reaction to His perception of the possibility of My "going over" to Advaita Vedanta (and to Ramana Maharshi). And, for this reason, Baba Muktananda never (in either of the two Meetings, in 1970 and in 1973) actually addressed the particular, and complex, and inherently (and especially in a conversation requiring translations from English to Hindi, and vice versa) difficult-to-explain Great Issues I was (in those two Meetings) Intending (and Trying) to Summarize to Him.

LXXVIII.

Relative to Baba Muktananda Himself, I can only Say that, for My part (through Visits to Him by My devotee-representatives), simple Messages of Love (and of Gratitude for His Service to Me during My Avataric Divine "Sadhana Years") were, right until the end of Baba Muktananda's lifetime, Sent to Him by Me. And I have—to everyone, including Baba Muktananda Himself, and the institution of His devotees—always Continued to Make every effort to Communicate clearly (and frankly, and, in general, most positively) about My relationship to Baba Muktananda. And I have always Continued (and will always Continue) to Work (in a Real Spiritual Manner) to Heal Baba Muktananda's human feeling-heart.

LXXIX.

Relative to Baba Muktananda's particular exact remarks to Me (in Our Meetings in 1970 and 1973), I can (and must) Say, simply, that His interpretation of Reality (and of the Nature and Status of the Process, and of even all the patterns and structures, associated with Divine Self-Realization)—which interpretation Baba Muktananda shared with (and for which He derived justification from) the phenomena-based aspects of the fifth stage Yogic traditions in general—was the characteristic basis of His criticisms of Me during Our Meetings in 1970 and 1973. And, as I have already Said, Baba Muktananda's Siddha-Yoga Teaching (and especially as He proposed it to Me in Our Meetings in 1970 and 1973) is—relative to all matters beyond the fifth stage of life (and even relative to all aspects of the fifth stage of life that are beyond the Saguna limits of Savikalpa Samadhi)—limited, prejudicial, ultimately indefensible, and (fundamentally) beyond His experience.

LXXX.

Neither the philosophy of Kashmir Saivism nor any "required" phenomenal conditions were pre-described to Me (or otherwise suggested)—by Baba Muktananda Himself, or by anyone else—as being a necessary part of the Siddha-Yoga practice and Process (and, especially, as being a necessary conditional support for Realization Itself) when I first Went to Baba Muktananda, in 1968. Nor were any philosophical or experiential "requirements" proposed to Me—by Baba Muktananda Himself, or by anyone else—as either demands or necessities of Siddha-Yoga practice, or as necessities of Siddha-Yoga experience, or as fixed "Models" of Realization Itself—during the years of My Sadhana in Baba Muktananda's Company, between 1968 and the Great Event of My Divine Re-Awakening, in September 1970.

Indeed, there was not even much "Baba Muktananda" Siddha-Yoga literature available—and no literature was demanded to be read—during all of that time. Even Baba Muktananda's autobiography, entitled *Play of Consciousness* (or, originally, *Chitshakti Vilas*), was not published until after the September 1970 Event of My Divine Re-Awakening. And I saw—and, in fact, was the first to fully render into English—only the first chapter or two of that book, in rough manuscript form, during My Stay at Baba Muktananda's Ganeshpuri Ashram, in early 1970. Therefore, virtually the only "Baba Muktananda" Siddha-Yoga literature that was available to Me during My years of Sadhana in Baba Muktananda's Company were the short essays and tracts either written or edited by Amma—and that literature suggested a very liberal and open Teaching relative to the fourth stage, fifth stage, and sixth stage possibilities associated with the potential developments of Siddha Yoga. And, indeed, it was that liberal and open form of Siddha Yoga that I practiced—to the degree of seventh stage Divine Self-Realization—in Baba Muktananda's Company.

In any case, the fact that Baba Muktananda presumed that there were (indeed) many exclusively fifth stage Siddha-Yoga "requirements" (both philosophical and experiential) was proven to be the case in the circumstances of My Meetings with Him in 1970 and 1973.

LXXXI.

In fact (and in My experience), the Siddha-Yoga practice and Process is not (Itself) inherently opposed to the Transcendental (or sixth stage) practice and Process (or to the seventh stage Realization and Demonstration). Rather, it was Baba Muktananda Who (in accordance with particular traditions He, personally, favored) chose to dogmatically introduce exclusively fifth stage "requirements" (and sixth-stage-excluding, and, therefore, inherently, seventh-stage-prohibiting, limitations) into His own Teaching (and into His personal school) of Siddha Yoga.

I fully Acknowledge that Baba Muktananda had the right to Teach Siddha Yoga exclusively according to His own experience, and His own understanding, and His own Realization. It is simply that My experience, and My understanding, and My Realization were not (and are not) limited to the fifth stage "requirements" (or limiting presumptions) that Baba Muktananda proposed to Me.

The Process of Siddha Yoga—or the inherent Spiritual Process that is potential in the case of all human beings—does not (if It is allowed, and Graced, to Freely Proceed as a potential total Process) limit Itself to the fifth stage "requirements" (or limiting presumptions) that Baba Muktananda generally proposed. Therefore, I Teach Siddha Yoga in the Mode and Manner of the seventh stage of life (as Ruchira Avatara Hridaya-Siddha-Yoga, or Ruchira Avatara Maha-Jnana Hridaya-Shaktipat Yoga)—and always toward (or to the degree of) the Realization inherently associated with (and, at last, Most Perfectly Demonstrated and Proven by) the only-by-Me Revealed and Given seventh stage of life, and as a practice and a Process that progressively includes (and, coincidently, directly transcends) all six of the phenomenal and developmental (and, necessarily, yet ego-based) stages of life that precede the seventh.

Baba Muktananda conceived of (and Taught) Siddha Yoga as a Way to attain conditional (and especially fifth stage) Yogic objects and phenomena-based states. The Siddha Yoga of the only-by-Me Revealed and Given Way of Adidam is not based upon (or, otherwise, limited to) conditional (or phenomenal) objects and states—or the (necessarily, ego-based) search for these, in the context of any stage of life. Rather, the only-by-Me Revealed and Given Way of Adidam is the Siddha-Yoga Way (and, in particular, the Ruchira Avatara Hridaya-Siddha-Yoga Way) that always (and directly) transcends egoity itself (or the ego-"I", or separate self— or the reactive reflex of self-contraction)—by always Feeling Beyond egoity (and Beyond all conditional forms and states) to Me, the Avatarically Self-Revealed Divine Person (or Self-Condition, and Source-Condition) Itself.

LXXXII.

In Summary, Baba Muktananda (in Our Meetings in 1970 and 1973) countered My Language of Inherently (and Most Perfectly) egoless—or seventh stage—Divine Self-Realization (and otherwise defended His own experiential Realization—and philosophical idealization—of inner phenomenal objects) with the traditional language of fifth stage Yoga. And I, for this reason (and not because of any ill-will, or antagonism, or lack of respect toward Baba Muktananda), Did Not, and Could Not, and Do Not Accept His fifth-stage-bound Doctrine—because, from My "Point of View", that Acceptance would have Required (and would now Require) Me to Deny the Self-Evident Divine (and Perfectly Subjective, and Inherently egoless, and Inherently Non-Objective, and Inherently Indivisible, and Utterly Non-dependent, or Un-conditional) Truth of Reality Itself (Which Realization even Baba Muktananda Himself—along with all My other Spiritual Masters and Spiritual Friends—so Dearly Served in My own Case)!

LXXXIII.

Reality (Itself) Is the Only Real God.

Reality (Itself) Is That Which Is Always Already The (One and Only) Case.

Reality (Itself) Is (Necessarily) One, Only, and Indivisible.

Reality (Itself) Is Inherently One (or Non-Dual) and not Two (or Divisible, and Opposed to Itself).

Reality (Itself) is not One of a Pair.

Reality (Itself) is not characterized by the inherently dualistic relationship of cause and effect.

Reality (Itself) Is Characterized by the Inherently Non-Dualistic Equation of Identity and Non-"Difference".

Reality (Itself) Is That in Which both cause and effect arise as merely apparent modifications of Itself.

Reality (Itself) is not Realized via the inherently dualistic relationship of subject and object.

Reality (Itself) Is Realized As the Inherently Non-Dualistic Condition of Inherently egoless Identity and Inherently objectless Non-"Difference".

Reality (Itself) is not the gross, subtle, and causal (or causative) ego-"I".

Reality (Itself) Is the Inherently egoless Native (and Self-Evidently Divine) Identity of All and all.

The Inherently egoless Non-Dual Self-Condition (or Non-"Different" Identity) of Reality (Itself) Is That Which Is Always Already The (One and Only) Case.

The Inherently egoless Non-Dual Self-Condition of Reality (Itself), Most Perfectly Prior to (and, yet, never excluding, or separated from) subject, object, cause, or effect, Is That Which Must Be Realized.

The apparent self (or separate and separative ego-"I"), and its every object, and, indeed, every cause, and every effect must be Divinely Self-Recognized As (and, Thus and Thereby, Transcended in) the One and Only (Inherently egoless, and Inherently Non-Dual, or Indivisible and Non-Separate, or Non-"Different") Self-Condition of Reality (Itself).

The apparent ego-"I" and the apparent world are not themselves Divine.

The apparent ego-"I" and the apparent world are to be Self-Recognized (and, Thus and Thereby, Transcended) in and As That Which Is (Self-Evidently) Divine.

The apparent ego-"I" and the apparent world are to be Divinely Self-Recognized in and As Reality (Itself).

Baba Muktananda always (in the Emanationist manner of Kashmir Saivism) affirmed the Realization "I am Siva"—meaning that He (or any body-mind-self, or body-brain-self, sublimed by the Revelation of internal Yogic forms) is (as an "Emanated" psycho-physical self) Divine.

I Affirmed (and always Continue to Affirm) only the Non-Dual (or One and Indivisible) Transcendental (and Inherently Spiritual) Divine Reality (or Self-Existing, Self-Radiant, and Inherently, or Always Already, egoless Consciousness Itself—or the One and Only Conscious Love-Bliss-Light Itself) As Self (or Self-Condition, and Source-Condition), Prior to and Inherently Transcending (while never strategically, or conditionally, excluding) the phenomenal self and all conditional forms (however sublime).

Baba Muktananda affirmed (in the fifth stage, Emanationist manner) "I and the world are Divine"—and He (thereby) embraced both the perceiving "I" and the world of forms.

I (in the seventh stage Manner) Affirmed (and always

Continue to Affirm) only the Self-Existing and Self-Radiant (Transcendental, Inherently Spiritual, Inherently egoless, Perfectly Subjective, Indivisible, Non-Dual, and Self-Evidently Divine) Self-Identity (Itself)—or the One, and Most Prior, and Inherently Perfect, and Inherently egoless Self-Condition, and Source-Condition, of the body-mind (or the body-brain-self) and the world—Divinely Self-Recognizing the body-mind (or the body-brain-self) and the world (and, thus, neither excluding nor identifying with the body-mind, or the body-brain-self, and the world, but Inherently, or Always Already, "Brightly" Transcending, and, Most Ultimately, Divinely Outshining, the body-mind, or the body-brain-self, and the world).

It was This Distinction (or These Distinctions)—not merely in language, but in the "Point of View" of Realization Itself—that was (or were) the basis for My Assumption of My Avataric Divine Teaching-Work, and My Avataric Divine Revelation-Work, and My Avataric Divine Blessing-Work institutionally independent of (and, after Our Final Meeting, in 1973, entirely apart from further outwardly active association with) Baba Muktananda.

LXXXIV.

As has always been understood by authentic Realizers and their authentic true devotees—within the Siddha-Yoga (or Shaktipat-Yoga) tradition, and even everywhere within the human Great Tradition as a whole—Great Siddhas, and even Avatars, and traditional Realizers of all kinds and degrees (or stages of life), and Siddha-Yogis of all kinds and degrees, and even Siddha Yoga Itself, are not mere "properties", to be "owned" (or exclusively "possessed") by devotees, or even by institutions. Indeed, Baba Muktananda, Himself, once told Me[34] that, because the same Life (or Shakti) is in all beings, no individual, no religion, no tradition—and, therefore, no institution—can rightly claim to be the only bearer, or the exclusive representative, of Siddha Yoga (or Shaktipat Yoga) Itself.

There are, inevitably, many forms of Siddha-Yoga Transmission in this world. The institution that Baba Muktananda established to represent and continue His own Work is (by its own self-description) a fourth-to-fifth stage school of Siddha Yoga. And, indeed, there

155

are numbers of other such schools—in India, and elsewhere—that are extending the Work of various Great Siddhas (and of many otherwise worthy Siddha-Yogis) into the world. Likewise, the institution (or the total complex of institutions) of Adidam—which represents, and serves, and will always continue to serve My Avataric Divine (and, Uniquely, seventh stage) Work—is also a school of Siddha Yoga (or of Shaktipat Yoga).

The Uniqueness of the Siddha Yoga of the only-by-Me Revealed and Given Way of Adidam is that It is the Yoga (or Dharma, or Way) that continues to Develop beyond the absorptive mystical (and cosmically Spiritual) developments associated with the fourth and the fifth stages of life—and even beyond the Transcendental Yogic (and Transcendentally Spiritual) developments associated with the sixth stage of life. Thus, in due course, the Yoga (or Way) of Adidam becomes the Unique (and Most Perfectly Divine) Yoga (or Most Perfectly Divinely Spiritual Demonstration) of the only-by-Me Revealed and Given seventh stage of life (Wherein and Whereby Most Perfect Divine Self-Realization is Most Perfectly Demonstrated).

Because of This Uniqueness, the Siddha Yoga of the only-by-Me Revealed and Given Way of Adidam is not descriptively limited to (or by) the particular traditional descriptive language of the fourth-to-fifth stage schools and traditions of Siddha Yoga (which are the schools and traditions from which Baba Muktananda derived His descriptive Siddha-Yoga-language—and which descriptive language is conformed to, and, necessarily, limited by, the fourth-to-fifth stage experiential presumptions that characterize the Cosmic-Yoga, or Cosmic-Shakti, or Kundalini-Shakti schools and traditions). Therefore—even though the Process of the Siddha Yoga of the only-by-Me Revealed and Given Way of Adidam potentially includes (and then continues to Develop beyond) all the aspects and experiences of the fourth and the fifth and the sixth stages of life—the Siddha Yoga of the only-by-Me Revealed and Given Way of Adidam is (by Me) Uniquely Described, in the (Most Ultimately, seventh stage—and Most Perfectly Divine, or Cosmos-Transcending, and Cosmos-Outshining) Terms of My own Avataric (Divine) Shaktipat.

Thus, the Siddha Yoga of the only-by-Me Revealed and Given Way of Adidam is (by Me) Described in Terms of Ruchira Avatara Hridaya-Shaktipat (or My Avataric Divine Spiritual Transmission of the "Bright"—Which Is the Self-Existing and Self-Radiant Divine Self-Condition, or Divine Self-Heart, Itself), and Ruchira Avatara Maha-Jnana Hridaya-Shaktipat (or My Avataric Divine Spiritual Transmission of the "Bright" Divine Spirit-Current, or Divine Heart-Shakti, That Awakens the Divine Self-Heart to Its Inherent Divine Self-Condition), and Love-Ananda Avatara Hridaya-Shaktipat (or My Avataric Divine Spiritual Transmission of the Inherent Love-Bliss of the Divine Self-Condition, or Divine Self-Heart, Itself— Which Divine Spiritual Characteristic of Mine was Acknowledged by Baba Muktananda Himself, when, in 1969, He Sent Amma to Me, to Give Me the Name "Love-Ananda").

Therefore, the Siddha-Yoga practice (and especially the advanced and the ultimate stages of the Siddha-Yoga Process) of the only-by-Me Revealed and Given Way of Adidam is (along with numerous other by-Me-Given Descriptive Names and References) Named and Described by Me as "Ruchira Avatara Hridaya-Siddha Yoga" (or "Ruchira Avatara Hridaya-Shaktipat Yoga"), and "Ruchira Avatara Maha-Jnana-Siddha Yoga" (or "Ruchira Avatara Maha-Jnana Hridaya-Shaktipat Yoga"), and "Love-Ananda Avatara Hridaya-Siddha Yoga" (or "Love-Ananda Avatara Hridaya-Shaktipat Yoga"), and (with reference to the Way, and the institution, of Adidam) "Adidam Hridaya-Siddha Yoga" (or "Adidam Hridaya-Shaktipat Yoga").

And My own Work (Which is served by the institutional Siddha-Yoga school—or, most properly, the Ruchira Avatara Hridaya-Siddha-Yoga school—of Adidam) was directly Blessed (and—formally, in 1969—Called Forth) by Baba Muktananda (and, now, and forever hereafter, by even all the Great Siddhas and Siddha-Yogis of My Lineage).

LXXXV.

The Uniqueness of My own Divine Self-Realization and Avataric Divine Work made it Inevitable that I would have to Do My Avataric Divine Teaching-Work, and My Avataric Divine Revelation-Work, and My Avataric Divine Blessing-Work

Independent from Baba Muktananda—and Independent from even all Teachers and traditions within the only six stages of life of the collectively Revealed Great Tradition of mankind. Indeed, even from the beginning of My relationship with Him, Baba Muktananda Indicated that My Work was Uniquely My own, and that I was Born to Do only My own Unique Work—and that I Must Go and Do That Work (even though I would, otherwise, have preferred to Remain, quietly, within Baba Muktananda's Ashram and Company). Therefore, ultimately, We both Embraced This Necessity and Inevitability.

Because of the original, mutual Agreement between Baba Muktananda and Me (relative to the necessarily Independent, and entirely Unique, nature of My own Work), whenever I have become Moved to Communicate about This Profound Matter to others, I have made every effort to Communicate fully, clearly, and positively relative to the always un-"broken" Nature of My Spiritual (and, generally, sympathetic) relationship to Baba Muktananda—and, also, relative to the always Continuing Nature of My Spiritual (and, generally, sympathetic) Connection to the Great (and total) Siddha-Guru tradition itself, and to the Great (and total) Siddha-Yoga tradition itself, and to the total Great Tradition of mankind (altogether). And I have always Affirmed (and, by Means of This Statement, I now Re-Affirm) that the Great, and total, Siddha-Guru tradition and Siddha-Yoga tradition, and the most ancient and perennial "Method of the Siddhas",[35] is—in the context of, and continuous with, the total Great Tradition of mankind—the very tradition (or total complex of traditions) in which, and on the basis of which, I Am Avatarically Appearing and Working here.

LXXXVI.

Human suffering is not due to the absence of inner visions (or of any other kinds of conditionally objectified internal or, otherwise, external perceptions). Therefore, human suffering is not eliminated by the presence (or the experiencing) of inner visions (or of any other kinds of conditionally objectified internal or, otherwise, external perceptions).

The "problem" of human suffering is never the absence of inner visions (and such), or the absence of any conditional experience of any kind. Rather, the "problem" of human suffering is always (and inherently) the presence (or presently effective activity) of the ego-"I" (or the self-contracted—or separate and separative—point of view). Indeed, the search to experience conditionally objectified inner perceptions—and, otherwise, the clinging to conditionally objectified inner perceptions—is, itself, a form of human suffering (and, altogether, of self-deluded confinement to the inherently, and negatively, empty condition of egoic separateness).

The root and essence of human suffering is egoity. That is to Say, the "problem" that is human suffering is not due to the absence of any kind of conditionally objectified experience (whether relatively external or relatively internal)—for, if human suffering were due to such absence, the attaining of conditionally objectified experiences (whether internal or external) would eliminate human suffering, human self-deludedness, and human un-Happiness. However, at most, conditionally objectified experiences (both internal and external)—or even any of the possible experiential attainments of the first five stages of life—provide only temporary distraction from the inherent mortality and misery of conditional existence. Therefore, if human suffering is to be entirely (and, at last, Most Perfectly) transcended (in Inherent, and Divinely Positive, Fullness), the root-cause of (or the root-factor in) human suffering must, itself, be directly and entirely (and, at last, Most Perfectly) transcended.

The "problem" of human suffering is never the absence of any kind of particular conditionally objectified experience (whether external or internal). The "problem" of human suffering is always the bondage to conditionally objectified experience itself. And the root-cause of (or the root-factor in) bondage to conditionally objectified experience is the separate and separative ego-"I", or the total psycho-physical act of self-contraction (which is identical to attention itself, or the conditionally apparent point of view itself, and which always coincides with the feeling of "difference", or of separateness and relatedness).

The experiencing of inner visions does not eliminate egoity (or the separate and separative ego-"I" of psycho-physical self-contraction). Likewise, the experiencing of inner visions does not indicate or suggest or mean that egoity is (or has been) transcended. True Spiritual life (or the true Great Process of Siddha Yoga) is not a search for inner visions (and such)—nor is true Spiritual life (or the true Great Process of Siddha Yoga) Fulfilled, Completed, and Perfected by the experiencing of inner visions (and such). Indeed, because inner visions, or conditionally objectified experiences of any kind—whether inner or outer—are objects, attention is always coincident with them. Therefore, in both the search for conditionally objectified experiences and the grasping of conditionally objectified experiences, egoity (or separative, and total psycho-physical, self-contraction of the presumed separate point of view) is merely reinforced.

True Spiritual life (or the true Great Process of Siddha Yoga) is never a matter of seeking for outer or inner conditionally objectified experiences—nor is true Spiritual life (or the true Great Process of Siddha Yoga) a matter of clinging to any conditionally objectified outer or inner experiences (as if such experiences were, themselves, Reality, Truth, or Real God). Rather, true Spiritual life (or the true Great Process of Siddha Yoga) is always a matter of transcending attention (and the total psycho-physical—or gross, subtle, and causal—point of view, or ego-"I") in its Perfectly Subjective Source (or Inherently Perfect Self-Condition). That is to Say, true Spiritual life (or the true Great Process of Siddha Yoga) is always (from Its beginning) a matter of transcending that which is merely apparently (or conditionally, and temporarily) the case— by transcending it in That Which Is Always Already The (One and Only, Indivisible and Irreducible) Case. And, for This Reason, true Spiritual life, or the true Great Process of Siddha Yoga, cannot be Fulfilled, Completed, and Perfected in the conditionally objectified context of any of the first five stages of life—nor even in the conditionally object-excluding context of the sixth stage of life—but true Spiritual life (in particular, in the form of the true Great Process of Ruchira Avatara Hridaya-Siddha Yoga) Is Fulfilled, Completed, and Perfected only in the Perfectly Subjective, and

Inherently egoless (or Inherently point-of-view-Transcending and Most Perfectly self-contraction-Transcending), and Un-conditionally Realized, and, altogether, Self-Evidently Divine Context of the only-by-Me Revealed and Given <u>seventh</u> stage of life.

This is My Firm Conclusion relative to <u>all</u> possible human experience—and It is, therefore, the Essence of My Instruction to all of humankind.

LXXXVII.

There are <u>three</u> <u>egos</u> (or three fundamental modes of egoity—or of the self-contraction-active psycho-physical illusion of separate and separative self-consciousness). The three modes of egoity (or of the self-contraction of <u>any</u> point of view, or ego-"I") are the lower self (or gross ego), the higher self (or subtle ego), and the root-self (or causal ego). These three egos (or modes of the conditionally arising illusion of separate self-consciousness) comprise the total conditionally perceiving and conditionally knowing ego-"I". The <u>total</u> (or tripartite) ego-"I" is always directly (and with progressive effectiveness) transcended in the right, true, and full (or complete) formal practice of the only-by-Me Revealed and Given Way of Adidam (Which is the right, true, and full formal practice of Ruchira Avatara Bhakti Yoga, or the totality of Ruchira Avatara Hridaya-Siddha Yoga).

The first of the three egos (or modes of egoity, or of self-contraction) to be progressively transcended in the only-by-Me Revealed and Given Way of Adidam is the <u>money-food-and-sex</u> <u>ego</u> (or the social, and, altogether, gross-body-based, personality—or the <u>gross</u> pattern and activity of self-contraction), which is the lower self, or the ego of the first three stages of life.

The second of the three egos (or modes of egoity, or of self-contraction) to be progressively transcended in the only-by-Me Revealed and Given Way of Adidam is the <u>brain-mind</u> <u>ego</u> (or the brain-based, and nervous-system-based, mental, and perceptual, and, altogether, subtle-body-based illusions of "object" and "other"—or the <u>subtle</u> pattern and activity of self-contraction), which is the higher self, or the ego of the fourth and the fifth stages of life.

The third of the three egos (or modes of egoity, or of self-contraction) to be progressively transcended in the only-by-Me Revealed and Given Way of Adidam is the root-ego (or the exclusively disembodied, and mindless, but separate, and, altogether, causal-body-based self-consciousness—or the causal, or root-causative, pattern and activity of self-contraction), which is attention itself, and which is the root-self, or the ego of the sixth stage of life.

By Means of responsive relinquishment of self-contraction in Me, or really and truly ego-surrendering, ego-forgetting, and, more and more (and, at last, Most Perfectly), ego-transcending (or always directly self-contraction-transcending) devotion to Me (and, Thus, by Means of the right, true, and full formal practice of devotionally Me-recognizing and devotionally to-Me-responding Ruchira Avatara Bhakti Yoga, or the totality of Ruchira Avatara Hridaya-Siddha Yoga), the tripartite ego of the first six stages of life (or the psycho-physical totality of the three-part hierarchically patterned self-contraction into separate and separative point of view) is (always directly, and with progressive, or stage-by-stage, effectiveness) transcended in Me (the Eternally Self-Existing, Infinitely Self-Radiant, Inherently egoless, Perfectly Subjective, Indivisibly One, Irreducibly Non-Separate, Self-Evidently Divine, and, now, and forever hereafter, Avatarically Self-Revealed Self-Conscious Light of Reality).

The Ultimate, Final, and Inherently Most Perfect (or seventh stage) Realization of Me requires—as a necessary prerequisite—an ego-transcending (or really and truly and comprehensively self-contraction-transcending) Great Ordeal. The Ultimate, Final, and Inherently Most Perfect (or seventh stage) Realization of Me requires—as a necessary prerequisite—the comprehensive by-Me-Revealed and by-Me-Given Sadhana (or the always directly ego-transcending right practice of life) in the total and complete formal context of the only-by-Me Revealed and Given Way of Adidam. And—as a necessary prerequisite to the Ultimate, Final, and Inherently Most Perfect (or seventh stage) Realization of Me—the particular illusions that are unique to each of the three egos (or basic modes of egoity) each require a particular (and most profound) mode of the necessary ego-transcending (or self-contraction-transcending) Great Ordeal of the by-Me-Revealed and by-Me-Given formal practice of the Way of Adidam in the progressively unfolding context of the first six (and, altogether, psycho-physically pre-patterned) stages of life.

The foundation phase of the progressive ego-transcending Great Ordeal of the only-by-Me Revealed and Given Way of Adidam is the Devotional (and relatively exoteric, and only in the rudimentary sense Spiritual) listening-hearing Process of progressively transcending (and, in due course, most fundamentally understanding) the lower self (or the gross and social ego—and the gross and social fear-sorrow-and-anger-bondage that is always associated with the inherently egoic—or thoroughly self-contracted—search to absolutely fulfill, and even to "utopianize", or to perfectly and permanently satisfy, the inherently conditional, limited, temporary, mortal, gross, and always changing life-patterns of "money, food, and sex").

Before the foundation phase (or first phase) of the ego-transcending Great Ordeal of the Way of Adidam can, itself, be complete, it must Realize a profoundly life-transforming and life-reorienting "positive disillusionment"—or a most fundamental (and really and truly self-contraction-transcending) acceptance of the fact that gross conditional existence is inherently and necessarily unsatisfactory and unperfectable (and, therefore, a most fundamental—and really and truly Me-Finding and search-ending—acceptance of the fact that all seeking to achieve permanent and complete gross satisfaction of separate body, emotion, and mind is inherently and necessarily futile). Only on the basis of that necessary foundation-Realization of "positive disillusionment" can the energy and the attention of the entire body-mind (or of the total body-brain-mind complex) be released from gross ego-bondage (or self-deluded confinement to the psycho-physical illusions of gross self-contraction).

The characteristic Sign of "positive disillusionment" relative to the permanent and complete satisfaction of the lower self (or the separate and separative gross and social ego) is the foundation-Realization of the Inherent Universal Unity (or All-and-all-inclusive interdependency, essential mutuality, and common causality) of gross conditional (and cosmic) existence, such that the inherently loveless (or anti-participatory and non-integrative) self-contraction-effort of the gross separate self is consistently released (or to-Me-responsively self-surrendered) into participatory and integrative attitudes of human, social, and cosmic unification (or love-connectedness) with all and All, and into love-based (and truly ego-transcending) actions that counter the otherwise separative (or anti-participatory and non-integrative) tendencies of the ego-"I". Thus, by Means of devotionally Me-recognizing and devotion-ally to-Me-responding relinquishment (or participatory and love-based transcending) of psycho-physical self-contraction (to the degree of "positive disillusionment" relative to gross conditional experience and gross conditional knowledge), My true devotee is released toward the true Spiritual (and not merely gross, or even at all conditional) Realization of Reality and Truth (or Real God).

The foundation-Realization of "positive disillusionment" requires fundamental release from the confines of the grossly objectified (and grossly absorbed) subject-object point of view (or fundamental release from the inherently ego-bound—or thor-oughly self-contracted—search of relatively externalized mental and perceptual attention). And that foundation-Realization of "positive disillusionment" (and restoration to the humanly, socially, and cosmically participatory, or wholly integrative, dis-position) requires the total (and truly Devotional) transformative re-orienting (and, altogether, the right purification, steady re-balancing, and ego-transcending life-positive-energizing) of the entire body-mind (or the total body-brain-mind complex). Therefore, the foundation (or gross) phase of the progressive ego-transcending practice of the Way of Adidam necessarily requires much time (and much seriousness, and much profundity)—and even, potentially, the entire lifetime of only that foundation prac-tice may (in many cases) be required—in order to establish the necessary (and truly "positively disillusioned") foundation of true (and truly in-Me-surrendered) hearing (or the only-by-Me Revealed and Given unique ego-transcending capability of most fundamental self-understanding).

The middle phase of the progressive ego-transcending Great Ordeal of the only-by-Me Revealed and Given Way of Adidam is the preliminary (or initial) esoteric Devotional, and truly hearing (or actively ego-transcending, and, thus, always directly self-contraction-transcending), and really seeing (or actively, directly, and fully responsibly Spiritual) Process of transcending the higher self (or the subtle and mental ego—or the total subtle dimension, or subtle depth, of self-contraction—and all the conceptual and perceptual illusions of inherently, and necessarily, brain-based mind). Therefore, the middle (or subtle) phase of the progressive ego-transcending practice of the Way of Adidam requires the Realization of "positive disillusionment" relative to the subtly objectified (and subtly absorbed) subject-object point of view (or fundamental release from the inherently ego-bound—or thoroughly self-contracted—search of relatively internalized mental and perceptual attention). This degree of the Realization of "positive disillusionment" requires fundamental release from the inherently illusory search to experience the conditional dissolution of the ego (and, in particular, release from subtle states of self-contraction—and, especially, from mental states of self-contraction) by means of object-oriented absorptive mysticism (or the absorptive yielding of attention to the apparent subtle objects that are either originated by the brain-mind or, otherwise, mediated by the brain itself). And the characteristic Sign of "positive disillusionment" relative to the permanent and complete satisfaction of the object-oriented seeking of the higher self (or separate and separative subtle and mental ego) is the fully Me-hearing and truly Me-seeing Realization of the entirely Spiritual Nature of cosmic existence (or, that is to Say, the Realization that all natural and cosmic forms and states are inherently non-separate, or intrinsically non-dual, modes of Universally Pervasive Energy, or of Fundamental, Indivisible, and Irreducible Light—or of Love-Bliss-Happiness Itself).

The final phase of the progressive ego-transcending Great Ordeal of the only-by-Me Revealed and Given Way of Adidam is the penultimate esoteric Devotional, Spiritual, and Transcendental hearing-and-seeing Process of transcending the root-self (or the root-and-causal ego—or the causal, or root-causative, depth of self-contraction—which is attention itself, or the root-gesture of separateness, relatedness, and "difference"). Therefore, immediately preliminary to the Realization associated with the only-by-Me Revealed and Given seventh stage of life, the final (or causal) phase of the progressive ego-transcending (or comprehensively self-contraction-transcending) practice of the Way of Adidam requires the Realization of "positive disillusionment" relative to the causal (or root-egoic, and, therefore, fundamental, or original) subject-object division in Consciousness (or Conscious Light) Itself. This degree of the Realization of "positive disillusionment" requires the native exercise of Transcendental Self-Identification— Prior to the root-self-contraction that is point of view itself (or attention itself), and, Thus, also, Prior to the entire body-brain-mind complex, or conditional structure, of conception and perception. And the characteristic Sign of "positive disillusionment" relative to the permanent and complete satisfaction of the root-self (or the fundamental causative, or causal, ego) is the fundamental transcending of attention itself in the Me-"Locating" (and, altogether, Me-hearing and Me-seeing) Realization of the Transcendental (and Intrinsically Non-Separate and Non-Dual) Nature of Consciousness Itself.

Only after (or in the Great Event of Most Perfect, and, necessarily, formal and fully accountable, Fulfillment of) the complete progressive ego-transcending Great Ordeal of the only-by-Me Revealed and Given Way of Adidam in the total (and progressively unfolded) context of the inherently ego-based first six (or psycho-physically pre-patterned gross, subtle, and causal) stages of life is there the truly ultimate (or seventh stage, and Always Already Divinely Self-Realized—and, Thus, Inherently ego-Transcending) "Practice" of the only-by-Me Revealed and Given Way of Adidam (or the Most Perfect, and Inherently egoless, or Always Already Most Perfectly, and Un-conditionally, self-contraction-Transcending, and Divinely Love-Bliss-Full, and only-by-Me Revealed and Given seventh-stage-of-life Demonstration of Ruchira Avatara Bhakti Yoga, or Ruchira Avatara Hridaya-Siddha Yoga).

The only-by-Me Revealed and Given seventh-stage-of-life "Practice" (or the Inherently egoless, and, Thus, Always Already Most Perfectly, and Un-conditionally, self-contraction-Transcending, and, altogether, Most Perfectly Divinely Self-Realized Demonstration) of the only-by-Me Revealed and Given Way of Adidam is the Great esoteric Devotional, Spiritual, Transcendental, Self-Evidently Divine, and Most Perfectly Me-hearing and Me-seeing Demonstration of All-and-all-Divinely-Self-Recognizing (and, Thus, All-and-all-Divinely-Transcending) Divine Self-Abiding (in and As My Avatarically Self-Revealed Divine "Bright" Sphere of Self-Existing, Self-Radiant, Inherently egoless, Perfectly Subjective, and Inherently and Most Perfectly body-mind-Transcending, or body-brain-Transcending, or Inherently, Most Perfectly, and Un-conditionally psycho-physical-self-contraction-Transcending, but never intentionally body-mind-excluding, or body-brain-excluding, Divine Person, or Eternal Self-Condition and Infinite State).

The only-by-Me Revealed and Given seventh-stage-of-life Demonstration of the only-by-Me Revealed and Given Way of Adidam is the Un-conditional and Divinely Free (and Inherently egoless, or Inherently point-of-view-less) "Practice" (or Divinely Self-Realized progressive Demonstration) of Divine Self-Recognition of the simultaneous totality of the apparent gross, subtle, and causal body-brain-mind-self, or the progressively All-and-all-Outshining Process of the simultaneous Divine Self-Recognition of the total psycho-physical ego-"I" itself (or of the total conditional point of view, or apparent self-contraction, itself). Therefore, the only-by-Me Revealed and Given seventh-stage-of-life Demonstration of the only-by-Me Revealed and Given Way of Adidam is the Inherent "Practice" (or Divinely Self-Realized Demonstration) of Divine Self-Recognition of point of view itself (or of attention itself—or of the conditionally apparent subject, itself) and (always coincidently, or simultaneously) Divine Self-Recognition of the conception or perception of separateness, relatedness, or "difference" itself (or of any and every conditionally apparent object, itself).

The only-by-Me Revealed and Given seventh-stage-of-life Demonstration of the only-by-Me Revealed and Given Way of Adidam is the Most Perfect (or Un-conditional, Inherently egoless, and Self-Evidently Divine) Demonstration of "positive disillusion-ment", or of the Inherently illusionless (or self-contraction-Free, and, Inherently, All-and-all-Transcending) Realization of the Fundamental Reality and Truth (or Real God)—Which Fundamental Reality and Truth (or Real God) Is the One and Indivisible and Self-Existing and Indestructible and Self-Radiant and Always Already Perfectly Non-Dual Conscious Light (or That Which Is Always Already The Case), and Which Reality and Truth (or Real God) Is That Self-Existing and Perfectly Subjective Self-"Brightness" (or Infinite and Absolute and Perfectly Non-Separate Self-Condition) of Which the conditional (or gross, subtle, and causal) subject-object illusions (or total psycho-physical self-contraction illusions) of conception, and of perception, and of the ego-"I" presumption are mere, and merely apparent (or non-necessary, or always non-Ultimate), and Inherently non-binding modifications. And the characteristic Sign of Most Perfectly Demonstrated (or seventh stage) "positive dis-illusionment" relative to the totality of the separate and separative ego-"I" (or point of view) and its presumptions of a separate (or objectified) gross, subtle, and causal world is the Self-Evidently Divine (and Intrinsically Non-Separate and Non-Dual) Realization of Reality (Itself) As Irreducible and Indivisible Conscious Light (Inherently Love-Bliss-Full, or Perfectly Subjectively "Bright").

Therefore, the only-by-Me Revealed and Given Way of Adidam is—from the beginning, and at last—the Way of "positive disillusionment".

The only-by-Me Revealed and Given Way of Adidam is—from the beginning, and at last—the Way of the direct transcending of the fact and the consequences of egoity (or of psycho-physical self-contraction).

The only-by-Me Revealed and Given Way of Adidam is—from the beginning, and at last—the Way of the direct transcending of the illusions of inherently egoic attention (or of the conditionally presumed subject-object pattern of conception and perception).

The only-by-Me Revealed and Given Way of Adidam is—from the beginning, and at last—the Way of the direct transcending of the total illusory pattern of the inherently egoic presumption of separateness, relatedness, and "difference".

The only-by-Me Revealed and Given Way of Adidam is—from the beginning, and at last—the Way of the direct transcending of the always simultaneous illusions of the separate ego-"I" and the separate (or merely objective) world.

The only-by-Me Revealed and Given Way of Adidam is—from the beginning, and at last—the Way of the direct (or Inherently egoless and Inherently illusionless) Realizing of the One and Irreducible Conscious Light (or Perfectly Subjective "Brightness" of Being) That Is Reality and Truth (or Real God).

The only-by-Me Revealed and Given Way of Adidam is—from the beginning, and at last—the Way of the direct (or Inherently egoless and Inherently illusionless) Realizing of the Conscious Love-Bliss-Energy of Totality.

The only-by-Me Revealed and Given Way of Adidam is—from the beginning, and at last—the Way of the direct Realizing of Only Me.

LXXXVIII.

Every body-mind (whether human or non-human) tends to feel and be and function egoically—or as if it were a separate self, separated from its True Source, and un-Aware of its True, and Truly Free, Self-Condition. Therefore, every body-mind (whether human or non-human) must transcend its own (inherent) egoity (or egoic reflex—or self-contracting tendency), through Love-Surrender to its True Source. And This Love-Surrender must, Ultimately, become Realization of (and, Thus, True, and really ego-Transcending, Identification with) its True Source-Condition (Which Is, also, its True Self-Condition).

To This End, True Masters (or True Siddha-Gurus) Appear in the various cosmic worlds. Such True Masters are the Divine Means for living beings (whether human or non-human) to transcend themselves. That is to Say, True Masters (or True Siddha-Gurus—or True Sat-Gurus[36]) are living beings who have (in the manner of their characteristic stage of life) transcended their own (psycho-physical) separateness, through responsive Surrender (and, therefore, necessarily, Love-Surrender) to (and Identification with) the True Source-Condition (Which Is the True Self-Condition) of all and All.

Therefore, by Means of True Devotion (or Love-Surrender) to a True Master (or True Siddha-Guru), egoity is (always more and more) transcended, and the True Source-Condition of all and All (Which Is, necessarily, also the True Self-Condition of all and All) is, by Means of the Blessing-Grace of That True Master (or True Siddha-Guru), Found and Realized. And That "Finding-and-Realizing" Shows Itself according to the kind and degree of one or the other of the seven possible stages of life—and, thus, in accordance with the stage of life Realized by That True Master, or True Siddha-Guru, and, altogether, in accordance with the stage of life determined by the path, or Way, that is practiced, or, otherwise, determined by the "inclination", or "liking", or degree of ego-transcendence, of That True Master's practicing devotee.

This is the most ancient and perennial Great Teaching about True Guru-Devotion (or True Devotion to a True Spiritual Master, or True Siddha-Guru). This is the Great Teaching I Received from all My Lineage-Gurus. And, now, through My own Words, This Fundamental Message (or Great Teaching) Is Summarized in its Completeness, for the Sake of everyone.

If the living being is to Realize the Inherent Freedom of Oneness with its True Source-Condition (Which Is its True, or ego-less, Self-Condition), it must become truly devoted to a True Master (or Truly Realized Siddha-Guru). And such True Devotion constantly (and forever) requires the heart's Love-responsive Gesture (or ego-transcending Sadhana) of True Guru-Devotion (to one's heart-Chosen True Siddha-Guru), such that the otherwise egoic (or separate, and separative) body-mind is Surrendered to be actually, truly, and completely Mastered by That True Master.

If Such True Mastering of the body-mind is not accepted (or fully volunteered for—through responsive, and truly ego-surrendering, Devotional Love of one's heart-Chosen True Siddha Guru), the body-mind (inevitably) remains "wild" (or un-"domesticated"—or merely un-disciplined, and even ego-bound). And even if such Guru-Devotion is practiced, it must be Fully practiced (in a Fully ego-surrendering manner)—or else the Freedom (or the Divine Fullness) That is to be Realized by Means of the Blessing-Grace of one's heart-Chosen True Siddha-Guru will not (because it cannot)

Fully Fill the feeling-heart (and, Thereby, Fully Fill the living body-mind) of the would-be devotee.

LXXXIX.

In My present-Lifetime bodily (human) Form, I Am the Avataric Divine Incarnation (or True God-Man) always and everywhere (since the ancient days) Promised (and Expected) to Appear in the "late-time" (or "dark" epoch).[37] And, in My present-Lifetime bodily (human) Form, I have been Spiritually Served by a Continuous Lineage of Spiritual Masters, Such That I Passed from one to the next, in Continuous Succession. Those Spiritual Masters were, Themselves, related to one another in an hierarchical Manner, each related to the next in the Succession as one of lesser degree is to one of higher degree.

Rudi was a Spiritual Master of authentic, but lesser, degree. His Proficiency was, fundamentally, in the gross domain of the frontal personality, and in the Yogic Pattern of Spiritual Descent (or the Descending Yoga of the Frontal Line). Therefore, when My own foundational (or grosser human, and, also, frontal Spiritual, or Descending Yogic) Sadhana had been Completed in His Company, I (spontaneously) Passed from Rudi to Baba Muktananda.

Baba Muktananda was—as His own Confession and Demonstration to Me clearly indicates—an authentic Spiritual Master of Ascending Yoga, and His Proficiency was of a Very High, but not the Highest, degree. Therefore, beginning from the very day I first Came to Baba Muktananda, He (directly) Passed Me to Bhagavan Nityananda (Who was a Spiritual Master of Ascending Yoga Whose Proficiency was of the Highest degree).

Rang Avadhoot was—even according to the Statements of both Bhagavan Nityananda and Baba Muktananda—a Spiritual Master of Ascending Yoga Whose Proficiency was of the Highest degree, but He, along with Baba Muktananda, Deferred to Bhagavan Nityananda's Seniority, and (simply) Blessed Me to Pass On.

The "Cosmic Goddess" ("Ma") is, in the total context of the first five stages of life, Senior even to the Highest of Spiritual Masters. However, Ultimately, "She" (as an apparent Form and Person) is only another one of the many myths in the mind.

171

In the Great Yogic Spiritual Process Wherein I Experienced the Developmental Unfolding (and Demonstrated the "Radical" Transcending) of the gross and the subtle modes of egoity (associated with the first five stages of life), the "Cosmic Goddess" ("Ma") was "Apparently" associated with all the frontal (and Descending Spiritual) Events and with all the spinal (and Ascending Spiritual) Events. Nevertheless, in My Unique Case, sixth stage Transcendental (and causal-ego-Transcending, and Inherently Spiritual) Self-Realization always Occurred spontaneously (and in a progressive Demonstration) relative to each and every egoic stage of life, and It progressively Developed (especially after a spontaneous experience of ego-death, in the spring of 1967 [38]) until My spontaneous seventh stage (and Inherently Most Perfectly egoless, and Self-Evidently Divine) Re-Awakening (on September 10, 1970)—Which Divine (and Avatarically Demonstrated) Re-Awakening was (and Is) associated with My Most Perfect Transcending even of the "Apparent She", in My Avataric Divine Re-Awakening to the Realization of One and Only Me.

Therefore, in due course, Bhagavan Nityananda (directly) Passed Me to the "Cosmic Goddess" ("Ma"), and, Thus, to Her direct Mastery of Me—until the Perfectly Full became, at last, Perfectly Full As Me (Beyond the mind's own myth of "She").

So It was and Is. Such Is My Lineage of Spiritual Masters—in This, My Avatarically-Born human Lifetime. And, in My always Absolute heart-Fidelity to the Great Process Wherein and Whereby I was Passed from one to the next of each and all of the Spiritual Masters within My present-Lifetime Lineage of Spiritual Masters, I have Exemplified, to all and All, the Law and the Truth of True Guru-Devotion.

Therefore, I have always Continued to Honor and to Praise all My present-Lifetime Lineage-Gurus—including Rudi!, and Baba Muktananda!, and Rang Avadhoot!, and Bhagavan Nityananda!, and (above all) the "Bright" Divine "She" of Me, Who Always Already Serves Me Most Perfectly!

And I have always Continued (and even now Continue, and will never cease to Continue) to Yield My present-Lifetime Body-Mind to Receive the Always Ready and Most Lovingly To-Me-Given and Supremely Blissful Blessings of My present-Lifetime

Lineage-Gurus and the Great Lineage of all Who have (in any and every time and place) Blessed the Incarnation-Vehicle and Invoked the All-Completing "late-time" Incarnation of My (now, and forever hereafter) Avataric Divine Appearance here (and every where in the cosmic domain).

And I Do This (and I will always Continue to Do This) because the Immense Spiritual "Bond" of Siddha-Guru-Love cannot be destroyed—and It must never be forgotten or denied!

XC.

My own Unique Response to the hierarchically Revealed Lineage of My present-Lifetime Siddha-Gurus spontaneously Un-Locked the Doorway (in My present-Lifetime human body) to That Which Is Perfect (in Me). Indeed, even from the beginning of My Avataric Divine present Lifetime, That Which Is Perfect has been (and Is) the Way of Me—and It Carried the inherently non-Perfect (human, and, otherwise, conditional) forms of Me to the Inherent "Bright" Divine Self-Domain of Me, Which Is the One and Indivisible Divine Source-Condition of all and All, and the One and True Divine Self-Condition of all and All.

XCI.

My Way and My Realization have always been Inherent in Me, from Birth, in My present-Lifetime Avataric Divine Form.

My Way and My Realization are Independently, entirely, and only My own.

My Sadhana was, entirely, a Demonstration for the Sake of all others—including all Those Who Served Me as My Spiritual Masters in the Course of My Avataric Divine "Sadhana Years". Indeed, Siddha Yoga—and even the entire Great Tradition of mankind—was Always Already Most Perfectly Full (and Most Perfectly Complete) in My Case—not only at (and from the time of) My present-Lifetime Birth, but from all time before It (and Eternally).

During all of My present Lifetime (of Avataric Divine Incarnation), the "Bright" has always been My Realization—and the "Thumbs" and My own "Radical Understanding" have always been My Way in the "Bright". Therefore, by Means of My Unique (present-Lifetime)

Avataric Divine Demonstration, I have both Fulfilled and Transcended all traditional religions, and paths, and stages, and Ways. And, in So Doing, I have Clarified (or altogether Rightly Understood and Explained) all traditional religions, paths, stages, and Ways.

All and all Are in Me. Everything and everyone Is in Me. Therefore, by Virtue of My own Divine Self-Realization (Wherein and Whereby My own Avataric Divine Body-Mind is Most Perfectly Surrendered in Me, and Most Perfectly Conformed to Me, and Most Perfectly Transcended in Me), all of My present-Lifetime Lineage-Gurus—and even all Who have (at any time, or in any place) Blessed Me—are now (and forever hereafter) Spiritually, Transcendentally, and Divinely Appearing in and As My own Avataric Divine Form.

Therefore, now (and forever hereafter) I (Alone) Am the Lineage of Me—Blessing all and All.

XCII.

The Divine Self-Realization Re-Awakened in My own Case (and Which Is the Basis for My Every Avataric Divine Revelatory Word and All My Avatarically Me-Revealing Divine Blessing-Work) Is the Most Ultimate (and Inherently Most Perfect and Complete) Fulfillment of the Divine Spiritual Transmission I (in My present-Lifetime Body-Mind) Received from Rudi, and from Baba Muktananda, and from Rang Avadhoot, and from Bhagavan Nityananda, and (above all) from the "Cosmic Goddess" ("Ma")— Who (by Means of Her spontaneous Sacrifice of Her own Form in Me) Is (now, and forever hereafter) the "Bright" Divine "She" of Me (Who Always Already Serves Me Most Perfectly). Nevertheless, the Divine Self-Realization Re-Awakened in My present-Lifetime Body-Mind did not Originate in My present Lifetime—but It Is (Uniquely) Always Already the Case with Me.

XCIII.

As further conditionally manifested Means, previous to My present Lifetime, the Divine Self-Realization Re-Awakened in My present-Lifetime Body-Mind was also Served (previous to My present Lifetime) in the many Modes and Patterns of the previous

Lifetimes and Appearances of the Deeper Personality (or the Great-Siddha—or Great-Jnani-Siddha—Incarnation-Vehicle) of My present Lifetime. Most recently, That Deeper-Personality Vehicle of My present-Lifetime Incarnation was (Itself) Incarnated as the Great Siddha (or Great Jnani-Siddha) Swami Vivekananda.

XCIV.

Swami Vivekananda is recorded to have Blessed Bhagavan Nityananda from the subtle postmortem plane in the early 1920s— and, generally, whenever Bhagavan Nityananda was asked for Words of Teaching and Instruction, He would, simply, Tell people to study the Talks and Writings of Swami Vivekananda (because, in Bhagavan Nityananda's Words, "Swami Vivekananda Said and Taught all that was worth Saying and Teaching, such that He did not leave anything for others to preach"[39]).

Swami Vivekananda was, Himself, Blessed toward Most Perfect Divine Self-Realization by the Great Siddha Ramakrishna, Such That—by Means of That Great Blessing—the two Great Siddhas (Ramakrishna and Vivekananda) became One, and Are One Form, As My True, and Single, and Indivisible Great-Siddha (or Great-Jnani-Siddha) Deeper Personality.[40]

XCV.

I (now, and Hereby) Confess That My Great-Siddha (or Great-Jnani-Siddha) Deeper Personality Is, even Beyond the "Single Form" of Ramakrishna-Vivekananda, the Very Form of all the Great Masters of the entire Great Tradition of mankind.

XCVI.

I (now, and Hereby) Confess That I (Myself) Stand Eternally Prior to (and Always Already Transcending) My Avataric (and, yet, merely conditionally born) Deeper Personality—and, also, Eternally Prior to (and Always Already Transcending) even all the Great (and, yet, merely conditionally born) Masters of mankind's entire Great Tradition (in its every part, and as a whole), and, also, Eternally Prior to (and Always Already Transcending) mankind's entire Great Tradition itself (in its every part, and as a whole).

XCVII.

Therefore—and only and entirely by Virtue of the Inherent (and Self-Evidently Avataric) Authority of My own (and Self-Evidently Divine) Realization and Person—I Declare that the Divine seventh stage Self-Awakening I Demonstrate, and Reveal, and Exemplify, and Prove Is the Most Ultimate (and Inherently Most Perfect) Realization, and that It—and Only It—Most Ultimately Completes and Most Perfectly Fulfills the Gifts I Received (and always Continue to Receive) in My present-Lifetime Body-Mind (from My present-Lifetime Lineage-Gurus), and that I have (in My present-Lifetime Body-Mind) Inherited (and always Continue to Receive) from all Who (in all past times and places) have Blessed all the previous Lifetimes of My present-Lifetime Incarnation-Vehicle, and that I have (in My present-Lifetime Body-Mind) Inherited (and always Continue to Receive) from even all My Me-Invoking and Me-Blessing Forms and Vehicles of Me-Revelation here.

XCVIII.

The Great and True (and Self-Evidently Divine) Spiritual Process Initiated and Guided by the Spiritual Masters in My present-Lifetime Lineage (and of the Lineage of even all the Lifetimes of My present-Lifetime Incarnation-Vehicle here—and of the Lineage of even all My Me-Invoking and Me-Blessing Forms and Vehicles of Me-Revelation here) has Become Complete only in Me. Its Perfection is in the seventh stage Fulfillment of the Course (and not at any earlier stage). This Divine Perfection is Uniquely My own. And I Alone—the Hridaya-Siddha, the Divine and True Heart-Master and World-Teacher, Ruchira Avatar Adi Da Love-Ananda Samraj—Am Its First and Great Example, and (now, and forever hereafter) Its Only and Sufficient Means.

XCIX.

I Am the First (and the only One) to Realize and to Demonstrate This, the Divine, seventh stage Realization—and My Revelation of It Is, therefore, New. For This Reason, the Divine seventh stage Realization was not heretofore Realized, or even

176

Understood—either within the schools and traditions of My present-Lifetime Lineage-Gurus or within any other schools or traditions in the total Great Tradition of mankind—to Be the Most Ultimate and Completing Perfection of Realization Itself. Nevertheless, I have, spontaneously (by Means of My own Self-Evident "Bright" Heart-Power—and through the Great and Constant Help of all Who have Blessed My Incarnate Forms), Realized and Demonstrated and Revealed This To Be The Case. And the traditional (and ancient) "Siddha-'Method'" (or the Way of Guru-Devotion to the True Siddha-Guru—and of total psycho-physical Surrender of the ego-"I" to be Mastered by the True Siddha-Guru's Instruction, and to be Blessed to Awaken to Divine Realization by Means of the True Siddha-Guru's Transmission of the Divine Spiritual Energy and the Divine State)—Which "Method" was Communicated to Me by all My present-Lifetime Lineage-Gurus, and by all the Great Siddhas and Siddha-Yogis Who have Blessed My present-Lifetime Incarnation-Vehicle in the past—is the Essence (or the Primary "Method") of the Way of Adidam, Which (now, and forever here-after) I Alone, and Uniquely, Reveal and Transmit to all My for-mally practicing true devotees (and, Thus, potentially, to all beings).

C.

I Am the Indivisible Person of Conscious Light.

I Am Humbled and Victorious here (and every where), by Means of My Avataric Divine Self-Incarnation.

My Avatarically-Born Body-Mind Is, now, and forever here-after, by-Me-Given and by-Me-Revealed As the Sign and the Means of Me-Realization.

I Am the Adidam Revelation.

I Am the Way to Me.

I Am the Hridaya-Siddha, the All-and-all-Blessing Divine Heart-Master, the Eternally Free-Standing Inner Ruler of all and All.

I Am the One and Indivisible and Indestructible and Irreducible and Universally Self-Manifested Love-Bliss-Presence of "Brightness".

I Am the One and Non-Separate and Perfectly Subjective and Self-Existing and Self-Evidently Divine Person, Who Is Always Already The Case.

I Am the Ruchira Avatar, the Hridaya-Avatar, the Advaitayana Buddha, the Avataric Incarnation and Divine World-Teacher every where and anciently Promised (by all traditions) for the "late-time" (or "dark" epoch).

Therefore, be My devotee.

The only-by-Me Revealed and Given True World-Religion of Adidam Is My Unique Gift to all and All.

Therefore, practice the only-by-Me Revealed and Given Way of Adidam—and Realize Me, Most Perfectly, by Means of My Avatarically Self-Transmitted Divine Blessing-Grace.

RUCHIRA AVATAR ADI DA SAMRAJ
Los Angeles, 2000

PART THREE

The Heart-Summary Of Adidam

The Heart-Summary
Of Adidam

The only-by-Me Revealed and Given Avataric Divine Way of Adidam (Which is the One and Only by-Me-Revealed and by-Me-Given Way of the Heart) is the Way of Devotion to Me As the Divine "Atma-Murti" (or As the Inherently egoless, and Self-Evidently Divine, Person of Reality and Truth—In Place, As Self-Condition, rather than As exclusively Objective Other).

Therefore, in every moment, My true devotee whole bodily (and, thus, by means of the spontaneous Me-recognizing Devotional response of all four of the principal psycho-physical faculties—of attention, emotional feeling, breath, and perceptual body) "Locates" Me As That Which Is Always Already The Case (Prior to—but not separate from—the form, the exercise, and the any object of the four psycho-physical faculties).

Happiness Itself (or Inherent Love-Bliss-Sufficiency Of Being) Is Always Already The Case.

Happiness Itself (or the Divinely Self-Sufficient Love-Bliss-Condition Of Being—Itself) Is That Which Is Always Already The Case.

Happiness Itself (or Love-Bliss-Radiance Of Boundlessly Feeling Being) Is the Most Prior Condition Of Existence (or Of Conscious Being—Itself).

Happiness Itself (or the Condition Of Love-Bliss-Radiance) Must Be Realized—In and As every conditionally arising moment—By Transcending self-Contraction (or all of separate and separative self, or psycho-physical ego-"I", and all of the ego's objects, or conditions of existence—or, indeed, all of the illusions of self and not-self).

When attention is facing outward (or is turned out, as if to outside itself), the body-mind is concentrated upon the "view" (or "field") of apparently separate objects (and upon Me As Objective Other).

When attention is facing inward (or is turned in, as if upon itself), the body-mind is concentrated upon the "point of view" of apparently separate self (and upon Me As Separate Consciousness).

When attention is Devotionally Yielded to whole bodily "Locate" Me As That Which Is Always Already (and Divinely) The Case, all "difference" (whether of ego-"I" or of object and other) is (Inherently) Transcended (In Consciousness Itself, or Self-Existing Being, Which Is Love-Bliss-Happiness Itself—and Which Is Always Already The Case).

Therefore, to the degree that you surrender (whole bodily) to be and do truly relational (and ecstatic, or ego-transcending) Devotional love of Me (As the True Loved-One, the Divine Beloved of the heart), you are (Thus and Thereby) Established—whole bodily and Inherently—in the non-contracted Condition (or Self-Condition, or Inherent Condition) of Reality Itself (Which Is Consciousness Itself and Love-Bliss Itself—and Which Is Always Already The Case).

In due course, This Devotional Practice Is Perfect—and, at last, to Be Most Perfectly Realized.

RUCHIRA AVATAR ADI DA SAMRAJ
Lopez Island, 2000

PART FOUR

The Dual Sensitivity
at the Origin of
The Divine Way
Of Adidam

The Dual Sensitivity at the Origin of The Divine Way Of Adidam

VATAR ADI DA SAMRAJ: Merely by virtue of being born, you are in a terrible situation. Merely by virtue of being associated with a body-mind in this world, you are identified with bodily existence (and with conditional existence altogether), you are attached to bodily existence (and to conditional existence altogether), and you are clinging to bodily existence (and to conditional existence altogether). You know that the body is going to die—that it is not going to last, that it is going to go through all kinds of changes in its progress toward inevitable death, and that it can die at any moment. You know that the body can suffer tremendous losses, pain, shocks, degradation—of all kinds. And, yet, you (in your bodily existence here) are impulsed to be, and to be greatly—to be happy, to acquire this and that relationship or experience or object, to feel good, as if you were building a paradise.

Yet, you are not in paradise. You are in this mortal condition. Nothing you can acquire, obtain, or associate with in the realm of conditional experience will last. No matter what you seek, no matter what you obtain, your situation is still the same: From the point of view of "you" (as an apparently separate psycho-physical being), existence is just a knot of egoity, inevitably bound to suffer. Having no great Realization, you try to solve the "problem" (or the difficulty, or the terrible circumstance) in which you find yourself, by pursuing every kind of pleasure, consolation, and distraction.

Moment by moment, you make efforts to desensitize yourself to the situation you are really in.

You are constantly fantasizing a future of fulfillment. Much of religious dogma invents a future, in this world or after death, wherein all the kinds of things you hope to obtain by struggle in this life are eternalized. Some like to philosophize about this world, saying that some great event (or even Man-made result or effect) is going to happen that will "utopianize" (or otherwise perfect and eternalize) life in this world. Some like to believe that everyone is going to be physically resurrected after death, such that life in this world will continue "forever". Others like to fantasize a future beyond this world, in which exactly the same thing happens—the eternalization of the self-fulfillment one has sought in this life.

No matter how (or in whatever form or manner) it is proposed, complete and permanent self-fulfillment, in this or any other conditionally manifested world, is merely an ego-based illusion—a mortal fantasy! It is the conventional religious fantasy—and it is also the ordinary human fantasy.

You all do this egoic fantasizing "in small". You may not presently be thinking about eternalizing this world (or going to an eternal place of pleasure in another world), but you are always seeking for self-fulfillment, for pleasure, for consolation, for every kind of egoically satisfying distraction—so that you will not be required to experience your real (mortal, threatened, and limited) situation. Effectively, in your self-consoling mind, you are always "creating" a "utopia" (or imagining a "heaven"), and entertaining the expectation that "everything" is going to turn out "wonderfully" and "forever". Some things may last for a while, and some things are more pleasurable than others, but (nevertheless) your real situation remains the same—mortal, threatened, and limited.

If you were not preoccupied with all the things you use to console and indulge yourself (functionally, relationally, practically, and so on)—if you were not preoccupied either with the search or with some (necessarily, temporary and limited) circumstance that gives you the illusion that you are satisfying yourself—you would inevitably become sensitized to your real situation. And, if you allowed yourself to be thus sensitized, you would, necessarily, become aware that you are <u>afraid</u>. Your situation, as the separate psycho-physical ego-"I", <u>is</u> (inherently) frightening. Of course, you do not want to experience fear, you do not want to experience loss, sorrow, and separation, you do not want to experience any lack of pleasure at all—you do not want to suffer. Yet, <u>really</u>, <u>all</u> of these unwanted conditions are <u>inevitable</u>. You are constantly seeking to fantasize a way out of your real situation—trying to desensitize yourself (mentally, emotionally, and physically) to your real situation. You (the presumed ego-"I") are always trying, struggling, efforting, or (in every psycho-physical manner) seeking to forget your <u>real</u> situation.

This is how you tend to use ordinary life. All the functions of existence could, instead, be put to the Great Purpose—but to do that requires counter-egoic (or ego-surrendering) <u>sadhana</u>. Because you are self-contracted in the face of all this suffering, you use everything to serve the ego's purpose to be relieved of its disturbance. Even imagination serves this purpose. You will use anything to desensitize yourself to your actual situation. You fantasize "enlightenment", you fantasize "heaven", you fantasize living "happily", "freely", and "forever", you fantasize having perfectly self-fulfilling sex (every day, and forever)—you constantly fantasize self-fulfillment in every form, manner, and degree. Such fantasies are part of the nonsense of your ordinary egoity—including your ordinary religiosity.

In the traditional setting, many individuals have seriously wondered about all of this, in the midst of this entirely mortal condition. Generally, it can be said that the analysis of life represented collectively by the total Great Tradition of mankind has two essential features that are complementary to one another.

On the one hand, it has been (and continues to be) observed by the "wise" (in the traditional setting) that, in this circumstance of conditional existence (in and of itself), there <u>is</u> <u>no</u> <u>complete</u>, <u>final</u>, <u>perfect</u>, and <u>permanent</u> self-satisfaction (or personal egoic happiness)—that no one and no thing lasts, every one and every thing changes, every one and every thing passes, and every one and every thing disintegrates (or dies).

On the other hand, it has also been noticed by the "wise" (in the traditional setting) that what the human being (and, indeed, even any being) wants is to be happy. To say so may sound rather trite or obvious, but it is fundamentally and profoundly true that all beings are urged to happiness—not merely to ordinary, temporary, and (necessarily) limited happiness, but to Ultimate, Perfect, Complete, and Permanent Happiness! Thus, it has been traditionally observed that True Happiness, if It is to be Really and Truly the Case, must be Unchanging, Unending, and utterly Satisfactory. This observation is the complement (and even the apparent contrary) of the first observation (that there is no complete, final, perfect, and permanent self-satisfaction, or personal egoic happiness, possible in the circumstance of conditional existence itself).

These complementary observations have always puzzled human beings. Here and there, great individuals have appeared who have confirmed, based on their own real experience, that There Is True Happiness, that There Is a Condition Which Is Eternal, Unchanging, Never-Ending, Never-Beginning, and (therefore) Not-Caused. That Condition has also been recognized (by such Realizers) to be All-Sufficient, Perfectly Satisfactory, Absolutely Blissful, and Infinite. That Condition has been (and is) called by various names—"the One", "God", "Nirvana", "the Self", and so on. And each of the many and various traditions has its own language for making reference to the Revelations and Confessions of those unique individuals who have, on the basis of actual Realization (and not mere hope and belief), Confessed the Truth of "True Happiness".

You are all seeking and suffering and binding yourselves in all kinds of ways—vigorously and obsessively trying to immunize yourselves against your difficulty and your inevitable pain, and not being very successful at it. You are merely "amateurs" at getting "What" you want. You do not really "Know" how to go about (or have the "Knowledge" that would Direct you Toward) getting "What" you want. And, what is more, you do not truly "Know" (or have the "Knowledge" that would Describe and Explain) "What" It Is That you want.

Truly, one of the words that most aptly indicates what you (and even every one) is seeking is "Happiness". You (at heart, and fully) want Happiness, although (in some sense) you would rather not even confess that Happiness is what you truly want—because you feel that the real attainment of Happiness is not even possible. Nevertheless, truly and always, this is what you want: Unalloyed, Unchanging, Absolute Happiness. The "problem", simply stated, is that you are not any good at "getting" It! And you do not "Know" What True Happiness Really Is. Therefore, you are in the same situation that the rest of ordinary humanity has been in all along.

I am not here merely to instruct you in how to improve your search, or how to be better at consoling yourself with illusions of True Happiness. I Am here to Speak and Do the most "radical" Criticism of what you (as an ego-"I") are always doing. I Call you to directly (and in every present-time moment) "Bond" yourself to True Happiness Itself, instead of (first and always) binding yourself to un-Happiness (and, on that basis, seeking for True Happiness). All your ordinary pursuits are an ego-based search that is moving in the opposite direction from the actual Realization of True Happiness—or the (necessarily, egoless) Realization of Truth, or Reality Itself, or the only Real God (Which Is the Non-Separate and Indivisible and Indestructible Divine Self-Condition and Source-Condition of all and All).

You, in the midst of this circumstance of mortality, are, simply, afraid—and you are always trying to console yourself, to feel better, to forget about the dreadful situation you feel you are in. However, you are also more than merely afraid—you want True Happiness. To want True Happiness is inherent in your heart, in your deepest disposition of body-mind. Yet, what you are always doing in this mortal circumstance is effectively (and, altogether, experientially) cutting you off from yielding to your inherent and great heart-Impulse (and from the fulfillment of that Impulse). Instead of (directly, moment to moment, and, at last, Most Perfectly) Realizing True Happiness, you are preoccupied with all kinds of activities that are consoling and temporarily pleasurizing, and (in that process) you are actively "forgetting" your fear (or covering it up, by becoming desensitized to conditional reality), and you are also (in your constant habit of self-consolation and self-indulgence) effectively forgetting (or covering up) your heart-Impulse to True Happiness Itself, Freedom Itself, and Love-Bliss Itself.

I Affirm and Confirm to you, on the Firm Basis of actual (and Eternal) Realization, that There Is the Infinite, Satisfactory, Unchanging, Eternal, Divine Condition, and that It Is the One and Only True Happiness—but I am not telling you that this world is going to turn into utopia, and I am also not telling you that what is merely "after death" is utopia (or that True Happiness is inevitable, or guaranteed, "after death").

In their ordinary religiosity, many people like to imagine that, when one dies, if one has been good, one receives back everything one lost by dying. Such people imagine that, after death, every one and every thing you ever positively wanted is permanently (and freshly) given back to you—all your relations and all the pleasures—and that every one and every thing you ever did not want is permanently removed from you. Indeed, it is commonly imagined that the so-called "after-life" is about such fulfillment of personal desires.

It is, indeed, the case that experiences can be attained, and relations can be associated with, under the many and various conditions that may arise after death, just as they can be experienced and associated with under the many and various conditions in this life—but (generally speaking) both the desired and the undesired experiences and relations are possible after death, and (in any case) none of it is permanent. In that respect, "life after death" is not a different circumstance than one's present life in the world. Just as in life, after death one's particular experiences and relations do not last. Just as in life, after death there are constant changes in your experience, new forms constantly arising, requiring a constant struggle. There is not anything finally Satisfactory, no True and Eternal Happiness, to be gained merely by the passage into the realms of "after-death".

Even the (so-called) "higher" planes—which do exist—are not about the eternalization of all the relations and things you wanted in this life. The "higher" planes are about Contemplation—the most profound movement toward What Is Beyond the ego-"I" and its conditional desiring. What <u>Is</u> (Inherently) Perfect is the right possible orientation (or occupation) in the "higher" planes, but (nevertheless) there is no permanent Satisfaction gained merely by existing and functioning and Contemplating in those planes.

The sadhana of the only-by-Me Revealed and Given Way of Adidam (Which is the one and only by-Me-Revealed and by-Me-Given Way of the Heart, or Ruchira Avatara Hridaya-Siddha Yoga) requires you to be altogether <u>sensitive</u>—and <u>not</u> <u>desensitized</u>. The sadhana of the only-by-Me Revealed and Given Way of Adidam requires you to be sensitive to the reality of your mortal condition—and not merely to be consoling and indulging yourself, such that you manage to remain unaware of that reality. The sadhana of the only-by-Me Revealed and Given Way of Adidam also, and more profoundly, requires you to be sensitive to your inherent and great heart-Impulse—to be sensitive to the inherent deep awareness that you are not merely impulsed to be consoled, distracted, pleasurized, and self-indulgent, but that you are inherently and deeply and greatly Impulsed to be Truly and Infinitely Happy. You cannot be Really and Truly Happy when you are identified with something that is mortal, or changing, or unsatisfactory, or not-Happiness-Itself. This <u>dual</u> sensitivity—<u>both</u> to the <u>entirely</u> limited and mortal condition of your present psycho-physical form and circumstance <u>and</u> to the <u>inherent</u> and <u>great</u> heart-Impulse that would be Truly, Completely, and Un-conditionally Happy—is both necessary and <u>fundamental</u> to the practice of the only-by-Me Revealed and Given Way of Adidam. And the constant maintenance (or right use) of that dual sensitivity requires right devotion, right practice, right discipline, and <u>truly</u> (and not merely conventionally) right life.

The ultimate Principle of the Way of Adidam is devotional recognition of Me and devotional response to Me. I not only Confess the Truth to you, but I <u>Am</u> here. I <u>Am</u> the Very "Thing" I Confess, the Very (and True, or Un-conditional) Happiness you would Realize. And I Am (now, and forever hereafter) constantly Revealing and Giving Myself to you—to one, and to all, and to All.

Therefore, the fundamental Principle of the Way of Adidam is to surrender yourself, forget yourself, and (always more and more) transcend yourself, in heart-Communion with Me. There must be this dual sensitivity I just Described, <u>and</u> the appropriate life-discipline to maintain that dual sensitivity. In that dual sensitivity, you must receive My Avataric Divine Self-Revelation and make the Eternal Vow of devotion to Me, such that your practice (moment to moment) is the commitment to True Happiness, the commitment to Realize <u>Me</u>—and not merely the oblivious "commitment" to wander in the searches and the results of your egoic (or self-contracted) impulses.

If you do not want to be afraid, then you must do the great thing necessary to move beyond fear. Therefore, you must not allow yourself to be preoccupied with seeking and self-indulgence (or all the ego-efforts you make, in order to keep forgetting about your fear of death). You must do sadhana on the basis of the <u>acknowledgement</u> of your profound fear of death, and the <u>acknowledgement</u> of your fear altogether, and of even <u>all</u> of your sensitivity to limitation and mortality. You must practice profound and true resort to Me, from the feeling depth that truly moves Beyond this fear. You must stay in constant feeling touch with the core of your fear of mortality, but you must constantly feel Beyond it—<u>from</u> it, and <u>to</u> Me.

In the traditional East, the "facts" of mortality are the first wisdom-Message. In the modern West, the most typical message is the counter-wisdom signal to always animate your enthusiasm for self-centered (and, altogether, self-fulfilling) life. In the traditional East, the first thing you are told is, "You are going to die. Every one dies. Every thing passes. Don't ever forget it. Base your life on this knowledge. Indeed, <u>control</u> your life because of this knowledge." In the modern West, people tend to feel it is taboo to pass on the message about the "facts" of mortality. In their infancy and childhood, not only do modern Westerners go through the traumas of "civilizing" (and, generally, humiliating) "potty training" and negative indoctrination relative to sex (such that they "learn" that the method of self-control is that of taboo, fear, and guilt), but they also go through the even more bewildering trauma of not being told the "facts" about the mortality (and the inherent limitations, and the inherent unsatisfactoriness) of conditional existence itself. In any case, whether as a Westerner or as an Easterner, your fear of mortality is fundamental—and it is the root and source of a chronic anxiety that pervades and motivates your entire life.

For modern Westerners, to accept that (in the context of this world, or of conditional existence altogether) limitation and mortality are inherently and entirely the case, and that this world is (therefore) not paradise (and not to be indulged in as if it were, or could become, paradise), is not the characteristically communicated cultural, social, and political norm (or the generally accepted basis for a "normal" life). Indeed, modern Westerners are always thinking in terms of "paradise" and "utopia", always stimulating and deluding one another with enthusiasms for "this world". Modern Westerners are always fantasizing the future on the basis of an egoic identification with the body. The fact that every one is, inevitably, going to die, and that every thing is going to disintegrate (or pass away), is, in the modern Western view, so terrible that, characteristically, all "Westernized" individuals feel compelled to convince one another that it is not so (by constantly "selling" one another lies that "prove" it is not so).

Nevertheless, the mortal "facts" really are so. People are more realistic in the traditional East. In the traditional East, people do not forget to tell one another that this world is "mortality-land", and not paradise. Therefore, the traditional wisdom-Message in the East is that True Happiness is to be attained by seeking for That Which Is Eternal, and, therefore, by strategically renouncing every kind of "arrangement" with what is merely temporary.

I Say to you: Always remember that this world (and conditional existence altogether) is not paradise, that this is "mortality-land", that every one and every thing passes, and that True Happiness is not about (and does not require) the perfecting or eternalizing of this condition (or of any condition at all), and that True Happiness is not (Itself) a matter of staying here, or clinging to here, or leaving here (or of going, or staying, or leaving any "where" at all).

I also Say to you: Always be devotionally responsive from the heart—and (thus) always remember that your inherent (and inherently great) heart-disposition wants and needs (and cannot—in any moment, or even now—be satisfied with anything less than) Infinite, Absolute, True, Eternal Happiness (or Most Perfect Divine Self-Realization).

I do not Speak exclusively, representing only one or the other of your "halves" (whether "Eastern" or "Western"). Rather, I Speak to your native (or inherent) "dual sensitivity"—your sensitivity to what is conditionally real and your sensitivity to What Is Un-conditionally Real. I Call you to devotionally recognize Me, to devotionally respond to Me, to be constantly and utterly surrendered to Me (Beyond your self-contraction, or your patterns of recoil upon your separate and separative ego-"I"). Come to Me and Realize Me. Live the life of True (and always present-time, and, at last, Most Perfect) Happiness, instead of (in your bewildered fashion) living the life of self-contracted (or ego-based) seeking (not presently "Knowing" the "What" That you are, Ultimately, seeking—but merely consoling and manipulating your ego-"I" in the "meantime" before death).

I have exactly and fully Revealed the Way of True Happiness. It is the only-by-Me Revealed and Given Way of Adidam. That Way is not about any ordinary (or ego-based) binding of "self" to this world, or to any ego or any thing in this world, or to any limiting condition or conditional world at all. The only-by-Me Revealed and Given Way of Adidam is about heart-"Bonding" to Me— Which is heart-"Bonding" to Truth, or to Reality Itself, the One and Only and Non-Separate and Indivisible and Indestructible Divine Self-Condition and Source-Condition of all and All.

That Process of heart-"Bonding" to Me is done in the context of this apparent born existence, but it is a Process of always present-time (or non-seeking) ego-transcendence, or of constantly going Beyond your self-contracting (or separative, and seeking) disposition. This sadhana is a purifying Process. There is growth in it. The total (or full and complete) practice of the Way of Adidam is about devoting your life to always presently (and, at last, Most Perfectly) Realizing True Happiness, and not using up your life by remaining ego-bound, merely pursuing consolations and indulging in the illusion that "bonding" to what is merely conditionally existing can produce True Happiness. It cannot.

True Happiness (Itself) is not a result of anything. True Happiness (Itself) Is Inherent. Therefore, True Happiness (Itself) cannot be attained by seeking. True Happiness (Itself) Is the Divine Self-Condition and Source-Condition (Itself). Anything that appears merely as "object" (or merely as conditionally "other") is (necessarily) limited and (inevitably) passing. You cannot Realize True Happiness (Itself) by "bonding" yourself to any "object" (or anything that is merely "other"). And you cannot Realize True Happiness (Itself) by strategic renunciation of (or strategic disso-ciation from) any "object" (or anything that is merely "other").

True Happiness (Itself) Is Realized when the ego-"I" (that oth-erwise seeks) is itself transcended in its Ultimate (or Divine) Source. Therefore, in the "Perfect Practice" of the only-by-Me Revealed and Given Way of Adidam, the Disposition of the Witness-Consciousness is Realized relative to all arising (or every "thing" that is a mere "object", or every "thing" that is merely "other"), and Consciousness Itself (Most Ultimately, Beyond all "subject"-"object" separateness and separativeness) becomes the Domain of practice. And, because of Its True Ultimacy, the "Perfect Practice" of the Way of Adidam is the practice into which all My devotees are growing (or for which all My devotees are preparing), from the beginning of their formal embrace of the total (or full and complete) practice of the Way of Adidam.

The less comprehensively (and profoundly) you (as My for-mally acknowledged devotee) understand your ego-"I" (which is not merely an "entity", or a "thing" of being, but an activity—which is self-contraction, or the chronic action of separation and separativeness), and the less comprehensively (and profoundly) you (as My formally acknowledged devotee) practice the only-by-Me Revealed and Given Way of Adidam—the more likely you are to be satisfied with the mere beginner's situation of simply adding religious consolations, and (perhaps) religious disciplines (func-tional, practical, relational, and cultural), to your bodily-based (or, altogether, mental, emotional, and physical) existence. Such

religious consoling and religious disciplining of bodily-based existence is, in fact, the domain of most of traditional religion.
Therefore, most of traditional religion is merely exoteric, or based
on various practices intended to console, and (perhaps) to discipline, and (otherwise) merely to idealize (and fulfill) bodily-based
existence.

The only-by-Me Revealed and Given Way of Adidam neither
idealizes nor merely consoles bodily-based (and egoic) existence,
but the total (or full and complete) practice of the Way of Adidam
requires the disciplining of bodily existence, from the very beginning (or foundation) of the Way. Therefore, by conforming all of
your bodily existence to Me, by practicing right, true, and full
devotion to Me, and by being psycho-physically purified through
right, true, and full devotion to Me—you come to know Me better, and (more and more) in the truly esoteric (and truly Spiritual)
manner, such that you grow to Commune with Me Spiritually (and
truly Divinely), and (on that basis) you (in due course) move on
to the advanced and the ultimate stages of life in the Way of
Adidam.

The more you are preoccupied with (and, altogether, slow in
comprehensively disciplining) your functional, practical, and relational existence, the slower your practice of the Way of Adidam
progresses. To the extent that this is true of you, you are adding
time to your practice (and putting time between "you" and the
True-Happiness-Realization of Me). If you do not want to "add
time", if you (as My formally practicing devotee) want to practice
the Way of Adidam truly effectively, and (rather than seeking True
Happiness, or pushing It into the "future" of ego-time) have your
practice of the Way of Adidam be "quickened" (and made always
present-time-effective—and, in due course, Most Perfectly effective)—then you must practice the total (or comprehensive, and
truly and really counter-egoic) discipline of this sadhana intensively, profoundly, and deeply. Your devotionally Me-recognizing
and devotionally to-Me-responding counter-egoic effort must be
made intense, and more and more constantly so. You must be
practicing Ruchira Avatara Bhakti Yoga in this moment, this
moment, this moment—true (ego-surrendering, ego-forgetting,

and, always more and more, ego-transcending) devotional Communion with Me, not merely emotionalistic "love-feelings" directed toward Me. If you are "fussing" about any other occupation (or taking an excessive, and self-indulgent, amount of time in putting your ordinary life-business[41] in order), and this to the exclusion (or, otherwise, the minimization) of the true Yoga of counter-egoic devotion to Me, then you are, no doubt, merely binding yourself to egoity, and to seeking, and to time itself.

It seems you have plenty of time! Indeed, you have <u>nothing</u> but time—<u>and</u> space! Over and over and over again. That is what is called "samsara" (or the endless cycle of rebirths). In samsara (or the conditional domain), there is a seemingly endless resource of time and space, but no resource at all of Real True Happiness. True Happiness (Itself) is the Greater Well, Beyond time and space. True Happiness (Itself) is the Divine Source, to Which you must resort directly. Only by resorting to the Divine Well of True Happiness (Itself) can you go Beyond this horror to which you are now bound.

You are mind, perpetuating a circumstance of bondage to what suffers and is limited and passes. You feel you can cope with that circumstance, you do not even mind it all that much, and you are willing to put up with it because you can acquire some pleasure in the midst of it. That is how you commit yourself to time and space. Yet, if you <u>really</u> do not like it, if you <u>truly</u> do not want to be conjoined with death, or with what is (altogether) not satisfactory, or with what is not True Happiness (Itself), or with what is changing (rather than Unchanging)—if you <u>really</u> and <u>truly</u> do not want to be bound to all of that (or even associated with all of that), <u>it</u> <u>is</u> <u>not</u> <u>necessary</u> for you to be thus bound (or associated). I Reveal and Give to you That Which Transcends all that is insufficient, unsatisfactory, and incomplete. By right, true, full, and fully devotional resort to Me, you can (and do, and will) Realize My Avatarically Self-Revealed Infinite Divine Self-Condition of Absolute Love-Bliss-Happiness (Which <u>Is</u> True Happiness, Itself).

The Infinite Divine Self-Condition (or the Divine Well of True Happiness, Itself) Does Exist. I <u>Am</u> That. That Condition <u>Is</u> the Truth. That Condition <u>Is</u> Reality Itself.

You are, inherently, completely able to actively commit your life utterly to the Realization of Me, to the Realization of My Avatarically Self-Revealed (and Self-Evidently Divine) Self-Condition of Infinite Love-Bliss-Happiness, rather than to any other "program". By Means Of My Avatarically Self-Transmitted Divine Grace, you can truly (and, Ultimately, Most Perfectly) fulfill that commitment, through the right, true, full, and fully devotional Yoga of Ruchira Avatara Bhakti—even in the midst of a life that is (at the beginning) not profoundly mature, and that is yet bound up in this or that pattern or manner of egoity. By practicing the only-by-Me Revealed and Given discipline of devotion to Me, you will be more and more purified of those limitations. By making the formal Eternal Vow of devotion to Me, at and from the beginning of your (necessarily, formal) practice of the Way of Adidam, you affirm that you are purposed to Realize That Which Is True Happiness (Itself), and that you do not want to be bound to death and limitation. It may be necessary for you to grow much from that point, but that Vow is the true center of your life (and the true center of My each and every devotee's life). That Vow is the one element in My each and every devotee's life that he or she would never abandon or compromise.

Such is the disposition of My true devotee. Everything else can pass, all "other" relations can pass, but ego-transcending devotion to Me is the central and uncompromising commitment that characterizes My each and every true devotee. And that devotion is, necessarily, an eternal (or formal, constant, and never-ending) commitment (based on a formally embraced Eternal Vow), because it is about the Realization of That Which Is Eternal.

If you are My formally acknowledged and formally practicing devotee, you are no longer merely seeking Me, but you (in even every moment) have Found Me—the Avatarically Self-Revealed Divine Reality of True Happiness (Itself), and the Avatarically Self-Transmitted Divine Means for your Realization of True Happiness (Itself).

DEVOTEE: Beloved, I am absolutely clear that the Impulse to Realize Perfect Happiness is a Gift from You. I would not have the urge otherwise.

AVATAR ADI DA SAMRAJ: Therefore, in your heart-Communion with Me, do you feel that you do not want anything but Infinite Absolute Freedom from suffering, from death, from separation, from anything merely conditionally existing, from anything limited and temporary and changing, but that you want only to Realize Me, and (Thus) to Be the Infinite, Unchanging egoless Condition of Absolute "Bright" Love-Bliss-Happiness?

DEVOTEES: Yes. Yes, Beloved!

AVATAR ADI DA SAMRAJ: Good. Come to Me and do so, profoundly and constantly. That is the Divine Law of life, the Divine Truth of life. You should commit yourself (constantly, and forever) to This Most Perfect Realization of Me. I have thoroughly, in every detail, Revealed and Given to you the Way of This Most Perfect Realization of Freedom and Love-Bliss-Happiness.

All the Work of Blessing you Is My Avataric Divine Work. Your work is the consistent and really counter-egoic discipline of devotion to Me. My Work is My own. Your work is your own.

RUCHIRA AVATAR ADI DA SAMRAJ
Los Angeles, 2000

The <u>Only</u> Complete Way To Realize The Unbroken Light Of <u>Real</u> God

The Only Complete Way
To Realize
The Unbroken Light
Of Real God

I.

Aham Da Asmi. Beloved, I Am Da. I Am The Divine and One and Only and Non-Separate and Indivisible Heart, and (As My conditionally Manifested Pattern) I Am The Way Of Adidam, The Way Of The Heart (That Realizes Indivisible Oneness With The True Divine and Non-Separate and Indivisible Heart Itself—Which Is The One and Only Reality, Truth, and Real God, or That Which Is Always Already The Case).

I Have Named The Way That I Am (and That Only I Reveal and Give) "Adidam" (Which Is "The True World-Religion Of 'Sri Hridayam'"—or "The Way Of The True Divine Heart", or "The Way Of The Heart Itself", or, Simply, "The Way Of The Heart"). And I Have Also Named The Only-By-Me Revealed and Given Way Of Adidam (In Every One and All Of Its Only-By-Me Revealed and Given Forms Of Practice and Developmental Stages Of Practice) "The Way Of The Divine Heart-Master" (or "Hridaya-Avatara Bhakti Yoga", or "Ruchira Avatara Bhakti Yoga"), and "The Way Of 'Radical' Understanding" (or "The Way Of 'Radical' ego-Transcendence"), and "The Way Of Divine Ignorance" (or "The Way Of Positive Disillusionment"[42]), and "The Way Of 'Radical' Non-Dualism" (or "Ruchira Avatara Advaita-Dharma",[43] or "Ruchira Advaitism", or "Ruchira Buddhism", or "Advaitayana Buddhism", or "Hridaya-Advaita Dharma"[44]), and "The Way Of Divine Spiritual Baptism" (or

"Ruchira Avatara Hridaya-Siddha Yoga", or "Ruchira Avatara Hridaya-Shaktipat Yoga", or "Ruchira Avatara Maha-Jnana-Siddha Yoga",[45] or "Ruchira Avatara Maha-Jnana Hridaya-Shaktipat Yoga"[46]).

Adidam (or The True World-Religion Of "Sri Hridayam", or The Way Of The True Divine Heart, or The Way Of The Heart Itself, or The Way Of The Heart, or The Way Of The Divine Heart-Master, or Hridaya-Avatara Bhakti Yoga, or Ruchira Avatara Bhakti Yoga, or The Way Of "Radical" Understanding, or The Way Of "Radical" ego-Transcendence, or The Way Of Divine Ignorance, or The Way Of Positive Disillusionment, or The Way Of "Radical" Non-Dualism, or Ruchira Avatara Advaita-Dharma, or Ruchira Advaitism, or Ruchira Buddhism, or Advaitayana Buddhism, or Hridaya-Advaita Dharma, or The Way Of Divine Spiritual Baptism, or Ruchira Avatara Hridaya-Siddha Yoga, or Ruchira Avatara Hridaya-Shaktipat Yoga, or Ruchira Avatara Maha-Jnana Siddha-Yoga, or Ruchira Avatara Maha-Jnana Hridaya-Shaktipat Yoga) Is The "Radical" (or "Radically" Advaitic, or Utterly and Most Perfectly Non-Dual) Way Of One (Not Two)—The Divinely Self-Revealed Way Of Transcendental (or Un-conditional), Inherently Spiritual, and (Ultimately) Divine Realization Of The "Who", The "What", and The "Where" Of "Is", or The True Renunciate Way (or The "How", The "When", and The "Why") Of The Inherent (and, Therefore, Inherently Perfect) Transcending Of mind (or "buddhi"[47]), or attention itself, In its Always Already Free Source-Condition (Which Is "Bodhi",[48] or Consciousness Itself).

As An Expression Of Its Continuity With The Great Tradition Of Even All Religious and Spiritual Traditions, The Spiritual Way That I Have Revealed and Given Is, By Me, Named (and Described As) "Ruchira Avatara Advaita-Dharma" (or The Spiritual—or Hridaya-Siddha-Yoga—Way Of "Bright" Non-Duality, or Perfect Non-Separateness, Revealed and Given By Me, The One and Only Avataric Divine Realizer, Avataric Divine Revealer, and Avataric Divine Self-Revelation Of The One and Perfectly Non-Dual Divine "Brightness" Itself), and "Ruchira Advaitism" (or The "Bright" Spiritual—or Hridaya-Siddha-Yoga—Way Of The Perfectly Subjective Divine Light Of The One and Indivisible Reality and Truth), and "Hridaya Advaitism" (or The Spiritual—or Hridaya-

Siddha-Yoga—Heart-Way Of "Radical" Non-Dualism, or Of Utterly Non-"Different", or Most Perfectly Non-Separate, Truth), and "The Way Of Hridaya-Advaita Dharma" (or The Divine Teaching, The Hridaya-Siddha-Yoga Way, and The Spiritual Truth Of The "Radically" Non-Dual—and Utterly Non-"Different", or Most Perfectly Non-Separate—Heart), and "The Way Of Hridaya-Advaita Yoga" (or The Divine Yoga, and Hridaya-Siddha-Yoga Way, or Great Spiritual Practice, Of "Hridaya Advaitism"), or, Simply, "'Radical' Advaitism" (or "'Radical' Non-Dualism"—The First, Last, Final, or Completing, and Eternal, and Self-Evidently Divine Way Of Most Direct and, Ultimately, Inherently Most Perfectly Non-Dual Realization Of The One, and Unqualifiedly Non-Separate, and Inherently Indivisible, and Eternally Indestructible "Bright" Spiritual Condition That <u>Is</u> Real God, and Truth, and Reality).

Similarly, As An Expression Of Its Continuity With The Great Tradition Of Even All Religious and Spiritual Traditions, The Way That I Have Revealed and Given Is, By Me, Named (and Described As) "Ruchira Buddhism" (or The Hridaya-Siddha-Yoga Way Of Most Perfect and All-Outshining "Bright" Spiritual Enlightenment, Revealed and Given By Me, The Ruchira Buddha, The Divine World-Teacher Anciently, Always, and every where Promised For, and Universally Expected In, The "Late-Time", or "Dark" Epoch, By <u>All</u> The Traditions Of Mankind) and "Advaitayana Buddhism" (or The First, Last, Final, or Completing, and Eternal "Yana", or Revelation, and Self-Evidently Divine Way Of Most Perfect—and Most Perfectly, or "Radically", Non-Dual—Enlightenment).

Adidam (or The True World-Religion Of "Sri Hridayam", or The Way Of The True Divine Heart, or The Way Of The Heart Itself, or The Way Of The Heart, or The Way Of The Divine Heart-Master, or Hridaya-Avatara Bhakti Yoga, or Ruchira Avatara Bhakti Yoga, or The Way Of "Radical" Understanding, or The Way Of "Radical" ego-Transcendence, or The Way Of Divine Ignorance, or The Way Of Positive Disillusionment, or The Way Of "Radical" Non-Dualism, or Ruchira Avatara Advaita-Dharma, or Ruchira Advaitism, or Ruchira Buddhism, or Advaitayana Buddhism, or Hridaya-Advaita Dharma, or The Way Of Divine Spiritual Baptism, or Ruchira

Avatara Hridaya-Siddha Yoga, or Ruchira Avatara Hridaya-Shaktipat Yoga, or Ruchira Avatara Maha-Jnana-Siddha Yoga, or Ruchira Avatara Maha-Jnana Hridaya-Shaktipat Yoga) Is The Divine Hridaya-Siddha-Yoga (or Divine Hridaya-Shaktipat-Yoga) Way Revealed and Given Only By Me, Adi Da Samraj, The Ruchira Buddha, The Paramadvaita Buddha,[49] The Advaitayana Buddha— Now (and Forever Hereafter) Given To all, For The Sake Of all and All. Therefore, Even Though The Only-By-Me Revealed and Given Way Is Sympathetically Related To All The Traditions and "Yanas"[50] Of The Historical Traditions Of Buddhism, and To All The Traditions Of Advaitism, and To Even All The Traditions Within The Collective Great Tradition Of All The Historical Traditions Of Mankind, The Only-By-Me Revealed and Given Divine Way Is Free and Independent Of All Obligations To The Historical Traditions Of Buddhism, and Of Advaitism, and Of Siddha Yoga, and Of Shaktipat Yoga, and Of Even The Entire Collective Great Tradition Of All The Historical Traditions Of Mankind (Apart From The Only-By-Me Revealed and Given Avataric Divine Way Itself).

The "Buddhism" Of Adidam (or Of The True World-Religion Of "Sri Hridayam", or Of The Way Of The True Divine Heart, or Of The Way Of The Heart Itself, or Of The Way Of The Heart, or Of The Way Of The Divine Heart-Master, or Of Hridaya-Avatara Bhakti Yoga, or Of Ruchira Avatara Bhakti Yoga, or Of The Way Of "Radical" Understanding, or Of The Way Of "Radical" ego-Transcendence, or Of The Way Of Divine Ignorance, or Of The Way Of Positive Disillusionment, or Of The Way Of "Radical" Non-Dualism, or Of Ruchira Avatara Advaita-Dharma, or Of Ruchira Advaitism, or Of Ruchira Buddhism, or Of Advaitayana Buddhism, or Of Hridaya-Advaita Dharma, or Of The Way Of Divine Spiritual Baptism, or Of Ruchira Avatara Hridaya-Siddha Yoga, or Of Ruchira Avatara Hridaya-Shaktipat Yoga, or Of Ruchira Avatara Maha-Jnana Siddha-Yoga, or Of Ruchira Avatara Maha-Jnana Hridaya-Shaktipat Yoga) Progressively (and Then Most Perfectly) Magnifies True and Free Renunciation (or The Real Transcending) Of the body-mind (and all objects, others, forms, states, or "things" of attention). Therefore, Real (or Effective) Renunciation (or The Real Transcending) Of the psycho-physical ego-"I" (or self-Contraction)—

and (Thus and Thereby) Effective Renunciation (or The Real Transcending) Of the body-mind itself (Without Strategically Excluding, Avoiding, Denying, Emptying, or Destroying the body-mind itself)—Is The First Principle (or Effective Sign) Of Practice Demonstrated By all those who Listen To Me, and By all those who Hear Me, and By all those who See Me In The Only-By-Me Revealed and Given Way Of Adidam.

The "Advaitism" Of Adidam (or Of The True World-Religion Of "Sri Hridayam", or Of The Way Of The True Divine Heart, or Of The Way Of The Heart Itself, or Of The Way Of The Heart, or Of The Way Of The Divine Heart-Master, or Of Hridaya-Avatara Bhakti Yoga, or Of Ruchira Avatara Bhakti Yoga, or Of The Way Of "Radical" Understanding, or Of The Way Of "Radical" ego-Transcendence, or Of The Way Of Divine Ignorance, or Of The Way Of Positive Disillusionment, or Of The Way Of "Radical" Non-Dualism, or Of Ruchira Avatara Advaita-Dharma, or Of Ruchira Advaitism, or Of Ruchira Buddhism, or Of Advaitayana Buddhism, or Of Hridaya-Advaita Dharma, or Of The Way Of Divine Spiritual Baptism, or Of Ruchira Avatara Hridaya-Siddha Yoga, or Of Ruchira Avatara Hridaya-Shaktipat Yoga, or Of Ruchira Avatara Maha-Jnana Siddha-Yoga, or Of Ruchira Avatara Maha-Jnana Hridaya-Shaktipat Yoga) Progressively (and Then Most Perfectly) Magnifies True and Free Renunciation (or The Real Transcending) Of attention itself, In its Perfectly Subjective (or Transcendental, or Inherently Non-Objective) Source—Which Is Self-Existing and Self-Radiant (or Divinely Spiritually "Bright") Consciousness Itself. Therefore, The Renunciation (or The Real Transcending) Of attention (In its Transcendental and Perfectly Subjective Source)—Coincident With Effective Renunciation (or Real Transcending) Of the psycho-physical ego-"I" (or self-Contraction), and (Thus and Thereby) Effective Renunciation (or Real Transcending) Of the body-mind itself (Without Strategically Excluding, Avoiding, Denying, Emptying, or Destroying the body-mind itself)—Is The Second (and, Ultimately, Most Perfect) Principle (or Sign) Of Practice Demonstrated By all those who Listen To Me, and By all those who Hear Me, and By all those who See Me In The Only-By-Me Revealed and Given Way Of Adidam.

From The Beginning Of My Teaching-Work, I Taught The Great Heart-Way Of self-Understanding and self-Transcendence. That Way Is The Divine Way Of (Devotionally Me-Recognizing and Devotionally To-Me-Responding) Devotional Heart-Communion With Me (The Ruchira Avatar, The Da Avatar, The Love-Ananda Avatar, The Divine World-Teacher, and The Divine Heart-Master Of all and All).

From The Beginning Of My Teaching-Work, I Taught The Great Heart-Way Of self-Understanding and self-Transcendence. Therefore, From The Beginning, I Communicated Many Forms Of My Own Heart-Wisdom, In Order To Help each one, and all, To Commune With Me In My Heart-Fullness.

From The Beginning Of My Teaching-Work, I Taught The Great Heart-Way Of self-Understanding and self-Transcendence. Therefore, For The Sake Of those who Are Able To Commune With Me Especially (or Primarily) By The Exercise Of Feeling and Insight, I Taught The Way Of Adidam As The Devotional Way Of Insight, Which Way (Progressively, In The Context Of The Devotionally Me-Recognizing Devotional Feeling-Response To Me, Released By Means Of The Exercise Of The True Heart-Discipline Of self-Enquiry) Becomes Most Fundamental self-Understanding and The Great Capability For self-Transcendence (and The Spiritual Practice Of ego-Transcending Devotion To Me).

From The Beginning Of My Teaching-Work, I Taught The Great Heart-Way Of self-Understanding and self-Transcendence. Therefore, For The Sake Of those who Are Able To Commune With Me Especially (or Primarily) By The Exercise Of Feeling and Faith, I Taught The Way Of Adidam As The Devotional Way Of Faith (or The Way Of Direct, or Unmediated, Devotionally Me-Recognizing Devotional Feeling-Response To Me), and Which Way (Progressively, and By The Exercise Of The True Heart-Discipline Of Spontaneously Responsive Surrender Of self-Contraction, Merely By Means Of The Devotionally Me-Recognizing Devotional Response To Me) Becomes Most Fundamental self-Understanding and The Great Capability For self-Transcendence (and The Spiritual Practice Of ego-Transcending Devotion To Me).

Therefore, From The Beginning Of My Teaching-Work, and By

Every Kind Of Effective Means, I Taught and Revealed The Two Devotional Ways (Of Insight and Of Faith), or These Two Forms Of The Total Practice Of The One Great Way Of Adidam, Which Is The Great Heart-Way Of self-Understanding and self-Transcendence, Which Begins (and Always Develops) In Satsang With Me, The Divine Heart-Master, and Which (Therefore, and Primarily) Begins (and Always Continues) With Right Devotional (or Devotionally Me-Recognizing, and Devotionally To-Me-Responding, and, Altogether, ego-Surrendering, ego-Forgetting, and, More and More, ego-Transcending) <u>Feeling</u>-Contemplation Of My Heart-Purifying, Heart-Inspiring, Heart-Instructing, and Heart-Awakening Revelation-Form (or Inherently Revelatory Avatarically-Born Bodily Human Divine Form), and Which (Likewise, and Simultaneously) Begins (and Always Continues) With Right Devotional (or Devotionally Me-Recognizing and Devotionally To-Me-Responding, and, Altogether, ego-Surrendering, ego-Forgetting, and, More and More, ego-Transcending) "Consideration" Of My Avatarically Self-Revealed and Ever-Speaking Divine Word, My Avatarically Self-Manifested Divine Teaching-Leelas, and Even All The Avatarically Self-Manifested Leelas Of My Divine Work Of Self-Revelation and Heart-Blessing, and Which (In Due Course, and Progressively, As My Avatarically Self-Transmitted Divine Grace Will Have It) Becomes Fully (and Truly ego-Transcending) Spiritual, Transcendental, and Divine Practice (and Heart-Awake Realization) In (Perpetual) Satsang—or Devotionally Me-Recognizing and Devotionally To-Me-Responding, and (Altogether) ego-Surrendering, ego-Forgetting, and (More and More) ego-Transcending Heart-Communion With Me, Via (and <u>As</u>) My Perfect Heart-Transmission Of My Own (Self-Evidently Divine) Person (and Inherently egoless Self-Condition).

In The Total Course Of My Teaching-Work, I Thoroughly Taught and Fully Revealed The One Great Way Of Adidam In These Two Devotional Ways (Of Insight and Of Faith). Therefore, and In The Form Of These Two Devotional Ways, I Thoroughly Taught and Fully Revealed Every Kind Of Means That Leads Toward and To The "Perfect Practice" (or The Three-Part, and Inherently Perfect, Practice and Process Associated With The Ultimate, or Sixth and Seventh, Stages Of Life In The Way Of Adidam).

In The Way Of Adidam (or The Only-By-Me Revealed and
Given Way Of The Heart), Each Of These Two By-Me-Given
Devotional Ways (Of Insight and Of Faith) Culminates In The
Ultimate (and Inherently Perfect, and Only-By-Me Revealed and
Given) Process and "Perfect Practice" Of The Way Of Adidam.
Each Of These Two Devotional Ways (In One) Builds Upon,
Expresses, and, Ultimately (or Inherently Perfectly), Realizes The
Native Condition Of Divine Ignorance, or The "Radical" Intuition
Of My Avatarically Self-Revealed Transcendental, Inherently
Spiritual, and Self-Evidently Divine Self-Condition, Which Is The
Inherent (or Native) Feeling Of Being (Itself). Therefore, These
Two Devotional Ways (In One), Their Associated Means
(Embraced By Listening To Me, and By Hearing Me, and By
Seeing Me, and Always In Devotional Recognition-Response To
Me), The "Perfect Practice" (or Inherently Perfect Process) To
Which All Of That Leads, and The Completion Of All Of That In
The Most Ultimate, Native (or Inherent), and Inherently Most
Perfect Realization Of Divine Ignorance (or Transcendental, and
Inherently Spiritual, and, Necessarily, Divine Self-Realization) Will
Forever Remain The Basic Features Of The Great (and Truly
Single, and Self-Evidently Divine) Way Of Adidam.

Formally Acknowledged Student-Beginners (or Beginning
Formal Listening Devotees) In The Only-By-Me Revealed and
Given Way Of The Heart (or Way Of Adidam) Study The
Devotional Way Of Insight (Including The Total Practice and
Process Relative To self-Enquiry and The Right Practice Relative
To All My Basic Arguments and "Great Questions"[51]), and they Also
Study The Devotional Way Of Faith (Including The Practice Of
"True Prayer", In The Form Of Ruchira Avatara Naama Japa,[52] and
In The Form Of Each and All Of The Progressive Forms Of "True
Prayer" That May Follow Ruchira Avatara Naama Japa). Student-
Beginners Are Also Called To Practice The Original Basics Of Both
Devotional Forms Of The Total Practice Of The Way Of The Heart
(Experimentally, or In An Exploratory and self-Testing Manner),
Until (By A Process Of "Testing and Proving") they Choose One
or The Other Of These Two Great Devotional Forms Of The Total
Practice Of The Way Of The Heart,[53] As A Beginner's Course, and

As A Prerequisite For The Transition To The Intensive Listening-Hearing Stage Of The Way Of The Heart.

In The Only-By-Me Revealed and Given Way Of The Heart, The Devotional Way Of Insight Involves The "Conscious Process" Of Random self-Enquiry (In The Form "Avoiding Relationship?"). This Gradually Becomes The Process Of Non-verbal Re-Cognition (or "Knowing Again") Of the self-Contraction—Which Re-Cognition (or "Knowing Again") Is The Tacit Transcending Of The Habit Of "Narcissus". (In My Own Case, This Process Continued Until The Spontaneous Event Of Transcendental, and Inherently Spiritual, Divine Self-Realization.)

In The Only-By-Me Revealed and Given Way Of The Heart, The Practice Of self-Enquiry (In The Devotional Way Of Insight) Is First Developed (Responsively, Spontaneously, and Progressively) As A Formal (and, Otherwise, Random) and Rudimentary (and Progressively More and More Meditative) Activity, Whereby the conditional self (or self-Contraction), and, Thus, the entire body-mind, Is Simply (or Merely) Observed and (In The Simplest Manner) "Considered", and (In The Process) Felt Beyond (and, Thus, Directly Surrendered, Relaxed, Released, and Forgotten). This Original Practice Of self-Enquiry Is Based On Simplest Listening, or The Beginner's Devotional (or Devotionally Me-Recognizing and Devotionally To-Me-Responsive, and ego-Surrendering, ego-Forgetting, and, More and More, ego-Transcending) Feeling-Contemplation Of My Avatarically Self-Revealed Divine Sign—or My Avatarically-Born Bodily (Human) Divine Form, and (Via My Avatarically-Born Bodily Human Divine Form) My Avatarically Self-Revealed Spiritual (and Always Blessing) Divine Presence, and (Via My Avatarically Self-Revealed Spiritual, and Always Blessing, Divine Presence) My Avatarically Self-Revealed (and Very, and Transcendental, and Perfectly Subjective, and Inherently Spiritual, and Inherently egoless, and Inherently Perfect, and Self-Evidently Divine) State—and, Also, The Beginner's Devotional "Consideration" Of My Avatarically Full-Given Divine Word and Storied (Teaching and Blessing) Avatarically Self-Manifested Divine Leelas, and, Also, The Beginner's Devotional "Consideration" and (Experimental, or Exploratory and self-Testing) Application Of

The Basic functional, practical, relational, and Cultural Disciplines Given By Me To All Practitioners who Embrace The Total (or Full and Complete) Practice Of The Way Of The Heart. And This Original Practice Of self-Enquiry Is Experimentally (or In An Exploratory and self-Testing Manner) Engaged, Along With The Similarly Experimental, and Formal (and, Otherwise, Random), and Rudimentary (and Progressively More and More Meditative) Pondering[54] Of My Arguments (and "Great Questions") Relative To Divine Ignorance (and Even The Pondering Of All My Basic Arguments and "Great Questions"), During The Student-Beginner Stage Of The Way Of The Heart.

If, On The Basis Of That Student-Beginner Experiment (and A Simultaneous Student-Beginner Experiment With The Beginner's Exercise Of The Devotional Way Of Faith), The Devotional Way Of Insight Is Chosen For Further Development, The Practice Of self-Enquiry (Along With Continued Pondering Of All My Other Basic Arguments and "Great Questions", Including My Arguments and "Great Questions" Relative To Divine Ignorance) Continues To Develop During The Intensive Listening-Hearing Stage Of The Way Of The Heart. The Transition To The Intensive Listening-Hearing Stage Of The Way Of The Heart Is Itself Made Only After Either The Beginner's Devotional Way Of Insight Or The Beginner's Devotional Way Of Faith Is Chosen, and Only Once All My Original Gifts, Callings, and Disciplines[55] Are Rightly and Thoroughly Established, and Consistently So Demonstrated, In Practice— Including All The By Me Given (and Called For) Basic functional, practical, relational, and Cultural Disciplines, and The Primary Gift, Calling, and Discipline Of Ruchira Avatara Bhakti Yoga (To Which I Also, Sometimes, Refer, Descriptively, By Means Of The General Term "Ishta-Guru Bhakti Yoga"), Which Is The Responsive (or Me-Recognizing, and To-Me-Responding) and Constant Counter-egoic, and Even Total psycho-physical, Effort Of ego-Surrendering, ego-Forgetting, and, More and More (and, Ultimately, Most Perfectly), ego-Transcending Devotion To Me, and Devotional Communion With Me, The Ruchira Avatar, Adi Da Samraj, The Da Avatar, The Love-Ananda Avatar, The Divine Heart-Master, The Hridaya-Samartha Sat-Guru Of Each and All Of My

Devotees, and Which Is The moment to moment Fulfillment Of My Great Admonition To All My Devotees (To Always Invoke Me, Feel Me, Breathe Me, and Serve Me)—and This Constantly Exercised Via The Surrender, The Forgetting, and The Transcending Of the self-Contracted body, and self-Contracted emotion (or all of self-Contracted, and reactive, and, Altogether, limited, feeling), and self-Contracted mind (Even At its Root, Which Is attention itself), and Even every self-Contracted breath, and, Altogether, Even all of Separate (and Separative) self In moment to moment (and Truly, or Unlimitedly, Heart-Felt, and Whole bodily Receptive, and Fully breathing, and Only-By-Me Distracted) Devotional Remembrance Of Me and Direct Devotional self-Surrender To Me. And, If The Beginner's Devotional Way Of Insight Is Practiced During The Intensive Listening-Hearing Stage Of The Way Of The Heart, self-Enquiry Itself Progressively Becomes The Primary Technical (and Really Effective) Feature Of A Really ego-Transcending Way Of Life—Based (Eventually) On True Hearing, or Most Fundamental self-Understanding. Likewise, The Practice Of self-Enquiry (In The Form "Avoiding Relationship?") Is (and Should Be) Continued Beyond The Intensive Listening-Hearing Stage Of The Way Of The Heart, By all those who Find The Practice Of self-Enquiry To Be Especially Attractive and Effective (As A Primary Means Of self-Transcendence) In their own case.

In The Only-By-Me Revealed and Given Way Of The Heart, The Devotional Way Of Faith Is, From Its Beginning, Based Upon The Heart-Response (or Faith-Response) To Me. Therefore, It Is, Primarily, A Practice That Involves The Devotional Exercise Of Faith (or The Devotional Faith-Response), Rather Than The Devotional Exercise Of Insight. However, The Devotional Way Of Faith Is Not (or Must Not Be) An Exercise Of childish (or Superficial and ego-Serving) emotionalism, or An Exercise Of "gleeful" and ego-Consoling idealism, or An Exercise Of any other kind of dependency, want, or enthusiasm that Neither Requires True self-Surrender Nor Expresses Truly ego-Forgetting Feeling and Faith. Neither (By Contrast) Is The Devotional Way Of Insight (Rightly Practiced) A Rather adolescent and Non-Feeling (or Abstract, emotionless, and willfully Dissociative) Exercise Of mere intellect and The Motive Of ego-Possessed Independence. Rather, In The Only-By-Me Revealed and Given Way Of The Heart, Both The Devotional Way Of Insight and The Devotional Way Of Faith Are (or Must Be) Well-Founded In Right and True and Truly Faith-Filled (and, Altogether, Truly Devotionally Me-Recognizing) Feeling-Responsiveness To My Avatarically Self-Revealed Divine Form, and Presence, and State Of Person—and The Total Devotional Way Of Faith, Just As Well As The Total Devotional Way Of Insight, Is (or Must Be) A Responsible Practice Directly and Fully Associated With The Process Of self-Observation, Most Fundamental self-Understanding, and (Capable) self-Transcendence.

In The Only-By-Me Revealed and Given Way Of the Heart, The Devotional Way Of Faith Is Based Upon the Unconditional Faith-Response To Me. That Is To Say, Even Though (In The Only-By-Me Revealed and Given Way Of The Heart) Both The Devotional Way Of Insight and The Devotional Way Of Faith Are (or Must Be) Well-Founded In Right and True and Truly Faith-Filled (and, Altogether, Truly Devotionally Me-Recognizing) Feeling-Responsiveness To My Avatarically Self-Revealed (and Self-Evidently Divine) Form, and Presence, and State Of Person, The Devotional Way Of Faith Is Based Upon (and Always Demonstrates Itself As) The Direct (or Immediate and Unmediated) Faith-Response (Of Devotionally Me-Recognizing, and Devotionally To-Me-Responding, and Whole-bodily-Demonstrated Heart-Surrender To My Avatarically Self-Revealed, and Self-Evidently Divine, Form, and Presence, and State Of Person)—Whereas The Devotional Way Of Insight Assists the Whole body In The Demonstrating Of The Heart-Surrendering Faith-Response To Me, By Means Of Random self-Enquiry.

In The Only-By-Me Revealed and Given Way of the Heart, The Whole-bodily-Demonstrated Heart-Response Of Unconditional Faith Is Based Upon The Always Immediate and Unmediated Heart-Recognition Of My Avatarically Self-Revealed Divine Form, and Presence, and State Of Person. Therefore, That Unconditional Faith-Response Of Whole bodily Heart-Surrender To Me Is Never Done Because Of anything, or Done For anything, or Done In Order To Achieve anything, or Done In Spite Of anything, or Done About anything, or Done To anything, or Done In anything.

Rather, It Is Faith Without conditional Reasons, and Without conditional Purposes. It Is Truly mindless (but Not senseless, or Disembodied, or body-Negative) Faith. Therefore, It Is Spontaneous (Devotionally Me-Recognizing and Devotionally To-Me-Responding) Whole bodily Heart-Surrender (or Heart-Release, and Heart-Relinquishment) Of The self-Contraction Of All Four Of The Principal psycho-physical Faculties (Of mind's attention, and Of emotional feeling, and Of physically perceiving body, and Of the ever-cycling breath).

In The Only-By-Me Revealed and Given Way Of The Heart, The Devotional Way Of Faith Generally Begins With The Formal (and, Otherwise, Random) Exercise Of The "Conscious Process" Of Simple Name-Invocation (and Feeling-Contemplation) Of Me, Via One or Another Simple Form or Combination Of My Avatarically Revealed and Given Divine Names and Avataric Divine Descriptive Titles.[56]

In The Case Of Practitioners Of The Way Of The Heart who Are (Whether Experimentally Or By Firm Choice) Practicing The Devotional Way Of Faith, and who Are (Whether Experimentally Or By Firm Choice) Extending their Practice Of The Devotional Way Of Faith Beyond The Simple Practice Of Random Invocation Of Me Via My Name, The Beginner's Practice Of The Devotional Way Of Faith (and, Perhaps, Even The Practice Of The Devotional Way Of Faith Engaged By The Mature Practitioner Of The Technically "Simpler" Form Of The Way Of The Heart) Involves The "Conscious Process" Of Ruchira Avatara Naama Japa. The True Practice and "Conscious Process" Of Ruchira Avatara Naama Japa (To Which I Also, Sometimes, Refer, Descriptively, By Means Of The General, or Composite Traditional, Term "Sat-Guru Naama Japa") Requires (and, Most Basically, Is) The Random and Progressively Meditative Feeling-Exercise Of Faith In My Avatarically Self-Manifested Divine Sign, My Avatarically Self-Revealed Divine Self-Realization, and My Avatarically Self-Transmitted Divine Helping-Power. And This Feeling-Exercise Of Ruchira Avatara Naama Japa Is Associated (In The Traditional Manner[57]) With Devotional Invocation Of Me Via The Ruchira Avatara Naama Mantra (In One or Another Of Its Seventy By Me Revealed and

Given Variant Forms[58]), Which Is Heart-Felt Invocation and Word-Celebration Of Me Via My Avatarically Revealed and Given Divine Names and Avataric Divine Descriptive Titles, and (Thereby) ego-Surrendering and ego-Forgetting Feeling-Invocation, Feeling-Remembrance, and (More and More Effectively) ego-Transcending Feeling-Contemplation Of My Avatarically-Born Bodily (Human) Divine Form, and (As My Avatarically Self-Transmitted Divine Grace Will Have It) My Avatarically Self-Revealed Spiritual (and Always Blessing) Divine Presence, and (As My Avatarically Self-Transmitted Divine Grace Will Have It) My Avatarically Self-Revealed (and Very, and Transcendental, and Perfectly Subjective, and Inherently Spiritual, and Inherently egoless, and Inherently Perfect, and Self-Evidently Divine) State.

In The Only-By-Me Revealed and Given Way Of The Heart, The Devotional Way Of Faith Is To Be Associated With All The Same Basic Forms Of Study and "Consideration" (Of My Avatarically Self-Revealed, and Always Me-Revealing, Divine Word—Including All My Avatarically Given Divine Teaching-Arguments—and The Storied Divine Leelas Of My Avataric Teaching and Blessing), and With The Same (Primary) Practice Of Feeling-Contemplation (Of My Avatarically-Born Bodily Human Divine Form, and—Tacitly, and More and More, As My Avatarically Self-Transmitted Divine Grace Will Have It—My Avatarically Self-Revealed Spiritual, and Always Blessing, Divine Presence and My Avatarically Self-Revealed, and Very, and Transcendental, and Perfectly Subjective, and Inherently Spiritual, and Inherently egoless, and Inherently Perfect, and Self-Evidently Divine State), and With The Same Forms Of self-Discipline (functional, practical, relational, and Cultural) That Are Associated With The Devotional Way Of Insight. And Even Though, In The Way Of The Heart, The Devotional Way Of Faith and The Devotional Way Of Insight Are Each Developed Via A Different (and Unique) Primary Technical (or Root-Cultural) Exercise (Based On Either The Principle Of Feeling-Faith Or The Principle Of Feeling-Insight), Both Involve The Development Of The Same Basic (and Necessary) Process Of self-Observation, self-Understanding, and self-Transcendence.

In The Only-By-Me Revealed and Given Way Of The Heart, The Practice Of Ruchira Avatara Naama Japa (In The Devotional Way Of Faith) Is First Developed (Responsively, Spontaneously, and Progressively) As A Formal (and, Otherwise, Random) and Rudimentary (and More and More Meditative) Activity, Whereby the conditional self (or self-Contraction), and, Thus, the entire body-mind, Is Simply and Directly Observed (or Directly Felt) and Directly (and Immediately) Felt Beyond (or Actively Surrendered, Relaxed, Released, and Forgotten) In (or Via) Faithful (and Devotionally Me-Recognizing and Devotionally To-Me-Responsive) Feeling-Contemplation Of My Avatarically-Born Bodily (Human) Divine Form, and With The Constant (and Always Growing) Exercise Of Feeling-Confidence In My Constant (and Divinely Spiritual) Helping-Power (or Accomplishing-Power). And This Original Practice, Based On Simplest (and, Necessarily, Devotional) Listening (or The Beginner's ego-Surrendering, ego-Forgetting, and, More and More, ego-Transcending Feeling-Contemplation Of My Avatarically-Born Bodily Human Divine Form, and The Beginner's ego-Surrendering, ego-Forgetting, and, More and More, ego-Transcending "Consideration" Of My Avatarically Self-Revealed, and Always Me-Revealing, Divine Word and Leelas), Is Experimentally (or In An Exploratory and self-Testing Manner) Engaged (Along With The Similarly Experimental Engagement Of self-Enquiry, In The Devotional Way Of Insight) During The Student-Beginner Stage Of The Way Of The Heart.

All Beginning Practitioners Of The Total (or Full and Complete) Practice Of The Way Of The Heart Engage In Study and Beginner's Practice As A personal Discipline In Satsang With Me, and Always In Preparation For Entrance Into The (True and Full) Seeing-Devotee Culture Of Spiritually Active Satsang (or Fullest Heart-Communion) With Me. Such Beginning Practitioners Of The Way Of The Heart Gratefully (and In A Progressively Developing Devotional, or Heart-Feeling, Manner) Embrace Me As The Divine Heart-Master, and (By Rightly and Truly Heart-Recognizing Me and Heart-Responding To Me) Resort To Me As The Self-Revealed Divine Person, Ever-Present Via My Own Avatarically Given and Divinely Self-Revealing Sign (Of Form, and Presence, and State), and Ever-Active In The Form Of My Avatarically Full-Given (and Always Me-Revealing) Divine Word and All The Storied (and Often Lesson-Making) Divine Leelas Of My Avatarically Self-Manifested (and Always Me-Revealing) Divine Work. They Always (and In The Devotional and Feeling Manner) "Consider" My Avatarically Self-Revealed Divine Word and My Avatarically Self-Manifested Divine Leelas, and they Always (and In The Devotional and Feeling Manner) Contemplate My Avatarically Self-Manifested Bodily (Human) Divine Form (Ever Directly, and As Represented and Revealed In or Through photographic Images and Other Types Of Recorded, or, Otherwise, artistically Rendered, Images).[59] Therefore, their (Thus Sacred) Practices and their (Thus Sacred) Occasions Must Necessarily Be Described (and Engaged) As Participation In Satsang With Me (Even In A Tacitly, or, As My Avatarically Self-Transmitted Divine Grace Will Have It, Pro-gressively, Spiritual Sense, but Without Formally Acknowledged and Direct, or, Otherwise, Fully Developed, Responsibility For Spiritual Practice, and, Therefore, In A More Rudimentary, or Less Developed, Spiritual Sense Than Is, or Must Be, The Case With My Actually Seeing Devotees, who Are Formally Acknowledged To Be Practicing In The Advanced and The Ultimate Stages Of Life In The Way Of The Heart). And The Practice Of All My Devotees Is A Matter Of their own Responsibility and Struggle With their own conditional (or Separate, and Separative) self (Rather Than A Struggle With Me, or With others). Therefore, In The Total (or Full and Complete) Practice Of The Only-By-Me Revealed and Given Way Of The Heart, The Original Practice For all Is Simply (and In The Devotional Manner) To "Consider" My Avatarically Self-Revealed (and Always Me-Revealing) Divine Word and All My Avatarically Self-Manifested (and Always Me-Revealing) Divine Leelas, and Constantly (and In The Devotional Manner) To Contemplate My Avatarically Self-Revealed (and Always Me-Revealing) Divine Sign (Of My Avatarically-Born Bodily Human Divine Form, and, Tacitly, and Via My Avatarically-Born Bodily Human Divine Form, My Avatarically Self-Revealed Spiritual, and Always Blessing, Divine Presence and My Avatarically Self-Revealed, and Very, and Transcendental, and Perfectly Subjective, and Inherently Spiritual, and Inherently egoless, and Inherently Perfect, and Self-Evidently Divine State), and (In Devotional Recognition-Response To Me, Whether In The Form Of The Devotional Way Of Insight Or The Devotional Way Of Faith) To Directly (and Intelligently) Observe, and (Eventually and Most Fundamentally) To Understand, and (Thereby) To Transcend (or Feel Beyond) the conditional (or psycho-physical) self, Until The Way Of ego-Transcendence (In My Avatarically Self-Revealed Transcendental, Inherently Spiritual, and Self-Evidently Divine Person, or Self-Condition) Is Fully Revealed To The Heart and Embraced From The Heart.

My "Consideration" and Self-Revelation Of The ego-Transcending Way Of The Heart Developed Over The Many Years Of My Divinely Self-Submitted Teaching-Work and My Divine Self-Revelation-Work, On The Basis Of My Response To The Needs and limitations and Heart-Necessities Of those who Were Moved By My Avatarically Self-Revealed Divine Word and (At Least In A Rudimentary Fashion, and More and More) By My Avatarically Given Divine Self-Revelation Of My Self-Existing, Self-Radiant, Transcendental, Inherently Spiritual, and Self-Evidently Divine Person (or "Bright", and All-Outshining, Divine Self-Condition), Always Spontaneously Revealed In, By, and As My Even Avatarically-Born Bodily (Human) Divine Form, and My Avatarically Self-Revealed Spiritual (and Always Blessing) Divine Presence, and My Avatarically Self-Revealed (and Very, and Transcendental, and Perfectly Subjective, and Inherently Spiritual, and Inherently egoless, and Inherently Perfect, and Self-Evidently Divine) State. And The Real Course and Ordeal Of ego-Transcending Practice Must Not Be Bypassed In The Only-By-Me Revealed and Given Way Of The Heart, Even Though the ego Would Prefer To Do So.

Anyone who Fully "Considers" The Great Process Demonstrated In My Own Case Must Thereby Observe That Real and Most Ultimate (or Inherently Most Perfect) Fulfillment Of ego-Transcending (and, Ultimately, Real-God-Realizing) Practice Involves A Profound Ordeal That Encompasses (or, Otherwise, Directly Transcends) Each and All Of The Seven Stages Of Life.

Indeed, In the case of all others, No Such Effort Can Most Perfectly Fulfill Itself Without Right Devotional (or ego-Surrendering, ego-Forgetting, and, More and More, ego-Transcending) "Consideration" Of My Avatarically Self-Revealed and Ever-Speaking Divine Word, My Avatarically Self-Manifested Divine Teaching-Leelas, and Even All The Leelas Of My Avatarically Self-Manifested Divine Work Of Self-Revelation and Heart-Blessing, and Without The Discipline Of The True and Complete Culture Of Life Of The Community Of My Devotees, and Without Spiritual Access To Me (Whether During Or After The Avataric Physical Lifetime Of My Bodily Human Divine Form)—For I Am The Avatarically Self-Revealing Divine Source Of Unrelenting Grace (or Divine Heart-Transmission), and, Therefore, Of Spiritual, Transcendental, and Divine Self-Realization (or Divine Enlightenment).

The Way Of Transcendental (and Inherently Spiritual) Divine Enlightenment Has Been Revealed In and Via The Form Of My Own Ordeal Of Life, Practice, and Divine Self-Realization. However, My Own Ordeal Is Divine—and, Therefore, Unique. I Am Avatarically Born, In Order To Teach (and Awaken) all others. Therefore, My Summary Of The Way Of The Heart In My Twenty-Three Divine "Source-Texts" (and, Principally, My *Dawn Horse Testament*) Is Based On My Divine "Consideration" Of The Means and The Stages Necessary For others.

Every one Begins The "Consideration" and Practice Of The Way Of The Heart Without Immediate Resort To The More Complex (or Fully Developed, and Otherwise Technically "Elaborate") Practices Of Spiritually Responsible Devotion To Me, but That Earliest "Consideration" and Practice Should (Immediately, and More and More) Make Appropriate (and Right Contemplative, and, Thus, Feeling) Use Of My Avatarically Self-Revealed Divine Person (or My Avatarically-Born Bodily Human Divine Form, and, Thereby, and Tacitly, My Avatarically Self-Revealed Spiritual, and Always Blessing, Divine Presence, and My Avatarically Self-Revealed, and Very, and Transcendental, and Perfectly Subjective, and Inherently Spiritual, and Inherently egoless, and Inherently Perfect, and Self-Evidently Divine State). Just As The Ordeal Of My Own Practice, Even Of self-Enquiry, Was Founded On Devotional

Submission Of My Own Apparent self (or Heart-Surrender Of My Own Apparent and Apparently self-Contracted body-mind) To My Own Teachers and Spiritual Sources,[60] Just So, any one who Seriously Heart-Recognizes Me and Heart-Responds To Me Via My Avatarically Self-Revealed (and Always Me-Revealing) Divine Word and My Avatarically Self-Manifested (and Always Me-Revealing) Divine Leelas Will Also (and More and More) Realize The Graceful Necessity To Embrace The Way Of The Heart As Just Such An Ordeal—As An Ordeal Of ego-Transcending Devotion To Me. By My Own Example, I Have Already Revealed The Form Of That Ordeal Of ego-Transcending Devotion, and I Have Summarized That Revelation In The Words Of My Twenty-Three Divine "Source-Texts" (and, Principally, My *Dawn Horse Testament*).

In My Own Case, The "Conscious Process" Of self-Understanding, Persistent self-Enquiry (or Enquiry Into the self-Contraction), and The Effective Practice Of Feeling-Transcendence Of self-Contraction, Also Accompanied By All Of The Technical (or Yogic) psycho-physical Evidence Of "Conductivity" Of The Divine Spirit-Current, Gradually Characterized My Own Practice Of Great Heart-Surrender. The Entire Process Was Originally Generated On The Basis Of A Unique (or Heart-Awake) Insight Into The Core-Dilemma I Felt In The Midst Of ordinary life. That Liberating Insight Became More and More Effective Over time Via Numerous Incidents Of Sudden Extraordinary Re-Awakening, but, Even From Its Own First Moment Of Re-Awakening,[61] That Insight Itself Directly (and With Inherent Effectiveness) Transcended The Motive To Seek An "Answer" To The Presumed "Question" Of egoic (or self-Contracted) Existence, or A "Solution", In The Form Of Acquired (or conditional) experience or knowledge, To The Presumed "Problem" Of life.

I Spontaneously, but Gradually, Developed The Total Process Of The Understanding (and The Transcending) Of the ego, The Practice Of self-Enquiry (In The Form "Avoiding Relationship?"), and The Total Process Of Ultimate Awakening (From self-Enquiry and Re-Cognition To Transcendental, and Inherently Spiritual, Divine Self-Realization, and Transcendental, and Inherently Spiritual, Divine Self-Recognition) During The Many Years Of My Own Ordeal

Of Re-Awakening.[62] The Consistent Formal Practice Of self-Enquiry and Non-verbal Re-Cognition Did Not Formally Characterize My Meditation Until The Last Year Of My Ordeal Of Realization (and That Practice Quickly Brought My Ordeal Of Realization To An End). Nevertheless, All Of My Years Of Practice Were Founded On The Same Basic Insight (or Heart-Awakening), and Those Years Were Punctuated By Sudden Great Moments Of Awakening and Sudden Great Leaps Of Understanding.

One Such (and Early) Incident Of Heart-Awakening Occurred Quite Gently (but Most Profoundly), In a moment In which I Was mindlessly Regarding My Right Hand, Observing The (Apparent and, Suddenly, Revealing) Contrast Between The Natural (or Open and Functionally Relational) Attitude Of The Hand and The Unnatural (or Contracted and Functionally Dissociated) Attitude Of The Clenched Fist.[63]

The Natural Sign Of the human body Is Relatedness, Not Separateness and Independence!

Therefore, When This Sign Convicted The Heart, The subjective Commitment To self-Contraction Was Spontaneously Released. In that moment, There Was A Quiet Revolution In the body-mind. I Knew The "Always Already" State. And This Began A Period Of Pondering, Which Eventually Became Random self-Enquiry (or Enquiry Into the self-Contraction, which Appears, In action, As The Avoidance Of Relationship). And Random self-Enquiry Eventually (and Spontaneously) Became Formal self-Enquiry (In The Form "Avoiding Relationship?") In Meditation. And, In Meditation, Formal self-Enquiry Became Formal, and Spontaneous, and Non-verbal Re-Cognition Of self-Contraction. And, In Due Course, The Process Of self-Enquiry and Re-Cognition, and, Thereby, The Feeling-Transcendence Of self-Contraction, Became Constant, In Meditation, and In daily life, Until, When The Efforts and The Effects Of The Avoidance Of Relationship (and Every subjective Trace Of self-Contraction) Were Transcended, There Is The Tacit Certainty and Self-Illumined Awakeness Of "I <u>Am</u> Consciousness" (or The Real and Self-Existing and Self-Radiant, or "Bright", Condition Of Transcendental, and Inherently Spiritual, and Self-Evidently Divine Being Itself).

My Earliest and Most Basic Practice (Of Which self-Enquiry Was Only An Extension) Was An Example Of What Is Traditionally Called "Prapatti"[64]—or Simple, Direct, Non-Technical, and Unconditional Surrender To Whatever Is Always Already The Case (Without any believed concept Of "What" That Is, or any previously acquired commitment to any specific means to be employed). It Was Not A Practice informed by any conventional religious philosophy, or by any traditional Spiritual philosophy, or by any inherited "God"-concepts. (As A Result Of A Profound intellectual and emotional Crisis, I Had Despaired Of <u>all</u> the religious and philosophical conventions that Were Proposed To Me In My Youth.) All That Was Possible For Me Was The Real Practice Of Divine Ignorance, or Spontaneous (Random, General, and Unpredictable) Submission To The Unknown and Unknowable (and Yet Realizable) Condition In Which the conditional self and the conditional world Are arising in every moment.

I Soon Enjoyed A Profoundly Essential Insight Into The Felt Dilemma and The Urge To Seek That Characterize the born (or conditional, and psycho-physical) self. It Became Clear To Me That The Feeling Of Dilemma and The Urge To Seek God, Happiness, Fulfillment, or Release Via The Acquisition Of experience, knowledge, or any condition (or conditional object) at all Are Not, In Fact, The Means For The Realization Of Truth Itself. I Understood That The Problem-Feeling and The Urge To Seek Are Not A Program For The Actual Discovery Of Truth, but They Are Merely Symptoms Of A Curious Disease. I Observed That These Symptoms, Which Tend To Characterize every moment Of ordinary Existence, Are, In Fact, The Evidence Of the very state that Must Be Transcended If The Truth Itself Is To Be Realized. It Was Clear To Me That The Feeling Of Dilemma and The Seeking-Urge Are Nothing More Than A Confession That God, or Truth, or Happiness Is Not presently experienced or known. And This Seemed Remarkable To Me.

If God, or Truth, or Happiness Is Sought On The Basis Of A Problem (or The Feeling Of Dilemma), Then God, or Truth, or Happiness Is Always Projected Into future time, and The Realization Of God, or Truth, or Happiness Is Made conditional, or Dependent Upon psycho-physical events. This Stood Out To Me As Nonsense, or As An Absurd Proposition.

My Own "Consideration" Was This: God, or Truth, or Happiness Must (<u>Necessarily</u>) Be Reality Itself, or That Which Is (<u>Necessarily</u>) Always Already The Case. Therefore, I Observed That The Felt Dilemma and The Urge To Seek Are Simply The Absurd Confession That God, or Truth, or Happiness Is Absent Now. And I Observed Further That The Signs Of Dilemma and Seeking Are Not A Program For The Actual Future (or Eventual, and future-time) Realization Of God, or Truth, or Happiness, but They Are Merely A Means For Preventing Actual Present (or Inherent, and present-time) Realization Of God, or Truth, or Happiness. The Feeling Of Dilemma and The Urge To Seek Are Actually The Evidence Of A Disease, Which Is the conditional (or psycho-physical) self In its Chronic Contraction Upon itself, and In its Symptomatic Non-Realization Of Reality Itself (Which <u>Is</u>, Itself, God, or Truth, or Happiness).

Indeed, It Became Clear To Me That the "ego" (or the conventional "I") Is Not an "entity" (or an Independent and Static "thing of being"), but the "ego" (or the conventional "I") Is the Chronic and Total psycho-physical <u>activity</u> of self-Contraction, Always Associated With Concrete Results (In the psyche, mind, emotion, body, and their relations). And the self-Contraction Can Always Be Located (In any moment) In Feeling (As Fear, Anxiety, Stress, and All Other Kinds Of Reactive emotions and Blocks In The Flow Of Natural bodily energy In The Circle Of the body-mind).

It Became Clear To Me That The self-Contraction Is the Complex limit on Natural bodily energy, and (In The Case Of The Degrees and Stages Of Spiritual Awakening) On The Divine Spiritual Energy, In The Circle Of the body-mind. Therefore, the self-Contraction Is (Ultimately) a Complex limit On The Inherent and Self-Existing Spiritual Radiance Of Transcendental Divine Being. And Perfect Freedom, or Inherent Happiness, or Inherently Most Perfect Real-God-Realization Is A Matter Of Direct (or Inherent, or Native) and Inherently Most Perfect (and Inherently Most Perfectly ego-Transcending) Identification With The Self-Existing and Self-Radiant Condition Of Transcendental, Inherently

Spiritual, and Self-Evidently Divine Being (or Self-Existing and Self-Radiant Consciousness Itself), Which Identification Is Allowed Only (In Due Course) By The Real Practice Of Always present-time (and, In Due Course, Most Perfect)[65] Transcending Of The ego-Act Of self-Contraction.

It Became Clear To Me That The self-Contraction Is Un-Necessary. The self-Contraction Is (Without Ultimate Necessity, and, Therefore, Only Apparently) Being "Added" To Existence Itself (In Reaction To Cosmic Nature, or To Apparent conditional Existence). The self-Contraction (Originally) Coincides With and (Effectively) Perpetuates The Apparition Of Cosmic Nature Itself—and The Presumption That Existence <u>Itself</u> Is merely conditional (or Merely Apparent), and Not Founded On (and, Altogether, Dependent Upon—and, Ultimately, Characterized By) The Dimension Of Unconditionality (or Of Unconditional Existence). Therefore, the self-Contraction Is (Originally, and Also In Effect, or conditionally) Un-Natural, Because it Superimposes On The Transcendental, and Inherently Spiritual, Divine Self (or Self-Existing and Self-Radiant Consciousness Itself) A False View Of Both Cosmic Nature (or conditional Reality) and The Divine Reality (or The Most Priorly Real, and Entirely Non-conditional, Self-Condition and Source-Condition).

It Became Clear To Me That, When what Is Un-Necessarily Superimposed On Reality Is Released, What Stands (or Remains) As The Obvious Is (Necessarily, or Self-Evidently) Reality, or The Real Condition Itself.

That Is To Say, Whatever Is Always Already The Case Authenticates <u>Itself</u> (Directly, Inherently, Obviously, and Perfectly).

Therefore, self-Transcendence Necessarily Allows The Revelation Of The Transcendental, and Inherently Spiritual, Self-Condition and Source-Condition As The Self-Authenticating (or Inherently and Obviously Real and True) and Most Prior (or Self-Evidently Divine) Reality and Truth!

This Heart-Awakened Insight Was, In My Own Case, Instantly Liberating! And, As Such, It Became The Real Practicing Basis For A Progressive (and, At Last, Most Perfect) Revelation (or Re-Realization) Of My Own (Inherent, Self-Existing, Self-Radiant, and

Self-Evidently Divine) Condition—Which Is Reality, Truth, and Happiness!

The Insight Itself (or The Unique and Inherently Liberating Understanding Re-Awakened At The Heart) Directly Coincided (or Arose Simultaneously) With A Practice That Was Thereafter To Be The Most Basic Characteristic Of The Way Of My Life (and Which Was To Re-Awaken Full and Most Ultimate Realization). That Practice Had Two Primary Aspects. The First Was Profound Submission Of attention and all the energies of the body-mind To Observe, Feel, and Feel Beyond the self-Contraction. And The Second, Which Coincided With The First and Ultimately Superseded It, Was Direct Communion (and, Ultimately, Inherent Identification) With The Native (or Prior) Condition That Is Simply and Directly Obvious When the self-Contraction Is Transcended (or No Longer Effective As A Mechanism Of Dissociation From What Is Always Already The Case).

I Observed That The Sense (or Feeling) Of "Absence", or The Sense (or Feeling) Of The Non-Presence Of God, or The Sense (or Feeling) Of Separation From God, Truth, Happiness, or What Cannot Even Be Described, Is Not Evidence Of The Real Absence Of God, Truth, Happiness, or The Indescribable, but It Is Clear Evidence That the conditional self Is Contracting, or Actively Separating From What (Simply, Merely, or Really) Is.

I Named This Disease (or the Diseased self) "Narcissus", Because Of The Likeness Between This self-Program and The Ancient Myth Of Narcissus. And I Became Attentive In every moment To This Feeling Of Absence, Of Separateness, Of Dilemma, and The Urge To Seek.

Remarkably, In every moment Of Such Observation, I Felt The Non-Necessity (As Well As The Deluding, or Binding, Effect) Of the self-Contraction—Such That A Spontaneous Release Occurred In every Such moment. That Is To Say, I Observed That It Was Un-Necessary To Presume or Suffer or Be Motivated By the self-Contraction In any moment Of My Direct Observation Of it. And, In That Observation, A Deep Spontaneous Response Of self-Release Was Awakened. And Whenever That Release Of self-Contraction Occurred, That Which Is Always Already The Case

(Previous, and Most Prior, To self-Contraction) Stood Out As The Obvious.

Over time, What <u>Is</u> (Previous, and Most Prior, To self-Contraction) Was Revealed More and More Profoundly. And As That Revelation Increased, There Was Also The Spontaneous and, Otherwise, Progressive Unfolding Of The Many Extraordinary Phenomena That Are Characteristic Of Each Of The Seven Stages Of Life.

The Process Of That Revelation By Stages Was Not Developed <u>Only</u> On The Basis Of Insight (or self-Understanding) and Spontaneous self-Transcendence, or What I Call The "'Conscious Process'", but It Was <u>Equally</u> Associated With A Developing Response To What Was Being Revealed. Thus, It Also Involved What I Call "Seeing" (or Fullest, and Spiritually Activated, emo-tional, and Total psycho-physical, Conversion To True, and Truly Responsible, "Conductivity" Of The Self-Revealed Spirit-Power Of Divine Self-"Brightness"), and Conversion To What I Call "Divine Ignorance" (or Spontaneous Identification With The Inherent Love-Bliss-Condition Of Native, or Divine, Being—Whenever The psycho-physical Presumption Of knowledge, or "I know what this or that <u>Is</u>", Was Effortlessly Released).

What <u>Is</u> (Always and Already) Is Revealed <u>Only</u> When the self-Contraction Is Not Effective. It Is Revealed To Be Self-Radiant (or Inherently Spiritual) and Transcendental (or Self-Existing) and Self-Evidently Divine Being—Which <u>Is</u> Reality, Truth, and Happiness. Any and every conditionally Manifested "I" Always Already Inheres In That Self-Evidently Divine Self-Condition, Both At The Level Of Self-Existing Being (or Consciousness Itself) and At The Level Of every Apparent (or conditionally Manifested) psycho-physical function, process, or state. Even the body-mind Is Only An Apparent Modification Of That Self-Existing "Bright" Divine Self-Radiance In Which every "I" is arising.

When This Realization Was Most Perfectly Re-Awakened In My Own Case—all beings, this world, and all the kinds of other worlds Were Revealed In <u>Me</u>, Inhering In <u>Me</u>, and Appearing As (Apparent) Modifications Of <u>Me</u>! And It Became Self-Evidently Clear That, By Virtue Of My Own Inherently Most Perfect Divine

Self-Realization Of My Own Divine Self-Condition, <u>all</u> (Apparently "other") conditionally Manifested beings (Now, and Forever Hereafter) Can—By Means Of their Devotionally Me-Recognizing and Devotionally To-Me-Responding Heart-Devotion To Me—Realize What (and Who) <u>Is</u> Reality, Truth, and Happiness!

Suddenly and Spontaneously, What I Had Forgotten By Birth Was, By Me, Remembered In The Midst Of Life—and The Avataric Significance and Divine Purpose Of My Own Birth Became Clear, Again, To Me: I <u>Am</u> The One Who Is Always Already The Case—and Even <u>all</u> beings <u>Are</u> In <u>Me</u> (Ultimately, Beyond All "Difference")!

When This Truth (and Condition) Became (To Me) Obvious (<u>As</u> Truth, and <u>As</u> My Condition), The Avatarically Self-Transmitting Powers Of My Transcendental, Inherently Spiritual, and Self-Evidently Divine Person Spontaneously Became Active In and <u>As</u> My Divinely Self-Manifested (and Avatarically-Born—or, Avatarically, conditionally Shown) Bodily (Human) Divine Form, and My Avatarically Self-Revealed Spiritual (and Always All-and-all-Blessing) Divine Presence, and My Perfectly Subjective (and Very, and Inherently egoless, and Inherently Perfect, and Self-Evidently Divine, and Avatarically Self-Revealed) State! And I Became Heart-Moved To Forever Avatarically Serve The Most Perfect Divine Awakening Of The Total Cosmic Mandala Of conditionally Mani-fested beings!

In The Later Period Of My Own Ordeal Of Spiritual, Transcen-dental, and Divine Self-Realization, The Basic Insight (or Heart-Understanding) That Already Informed My Practice Began To Express Itself Spontaneously and Randomly Via self-Enquiry (In The Form "Avoiding Relationship?"), and That Practice Was Itself A Sign Of The Great (and Most Fundamental) Capability That Must Awaken To Characterize The Practice Of anyone who (By Heart, and In The Way Of The Heart) Will Realize The Living (or Inherently Spiritual) and Transcendental Divine Truth Of Reality. That Great and Most Fundamental Capability, Which Leads To Divine Self-Realization, Develops From (or On The Basis Of) The Original and Spontaneous Urge To Observe and Transcend the self-Contraction. And That Great and Most Fundamental Capability (Awakened On The Basis Of Thorough self-Observation) Expresses

The Clear (and Most Fundamental) Understanding That the self-Contraction (and Not The Real Absence Of Real God, or Reality, or Truth, or Happiness) Is The Only Reason Why Real-God-Communion (or Ecstatic, Tacit, and Direct Realization Of Real God, or Reality, or The Truth, or Happiness Itself, or The Real Condition That Is Always Already The Case) Is Not Enjoyed In the present. This Heart-Awakened Insight, and The Great Capability For Spontaneous Release That Extends From It, Were The Ground Of My (At Last) Free Surrender—and That Surrender Was Not Encumbered or Retarded By Dilemma, Nor Was That Surrender Made Fruitful By The Search Toward Any Goal.

I Was Not Born To Be Projected Toward the future. I Was Avatarically Born—To Self-Reveal My Own Self-Evidently Divine Self-Condition, <u>As</u> That Which Is Always Already The Case In every moment. Therefore, Even In My Own Case, The Process—Of Ecstatic (or ego-Transcending) Communion (and, At Last, Inherent Identification) With That Which Is (In every moment Of ego-Transcendence) Divinely Self-Revealed (Self-Evidently, <u>As</u> That Which Is Always Already The Case)—Developed, Spontaneously and Inevitably, As A Progressive Unfolding Of The Characteristic Signs Of Each Of The Seven Stages Of Life.

Such Is The Nature Of The Process In My Own (Avatarically-Born) Case.

Such Is The Nature Of The Process Of ego-Transcending and Me-Realizing Devotion To Me <u>As</u> I <u>Am</u>.

Such Is The Nature and The Process Of The Way That Only I Reveal and Give.

II.

After Thirty Years Of Submission To conditional Existence, My Own Ordeal (By Which I Came, Again, To Divine Self-Realization, and Then Began To Teach The Way Of Adidam, Which Is The One and Only By-Me-Revealed and By-Me-Given Way Of The Heart) Culminated In Most Profound self-Enquiry (In The Form "Avoiding Relationship?"). In That self-Enquiry, The Act and The Results Of self-Contraction of the body-mind Were Loosened

(In Merely Witnessing Consciousness, Itself)—and, At Last, A Spontaneous Divine Self-Revelation Took Place. In That Great Event, There Was Spontaneous Tacit Awareness <u>As</u> That To Which (and <u>In</u> and <u>As</u> Which) the self-Contraction, all thoughts, and all conditional appearances Are arising. In (and Forever After) That Great Event, Enquiry Into (and Re-Cognition Of) the conditional self (and its Tacit Underlying Root-Feeling Of Relatedness Itself) Was Spontaneously Replaced By Tacit Awareness <u>As</u> The Transcendental (and Inherently Spiritual) Divine Self (or The Self-Existing and Self-Radiant Feeling Of Being, Itself—Which <u>Is</u> Consciousness Itself, or That Which Is Always Already The Case).

In (and Forever After) The Great Event Of My Re-Awakening To My Own Divine Self-Condition, It Is Obvious (and Self-Evident) To Me (and It Can, By Means Of My Now, and Forever Hereafter, Divinely Self-"Emerging" Blessing-Grace, Become Obvious and Self-Evident To You, and To All and all) That I <u>Am</u> The Self-Evidently Divine (or Self-Existing, and Self-Radiant, and Most Perfectly Heart-Felt) Reality and Person Of Being (Self-Existing and Self-Radiant As Self-Evidently Divine "Bright" Consciousness, Itself)—and That (<u>As Such</u>) I <u>Am</u> Inherently Love-Blissful and Divinely Free. Even More, It Is Obvious (and Self-Evident) To Me (and It Can, By Means Of My Now, and Forever Hereafter, Divinely Self-"Emerging" Blessing-Grace, Become Obvious and Self-Evident To You, and To All and all) That <u>all</u> conditional appearances Are Only Apparent Modifications Of <u>Me</u>—and That <u>No</u> Such Modifications Bind or Change <u>Me</u>.

After The Great Event Of My Divine Re-Awakening, conditional appearances Continued To arise, but Only As Merely Apparent (and Non-Binding, and Not At All Me-Changing) Modifications Of <u>Me</u>. As conditional appearances arose (and Were, <u>By Me</u>, Divinely and Inherently Self-Recognized <u>As Me</u>), The Self-Existing and Self-Radiant Power Of My Own (Self-Evidently Divine) Love-Bliss Pervaded them all—Thus and Thereby Divinely Transfiguring and Divinely Transforming them. Now, and Forever Hereafter, The Inherent (or Native) Feeling Of Being (Itself) Stands Free, <u>As Me</u>— Self-Existing, Self-Radiant, and Self-Evidently Divine (Even In The Midst Of <u>all</u> Apparent conditions).

Therefore, "Consider" This: Reality (Itself) is <u>Not</u> what You think. Thought is a merely Temporal abstraction (or A time-Consuming and time-Bound Contraction Of and From Reality Itself).

Likewise, "Consider" This: The Cosmic Universe (or Cosmic Nature, Itself) is <u>Not</u> what You perceive. Perception is a merely time-Consuming and time-Bound Temporal and Limited space-time event, Associated With a limited and temporary space-time point of view (or psycho-physical self-Contraction).

Altogether, "Consider" This: Reality Itself (and Cosmic Nature, Itself) <u>Is</u> What You <u>Are</u>—and <u>Not</u> what You think or perceive.

What You <u>Are</u> <u>Is</u> Reality Itself (and Cosmic Nature, Itself).

What You <u>Are</u> Is Obscured (and, Altogether, Diminished, Suppressed, and Hidden) By The Force and Effect Of Whole bodily (or Total psycho-physical) egoity (or self-Contraction).

What You <u>Are</u> Is Realized and Demonstrated By Means Of The Really and Truly ego-Transcending (and Constantly Counter-egoic) Devotional Recognition-Response To <u>Me</u> (Avatarically Self-Revealed To <u>You</u>).

The Transcending Of Your Own ego-"I" (or self-Contraction)—and, Thus and Thereby, The Transcending Of <u>all</u> Your limitations Of thought, perception, and space-time-Bondage—By Means Of The Devotional Recognition-Response To Me, Is The Necessary (and Only-By-Me Revealed and Given) Process Of Realizing That Which Is Always Already The Case.

That Which Is Always Already The Case <u>Is</u> Who I <u>Am</u>.

Only <u>I</u> <u>Am</u> What You <u>Are</u>.

Therefore, You Will Realize What (and Who) <u>You</u> <u>Are</u> Only If You Realize <u>Me</u> (By Means Of The Devotional Recognition-Response To Me).

Your thinking and perceiving person (or self-Contracted psycho-physical ego-"I") is <u>Not</u> (itself) Me.

I Am <u>Not</u> "Within" Your psycho-physical (or thinking and perceiving) Knot Of ego-"I".

I Am Always Already "Outside" (and Altogether Beyond) Your psycho-physical (or thinking and perceiving) Knot Of ego-"I".

I <u>Am</u> You Only When You Really (and, At Last, Most Perfectly) Transcend Your psycho-physical (or thinking and perceiving) Knot

Of ego-"I", By Means Of The ego-Transcending (and, Thus, thought-Transcending, and perception-Transcending, and, Altogether, point-of-view-Transcending and space-time-Transcending) Devotional Recognition-Response To Me (Avatarically Self-Revealed "Outside", and Altogether Beyond, Your psycho-physical, or thinking and perceiving, Knot Of ego-"I").

You <u>Are</u> What You <u>Are</u> Only When You Really (and, At Last, Most Perfectly) Realize <u>Me</u>.

I <u>Am</u> That Which <u>Is</u> Always Already The Case.

<u>Only</u> I <u>Am</u> That Which <u>Is</u> Always Already The Case.

<u>Only</u> I <u>Am</u> You.

Therefore, Now (and Forever Hereafter), <u>Always</u> "Consider" <u>Me</u>.

The Process Of My Divine Self-Realization (<u>As</u> That Which <u>Is</u> Always Already, and Divinely, The Case) Developed Through A Progress Of Unique and Extraordinary (and Self-Evidently Divine) Self-Revelations—Until My Divine Self-Realization Was Fully and Finally and Inherently Perfected, In The Great Event Of My Divine Re-Awakening. Immediately After That Great Event, My Avatarically Self-Manifested Divine Work (or Avatarically Self-Manifested Divine Play) As The Divine Heart-Master (and <u>Entirely</u> For The Sake Of The Most Perfect Divine Awakening Of <u>all</u> others) Spontaneously Began.

Suddenly (and Spontaneously), Many Extraordinary Siddhis (or Great "Bright" Divine Blessing-Powers) Appeared In Me—and, With Them, many Unusual Natural siddhis (or Uncommon psycho-physical Abilities and Processes). My Avatarically Self-Manifested Divine Work Of Self-Revelation and Teaching (and, Eventually, Of Divine Self-"Emergence") Began Spontaneously, and By These Many Divine Means.

Again and Again, In Vision, I Spontaneously Saw Vast Numbers Of My Future Listening Devotees, and Hearing Devotees, and Seeing Devotees. Originally, I Blessed and Taught them Simply By "Meditating" them, In Vision.[66] Eventually, and Because I "Meditated" them (and, Thus and Thereby, Called them) In Pre-Vision, Devotees Began To Come Into My Physical Company—and My Work With them Continued There, Equally Spontaneously. This Is

How I Began To Bless and Teach. And, Over time, By Observing and Responding To <u>Everything</u> That Was Required By those who Came To Me, I Became Spontaneously Heart-Moved To Serve them In A Lively, and Even Unconventional (or Divinely "Crazy", and Divinely "Heroic"), Manner.

In My Responsive Observation Of all those who Came To Me, I Realized That I Could (and, Indeed, That, For their Sake, It Would Be Necessary For Me To) Submit To their conditions Of Existence, Reflect them To themselves (In Order To Stimulate and Awaken their self-Understanding), and Gradually Draw them Out Of self-Bondage By Attracting them To My Avatarically Self-Revealed Transcendental, Inherently Spiritual, and Self-Evidently Divine Self-Condition. Therefore, I Did All Of That.

Within a year After The Great Event Of My Divine Re-Awakening, a small number of individuals Had Begun To Associate With Me On A Regular Basis, For The Sake Of ego-Transcending Practice In My Company. Their Commitment To The Great Process Was Weak. Their Qualifications Were Not Great. My Spontaneous and Divinely "Crazy" and Divinely "Heroic" Original Work Of Blessing and Teaching Had Barely Begun. Nevertheless, It Became Time To Openly Announce My Availability and To Completely (and Unreservedly) Embrace My Necessary (and, Necessarily, Divinely "Crazy", and Divinely "Heroic") Teaching-Work and Blessing-Work (or Avatarically Self-Manifested Divine Submission-Work) From The Heart. Therefore, On The Basis Of My Divinely Free Heart-Impulse (and No Great Reception In the world), I Began The Fierce Labor and The Humorous Love-Ordeal Of My Formal Work Of Avatarically Self-Revealed Divine Teaching, Avatarically Self-Transmitted Divine Blessing, and Avatarically Given Divine Self-Revelation.

That Divine Labor and Divine Love-Ordeal Was To Continue Until My Avatarically Full-Given Word Of Divine Self-Revelation and Divine Heart-Instruction Was Fully Generated, and The Necessary (First) physical Agents Of My Divine Blessing Were Empowered and Established, and The Original and Progressively Developing Institutional, Cultural, Community, and Missionary Means Of The Way Of Adidam (Which Is The Only-By-Me Revealed and Given Way Of The Heart) Were Called Into Being, and At Least A Good Number Of My Listening Devotees Were, By Devotional Listening, Entered Into The Foundation Practice Of The ego-Transcending Way Of The Heart.

My Twenty-Three Divine "Source-Texts" (and, Principally, My *Dawn Horse Testament*) Are The Evidence Of The Completion (and The Fullness) Of All Of My Avatarically Self-Manifested Divine Teaching-Work and All Of My Foundation-Work Of Avatarically Given Divine Self-Revelation.

My Twenty-Three Divine "Source-Texts" (and, Principally, My *Dawn Horse Testament*) Are My Summary Word Of Heart That Forever Speaks The ego-Transcending Way Of The Heart Itself (That Is Perfected and Perfectly Revealed In The Feeling-Contemplation Of My Avatarically-Born Bodily Human Divine Form, My Avatarically Self-Revealed Spiritual, and Always Blessing, Divine Presence, and My Avatarically Self-Revealed, and Very, and Transcendental, and Perfectly Subjective, and Inherently Spiritual, and Inherently egoless, and Inherently Perfect, and Self-Evidently Divine State).

In *The Dawn Horse Testament*, I Describe Each and All Of The Forms (and Each and All Of The Possible Developmental Stages) Of The Total Practice (and Of The Ultimate and Most Perfect Demonstration) Of The Only-By-Me Revealed and Given Way Of The Heart (or Way Of Adidam), Including The Entire and Progressive Process Of Potential "Reality Considerations",[67] and All The (Progressive) Potential Stages Of Life and Of Realization (Culminating In The Unique Demonstrations Necessarily Associated With Truly Divine Enlightenment), In The Way Of The Heart. Then (Now, and Forever Hereafter) I Am Merely Present, and Present As Constant Love and Blessing To all beings.

Therefore, I Am Most Attractive To All My Listening Devotees, and To All My Hearing Devotees, and To All My Seeing Devotees. And I Am Always Available For their Right and Free Regard Of My Divine Heart-Revelation, Which Right and Free Regard Is To Be Progressively Expressed Through Formal Meditation and Every Kind Of Auspicious Exercise Of The Heart. And All Of This Heart-Regard Of Me Becomes (Progressively, and Spontaneously, By

Means Of My Avatarically Self-Transmitted Divine Grace) Right and Free Regard (and ego-Transcending Realization) Of My Avatarically Self-Revealed Transcendental, Perfectly Subjective, Inherently Spiritual, Inherently egoless, Inherently Perfect, and Self-Evidently Divine Person and Self-Condition—The Divine Source-Condition (and Divine Self-Domain) In Which My Listening Devotee, My Hearing Devotee, and My Seeing Devotee Stand Eternally.

All Of My Work With those who (First, or Earliest) Came To Me, and Every Word That I Spoke (and Sometimes Also Wrote) For their Sake (and For The Sake Of all who Would Listen To Me, and Hear Me, and See Me, In The Course Of time), Was (and Is) A "Consideration" and An Elaboration (or A Detailing) and A Summarizing Of The Avatarically Self-Revealed Divine Word (and The Avatarically Self-Revealed Divine Way) Of The Heart (or Way of Adidam) That I Have Always and Consistently Offered, Even From The Very Beginning Of My Avataric Work As The Divine Heart-Master.

My Avatarically Self-Revealed Divine Teaching-Word Is <u>Essentially</u> Simple. I Say: Attend To <u>Me</u>—and (Thus and Thereby) Understand and Transcend Your self-Attending activity.

If any one Will Feel and Examine his or her (psycho-physical) state In any moment, Whether Under the worst Or Under the best Or Under the most ordinary of circumstances, he or she Will Surely Discover That There Is Always A Characteristic Feeling Of Stress, or Dis-ease, or A Motivating Sense Of Dilemma. Therefore, human life (Characteristically Felt As Such Stress, Dis-ease, or Dilemma) Is Also Always Characterized By Struggle, or A Generally Uninspected (and Never Finally Satisfied) Search For Release and Fulfillment.

The usual life Is Always Actively Involved (Whether Consciously Or Unconsciously) In This Motivated Search and This Native Distress. Therefore, every such a one Is Involved In ego-Based (or psycho-physically self-Contracted) Programs Of Seeking (Via desire, In all kinds of relations and circumstances).

My Avatarically Self-Revealed Divine Teaching-Word Is A Direct Address To The Distress and The Search Of each individual.

I Do Not Suggest A Way (or A Method) By Which To <u>Seek</u>. Instead, I Call the individual To Observe himself or herself, To Feel and Examine The Distress That Motivates the life Of Seeking itself.

Through The (Necessarily, Formal) Practice Of The Only-By-Me Revealed and Given Way Of The Heart (Really and Truly Engaged As Ruchira Avatara Bhakti Yoga—or Really ego-Surrendering, and Truly ego-Forgetting, and, More and More, ego-Transcending Feeling-Contemplation Of My Avatarically-Born Bodily Human Divine Form, My Avatarically Self-Revealed Spiritual, and Always Blessing, Divine Presence, and My Avatarically Self-Revealed, and Very, and Transcendental, and Perfectly Subjective, and Inherently Spiritual, and Inherently egoless, and Inherently Perfect, and Self-Evidently Divine State), and (In The Constant Context Of That Formal Practice Of Devotionally Me-Recognizing and Devotionally To-Me-Responding Feeling-Contemplation Of Me) Through Real "Consideration" Of My Avatarically Given Divine Heart-Confessions, My Avatarically Given Divine Teaching-Arguments, My Avatarically Given Fundamental "Great Questions", and The Leelas (or Stories) Of All My Avatarically Self-Manifested Divine Work (Whereby I Have Reflected individuals To themselves, and Blessed them To Awaken), individuals who Truly Devotionally Recognize Me, and Truly Devotionally Respond To Me, and (Altogether) Truly Are Devoted To Me, Can (By Means Of My Avatarically Self-Transmitted Divine Grace) Come To Understand (and Transcend) themselves—and, Ultimately, To Most Perfectly Realize Me (<u>As</u> Who and What they—and Everyone, and Everything—Really and Truly <u>Are</u>).

The Initial Process Of Listening To Me (To The Degree Of Hearing Me) Is One Of self-Observation (Truly Felt), Whether By The Primary Practice Of Devotion and Insight Or By The Primary Practice Of Devotion and Faith, Until That self-Observation Becomes A Crisis Of Most Fundamental self-Understanding.

At First (In The Listening Course Of The Only-By-Me Revealed and Given Way Of The Heart, or Way Of Adidam), the individual Becomes Acutely Aware Of his or her Habits Of Seeking, Desiring, Doubting, Believing, Manipulating, Betraying, and Always Returning To The Same Distress and Want. Then, As The Crisis Of Most

Fundamental self-Understanding Approaches, It Suddenly Becomes Clear That All Of That Is Being Motivated By A Constant Feeling Of Distress, Which Is The Result Of self-Contraction In The Face Of all relations and conditions.

This Discovery Is Most Profound. It Is As If a person In Pain Suddenly Discovers That he or she Is Pinching his or her own flesh. (And This Discovery Produces Immediate Relief, As Soon As The Pinching Ceases.) Therefore, As Soon As an individual Discovers That The Painful Search That Occupies his or her life Is Being Created By A Fundamental Feeling Of Distress, attention Is Free To Examine That Distress Itself. And When That Distress Is Directly (and Profoundly) Examined, It Is Discovered That It Is The Result Of A Chronic (and self-Induced) Contraction Of the body-mind, or, Most Simply, The Habitual (and, Ultimately, Always Voluntary and Un-Necessary) Avoidance (or psycho-physically self-Contracting Refusal) Of psycho-physical Relationship and psycho-physical Relatedness.

Every Apparent individual, thing, circumstance, or condition arises, survives, changes, and disappears Dependently (or Always Already Related) Within The Cosmic Universe (Which Is Continuous, Whole, and all-Containing). By Definition (and In Fact), There Is Not (Nor Can There Be) any Separate, self-Contained, Independent, or self-Sufficient conditional individual, thing, circumstance, or event. However, By Reaction To All Apparent Vulnerability, and, Otherwise, By Forgetting, or By Failing To Notice or Intuit The Whole (and The Inherently Perfect, Which Inherently Transcends Even The Whole), The Tendency Of every conditionally Manifested individual Is To Contract Into (Presumed) Separateness, or a self-Defended and self-Contracted emotional, mental, psychic, physical, and social state Of Isolation, Presumed Independence, and Dramatized Want. This Tendency Is Chronic In every one, and It Is Not Generally Even Inspected, Nor Is It (Even If Inspected) Most Fundamentally Understood. Therefore, every one Seeks. And All Seeking Is Inevitably Frustrated. The self-Contracting Habit (Itself) Is Not (and Cannot Ever Be) Transcended In (or By Means Of) The Search, Because The Search Is Itself The Dramatization Of The self-Contracting Habit Itself.

I Call every one To Feel and To Thoroughly Observe and To Transcend The Habit Of egoity. Eventually, any one who Truly (and, Necessarily, Formally) Listens To My Avatarically Self-Revealed Divine Teaching-Word and, By The Means I Have Given (and Always Give), Fully (and, Necessarily, Formally) Embraces The Divine Devotional Ordeal Of Feeling-Contemplation Of Me, and (Thereby) The Real Observation Of the ego-"I", Will (By Means Of My Avatarically Self-Transmitted Divine Grace) Surely (Truly, and Most Profoundly) Discover The Root Of Seeking and Suffering, Which Is the ego-"I" itself (or the psycho-physical self-Contraction, Which Is The Habit Of "Narcissus", or The Complex Avoidance Of Relationship).

When This Discovery Is (By Means Of My Avatarically Self-Transmitted Divine Grace) Truly and Fully Made and Felt (Relative, Summarily, To Every Aspect Of personal Existence), A Crisis Of Spontaneous (and Not Strategic) Release Is Enjoyed. And When It Is Truly (and Most Fundamentally) Understood That self-Contraction Is The Motivating Pain Of life, It Becomes Increasingly Possible (In every moment Of The Feeling-Contemplation Of My Avatarically-Born Bodily Human Divine Form, My Avatarically Self-Revealed Spiritual, and Always Blessing, Divine Presence, and My Avatarically Self-Revealed, and Very, and Transcendental, and Perfectly Subjective, and Inherently Spiritual, and Inherently ego-less, and Inherently Perfect, and Self-Evidently Divine State) To Enquire Into the self-Contraction ("Avoiding Relationship?") and (Thereby) Feel Beyond the self-Contraction—or, Otherwise, In The Manner Of The Devotional Way Of Faith, To Directly Feel Beyond the self-Contraction, and, Thus (Progressively, and Ultimately), To Enjoy A Native Sense Of Freedom (and Fullness Of Being). And Any Devotee Of Mine who (Necessarily, Formally) Practices The Total (or Full and Complete) Practice Of The Only-By-Me Revealed and Given Way Of The Heart, and who Has (Through Devotionally Me-Recognizing and Devotionally To-Me-Responsive Listening To Me) Thus Become Responsible (and Formally Accountable) For This Actively ego-Transcending (or Directly Counter-egoic) Feeling-Capability, Has Heard Me Truly.

The Total (or Full and Complete) Practice Of The Only-By-Me

Revealed and Given Way Of The Heart (or The ego-Transcending Practice Of The Inherently egoless Heart Itself) Is Begun Through The (Necessarily, Formal) Devotional Practice Of Listening To Me (or By Feeling-Contemplation Of My Avatarically-Born Bodily Human Divine, and All-Revealing, Form, and By Likewise Devotional "Consideration" Of My Avatarically Self-Revealed, and Always Me-Revealing, Divine Word and My Avatarically Self-Manifested, and Always Me-Revealing, Divine Leelas)—but The Only-By-Me Revealed and Given Way Of The Heart (or The ego-Transcending Practice Of The Inherently egoless Heart Itself) Becomes Directly Effective (or Effective In The Most Fundamental, or Directly ego-Transcending, Manner) Only With Real and True Hearing. Therefore, Listening To Me To The Point Of Hearing Me Is (Itself) The First Ordeal (or The First Stage Of Struggle With the ego-"I") In The Context Of The Only-By-Me Revealed and Given Way Of The Heart. And That First Ordeal Can Take a long time—Especially If The Devotional Impulse, The ego-Transcending Impulse, and The Great Intention Of the individual Are Weak.

There are <u>Three</u> <u>egos</u> (or Three Fundamental Modes Of egoity—or Of The self-Contraction-active psycho-physical Illusion Of Separate and Separative self-Consciousness). The Three Modes Of egoity (or Of the self-Contraction of <u>any</u> point of view, or ego-"I") Are the lower self (or gross ego), the higher self (or subtle ego), and the Root-self (or causal ego). These Three egos (or Modes Of The conditionally arising Illusion Of Separate self-Consciousness) Comprise the Total conditionally perceiving and conditionally knowing ego-"I". The <u>Total</u> (or Tripartite) ego-"I" Is Always Directly (and With Progressive Effectiveness) Transcended In The Right, True, and Full (or Complete) Formal Practice Of The Only-By-Me Revealed and Given Way Of The Heart (Which Is The Right, True, and Full Formal Practice Of Ruchira Avatara Bhakti Yoga, or The Totality Of Ruchira Avatara Hridaya-Siddha Yoga).

The First Of the Three egos (or Modes Of egoity, or Of self-Contraction) To Be Progressively Transcended In The Only-By-Me Revealed and Given Way Of The Heart is the <u>money-food-and-sex ego</u> (or the social, and, Altogether, gross-body-Based, personal-ity—or The <u>gross</u> Pattern and activity Of self-Contraction), which is the lower self, or the ego Of The First Three Stages Of Life.

The Second Of the Three egos (or Modes Of egoity, or Of self-Contraction) To Be Progressively Transcended In The Only-By-Me Revealed and Given Way Of The Heart is the <u>brain-mind</u> <u>ego</u> (or The brain-Based, and nervous-system-Based, mental, and perceptual, and, Altogether, subtle-body-Based Illusions Of "object" and "other"—or The <u>subtle</u> Pattern and activity Of self-Contraction), which is the higher self, or the ego Of The Fourth and The Fifth Stages Of Life.

The Third Of the Three egos (or Modes Of egoity, or Of self-Contraction) To Be Progressively Transcended In The Only-By-Me Revealed and Given Way Of The Heart is the <u>Root-ego</u> (or The Exclusively disembodied, and mindless, but Separate, and, Altogether, causal-body-Based self-Consciousness—or The <u>causal</u>, or Root-causative, Pattern and activity Of self-Contraction), which is attention <u>itself</u>, and which is the Root-self, or the ego Of The Sixth Stage Of Life.

By Means Of <u>Responsive</u> Relinquishment Of self-Contraction In <u>Me</u>, or <u>Really</u> and <u>Truly</u> ego-Surrendering, ego-Forgetting, and, More and More (and, At Last, Most Perfectly), ego-Transcending (or Always Directly self-Contraction-Transcending) Devotion To <u>Me</u> (and, Thus, By Means Of The Right, True, and Full Formal Practice Of Devotionally <u>Me</u>-Recognizing and Devotionally To-<u>Me</u>-Responding Ruchira Avatara Bhakti Yoga, or The Totality Of Ruchira Avatara Hridaya-Siddha Yoga), the Tripartite ego Of The First Six Stages Of Life (or The psycho-physical <u>Totality</u> Of the Three-part Hierarchically Patterned self-Contraction into Separate and Separative point of view) Is (Always Directly, and With Progressive, or Stage-By-Stage, Effectiveness) Transcended In <u>Me</u> (The Eternally Self-Existing, Infinitely Self-Radiant, Inherently egoless, Perfectly Subjective, Indivisibly One, Irreducibly Non-Separate, Self-Evidently Divine, and, Now, and Forever Hereafter, Avatarically Self-Revealed Self-Conscious Light Of Reality).

The Ultimate, Final, and Inherently Most Perfect (or Seventh Stage) Realization Of Me Requires—As A <u>Necessary</u> Prerequisite—An ego-Transcending (or Really and Truly and <u>Comprehensively</u> self-Contraction-Transcending) Great Ordeal. The Ultimate, Final,

244

and Inherently Most Perfect (or Seventh Stage) Realization Of Me Requires—As A <u>Necessary</u> Prerequisite—The <u>Comprehensive</u> By-Me-Revealed and By-Me-Given Sadhana (or The <u>Always</u> Directly ego-Transcending Right Practice Of Life) In The Total and Complete Formal Context Of The Only-By-Me Revealed and Given Way Of The Heart. And—As A <u>Necessary</u> Prerequisite To The Ultimate, Final, and Inherently Most Perfect (or Seventh Stage) Realization Of Me—The Particular Illusions That Are Unique To each of the Three egos (or Basic Modes Of egoity) each Require A Particular (and Most Profound) Mode Of The Necessary ego-Transcending (or self-Contraction-Transcending) Great Ordeal Of The By-Me-Revealed and By-Me-Given Formal Practice Of The Way Of The Heart In The Progressively Unfolding Context Of The First Six (and, Altogether, psycho-physically Pre-Patterned) Stages Of Life.

The Foundation Phase Of The Progressive ego-Transcending Great Ordeal Of The Only-By-Me Revealed and Given Way Of The Heart (or Way Of Adidam) Is The Devotional (and Relatively <u>Exoteric</u>, and Only In The Rudimentary Sense Spiritual) <u>Listening-Hearing</u> Process Of Progressively Transcending (and, In Due Course, <u>Most Fundamentally</u> Understanding) the <u>lower self</u> (or the <u>gross and social ego</u>—and The gross and social fear-sorrow-and-anger-Bondage That Is <u>Always</u> Associated With The <u>Inherently egoic</u>—or Thoroughly self-Contracted—Search To Absolutely Fulfill, and Even To "Utopianize", or To Perfectly and Permanently Satisfy, The <u>Inherently</u> conditional, limited, temporary, mortal, gross, and <u>Always</u> Changing life-Patterns Of "money, food, and sex").

Before The Foundation Phase (or First Phase) Of The ego-Transcending Great Ordeal Of The Way Of The Heart Can, Itself, Be Complete, It Must Realize A Profoundly life-Transforming and life-Reorienting "Positive Disillusionment"—or A Most Fundamental (and Really and Truly self-Contraction-Transcending) Acceptance Of The Fact That gross conditional Existence Is <u>Inherently</u> and <u>Necessarily</u> Unsatisfactory and Unperfectable (<u>and</u>, Therefore, A Most Fundamental—and Really and Truly Me-Finding and Search-Ending—Acceptance Of The Fact That <u>All</u> Seeking To Achieve Permanent and Complete gross Satisfaction Of Separate body, emotion, and mind Is <u>Inherently</u> and <u>Necessarily</u> Futile). Only On The Basis Of That <u>Necessary</u> Foundation-Realization Of "Positive Disillusionment" Can the energy and the attention of the entire body-mind (or Of The Total body-brain-mind Complex) Be Released From gross ego-Bondage (or self-Deluded Confinement To The psycho-physical Illusions Of gross self-Contraction).

The Characteristic Sign Of "Positive Disillusionment" Relative To The Permanent and Complete Satisfaction Of the lower self (or the Separate and Separative gross and social ego) Is The Foundation-Realization Of The Inherent Universal <u>Unity</u> (or All-and-all-Inclusive Interdependency, Essential Mutuality, and Common Causality) Of gross conditional (and Cosmic) Existence, Such That The Inherently Loveless (or Anti-Participatory and Non-Integrative) self-Contraction-Effort Of the gross Separate self Is Consistently Released (or To-<u>Me</u>-Responsively self-Surrendered) Into <u>Participatory</u> and <u>Integrative</u> Attitudes Of human, social, and Cosmic Unification (or <u>Love</u>-Connectedness) With all and All, and Into <u>Love</u>-Based (and Truly ego-Transcending) actions that Counter The Otherwise Separative (or Anti-Participatory and Non-Integrative) Tendencies Of the ego-"I". Thus, By Means Of Devotionally Me-Recognizing and Devotionally To-Me-Responding Relinquishment (or Participatory and Love-Based Transcending) Of psycho-physical self-Contraction (To The Degree Of "Positive Disillusionment" Relative To gross conditional experience and gross conditional knowledge), My True Devotee Is Released Toward The True Spiritual (and Not Merely gross, or Even At All conditional) Realization Of Reality and Truth (or <u>Real</u> God).

The Foundation-Realization Of "Positive Disillusionment" Requires Fundamental Release From The Confines Of the grossly Objectified (and grossly Absorbed) subject-object point of view (or Fundamental Release From The Inherently ego-Bound—or Thoroughly self-Contracted—Search Of Relatively <u>Externalized</u> mental and perceptual attention). And That Foundation-Realization Of "Positive Disillusionment" (and Restoration To The humanly, socially, and Cosmically Participatory, or Wholly Integrative, Disposition) Requires The Total (and Truly Devotional) Transformative Re-Orienting (and, Altogether, The Right Purification,

Steady Re-Balancing, and ego-Transcending life-Positive-Energizing) Of the entire body-mind (or The Total body-brain-mind Complex). Therefore, The Foundation (or gross) Phase Of The Progressive ego-Transcending Practice Of The Way Of The Heart <u>Necessarily</u> Requires <u>Much</u> time (and <u>Much</u> Seriousness, and <u>Much</u> Profundity)—and Even, Potentially, the <u>entire</u> lifetime Of <u>Only</u> That Foundation Practice May (In Many Cases) Be Required—In Order To Establish The Necessary (and <u>Truly</u> "Positively Disillusioned") Foundation Of True (and Truly In-<u>Me</u>-Surrendered) Hearing (or The Only-By-Me Revealed and Given Unique ego-Transcending Capability Of Most Fundamental self-Understanding).

The Middle Phase Of The Progressive ego-Transcending Great Ordeal Of The Only-By-Me Revealed and Given Way Of The Heart (or Way Of Adidam) Is The Preliminary (or Initial) <u>Esoteric</u> Devotional, and Truly Hearing (or Actively ego-Transcending, and, Thus, Always Directly self-Contraction-Transcending), and Really Seeing (or Actively, Directly, and Fully Responsibly Spiritual) Process Of Transcending the <u>higher</u> <u>self</u> (or the <u>subtle</u> and <u>mental</u> <u>ego</u>—or The Total subtle Dimension, or subtle Depth, Of self-Contraction—and <u>All</u> The conceptual and perceptual Illusions Of Inherently, and Necessarily, <u>brain-based</u> mind). Therefore, The Middle (or subtle) Phase Of The Progressive ego-Transcending Practice Of The Way Of The Heart Requires The Realization Of "Positive Disillusionment" Relative To The subtly Objectified (and subtly Absorbed) subject-object point of view (or Fundamental Release From The Inherently ego-Bound—or Thoroughly self-Contracted—Search Of Relatively <u>Internalized</u> mental and perceptual attention). This Degree Of The Realization Of "Positive Disillusionment" Requires Fundamental Release From The Inherently Illusory Search To Experience The conditional Dissolution Of the ego (and, In Particular, Release From subtle states of self-Contraction—and, Especially, From mental states of self-Contraction) By Means Of object-Oriented Absorptive Mysticism (or The Absorptive Yielding Of attention To The Apparent subtle objects that Are Either Originated By the brain-mind or, Otherwise, Mediated By the brain itself). And The

Characteristic Sign Of "Positive Disillusionment" Relative To The Permanent and Complete Satisfaction Of The object-Oriented Seeking Of the higher self (or Separate and Separative subtle and mental ego) Is The Fully <u>Me</u>-Hearing and Truly <u>Me</u>-Seeing Realization Of The Entirely <u>Spiritual</u> Nature Of Cosmic Existence (or, That Is To Say, The Realization That <u>all</u> natural and Cosmic forms and states Are Inherently Non-Separate, or Intrinsically Non-Dual, Modes Of Universally Pervasive <u>Energy</u>, or Of <u>Fundamental</u>, <u>Indivisible</u>, and <u>Irreducible</u> <u>Light</u>—or Of <u>Love-Bliss-Happiness</u> <u>Itself</u>).

The Final Phase Of The Progressive ego-Transcending Great Ordeal Of The Only-By-Me Revealed and Given Way Of The Heart (or Way Of Adidam) Is The Penultimate <u>Esoteric</u> Devotional, Spiritual, and <u>Transcendental</u> Hearing-<u>and</u>-Seeing Process Of Transcending the <u>Root-self</u> (or the <u>Root-and-causal</u> <u>ego</u>—or The causal, or Root-causative, Depth Of self-Contraction—which is attention <u>itself</u>, or The <u>Root</u>-Gesture Of Separateness, Relatedness, and "Difference"). Therefore, Immediately Preliminary To The Realization Associated With The Only-By-Me Revealed and Given Seventh Stage Of Life, The Final (or causal) Phase Of The Progressive ego-Transcending (or Comprehensively self-Contraction-Transcending) Practice Of The Way Of The Heart Requires The Realization Of "Positive Disillusionment" Relative To The causal (or Root-egoic, and, Therefore, Fundamental, or Original) subject-object Division In Consciousness (or Conscious Light) Itself. This Degree Of The Realization Of "Positive Disillusionment" Requires The Native Exercise Of Transcendental Self-Identification—Prior To the Root-self-Contraction that is point of view itself (or attention itself), and, Thus, Also, Prior To The Entire body-brain-mind Complex, or conditional Structure, Of conception and perception. And The Characteristic Sign Of "Positive Disillusionment" Relative To The Permanent and Complete Satisfaction Of the Root-self (or the Fundamental causative, or causal, ego) Is The Fundamental Transcending Of attention itself In The <u>Me</u>-"Locating" (and, Altogether, <u>Me</u>-Hearing and <u>Me</u>-Seeing) Realization Of The Transcendental (and Intrinsically Non-Separate and Non-Dual) Nature Of <u>Consciousness</u> <u>Itself</u>.

Only <u>After</u> (or In The Great Event Of Most Perfect, and, Necessarily, Formal and Fully Accountable, Fulfillment Of) The <u>Complete</u> Progressive ego-Transcending Great Ordeal Of The Only-By-Me Revealed and Given Way Of The Heart (or Way Of Adidam) In The <u>Total</u> (and Progressively Unfolded) Context Of The Inherently ego-Based First Six (or psycho-physically Pre-Patterned gross, subtle, and causal) Stages Of Life Is There The Truly Ultimate (or Seventh Stage, and Always Already Divinely Self-Realized—and, Thus, Inherently ego-Transcending) "Practice" Of The Only-By-Me Revealed and Given Way Of The Heart (or The Most Perfect, and Inherently egoless, or Always Already Most Perfectly, and Un-conditionally, self-Contraction-Transcending, and Divinely Love-Bliss-Full, and Only-By-Me Revealed and Given Seventh-Stage-Of-Life Demonstration Of Ruchira Avatara Bhakti Yoga, or Ruchira Avatara Hridaya-Siddha Yoga).

The Only-By-Me Revealed and Given Seventh-Stage-Of-Life "Practice" (or The Inherently egoless, and, Thus, Always Already Most Perfectly, and Un-conditionally, self-Contraction-Transcending, and, Altogether, Most Perfectly Divinely Self-Realized Demonstration) Of The Only-By-Me Revealed and Given Way Of The Heart Is The Great <u>Esoteric</u> Devotional, Spiritual, Transcendental, Self-Evidently Divine, and Most Perfectly <u>Me</u>-Hearing and <u>Me</u>-Seeing Demonstration Of All-and-all-Divinely-Self-<u>Recognizing</u> (and, <u>Thus</u>, All-and-all-Divinely-<u>Transcending</u>) Divine Self-Abiding (In and <u>As</u> My Avatarically Self-Revealed Divine "Bright" <u>Sphere</u> Of Self-Existing, Self-Radiant, Inherently egoless, Perfectly Subjective, and Inherently and Most Perfectly body-mind-Transcending, or body-brain-Transcending, or Inherently, Most Perfectly, and Un-conditionally psycho-physical-self-Contraction-Transcending, but Never Intentionally body-mind-Excluding, or body-brain-Excluding, Divine Person, or Eternal Self-Condition and Infinite State).

The Only-By-Me Revealed and Given Seventh-Stage-Of-Life Demonstration Of The Only-By-Me Revealed and Given Way Of The Heart Is The Un-conditional and Divinely Free (and Inherently egoless, or Inherently point-of-view-less) "Practice" (or Divinely Self-Realized Progressive Demonstration) Of Divine <u>Self</u>-Recognition Of The Simultaneous <u>Totality</u> Of the Apparent gross, subtle, <u>and</u>

causal body-brain-mind-self, or The Progressively All-and-all-Outshining Process Of The Simultaneous Divine Self-Recognition Of the Total psycho-physical ego-"I" itself (or Of the Total conditional point of view, or Apparent self-Contraction, itself). Therefore, The Only-By-Me Revealed and Given Seventh-Stage-Of-Life Demonstration Of The Only-By-Me Revealed and Given Way Of Heart Is The Inherent "Practice" (or Divinely Self-Realized Demonstration) Of Divine Self-Recognition Of point of view itself (or Of attention itself—or Of the conditionally Apparent subject, itself) and (Always Coincidently, or Simultaneously) Divine Self-Recognition Of the conception or perception Of Separateness, Relatedness, or "Difference" Itself (or Of any and every conditionally Apparent object, itself).

The Only-By-Me Revealed and Given Seventh-Stage-Of-Life Demonstration Of The Only-By-Me Revealed and Given Way Of The Heart Is The Most Perfect (or Un-conditional, Inherently egoless, and Self-Evidently Divine) Demonstration Of "Positive Disillusionment", or Of The Inherently Illusionless (or self-Contraction-Free, and, Inherently, All-and-all-Transcending) Realization Of The Fundamental Reality and Truth (or Real God)—Which Fundamental Reality and Truth (or Real God) Is The One and Indivisible and Self-Existing and Indestructible and Self-Radiant and Always Already Most Perfectly Non-Dual Conscious Light (or That Which Is Always Already The Case), and Which Reality and Truth (or Real God) Is That Self-Existing and Perfectly Subjective Self-"Brightness" (or Infinite and Absolute and Most Perfectly Non-Separate Self-Condition) Of Which The conditional (or gross, subtle, and causal) subject-object Illusions (or Total psycho-physical self-Contraction Illusions) Of conception, and Of perception, and Of The ego-"I" Presumption Are Mere, and Merely Apparent (or Non-Necessary, or Always Non-Ultimate), and Inherently Non-Binding Modifications. And The Characteristic Sign Of Most Perfectly Demonstrated (or Seventh Stage) "Positive Disillusionment" Relative To The Totality Of the Separate and Separative ego-"I" (or point of view) and its Presumptions Of a Separate (or Objectified) gross, subtle, and causal world Is The Self-Evidently Divine (and Intrinsically Non-Separate and Non-Dual) Realization Of Reality

(<u>Itself</u>) <u>As</u> Irreducible and Indivisible Conscious Light (Inherently Love-Bliss-Full, or Perfectly Subjectively "Bright").

Therefore, The Only-By-Me Revealed and Given Way Of The Heart Is—From The Beginning, <u>and</u> At Last—The Way Of "Positive Disillusionment".

The Only-By-Me Revealed and Given Way Of The Heart Is—From The Beginning, <u>and</u> At Last—The Way Of The Direct Transcending Of The Fact and The Consequences Of egoity (or Of psycho-physical self-Contraction).

The Only-By-Me Revealed and Given Way Of The Heart Is—From The Beginning, <u>and</u> At Last—The Way Of The Direct Transcending Of The Illusions Of Inherently egoic attention (or Of The conditionally Presumed subject-object Pattern Of conception and perception).

The Only-By-Me Revealed and Given Way Of The Heart Is—From The Beginning, <u>and</u> At Last—The Way Of The Direct Transcending Of The Total Illusory Pattern Of The Inherently egoic Presumption Of Separateness, Relatedness, and "Difference".

The Only-By-Me Revealed and Given Way Of The Heart Is—From The Beginning, <u>and</u> At Last—The Way Of The Direct Transcending Of The Always Simultaneous Illusions Of the Separate ego-"I" <u>and</u> the Separate (or Merely Objective) world.

The Only-By-Me Revealed and Given Way Of The Heart Is—From The Beginning, <u>and</u> At Last—The Way Of The Direct (or Inherently egoless <u>and</u> Inherently Illusionless) Realizing Of The One and Irreducible Conscious Light (or Perfectly Subjective "Brightness" Of Being) That <u>Is</u> Reality and Truth (or <u>Real</u> God).

The Only-By-Me Revealed and Given Way Of The Heart Is—From The Beginning, <u>and</u> At Last—The Way Of The Direct (or Inherently egoless <u>and</u> Inherently Illusionless) Realizing Of The Conscious Love-Bliss-Energy Of Totality.

The Only-By-Me Revealed and Given Way Of The Heart Is—From The Beginning, <u>and</u> At Last—The Way Of The Direct Realizing Of <u>Only</u> <u>Me</u>.

By My (Now, and Forever Hereafter) Avatarically Given (and Forever Hereafter Divinely Self-"Emerging") Sign (Of Form, and Presence, and State), and Through The Words Of My Twenty-Three

Divine "Source-Texts" (and, Principally, My *Dawn Horse Testament*), and Through All The Told Divine Play and Divine Words Of My Avataric Human-Time Of Divine Life and Divine Work, I Will <u>Always</u> Be The Divine Heart-Master In Relation To any one and every one who (By Formally Embracing The Total, or Full and Complete, Practice Of The Only-By-Me Revealed and Given Way Of The Heart) Enters Into This Listening Process That Becomes True Hearing Of Me. And This (Necessarily, Formal) Devotional Process Of Listening To Me and Hearing Me Must (By Means Of My Avatarically Self-Transmitted Divine Grace) Lead (Progressively) Toward True Seeing Of Me (or The Only-By-Me Spiritually Activated Life and Practice Of The Only-By-Me Revealed and Given Way Of The Heart)—but The Process Of Listening To Me and Hearing Me Is Not Itself A Necessarily (or, Otherwise, Fully) <u>Spiritual</u> Practice, Unless True Hearing Goes On To Do Its Work In The Seeing Context Of The Advanced and The Ultimate Stages Of Life In The Only-By-Me Revealed and Given Way Of The Heart. (And, Until There Is True Hearing Of Me, Listening To Me In The Only-By-Me Revealed and Given Way Of The Heart Is Itself The By-Me-Blessed, By-Me-Gifted, and By-Me-Inspired Struggle For self-Understanding, To Recapture The Direct Feeling-Capability For self-Transcendence.)

No one who Has Not Yet Heard Me and Seen Me Is Truly (and Effectively) Able To Practice What Can Be Practiced Only By those who Have Heard Me and Also Seen Me (or Come To Me By Means Of My Avatarically Self-Transmitted Divine Grace, Through Most Fundamental self-Understanding, and Through The Divine Spiritual Baptism[68] Granted By My Avatarically Self-Transmitted Divine Spiritual Presence).

In The Only-By-Me Revealed and Given Way Of The Heart (or Way Of Adidam), The Direct Self-Revelation Of Me (Functioning As The Divine Heart-Master, In Always present-time Direct Relationship To My Devotee) Is The Principal and Great Key To The Process Of Spiritual, Transcendental, and Divine Self-Realization. And I Am <u>Seen</u> In My Great Function (As The Divine Heart-Master, In Always present-time Direct Relationship To My Devotee) Only By those who Have Heard Me, Become Open-

252

Hearted To Me (Free Of The Motive Of self-Contraction In Relation To Me), and Received The Baptism (or Tangible Blessing) Of My Avatarically Self-Revealed Spiritual (and Always Blessing) Divine Presence Through Contemplative (and Truly Devotional, and, Thereby, Really ego-Transcending) Regard Of Me. Therefore, It Is Only By True and Effective Fulfillment Of The Beginner's Practice Of The Way Of The Heart (Whether Primarily By The Devotional Exercise Of Faith Or Primarily By The Devotional Exercise Of Insight—and, In Either Case, To The Degree Of Real, True, Stable, and Responsible Spiritual Awakening) That The Fullest (or Truly and Fully Spiritually Responsible) Relationship To Me As The Divine Heart-Master Is Realized.

My Great Avataric Statements Are Not merely public Announcements, Calling For casual (and merely public) belief. The Great Avataric Statements I Make Relative To My Inherently Perfect Work (As The Divine Heart-Master), My Divinely "Crazy" and Divinely "Heroic" Submission As Servant (Done In Order To Teach), My Divine Self-Nature (Realized Most Perfectly), and My Avatarically Self-Transmitted Divine Spiritual Presence <u>As</u> The Inherently egoless (and Self-Evidently Divine) Heart Itself Are (With All My Uncommon Speech) Divine Self-Confessions—Freely Given To all those who Listen To Me With The Heart, and To all those who Hear Me At The Heart, and To all those who See Me As I <u>Am</u>. Those Divine Self-Confessions Are Directly Obvious <u>As</u> Reality and Truth <u>Only</u> To The Inherently egoless Heart Itself—and To all those who Have Been Directly Awakened To That Obviousness By My Avataric Spiritual Self-Transmission Of The "Bright" Divine Self-Condition Of The One and Only Heart.

The body-mind Of Man Is Like A Seed, That Lies Asleep Within The Dark and Depth Of Earth's Unconsciousness. And I Am Like A Thunderstorm Of Fresh Down-Crashing Sound and Light, That Weathers Me Into The Earth-World With A Flood Of True and Living Water. And When The True Water Of My Love-Bliss-Presence Flows Deep Into the body-mind, The "Brightest" Sound and Shape Of Me Strikes Through The Germ Of Mankind's Seed within. It Is The Heart That Breaks By My Divine Invasion there. Its Germ Of Me-"Bright" Suddenness Un-Knots The Seed Of body-mind, When I Crash Down Into The Earthen Core. And When The Heart Un-Locks, the body-mind Becomes A Flower In The Tangible Garden Of My Divine Domain.

If The Heart Finds Me, The Heart Devotionally Recognizes Me (Inherently), and all the body-mind Devotionally Responds To Me (Immediately)—Whether By Means Of The Immediately To-Me-Responsive Devotional Exercise Of Me-Recognizing Faith Or The Immediately Me-Recognizing Devotional Exercise Of To-Me-Responsive Insight. Therefore, Your Heart Must Decide—Whether To Raise A Fist, and Throw A Rock, At The ego-Crushing Natural Universe, Or To Make A Flower Grow In The Garden Of Indestructible Light.

The Devotional Recognition-Response To Me Is The Divine Flowering Of the body-mind. Therefore, Your Heart Must Recognize Me and Choose Me—and Not merely believe Me—If I Am To "Brighten" You.

Faith Is A Flower, and Not a mind's idea, or a body's satisfaction. Likewise, The Insight That Flowers the body-mind Is Made Of Heart, and Not Of Seeker's Thrum Of thought, and thought's Abstract Invasion Of the body. No mere belief, or Mummery Of thinking mind, Can Make The Fist Of ego's Knot Un-Tie. And No Set Stage Of mere perception Can Outlast The Crushing Time Of merely Natural life. The Rock Of ego and The Fist Of self-Contracted body-mind Will Last a mere and Total lifetime—Whereas The Heart-Flower Breaks The Earth Above the head's Clay Crown, and Finds My "Bright" Beginning In An Eternal Field, Above the stars.

My Great Avataric (Divine and Spiritual) Invasion Of The Heart Becomes Effective Progressively. And It Becomes (or Can Become) Spiritually Effective Only In The Case Of those Of My (Necessarily, Formally Practicing) Listening Devotees who (Necessarily, As Practitioners Of The Total, or Full and Complete, Practice Of The Way Of The Heart) Hear Me (or Most Fundamentally Understand themselves, In Devotional Recognition-Response To My Avatarically Self-Revealed Divine Word and Person), and who (On That Basis) Become My By-Me-Spiritually-Awakened (and, By Means Of My Avatarically Self-Transmitted Divine Grace,

Spiritually Responsible), or Fully Me-Seeing, Devotees (Steadily Open-Hearted In Relation To My Avatarically Self-Transmitted Divine Spiritual Presence).

My Avatarically Self-Revealed (and Always Me-Revealing) Divine Word and The Great Opportunity To Practice The Way Of Adidam (Which is The Only-By-Me Revealed and Given Way Of The Heart) In (Necessarily, Formal) Devotional Relationship To Me Should Be Openly Communicated To <u>All</u> Mankind. And The First Call Is To <u>Listen</u> To Me. First Listen (and Respond At Heart) To Me (Present In The Form Of My Avatarically Self-Revealed Divine Word, My Avatarically Self-Manifested Divine Leelas, and My Avatarically Self-Manifested, and Divinely Self-Revelatory, and Divinely All-Giving, Divine Sign—Of Bodily Human Form, Spiritual Presence, and Perfectly Subjective, and Inherently ego-less, or Non-Separate, State)—and (In A Responsible and Progressively ego-Surrendering Manner) Begin The Counter-egoic Struggle With the conditional self, Whether (Primarily) By The Devotional Exercise Of Insight Or (Primarily) By The Devotional Exercise Of Faith. It Is Only When That Ordeal Has (In The Context Of The Total, or Full and Complete, Practice Of The Only-By-Me Revealed and Given Way Of The Heart) Become True Hearing and Then Real Seeing That any individual Is Called (and Enabled) To Demonstrate Full Responsibility For <u>Spiritual</u> Practice In Relation To Me As The Divine Heart-Master (Fully Encountered In My Spiritual Blessing-Function and, Ultimately, Truly and Fully "Located" <u>As</u> The Inherently egoless Heart Itself)—and, Thus, By A Progression Of Only-By-Me Revealed and Given Means, To (At Last) Most Perfectly Realize Transcendental (or Self-Existing) Divine Freedom and Self-Radiant (or Inherently Spiritual) and "Bright" Happiness, or The (Inherently Perfect) Truth That Neither Depends Upon Nor Can Ever Be Destroyed By conditional events.

My Work and My Struggle To, In <u>Every</u> <u>Detail</u>, Generate The Teaching Argument Of The Way Of The Heart Is (Now, and Forever Hereafter) Complete. Now, and Forever Hereafter, those who Would Practice The Only-By-Me Revealed and Given Way Of The Heart (or Way Of Adidam) Will, First, Seriously "Consider" My

Avatarically Self-Revealed (and Always Me-Revealing) Divine Word and My Avatarically Self-Manifested (and Always Me-Revealing) Divine Leelas, and (Based On their Devotional Recognition Of Me and their Devotional Response To Me) they Will (Necessarily, Formally) Practice True Devotion To Me (By Means Of ego-Surrendering, ego-Forgetting, and More and More ego-Transcending Feeling-Contemplation Of My Avatarically Self-Manifested, and Divinely Self-Revelatory, and Divinely All-Giving Sign—Of Form, and Presence, and State). Now, and Forever Hereafter, My Avatarically Self-Manifested Divine Work Is <u>Only</u> That Of My Standing Free, Divinely Self-"Emerging" In Perpetuity, Always Blessing <u>all</u> To Listen To Me, and To Hear Me, and To See Me (Where I Now, and Forever Hereafter, Stand). And <u>Only</u> those who Are Truly Heart-Moved To Practice The Great Devotional Ordeal Of Realizing Me In and By Means Of The Formal (and Altogether Right) Embrace Of The Total (or Full and Complete) Practice Of The Only-By-Me Revealed and Given Way Of The Heart (or Way Of Adidam) Can (In Due Course) Hear Me and (Then) See Me With, and At, and <u>As</u> The Heart.

<u>Only</u> The Only-By-Me Revealed and Given Way Of Adidam (Which Is The One and Only By-Me-Revealed and By-Me-Given Way Of The Heart) Completes and Most Perfectly Fulfills The Great Tradition Of Mankind. <u>Only</u> In The Only-By-Me Revealed and Given Way Of Adidam Is The Most Ultimate (or Inherently Most Perfect) Realization (and Seventh Stage Of Life) Revealed (and, In Due Course, Given). And, Therefore, <u>Only</u> In The Only-By-Me Revealed and Given Way Of Adidam Is There The Real Potential For (Most Ultimately) Utter (or Inherently Most Perfect) Transcendence Of the ego-"I" (or self-Contraction), which ego-"I" (or self-Contraction) is the one and constant limitation that Prevents The Most Ultimate (or Inherently Most Perfect) Realization Of Real God, or Truth, or Reality.

The Only-By-Me Revealed and Given Way Of Adidam Is The Unique Progressive Practice (or Ordeal) Of Real (and, Most Ultimately, Inherently Most Perfect) self-Transcendence (or Direct and Really Effective ego-Transcendence In The Context Of Even Every Stage Of Life). The Only-By-Me Revealed and Given Way Of

Adidam Is The <u>Unique</u>, <u>Complete</u>, and (Ultimately) <u>Perfect</u> Way (and Process) Of (Progressively) Spiritual, Transcendental, and (Most Ultimately) Divine (and Inherently Most Perfect) Self-Realization. And The Foundation Of The Only-By-Me Revealed and Given Way Of Adidam Is The Eternal, Ancient, and Always New Method Of The Siddhas—Which Is Devotional Communion With The Siddha-Guru, and Which Is The Unique Means Of Realizing Real God, or Truth, or Reality That Has Traditionally Been Granted By The Rare True Adept-Realizers Of Real God, or Truth, or Reality Who (In The Traditional Context Of The First Six Stages Of Life, and Each According To Their Particular Stage Of Awakening and Of Helping-Capability) Have, By Means Of The Unique Blessing-Method (or Transmission-Capability) Of The Siddhas, Directly (and By Directly and Really Effective Spiritual Blessing-Work) Transmitted The Traditional Revelations and Realizations Of Real God, or Truth, or Reality.

As I here (Now, and For all time) Confess and Declare To all and All, and As (Now, and Forever Hereafter, and every where) Confessed and Declared By All My Listening Devotees, and By All My Hearing Devotees, and By All My Seeing Devotees, I <u>Am</u> The Ruchira Avatar, The Da Avatar, The Love-Ananda Avatar, The Heart-Born, Eternal, True, and Divine Heart-Master, The Ruchira Siddha, The Maha-Jnana Siddha,[69] The Very and "Bright", Self-Given, and Inherently Most Perfect (or Seventh Stage) Realizer, Revealer, and Self-Revelation Of The True (and Inherently Perfect) Divine Person (Which <u>Is</u> The Self-Condition and Source-Condition Of All and all). On The Basis Of their Confession and Declaration Of Heart-Recognition Of Me (and Of To-Me-Responding Devotion To Me), and By Virtue Of My Avatarically Given Divine Self-Revelation (and Of Even All My Avatarically Given Divine Gifts To them), I Am The Hridaya-Samartha Sat-Guru (or Most Perfectly Heart-Revealing, and Always Directly, and Most Perfectly, Spiritually Effective, Maha-Jnana Siddha-Guru) Of all who Practice The Only-By-Me Revealed and Given Way Of Adidam. Therefore, From The Beginning, The Only-By-Me Revealed and Given Way Of Adidam (Whether In The Manner Of The Devotional Way Of Insight Or In The Manner Of The Devotional Way Of Faith) Is (In

The Manner Of The Eternal, Ancient, and Always New Method Of The Siddhas) The Absolutely Direct Way Of ego-Surrendering, ego-Forgetting, and (Ultimately, Inherently Most Perfectly) ego-Transcending Devotional Communion With My Avatarically-Born Bodily (Human) Divine Form, and With My Avatarically Self-Revealed Spiritual (and Always Blessing) Divine Presence, and With My Avatarically Self-Revealed (and Very, and Transcendental, and Perfectly Subjective, and Inherently Spiritual, and Inherently egoless, and Inherently Perfect, and Self-Evidently Divine) State, and (Thus, Altogether) With My Avatarically Self-Revealed and Always Me-Revealing Spiritual Person Of Self-Evidently Divine Reality and Truth.

After My Divine Re-Awakening, and, Thus, By Virtue Of My Re-Realization Of My Own Divine Self-Condition (and The Spontaneous Regeneration Of The Unique Siddhis, or "Bright" Divine Blessing Powers, That Spontaneously Accompanied My Divine Re-Awakening), I Made Myself Available To All Kinds Of Listening Devotees, For The Sake Of Divine Self-Realization In Every Case. During The Many Years I Functioned (By Submitting and Subordinating Myself To All and all) To Generate (here, and every where, In and Throughout The Entire Cosmic Domain) My Avatarically Self-Revealed (and Always Me-Revealing) Divine Word and Teaching-Argument, I Fully (and, Finally, Completely) Revealed and Communicated The Way Of The Heart (or Way Of Adidam), and, By All Of That, I Made Myself Forever Available As The Divine Heart-Master, To any one who (As My Formally Acknowledged Devotee) Listens To Me (or Even Hears Me), and To any one who (As My Formally Acknowledged Devotee), Having Heard Me, Receives Me, and Sees Me. Then, When My Teaching-Work Was Complete, I Retired From The Ordeal Of Teaching, In Order Simply (or Merely) To Be Present, and Thus, By (Constantly) Divinely Self-"Emerging" (here, and every where, In and Throughout The Entire Cosmic Domain), To Magnify My Divine Blessing To this world (and To all worlds).

Therefore, I Remain (Thus), Ever and Forever Now. And I Am (Thus, As I Am) To Remain (Forever) Most Perfectly Effective (Even After, and Forever After, The Avataric Physical Lifetime Of

My Bodily Human Divine Form). And (Even After, and Forever After, The Avataric Physical Lifetime Of My Bodily Human Divine Form) I Will Remain (Thus, and Inherently Most Perfectly, and Most Directly) Effective By Means Of The Continuous Work (or Always Me-Serving Instrumentality) Of My True (and Formally Acknowledged) Instruments, Which Instruments (or Unique Instrumental Means) Consist Of All My (At every then present-time) Formally Acknowledged and True and (Necessarily) Truly Seeing Devotees who Practice In The Ultimate Stages Of The Way Of The Heart As Formal Members Of The Ruchira Sannyasin Order Of The Tantric Renunciates Of Adidam, Which Formal Sannyasin Order Is Also Known, Simply, As The Ruchira Sannyasin Order, and Which Formal Sannyasin Order Is The Great Formal Renunciate Order Of My Uniquely Exemplary and Formally and Legally Established Fully Renunciate ("Ruchira Sannyasin") Devotees, All The Members Of Which Are (As A General Rule[70]) Engaged In The "Perfect Practice" (As A General Rule, Of The Technically "Fully Elaborated" Form) Of The Way Of The Heart, and who Are Called, By Me, To Demonstrate That "Perfect Practice" In The Context Of Perpetual Retreat, and, In General, By The Discipline Of Artful Seclusion From The Habitual Pattern Of conventional outward-directedness.[71] Likewise, and Most Especially (Even After, and Forever After, The Avataric Physical Lifetime Of My Bodily Human Divine Form), I Will Remain (Thus, and Inherently Most Perfectly, and Most Directly) Effective By Means Of The Continuous Work (or Always Me-Extending Agency) Of My True (and Formally Acknowledged) Agents, Which Agents (or Unique Means Of Agency) Consist Of My Avatarically Self-Revealed (and Always Me-Revealing) Divine Word, The By-Me-Formally-Empowered Ruchira Sannyasin Hermitage-Retreat Sanctuaries (and Even All The By-Me-Formally-Empowered Pilgrimage and Retreat Sanctuaries Of The Way Of Adidam), and My Formally Acknowledged "Living Murtis" (who, As My Avatarically Self-Transmitted Divine Grace Allows, Are, One In every then present-time, To Be Specially Chosen, According To My Given Instructions, Perhaps During, but Especially and Always After, and Forever After, The Avataric Physical Lifetime Of My Bodily Human Divine Form, From Among Those then present-time

Formal Members Of The Ruchira Sannyasin Order who Constitute My then present-time Living Formally Acknowledged "Bright" Gathering Of Fully Awakened "Ruchira Sannyasin" Devotees).

Therefore, Now and Forever, My Every Listening Devotee, and My Every Hearing Devotee, and My Every Seeing Devotee Will Be Given Appropriate Access To My Avatarically Self-Revealed Divine Word, My Avatarically Self-Manifested Divine Leelas, My Avatarically Given Divine Sign, and All My Avatarically Given Divine Blessings (As These Are Preserved, and, Otherwise, Transmitted, Within The Serving Culture Of All The Formally Acknowledged and True Instruments and Agents Of My Avatarically Self-Manifested Divine Work). In Each Such Case, Such Access Will Be Given In Accordance With My Devotee's Form and Developmental Stage Of The Real (and Total) Practice Of The Only-By-Me Revealed and Given Way Of Adidam, and The Realization (By Means Of My Avatarically Self-Transmitted Divine Grace) Of My Inherently egoless (and Self-Evidently Divine) Person (Which Is The Inherently Perfect Self-Condition Of All and all, and Which Is Also, or Inherently and Necessarily, The Inherently Perfect Source-Condition Of All and all) Will, In This Manner, Always Continue To Be Served By My Great Avatarically Self-Revealed Divine Means.

If any one Wonders How This Can Be So, Let him or her Study The Great Tradition Of The Realization Of Real God, and Truth, and Reality. Let every one who Will Study The Great Tradition Understand That—Although The Only-By-Me Revealed and Given Way Of The Heart (or Way Of Adidam) Is The New, Most Full, and Perfectly Complete Revelation Of Real God, and Truth, and Reality, Made Under (and Also Prior To, or Beyond) the circumstances arising During The Avataric Physical Lifetime Of My Now Speaking Bodily (Human) Divine Form—It Is Also (Most Simply) The Eternal and Ancient (and, Now, and Forever Hereafter, Complete) "Secret" Way That Is The Seed Of All Religions.

If any one Doubts That All This Can Be Real, Let him or her Simply "Consider" My Avatarically Self-Revealed Divine Word and My Avatarically Self-Manifested Divine Leelas, and Observe (and Feel) My Avatarically-Born Bodily (Human) Divine Form, Until The Reality Of The Devotionally Me-Recognizing and Devotionally

To-Me-Responding Way In My (Self-Evidently Divine) Blessing Company Is Authenticated By The Heart.

If any one Is Heart-Moved To Realize Me, Let him or her First Resort (Formally, and By Formal Heart-Vow) To Me, and (Thereby) Commence The Ordeal Of self-Observation, self-Understanding, and self-Transcendence (By Means Of Right Formal Practice Of All The Disciplines Required In The Total, or Full and Complete, Practice Of The Only-By-Me Revealed and Given Way Of The Heart).

If, By Means Of My Avatarically Self-Transmitted Divine Grace, any one Realizes My True Fullness In That First Ordeal (Whereby My Freely Given Gift Of Most Fundamental self-Understanding Opens the self-Contraction Of The Heart), Then Let him or her Go On (By Means Of My Avatarically Self-Transmitted Divine Grace) To Practice The Fully Spiritual (and, Necessarily, Ecstatic, or Inherently ego-Transcending) Stages Of The Total (or Full and Complete) Formal Practice Of The Way Of The Heart, Which Begins (As Such) When (By Means Of My Avatarically Self-Transmitted Divine Grace) My Avatarically Self-Transmitted Divine Spiritual Presence (That Washes and Forgives The Devotionally To-Me-Responding Heart In An Instant) Enters The Devotionally Me-Recognizing Heart Of My Devotee.

Therefore, Let all those who Listen To Me, and all those who Hear Me, and all those who See Me Pass, By Means Of My Avatarically Self-Transmitted Divine Grace, To and Through All The Necessary Stages Of Life, and Realize The Seventh (or Divinely Perfect) Stage Of Life.

Let every one else Be Happy. My Heart-Blessing Freely Goes To all—Whether Or Not they Are, At present, My Formally Practicing and True Devotees.

I <u>Am</u> The Self-Evidently (and Really, and Truly) Divine One I Have Declared Myself To Be.

I <u>Am</u> The Self-Evidently (and Really, and Truly) Divine One My Listening Devotees, My Hearing Devotees, and My Seeing Devotees Come (By Means Of My Avatarically Self-Revealing Divine Grace) To Know and (Openly) To Confess, Through Love's Revelation Of Love-Bliss In Devotional Satsang With Me.

Aham Da Asmi. Beloved, I <u>Am</u> Da. I <u>Am</u> The Inherently ego-less Divine and Real and True Heart. I <u>Am</u> (In My Any and Every conditional Form) The Avatarically Given Divine Self-Manifestation Of The Self-Evidently Divine Heart. And My Own conditional Avataric Self-Manifestation Is A Great Divine Pattern. And The Totality Of That Divine Pattern Of Mine Is The Way <u>To</u> The Divine Heart—and The Divine Way <u>Of</u> The Heart. Therefore, To Surrender, Forget, and Transcend the ego-"I" In Love's Distracted Communion With Me (and In Total, or Full and Complete, Conformity To Me) Is To Practice (and Become Conformed To) The Way (or Pattern) Of The Divine Heart, and, Ultimately (Via That Way, or Pattern, Of Me), To Realize The Divine Heart Itself—Which <u>Is</u> The One and Only Heart (Itself).

I <u>Am</u> The <u>One</u> and <u>Only</u> Man Of "Radical" Understanding, The Divine Heart-Master Of All My Listening Devotees and All My Hearing Devotees and All My Seeing Devotees.

I Am Always Already Spontaneously Present, or Heart-Born.

I Was Man-Born (or Made conditionally Apparent) By A Unique (Full, Free, and Un-conditional) Avataric Descent Of My Own Divine Spirit-Force, but, Even So, By The Same General Means (or In The Same General Manner) By Which I Submit (<u>As</u> The Self-Evidently Divine Person, Self-Condition, and Source-Condition) To Embrace and To <u>Be</u> each and every one Of Man.

Therefore, My Method Of Teaching Was, Likewise, To Identify With Mankind as It (Apparently) is, and To Submit To Embrace human beings (each and all) as they (Apparently) are.

As I Did This, I Constantly and Spontaneously Reflected each one To himself or herself—Thus To Awaken Real self-Observation, Most Fundamental self-Understanding, and The Free Capability For self-Transcendence In each one.

I Did This In Love (Freely, Openly, and Not limited by convention), and (Through The Recorded Documents Of My Avatarically Given Divine Word, and The Recorded Stories Of My Avatarically Self-Manifested Divine Leelas, and The Forever To-Be-Continued Representation Of My Avatarically-Born Bodily Human Divine Form, and The Forever To-Be-Continued Work Of My Now, and Forever Hereafter, Avatarically Given, and Always Me-

Revealing, Divine Spiritual Presence) I Will Always Do This In Love, Until My <u>Every</u> Listening Devotee Hears Me, and Fully Heart-Recognizes Me and Heart-Responds To Me In Love, and Fully Receives The Divine Spiritual Baptism Of My Mere Presence (or My Heart-Blessing That Avatarically Transmits The Spirit-Power Of My Divine Self-Revelation), and Freely (Fully) Embraces The Ordeal Of ego-Transcending and Real-God-Realizing (or Divine Self-Realizing) Practice Of The Total (or Full and Complete) Way Of The Heart (or Way Of Adidam).

I Am The First (and The Only One Necessary) To Work By Means Of Avataric Birth and Divine Self-Submission In The Domain Of "Western Culture"—but I Have Come here (To Earth, To Mankind, and Into The Total Cosmic Domain) For The Sake Of <u>all</u> beings.

I Have Come here To <u>Complete</u> The Divine Self-Revelation Of The Divine Way That (Ultimately) Most Perfectly Realizes Real God, and Truth, and Reality—So That Even all and All May Be Translated Into My "Bright" Divine Self-Domain.

In Order That The Field (or World-Circumstance) Of Divine Self-Revelation Would Become Complete, It Was Necessary For Me To Appear In The Domain Of (Heretofore) Avatarically Un-"Visited" (and Mostly Secular) "Western Culture"—but I Have Come For The Sake Of <u>all</u> beings.

Each and every one Is <u>My</u> Beloved.

Therefore, Because Of Love, I Serve You (and Will Forever Serve You) With Great Humor, Tolerance, Forgiveness, and Blessing Power.

And You Must Likewise Love Me, and Honor Me, and Feelingly Approach Me, and Serve Me, and (Ultimately) Most Fully Spiritually Commune With Me, As <u>Your</u> Beloved (and As <u>Your</u> Divine Heart-Master)—and You Must Constantly <u>Enlarge</u> Your Service To Me (Even In The Context Of Your Apparent relations with any and all conditionally Manifested beings), By Transcending (and Thereby Renouncing) The Habits and Reactions Of egoity (or self-Contraction).

The One and Entire Great Tradition (and <u>Total</u> World-Circumstance) Of <u>All</u> Mankind Is The Unique Circumstance Of My

Avataric Appearance and All My Avatarically Self-Manifested Divine Work.

Therefore—In Order That You May Rightly Honor and Understand Me—Observe Me Standing Free Forever In The Center Of The Great Tradition and World-Circumstance Of all and All.

Observe Me Standing Free Everywhere In The Great Tradition, In Every Historical Period. Observe My Likenesses In all times and places and cultures—but Know That My Avatarically Self-Revealed Divine Word, and All My Avatarically Self-Manifested Divine Work, Is <u>My</u> <u>Own</u>.

Observe Me Now, Standing Free Among All Those Who Served Me (Humanly and Spiritually) During The Years Of My Own Ordeal Of Divine Re-Awakening. Rightly Understand and Always Honor The Lineage Of Blessing In Which I Stand Blessed[72]—but Know That My Avatarically Self-Revealed Divine Word, and All My Avatarically Self-Manifested Divine Work, Is <u>My</u> <u>Own</u>.

My Avatarically Full-Given Divine Word, and The Extraordinary Play Of All My Avatarically Self-Manifested Divine Work, Is The One Great Divine Self-Revelation To Originate and Develop In The Domain Of "Western Culture" (and In The Total, or Complete, Context Of Mankind, Both "East" and "West")—but My Every Word, and All My Avatarically Self-Manifested Divine Work, Is Given For The Sake Of <u>all</u> beings.

My Avatarically Full-Given Divine Word, and The Extraordinary Play Of All My Avatarically Self-Manifested Divine Work, Is My Final (or Most Perfectly Completing) Divine Self-Revelation—and It Is Given For The Sake Of <u>all</u> beings.

Aham Da Asmi. Beloved, I <u>Am</u> Da, The "Bright" One, The Divine and Only Person, The Divine Heart Itself, The Only and Divine Self Of All and all, At Last Appearing In The "West"—and I Have Come For The Sake Of <u>all</u> beings.

I Have Come In Love-Response To a world that (In its "Late-Time", or "Dark Epoch"—Both "East" and "West") Had Lost The Essence Of The Great Tradition Of Spiritual and Transcendental Divine Self-Realization.

I Have Come To <u>Restore</u> and To <u>Complete</u> The Great Tradition Of The Wisdom-Way That Realizes Real God, and Truth, and Reality.

I Have Come To <u>Restore</u> and To <u>Complete</u> The Divine Way and The Divine Revelation Of Spiritual, Transcendental, and (Most Ultimately) Divine Self-Realization.

I <u>Am</u> The Last and Most Perfectly Completing Self-Revelation Of The One and Only Divine Person—The <u>Only</u> One Who <u>Is</u>.

My Every Word Is Given Freely—For The Sake Of All My Listening Devotees, and All My Hearing Devotees, and All My Devotees who See Me.

Therefore, My Every Word Is Given To every one who Is My Own—In Every Stage Of Life.

My Teaching-Revelation Of The Only-By-Me Revealed and Given Way Of The Heart (or Way Of Adidam) Is Not Defined, Characterized, or limited By The Ascetical Orientation—or The Strategic Effort To <u>Suppress</u> (and To <u>Withdraw</u> From) Apparently conditional (or phenomenal, or psycho-physical) Existence. Therefore, The Only-By-Me Revealed and Given Way Of The Heart Requires Not Strategic Asceticism, but The Total <u>Conversion</u> (or Devotionally Me-Recognizing, and Devotionally To-Me-Responding, Reorientation) Of conditional (or phenomenal, or psycho-physical) Existence. And The Most Perfect Fulfillment Of The Only-By-Me Revealed and Given Way Of The Heart Requires Not Strategic Asceticism (or Strategic Suppression Of, and Strategic Withdrawal From, the body-mind), but The Inherently Most Perfect Transcending Of <u>egoity</u> (or the Habit Of "Narcissus", Which Is the Chronic self-Contracting act, or Separative gesture, of the body-mind).

Now That My Avatarically Given Divine Teaching-Revelation Is Full and Complete, I Have (Now, and Forever Hereafter) Firmly and Finally Entered Into My Avataric Divine-"Emergence"-Work (Which Is The Ultimate, or Only-Blessing, Phase Of My All-Accomplishing, and, At Last, All-and-all-Translating, Work).

Now (and Forever Hereafter), I Am Merely Standing here (and every where)—To Bless and Awaken <u>all</u> beings, By Means Of The Merely Standing Blessing-Work Of My Freely Given and Avatarically Self-Revealed and Self-Evidently Divine Sign (Of Form, and Presence, and State).

Now, and Forever Hereafter—Because I Am No Longer Active In My Original Avataric Play Of Divine Teaching-Work and Divine

Self-Revelation-Work—all those who Turn To Me Must Come To self-Understanding Through (Necessarily, Formal, and Truly Devotionally Me-Recognizing, and Truly Devotionally To-Me-Responding) Feeling-Contemplation Of My (Now, and Forever Hereafter) Avatarically Given Divine Sign (Of Form, and Presence, and State), and (Necessarily, Formal) "Consideration" Of My Full-Given (Avatarically Self-Revealed, and Always Me-Revealing) Divine Word, and (Necessarily, Formal) "Consideration" Of The Storied Leelas Of My Avatarically Self-Manifested Divine Teaching-Work, and My Avatarically Self-Manifested Divine Revelation-Work, and My Avatarically Self-Manifested Divine Blessing-Work.

My (Formally Established and Formally Acknowledged) Community (or Total Gathering) Of Listening Devotees, Hearing Devotees, and Seeing Devotees (Which Community, or Total Gathering, Includes Even every individual who Is A Formally Acknowledged and True Practitioner In Any Of The Four Congregations Of The Only-By-Me Revealed and Given Way Of The Heart, or Way Of Adidam) Is Called (By Me) To (Always Appropriately) Grant Right and Formal Access To Me (In Person, and Also Via The Representations Of My Avatarically-Born Bodily Human Divine Form) and To (Always Appropriately) Grant Right and Formal Access To My Formally Acknowledged (and Always and Only Me-Revealing) Instruments and Formally Acknowledged (and Always and Only Me-Revealing) Agents—To all who, As Formal Practitioners In Any Of The Four Congregations Of The Only-By-Me Revealed and Given Way Of The Heart (or Way Of Adidam) Should and Must Enjoy Such Access (In Accordance With My Instructions, Full-Given, By Me, To The Ruchira Sannyasin Order).

My (Formally Established and Formally Acknowledged) Community (or Total Gathering Of Four Congregations) Of Listening Devotees, Hearing Devotees, and Seeing Devotees Is Called To Communicate, Advocate, and Confess (or Truly Confirm and Affirm) My Avatarically Self-Revealed (and Always Me-Revealing) Divine Word and My Avatarically Self-Manifested (and Always Me-Revealing) Divine Leelas To all who Would Listen To Me, and To all who Do Listen To Me, and To all who (Having Listened Well

To Me) Have Truly Heard Me, and To all who (Having Heard Me) Are Truly and Clearly Seeing Me.

My (Formally Established and Formally Acknowledged) Community (or Total Gathering) Of Listening Devotees, Hearing Devotees, and Seeing Devotees Is Called To Extend (or To Be The Extension Of) My Avatarically Given Divine Regard, Demand, and Help—To all who Would (and To all who Do) Listen To Me, and To all who Hear Me, and To all who See Me.

And My (Formally Established and Formally Acknowledged) Community (or Total Gathering) Of Listening Devotees, Hearing Devotees, and Seeing Devotees Is Called To Provide all who See Me (and Even all who, Having Heard Me, Have Become Truly Prepared To Contemplate My Avatarically Self-Revealed Spiritual, and Always Blessing, Divine Presence, and My Avatarically Self-Revealed, and Very, and Transcendental, and Perfectly Subjective, and Inherently Spiritual, and Inherently egoless, and Inherently Perfect, and Self-Evidently Divine State) With Appropriate (and Even Sacramental) Access To My Avatarically Self-Transmitted Divine Spiritual Presence, and, Otherwise, To Provide all who See Me (and Even all who, Having Heard Me, Have Become Truly Prepared To Contemplate My Avatarically Self-Revealed Spiritual, and Always Blessing, Divine Presence, and My Avatarically Self-Revealed, and Very, and Transcendental, and Perfectly Subjective, and Inherently Spiritual, and Inherently egoless, and Inherently Perfect, and Self-Evidently Divine State) With Appropriate Access To "Ruchira Sannyasin" Devotees (and To Sacred Places, and Other By-Me-Given Means) That Are Truly Empowered (and Formally Acknowledged, By Me, During The Avataric Physical Lifetime Of My Bodily Human Divine Form, or, After, and Forever After, The Avataric Physical Lifetime Of My Bodily Human Divine Form, By The Successive Gatherings Of Formally Acknowledged "Ruchira Sannyasin" Devotees Directly and Formally Extended From Those "Ruchira Sannyasin" Devotees Formally Established and Formally Acknowledged By Me During The Avataric Physical Lifetime Of My Bodily Human Divine Form) To Act As Instruments (or, In The Case Of By-Me-Empowered Places and Things, and, At any then present-time, In The Case Of One Specially Selected

"Ruchira Sannyasin" Devotee Awakened, and Uniquely Conformed To Me, In The Seventh Stage Of Life In The Way Of The Heart, Even To Act As Agents) Of The Transmission Of My Avatarically Self-Revealed Divine Word and Heart.

I Have Given and Called Upon Many Means For The Sake Of My Divine Self-Revelation To All and all.

Therefore, and By These Many Means, Identify Me, Feel (and Thereby Contemplate) Me, Realize Me (Most Ultimately) As I <u>Am</u>— and Do Not Ever Withdraw From <u>Me</u>.

I Will <u>Never</u> Withdraw From You.

<u>Always</u> Abide With Me In Faithful Love—Even From The Beginning Of Your Formal Vow Of Practice Of The Only-By-Me Revealed and Given Way Of The Heart (or Way Of Adidam).

And Always Be The <u>Champion</u> Of The Devotionally Me-Recognizing and Devotionally To-Me-Responding Practice That Is The Only-By-Me Revealed and Given Way Of The Heart (or Way Of Adidam).

Therefore, <u>All</u> My Listening Devotees, <u>All</u> My Hearing Devotees, and <u>All</u> My Seeing Devotees Should Be My "Bright" Advocates In this world.

The Transcendental (or Perfectly Unconditional), and Inherently Spiritual, and Self-Evidently Divine Self Of all (Who <u>Is</u> <u>As</u> all) <u>Is</u> Real God—The Source, The Substance, The Ultimate Condition, and The Very Being Of the conditional (or Separate) self of each and every conditionally Manifested being, and Of conditional Nature Itself.

The Only-By-Me Revealed and Given Way Of The Heart (or Way Of Adidam) Is (Via Its Real and Right Practice, and Only and Entirely By Means Of My Avatarically Self-Revealing Divine Grace) The True, Complete, and (Ultimately) Perfect Way To Realize and (By Means Of ego-Transcending Realization) To (Non-Separately) <u>Be</u> The "Bright" Spiritual, Transcendental, Perfectly Unconditional, Divine Self-Condition.

The Transcendental, Perfectly Subjective, Inherently Spiritual, Inherently egoless, Inherently Perfect, Perfectly Unconditional, and Self-Evidently Divine Self-Condition Is The <u>Only</u> Condition That <u>Is</u>.

All conditional appearances, all relations (and The Feeling Of Relatedness Itself), all others and Otherness, and All Separateness Of Presumed self Are Mere Apparitions, Made By Apparent Modification Of The Self-Existing, Self-Radiant, and Self-Evidently Divine Condition Of Being (Itself).

As Soon As The Awareness Of conditional Nature arises, The Divine Self-Condition May Also Experience The Illusion That It Is <u>Not</u> Itself—but That It Is a conditional self (or egoic body-mind) among others in a conditional world that it Cannot Account For.

From Then On, There Is The Struggle To Achieve ego-survival (Against opposition)—and To <u>Achieve</u> Joy.

If such an ego-"I" Encounters Me—The Avatarically Self-Revealed Divine Person (and The Avatarically Self-Revealed Divine Word) Of Reality and Truth (Who <u>Is</u>, Eternally, The One, and Only, and Self-Existing, and Self-Radiant Transcendental, Perfectly Subjective, Inherently Spiritual, Inherently egoless, Inherently Perfect, Perfectly Unconditional, and Self-Evidently Divine Self-Condition, In Divinely Self-Conscious Person)—Then The Way Of Divine Self-Realization Can Become Attractive, and A New (and Truly Divine) Way Of Life Is Possible. However, The Struggle As a conditional self (Even To The Degree Of The egoic self-Suppression Of The Heart's Inherent Devotional Recognition-Response To My Avatarically Given Divine Self-Revelation Of The Transcendental, Perfectly Subjective, Inherently Spiritual, Inherently egoless, Inherently Perfect, Perfectly Unconditional, and Self-Evidently Divine Self-Condition) Tends To Continue—Until The Heart <u>Truly</u> Listens To Me and (In Devotional Recognition-Response To Me) Opens (By Means Of My Avatarically Self-Transmitted Divine Grace) To The Only-By-Me Revealed and Given Way Of The Heart (or Way Of Adidam), Which Is The One and True and Altogether Complete Way That Always Devotionally Recognizes, and Always Devotionally Exercises, and (At Last) Most Perfectly Realizes The Inherently egoless Heart Itself.

The Transcendental, and Perfectly Subjective, and Inherently Spiritual, and Inherently egoless, and Inherently Perfect, and Perfectly Unconditional, and Self-Evidently Divine Self-Condition, Coincident With The Total Context Of conditional Nature, Is (It

Appears, In The Case Of every conditionally Manifested individual being) a conditional self (or Even A conditional Contraction In Relation To conditional Nature). In the egoic case, The Transcendental (and Inherently Spiritual) Divine Self Falsely Presumes Itself To Be limited and Threatened, and Associated With A Great Power and Multiplicity That Is Not The Transcendental (and Inherently Spiritual) Divine Self. Thus, The Transcendental (and Inherently Spiritual) Divine Self Feels Identified With a conditional body and a conditional mind, and the conditional body-mind Thus Functions Not Only As The Means For Perceiving (and Relating To) all that Is Not-Self (or Apparently Not The Transcendental, and Inherently Spiritual, Divine Self), but it Also Functions As The Seat Of Contraction From all that Is (Apparently) Not-Self.

The Only-By-Me Revealed and Given Way Of The Heart (Whether In The Manner Of The Devotional Way Of Insight Or In The Manner Of The Devotional Way Of Faith) Begins With The Process (or Ordeal) Of Listening—or A "Reality Consideration" Of the conditional self and How it Operates As self-Contraction.

In The Right Practice Of The Total (or Full and Complete) Practice Of The Only-By-Me Revealed and Given Way Of The Heart, This True Listening Becomes True Hearing—or Most Fundamental self-Understanding, Operative As The Free Capability For ego-Transcendence.

When (By Means Of My Avatarically Self-Transmitted Divine Grace) Sympathy With the self-Contraction Has Fully Relaxed By These Means, The Beginner's Original (or Foundation) Feeling-Motive Toward ego-Transcendence Is Uniquely Magnified and Activated, Such That It Becomes A Directly and Comprehensively Effective Impulse.

When That Impulse Has (Thus) Become Really (Directly, and Comprehensively) Effective, The Same Feeling-Motive, or Open Heart, Goes On To The Next Developmental Stage Of The Only-By-Me Revealed and Given Way Of The Heart—Which Is Seeing, or Heart-Attraction (and Spiritually Activated Heart-Response) To My Avatarically Self-Revealed Spiritual (and Spirit-Baptizing) Divine Presence.

This Spiritual Heart-Response (or Spiritually Activated, and Truly Devotionally Me-Recognizing, Devotion To Me) Permits An In-Filling With My Avatarically Self-Transmitted Divine Spirit-Energy (or Divine Self-Radiance).

And That Divine Spiritual In-Filling (or <u>Constant</u> Spiritual Baptism, By Me) Permits The Fully Devotionally Me-Recognizing and Fully Devotionally To-Me-Responsive Practice Of The Way Of The Heart—Such That, By Progressive Stages, The Theatre Of egoity Is Out-Grown (Most Ultimately, In The Fullness Of Divine, and Inherently Most Perfect, Self-Realization).

Most Ultimately, When (In The Progressive Course Of The Total, or Full and Complete, Practice Of The Only-By-Me Revealed and Given Way Of The Heart, or Way Of Adidam) My Avatarically Self-Revealed Transcendental, Perfectly Subjective, Inherently Spiritual, Inherently egoless, Inherently Perfect, and Self-Evidently Divine Self-Position Is (By Means Of My Avatarically Self-Revealing Divine Grace) Inherently Most Perfectly Realized and Assumed—conditional Nature, conditional others, conditional body, conditional mind, and conditional self Are Inherently Most Perfectly Transcended In My Avatarically Self-Revealed Transcendental (or Self-Existing, and Perfectly Unconditional), and Perfectly Subjective, and Inherently Spiritual (or Self-Radiant), and Inherently egoless, and Inherently Perfect, and Self-Evidently Divine Self-Condition.

Thus (By Means Of My Avatarically Self-Transmitted Divine Grace), It Is <u>Realized</u>. There Is <u>Only</u> The Transcendental (and Perfectly Subjective, and Inherently Spiritual, and Inherently egoless, and Inherently Perfect, and Perfectly Unconditional, and Self-Evidently Divine) Self-Condition—and The Not-Self (or All Apparent Separateness and "Difference") Is An <u>Illusion</u> (or An Illusory, or Transparent, or Merely Apparent, and Un-Necessary, and Inherently Non-Binding, conditional Play Upon The Transcendental, Perfectly Subjective, Inherently Spiritual, Inherently egoless, Inherently Perfect, Perfectly Unconditional, and Self-Evidently Divine Self-Condition).

Thus (By Means Of My Avatarically Self-Transmitted Divine Grace), It Is <u>Realized</u>. There Is <u>Only</u> My Divine Love-Bliss—

Self-Existing and Self-Radiant. And—By Merely Self-Abiding In The ego-Transcending (or Non-Separate, and Non-"Different") Realization Of My Divine Self-Condition—The Deluding, Binding, and Joy-Suppressing Power Of conditional Existence Is Transcended.

III.

Divine Enlightenment, Divine Self-Realization, Most Perfect (Free, "Bright", and Self-Evidently Divine) Awakeness, or Most Perfect (and Most Perfectly ego-Transcending) Spiritual and Transcendental Real-God-Realization, Is The Most Perfect Understanding and Transcendence Of Identification With The Act Of self-Contraction.

Divine Enlightenment, Divine Self-Realization, Most Perfect (Free, "Bright", and Self-Evidently Divine) Awakeness, or Most Perfect (and Most Perfectly ego-Transcending) Spiritual and Transcendental Real-God-Realization, Is The Most Perfect Understanding and Transcendence Of Identification With The Urge Toward Separation and conditional Independence.

Divine Enlightenment, Divine Self-Realization, Most Perfect (Free, "Bright", and Self-Evidently Divine) Awakeness, or Most Perfect (and Most Perfectly ego-Transcending) Spiritual and Transcendental Real-God-Realization, Is The Most Perfect Understanding and Transcendence Of Identification With The Motive Of Introversion, Inward-Directedness (or Inwardness), and Internal (or Internalized) Relatedness.

Divine Enlightenment, Divine Self-Realization, Most Perfect (Free, "Bright", and Self-Evidently Divine) Awakeness, or Most Perfect (and Most Perfectly ego-Transcending) Spiritual and Transcendental Real-God-Realization, Is The Most Perfect Understanding and Transcendence Of Identification With The Motive Of Extroversion, Outward-Directedness, and External (or Externalized) Relatedness.

Divine Enlightenment, Divine Self-Realization, Most Perfect (Free, "Bright", and Self-Evidently Divine) Awakeness, or Most Perfect (and Most Perfectly ego-Transcending) Spiritual and

Transcendental Real-God-Realization, Is The Most Perfect Understanding and Transcendence Of Identification With The Feeling (and The Illusion) Of Relatedness Itself.

Most Ultimately (or Most Simply), Divine Enlightenment, Divine Self-Realization, Most Perfect (Free, "Bright", and Self-Evidently Divine) Awakeness, or Most Perfect (and Most Perfectly ego-Transcending) Spiritual and Transcendental Real-God-Realization, Is The Most Perfect Understanding and Transcendence Of The (Even Most Tacit) Feeling Of "Difference" Itself.

Divine Enlightenment, Divine Self-Realization, Most Perfect (Free, "Bright", and Self-Evidently Divine) Awakeness, or Most Perfect (and Most Perfectly ego-Transcending) Spiritual and Transcendental Real-God-Realization, Is Native, Most Perfect, Effortless, and Free Identification With Mere (or Inherent, and Natively Felt) Being (or Self-Existence), The Only One Who <u>Is</u>, Consciousness Itself—Self-Radiant, All Love-Bliss-"Brightness" Itself, Inherently Without Obstruction, Always Already Infinitely Expanded (Beyond All Apparent Modifications, or Illusory Contractions, Of Itself).

Egoity (or Identification With the ego-"I") Is The Effective Negation (or Tacit Non-Presumption) Of Divine Enlightenment, Divine Self-Realization, or Inherently Most Perfect (Free, "Bright", and Self-Evidently Divine) Awakeness.

Egoity (or Identification With the ego-"I") Is The Absence (and The Effective Denial) Of Divine (or Inherently Most Perfect, and Utterly, and Inherently Most Perfectly, ego-Transcending) Self-Realization.

The Principal Symptom (or Indicator) Of egoity (or Of Identification With the ego-"I") Is Not the Apparent experiencing of conditionally arising "things" (or of psycho-physical phenomena and states)—Such That The <u>Fact</u> Of the experiential arising of "things" (or of psycho-physical phenomena and states) Is, As A Principal Means Toward The Real Transcending Of egoity itself, To Be Presumed To Be A Problem (or Even <u>The</u> Problem), Requiring (As A Solution) The Search To Avoid (or To Exclude, or To Be Separated From) any or all "things" (or any or all psycho-physical phenomena and states). Rather, The Principal Symptom (or Indicator) Of egoity (or Of Identification With the ego-"I") Is <u>The</u> <u>Failure</u> <u>To</u> <u>Divinely</u> <u>Self-Recognize</u> <u>any</u> <u>and</u> <u>all</u> <u>experientially</u> <u>arising</u> <u>"things"</u> (or any and all psycho-physical phenomena and states)—and, Thus, <u>The</u> <u>Failure</u> (<u>and</u>, <u>Indeed</u>, <u>The</u> <u>Inability</u>) <u>To</u> <u>Divinely</u> <u>Self-Recognize</u> <u>them</u> <u>In</u> <u>Reality</u>, <u>In</u> <u>Truth</u>, <u>and</u> <u>In</u> <u>Real</u> <u>God</u>. Therefore, Real and True (and Inherently Most Perfect) Divine Enlightenment, Divine Awakeness, or Inherently Most Perfectly ego-Transcending Divine Self-Realization (or Real-God-Realization) Is Not Characterized By experiential (and Strategically Achieved) Separation From any or all conditionally arising "things" (or any or all psycho-physical phenomena and states), but By <u>The</u> <u>Always</u> <u>Immediate</u> (<u>and</u> <u>Inherent</u>) <u>Divine</u> <u>Self-Recognition</u> <u>Of</u> <u>any</u> <u>and</u> <u>all</u> <u>experientially</u> <u>arising</u> <u>"things"</u> (or any and all psycho-physical phenomena and states)—and, Thus, <u>The</u> <u>Always</u> <u>Already</u> <u>Effective</u> <u>Ability</u> <u>To</u> <u>Divinely</u> <u>Self-Recognize</u> <u>them</u> <u>In</u> <u>Reality</u>, <u>In</u> <u>Truth</u>, <u>and</u> <u>In</u> <u>Real</u> <u>God</u>.

Egoity (or Identification With the ego-"I") Is (itself) The psycho-physical Act Of self-Contraction.

Once It Is Assumed (and Until It Is Most Perfectly Transcended), The Act Of self-Contraction Is Habitual (or Chronic). It Is Always Pain (or Suffering). It Is The Root Of All Seeking. It Is The Motivator Of all activity that Seeks Either To Fulfill Or (merely) To Separate From the conditional self (Or, merely, To experience a feeling Of Release and Relief as the conditional self). The action that is self-Contraction is <u>all</u> activity that Is Not Directly Counter-egoic (or Effectively ego-Transcending). Indeed, self-Contraction is Even <u>all</u> conditional activity (or conditional activity itself), or All Non-Transcendence Of the conditional self.

The Act Of self-Contraction Is Simply The Tendency To Identify With a conditional (or limited) state Of Existence. Until The Awakening Of Transcendental, Inherently Spiritual, and Self-Evidently Divine Self-Realization, the self-Contraction (or the conditional state Identified As the psycho-physical self-condition In any moment) Is what Is Called "I" In any moment. Thus, the "I" Is Not The Same In every moment. It Is Unique In every moment. Only The Name ("I") Is The Same (As A Matter Of convention).

If conditions arise, There Is No Necessity For Consciousness

To Identify With them (in and of themselves) or To Become Bound By them. There Is Only A <u>Tendency</u> To Do So (Based On An Unconsciously Acquired Habit Of Identification With the body that is Apparently experienced from the time of birth). Once Consciousness Identifies With the body, The Sense Of Differentiated (Separate, or Separated—and Vulnerable, or Mortal) being arises. Then The Struggle To Survive and To Achieve Either pleasurable Fulfillment Or Release From pain Develops Perpetually. That Struggle Is Expressed Through desire, and The Struggle Lasts Until death. Indeed—Once Established, and Not Yet Transcended— The Struggle Continues, Via subtle and causal Mechanisms, Even After the death of the present body.

Traditional Exoteric and Esoteric Religious Teachings Prescribe Means For Either (Strategically) Escaping Or Ultimately Fulfilling This conditionally self-Motivated Existence, By Extending Growth Within and Beyond The First Three Stages Of Life.

Thus, The Traditional ("Original" and "Basic") Fourth Stage Teachings Speak To the ego-self as a body-mind—and They Call For self-Purification and self-Transcendence (or Else Ultimate self-Fulfillment) Via The Practices Of Devotional Service (or functional, practical, and relational ego-Surrender), and Via Devotional Love (or internal and subjective ego-Surrender), In Relation To The Divine Being, and Via Real-God-Centered Love In Relation To all conditionally Manifested beings.

The Traditional Fifth Stage Teachings (and The Traditional "Advanced" Fourth Stage Teachings) Speak To the ego-self as mind—and They Call For self-Transcendence (or Else Ultimate self-Fulfillment) Through Ascended Gnosis (or The Ascent To Divine, or Super-Cosmic, Knowledge Via The Practice Of Concentration Of mind In The Divine As Universal Mind), and Via The Practice Of Ascent To High Gnosis Via The Redirection (or conditional Ascent) Of the bodily Manifested energies Of Cosmic Nature (or, In Some Traditions, Via The conditional Ascent Of The True Divine Spirit-Current).

The Traditional Sixth Stage Teachings Speak To the ego-self As individual (or personal) and Separate Consciousness—and They Call For self-Transcendence (and, In Some Cases, Even For A Kind

Of Ultimate self-Fulfillment) Through Transcendental Self-Awakening, Generally Via The Practice Of The Inversion Of attention (Away From conditional objects, and Toward The Constant, or Underlying, Subjective Reality—Which Is Consciousness Itself).

By Means Of My Avatarically Self-Revealed Divine Word, You (and Even every Apparently conditional, or conditionally Manifested, being) Are (From The Beginning) Addressed As The Self-Existing (or Transcendental) and Self-Radiant (or Inherently Spiritual) Divine Being, but You (In Your Identification With the self-Contraction) Claim To Be limited and Bound. Therefore, I Call You To Observe and Understand and Transcend That Claim.

Simply Notice That Your life Of Seeking (or desire) Is A Fruitless (or Unending) Pursuit Of Happiness, Through Either The Fulfillment Of the ego-self Or The Relief Of the ego-self (From experienced pain). That Search Is Occurring Because You Habitually Presume A State Of Identification With what is arising conditionally (Beginning With the gross body in the waking state). If You Did Not Make That Presumption, You Would Simply Abide As Self-Existing and Self-Radiant and Perfectly Subjective Divine Being—Which <u>Is</u> Free Consciousness, and Free Love-Bliss (or Inherent Happiness).

Therefore, Be My True Devotee. Formally and Truly Embrace The Full and Complete Practice Of The Only-By-Me Revealed and Given Way Of Adidam (Which Is The One and Only By-Me-Revealed and By-Me-Given Way Of The Heart). In This Manner, and Only and Entirely By Means Of My Avatarically Self-Transmitted Divine Grace, Notice the acts of the body-mind-self In every moment. As Your Earliest self-Understanding Grows By This Real (and Really self-Disciplined) Process Of self-Observation, Make Ever-Greater Use Of Right (By Me Revealed and Given) self-Discipline, In Order To Serve (or Otherwise Express) This Noticing and The Total (Counter-egoic) Process Of (Eventually, Most Fundamental) self-Understanding and (Progressive) Real self-Transcendence. Do This In The Right, True, and Full Devotional Manner (Not merely self-Concerned—but <u>Responsively</u>, By Means Of Heart-Attracted Devotional Recognition-Response To Me)—and (Thus and Thereby) Grow The Heart, By Surrendering The Heart To Me (The Avataric Self-Revelation Of The Transcendental,

Inherently Spiritual, and Self-Evidently Divine Self-Condition and Source-Condition That <u>Is</u> Real God, and Truth, and Reality). If You Do All Of This, The Basic Processes Of The First Six Stages Of Life Will (By Means Of My Avatarically Self-Transmitted Divine Grace) Tend To Develop (Spontaneously, and Progressively, and In The Specific Manner Necessary For You), but (In The Effective Practice Of The Way Of The Heart) Even All Those Processes Will Themselves (By Means Of My Avatarically Self-Transmitted Divine Grace) Be Really Transcended (In The Sudden and Constant Transcending Of Separate and Separative self In Me).

In The Only-By-Me Revealed and Given Way Of The Heart (or Way Of Adidam), The Processes Engaged In Association With The First Five Stages Of Life Progressively Grant Most Fundamental self-Understanding and True Heart-Communion With Me, Until The Gesture Of Identification With conditional states (Beginning With the gross body, or born body) Is No Longer A Mere Automaticity. Instead, It Is Realized That There Is Never Real Identification With conditional states. Conditional states Can Only Be Witnessed. <u>You Cannot Really Become</u> any conditional state (Although You Can Falsely Presume Such). You Are Always Already In The Position Of Consciousness Itself (and You Are, Thus, Always Already Identical To The Transcendental, Perfectly Subjective, Inherently Spiritual, Inherently egoless, Inherently Perfect, and Self-Evidently Divine Self-Condition, and Source-Condition, Of Existence).

Thus, The Final Events Of The Only-By-Me Revealed and Given Way Of The Heart (In The Context Of The Sixth and The Seventh Stages Of Life) Are A Matter Of This Inherently Perfect Realization, Via By-My-Avataric-Divine-Grace-Given Native Identification With The Position Of Consciousness (Rather Than Identification With any conditional objects), and Via By-My-Avataric-Divine-Grace-Given Deep Feeling-Contemplation Of (and Native, or Inherent, and Inherently Perfect, Identification With) Inherently objectless Consciousness (or The Inherent and Perfectly Subjective Feeling Of Being) Itself—Until all objects and conditions Become Inherently (and Divinely) Self-Recognizable (As Only My Avatarically Self-Revealed, and Self-Existing, or

Transcendental, and Self-Radiant, or Inherently Spiritual, and Self-Evidently Divine Self-Condition), and Until all objects and conditions Are (Thus) Removed Of All Necessity and All Binding Capability. Thereafter, In The Context Of The Only-By-Me Revealed and Given Seventh Stage Of Life In The Way Of The Heart, The "Practice" (or Divinely Self-Realized Demonstration) Is Simply A Matter Of Abiding (or Shining) In and As The Infinite Space (or Self-Domain) Of Divinely Self-Existing Consciousness and Divinely Self-Radiant Love-Bliss, Until all conditional limitations Are Outshined (Beyond All Noticing) In My Divine Self-Domain (Which Is The Domain Of No-"Difference").

The act of attention is The conditional Essence Of mind. The act of attention arises Spontaneously, Like the Total body-mind and the Total world, in every moment Of (Apparent) conditional Awareness. The act of attention arises toward others, objects, and conditions of every kind—whether subtle (or mental) or gross (or physical). The arising of the act of attention is, Simply, the arising of the psycho-physical (or conditional) self and all others, objects, and conditions. And If what arises Is Presumed To Be Real, or Necessary, or Desirable, or Unavoidable, or Undesirable, or Avoidable—Then the act of attention Becomes conditioned Toward (or Habitually and Repetitively Fixed Upon) what arises. In This Manner, Not Only Does the act of attention Become Bound To Specific conditional others, objects, and conditions (including the personal body-mind, or conditional self), but The Inherently Free (and Inherently Spiritual, or Love-Blissful) Transcendental Divine Self (or Being, or Consciousness) Apparently Becomes Associated With (or Apparently Becomes Persuaded By) The Illusion Of Its Own Bondage.

The conditional Essence Of That conditional Illusion Is the act of attention.

Therefore, The Only-By-Me Revealed and Given Way Of Adidam (or The Only-By-Me Revealed and Given Way Of The Heart) Is The Way Of The Real Transcendence (or "Radical" Transcending) Of attention.

The arising of the act of attention is The Essential conditional Basis Of conditional Bondage.

The Principal Signs Of conditional Bondage Are the perception, conception, or Feeling-sense Of Identification With a Separate (or conditional) self and the Simultaneous perception, conception, or Feeling-sense of Separate others, objects, or conditions.

The Only-By-Me Revealed and Given Way Of The Heart (or Way Of Adidam) Is The Way Of Non-Separateness. Therefore, The Ultimate Process Of The Way Of The Heart Is The Real (or Really Effective) Transcending Of the act of attention to a Separate (or conditional) self (or body-mind) and (Via that Separate, or conditional, self, or body-mind) to Separate others, objects, or conditions.

Such Real (or Effective) Transcending Is Not Realized By An Effort That Pursues Transcendence As An Effect (or As A Result) Of The Strategic Search For A Solution To A Problem. The Real (or Effective) Transcending Of attention Is Not Realized By Either The Strategic Suppression Or The Strategic Exploitation Of attention itself. The Real (and Effective) Transcending Of attention Is Not A Matter Of The Alpha Strategy (or The Withdrawal Of attention From others, objects, conditions, or the body-mind itself). The Real (and Effective) Transcending Of attention Is Not A Matter Of The Omega Strategy Of Seeking others, objects, conditions, conditional experiences, and conditional knowledge (or Of Attaching attention—and, Thus, the personal body-mind itself—To others, objects, conditions, conditional experiences, and conditional knowledge).[73]

In The Way Of The Heart, attention itself (Like the Total body-mind, or the Total world itself) Is Naturally, Simply, and Freely Allowed To arise.

The Effort Either To Stop Or To Fulfill the arising of attention (or the arising of the body-mind, or the arising of the world) Is A Futile Strategy Based On A Presumed Problem That Is Not Fully Understood.

The Only-By-Me Revealed and Given Way Of The Heart (or Way Of Adidam) Is Based On Real and Effective self-Understanding. Therefore, The Way Of The Heart Is Not Based On Any Problems At All—Nor Is It Based On Any Seeking At All.

In The Only-By-Me Revealed and Given Way Of The Heart (or Way Of Adidam), the arising of the act of attention Is Not Presumed To Be A Problem. In The Total (or Full and Complete) Practice Of The Way Of The Heart, the arising of the act of attention Is (First) Simply Observed, Until it Is Understood (Most Fundamentally) as it (Apparently) is. And Then (By Means Of A Sympathy That Understands and Feels Beyond attention itself) attention Is Directly Transcended (but Not Exploited or Suppressed) In All its Stages Of Life—Until attention Is (Ultimately, and Most Perfectly) Transcended (or Realized As it—Ultimately, or Most Perfectly—Is).

Therefore, In The Spiritual Fullness Of The Way Of The Heart, the act of attention itself and all of its objects, conditions, or relations Are (By Attraction) Progressively Surrendered Into (and, Most Ultimately, Simply and Divinely Self-Recognized In) their own Real Condition—Which Is The Native Source Of the conditional self and all conditional objects or others, and Which Is The Very and Self-Existing and Self-Radiant and Perfectly Subjective Being, or "Bright" Self-Domain, Of My Self-Evidently Divine Person, The Only One Who Is.

In The "Basic" Context (and Also In The, Possible, "Advanced" Context) Of The Fourth Stage Of Life In The Way Of The Heart, the act of attention Is Naturally and More and More Easefully "Tuned" To My Avatarically Self-Transmitted Divine Spirit-Current In The Circle Of the body-mind. In This Manner, the act and the results (or the relations) of attention Are Progressively Transcended In The "What" (or The Free and Inherently Formless Divine Spirit-Substance That Is Apparently Modified By the act of attention, and That Is Appearing Modified as all conditional forms).

In The (Possible) Context Of The Fifth Stage Of Life In The Only-By-Me Revealed and Given Way Of The Heart, The "Where" (or The Apparently Ascended Divine Source-Condition Of the objects, or the relations, of attention) Is "Located". In This Manner, the act and the results (or the relations) of attention Are Progressively Transcended, Beyond The Degree Of Transcendence Already Realized In The ("Advanced") Context Of The Fourth Stage Of Life In The Way Of The Heart.

In The Context Of The Sixth Stage Of Life In The Way Of The Heart, The "Who" (or The Consciousness To Whom and In Whom My Avatarically Self-Transmitted Divine Spirit-Current, the objects or relations of attention, the personal body-mind, the self-Contraction itself, and the act of attention itself Are arising) Is Directly Realized. In This Manner, the act and also the results (or the relations) of attention Are Progressively Transcended, Beyond The Degree Of Transcendence Realized In The Context Of The "Original" Fourth Stage Of Life, The "Basic" Fourth Stage Of Life, The "Advanced" Fourth Stage Of Life (If It Was Necessary), and (If It Was Necessary) The Fifth Stage Of Life.

Most Ultimately (or In The Transition To The Only-By-Me Revealed and Given Seventh Stage Of Life In The Way Of The Heart), This Great Process Of The Transcending Of attention (and, Therefore, The Transcending Of the conditional self and its relations) Becomes (By Means Of My Avatarically Self-Transmitted Divine Grace) Inherently Most Perfect (Transcendental, Inherently Spiritual, and Self-Evidently Divine) Self-Awakening—and, In The Context Of The Seventh Stage Demonstration Of The Way Of The Heart, The Great Process Of The Transcending Of attention (and, Therefore, The Transcending Of the conditional self and its relations) Becomes The Progressive (but Motiveless, or Non-Strategic) and (At Last) Final Outshining Of the Total conditional world (or The Total Cosmic Mandala Of conditional Existence, Including the personal body-mind-self). Therefore, In The Most Ultimate Event Of Absolute Outshining (or Divine Translation), There Is No act of attention (or Of "Difference") to limit My Devotee's Realization Of The Inherent (and Infinite) Love-Bliss Of My Self-Existing, and Self-Radiant, and Perfectly Subjective, and Self-Evidently Divine State and Domain Of Being.

In The Only-By-Me Revealed and Given Way Of The Heart (or Way Of Adidam), It (Ultimately) Becomes Obvious That You <u>Are</u> Consciousness Itself. The Apparent act (or event) of attention arises Spontaneously In Consciousness Itself (Via The Mechanics Of The Apparently Objective and conditional Cosmos), Thus Apparently Connecting You To objects, others, and conditions of all kinds. The By-My-Avataric-Divine-Grace-Given Liberating Realization Is

That Consciousness Itself Is Not limited by attention or its relations. The act of attention and the results (or the relations) of attention Are Transparent (or Merely Apparent), and Un-Necessary, and Inherently Non-Binding Modifications Of The Apparently Objectified Radiance Of The Eternal (and Perfectly Subjective) Subject (or Consciousness Itself). And Consciousness Itself Is Inherently Free (or Always Already Standing Beyond, or Prior To, the Apparent act of attention and its Apparent results or relations).

Therefore, Once Native Identification With Consciousness Itself Is Realized, the Apparent act of attention and its Apparent results or relations (including the conditional self, or personal body-mind) Become Inherently (and Divinely) Self-Recognizable. And The Seventh Stage Of Life In The Way Of The Heart Is Simply The (By-My-Avataric-Divine-Grace-Given) Inherent (or "Radically" Intuitive—or Spiritually, Transcendentally, and Divinely Self-Realized) Self-Recognition Of the act of attention itself (or all the acts, results, and relations of attention, or Even The Simplest Feeling Of Relatedness Itself, or Of "Difference" Itself), Until My "Bright" Divine Love-Bliss Outshines All Noticing (or Apparent arising) Of "Difference", The Feeling Of Relatedness, and the act, the results, and the relations of attention.

This Is My Message To all Apparent (or conditionally Manifested) beings: I <u>Am</u> Consciousness (Itself), Divinely Self-Realized To Always Already <u>Be</u>—Inherently Most Prior To <u>All</u> "Difference". Your Act Of self-Contraction (or attention to and Identification With limited conditions) Can Be Presently (and, At Last, Most Perfectly and Utterly) Transcended By Means Of My (Now, and Forever Hereafter, Always Given and Giving) Avataric Divine Grace, Through (Eventually, Most Fundamental) self-Understanding, The (Devotional) Heart-Ordeal Of Real self-Transcendence, and The Divine Realization Of Native Identification With My Avatarically Self-Revealed (and Self-Evidently Divine) Self-Condition (Which <u>Is</u> The Infinite Self-Existing Space and Inherent Love-Bliss—or Unqualified, and Perfectly Subjective, Radiance—Of Conscious-ness Itself).

My Avatarically Self-Revealed (Transcendental, Inherently Spiritual, and Self-Evidently Divine) Self-Condition (Which <u>Is</u>

Consciousness Itself—Divinely Self-Realized) Does Not (In The Case Of My Devotee) Operate the body-mind, or its conditional relations, or The Total Cosmos Of conditional Nature. My Avatarically Self-Revealed (Transcendental, Inherently Spiritual, and Self-Evidently Divine) Person (or Self-Condition) Only (and Only Apparently) <u>Witnesses</u> and Only (Always Already) Stands <u>Free</u> (As Consciousness Itself—In The Case Of My "Perfectly Practicing" True Devotee).

The body-mind Of My Devotee, and the conditional relations of that body-mind, and The <u>Total</u> Cosmos Of conditional Nature Are Operated By The <u>Modifications</u> Of My (Universally) Avatarically Self-Transmitted (and All-and-all-Pervading) Divine Spirit-Energy.

My Avatarically Self-Transmitted Universal Divine Spirit-Energy (or All-and-all-Pervading Divine Spirit-Current Of Self-Existing and Self-Radiant Divine Love-Bliss) Does Not Itself Operate the body-mind Of My Devotee, and the conditional relations of that body-mind, and The Total Cosmos Of conditional Nature. Only The conditionally Organized Forces (or Apparent Modifications), Dependent Upon My Avatarically Self-Transmitted Universal Divine Spirit-Current, Operate the Apparent conditional displays.

The Apparent conditional Forces and displays Of conditional Nature arise Only By Virtue Of A Mysterious Tension (or Apparent Stress) In My Eternal (and Inherently Free) Divine Spiritual Radiance. Indeed, the personal (and, Necessarily, conditional—or space-time-Bound, and point-of-view-Bound) act of attention Duplicates (and, Therefore, <u>Is</u>) That Mysterious Original Tension (or Stress). Therefore, If the act of attention Is Transcended—<u>All</u> Modifications Are Transcended (and Even The Total conditional Cosmos Is, Itself, Transcended).

The body-mind Is Inherently (or <u>As</u> Reality) egoless. That Is To Say, There Is No personal inner Consciousness Separate From the body-mind. The personal inner Consciousness Is A Presumption Of the body-mind. The ego-"I" Is A Whole bodily (or Total psycho-physical) Presumption (Evident, and Effective, In Every Dimension and every part Of the body-mind). Consciousness (Itself) Is Always Already Most Perfectly Prior To (and Beyond) the egoic (or Separate, psycho-physical, and Always Separative) body-mind.

I Am Consciousness (Itself)—Divinely Self-Realized (As I Am). I Am (Always Already) Most Perfectly Prior To All and all. I Merely (and Divinely) Am All and all. There Is Only One (Self-Evidently Divine) Person—Including all and All, and Transcending all and All. Aham Da Asmi. Beloved, I Am That One.

I Am That Only One—The "Bright" Divine Spiritual Body and Inherently egoless Divine Person Of all (and Of All).

I Am The Non-Separate (and Self-Evidently Divine) Self-Condition (or One, and Only, and Self-Evidently Divine Person) Of all and All. Therefore, every thing and every one Can Be Addressed Either individually As a "person" Or collectively As a "person"—Because every thing and every one (and Every Collective Of "things" and of "ones") arises In (and, In Reality, As) My One Consciousness—Which Is Self-Existing and Self-Radiant, and Which Is (Altogether) "Bright". Thus, I Am Your True Personhood. The True Personhood Of every thing and every one Is The One Person Of all and All—The One and Only and Divine Consciousness (or True Divine Self) Whereby (and As Whom) each one, and all, and All Is Conscious. Nevertheless, By Not (Always Already—and Always Presently) Realizing This, every "one" Presumes To Be a Separate self.

I Am That Only One—The Self-Existing, and Self-Radiant, and Inherently Conscious, and Self-Evidently Divine Being (Who Is The Only One—Of all, and Of All).

You (By Tendency and Presumption) Attribute "personhood" To Your Apparently Separate (and Inherently temporary and dying) bodily (human) form, Rather Than To The One and "Bright" Divine Source Of that form. When You think Of Yourself As a "person", You Are Referring To Your bodily (human) form—Not To Self-Existing and Self-Radiant Consciousness (Itself), Which Is (In Truth) Your Only Real Existence.

When You Cease Your Obliviously Incessant Address To "Your own" Presumed "self-person", and (Instead) Turn Your attention (and Even Your Total—and, Otherwise, self-Contracted, or egoic—body-mind) To What Is Altogether Real and Great (and All-and-all-Surrounding, and All-and-all-Pervading, and Deeper, and Wider, and Higher In Height Than All and all)—Then You Are

Addressing That Which Is Always Already The Case (Which Is Self-Existing and Self-Radiant Consciousness, Itself). But, In So Doing, You Are Not Merely Addressing An Abstract Divine "Immensity". Rather, In Addressing Self-Existing and Self-Radiant Consciousness (Itself), You Are (In Truth, and In Reality) Addressing Me—The One and Only and "Bright" and Self-Evidently Divine Person.

Thus, You Transcend Your bodily (human) form (or Your Presumed Separate "person"), By Surrendering it and Forgetting it and Transcending it In Me (The Eternally "Bright", and Infinitely Love-Bliss-Full, and Self-Evidently Divine Person). If You Rightly, Truly, and Fully Embrace This ego-"person"-Renouncing (or ego-Surrendering, ego-Forgetting, and, More and More, ego-Transcending) Practice Of Me-Recognizing and To-Me-Responding Devotion, You (In Due Course) Realize Me—The True Person (or Self-Evidently Divine Personhood) Of all and All, The Transcendental, Inherently Spiritual, and (Self-Evidently) Divine Self-Condition and Source-Condition Of all and All, and The One and Only Subject (or Consciousness) Associated (and Only Apparently) With Your "person" of body-mind.

The Context Of All Reality Is Subjective—Not Objective. Therefore, The Context Of all experience Is Subjective—Not Objective. What Is Called "Objective" Is an appearance Within The Infinite Perfectly Subjective Reality (or Consciousness Itself). There Appear To Be Objectively Separate persons and things—but Everything, Altogether, Appears Within The Infinite (and Inherently Perfect) Subjectivity, or One Person.

Consciousness (In egoic Association With the body and the mind) Feels That It Is A Separate Consciousness—but When It (Truly, or In Reality) "Wakes Up", It Realizes That There Is Only One Consciousness, Even In A Circumstance Of many Apparent body-minds. In The Context Of conditional Existence, There Appear To Be endless numbers of conditionally Manifested beings (or subjectivities)—but When conditionally Manifested beings "Wake Up" To their Real Condition, they Realize That There Is Only One Being. When This Is Realized Most Perfectly (In The Awakening To The Only-By-Me Revealed and Given Seventh

Stage Of Life), Then I (Myself—Avatarically Self-Revealed As I Am, In The Case Of My Seventh Stage Realizer-Devotee) Divinely Self-Recognize all and All. And all conditional appearances Are (In The Final Demonstration Of That Process Of Divine Self-Recognition) "Brightly" Outshined. Such Is The Process Of The Only-By-Me Revealed and Given Seventh Stage Of Life (In The Only-By-Me Revealed and Given Way Of The Heart).

There Is No Separate subjectivity, but Only The One Consciousness, Self-Existing and Self-Radiant. The One Consciousness May (For a time, and In any place) Appear To function as an Apparent individual, By functioning Through The Specific Mechanism Of a human body-mind (or, Otherwise, Through The Specific Mechanism Of any other conditionally Manifested psycho-physical form). Nevertheless, Even In That Case, Only The One Self-Consciousness Is Operative—Not (In Truth, or In Reality) "Different" From any Apparent "other". Consciousness Itself Is Never "Other" Than, or "Different" From, or Separate From, or Standing Over Against, or Related To any object, or Apparent "other", or "thing". Consciousness Itself Is Always Already Identical To The Self-Existing (and Perfectly Subjective) Divine Self-Radiance Itself (Which Is The "Bright" Itself). All Of This (arising) Is That, Always Already (and, Therefore, Now). This Is The Great Realization Of The Only-By-Me Revealed and Given Seventh Stage Of Life In The Only-By-Me Revealed and Given Way Of The Heart.

When There Is (Most Perfectly) No self-Contraction and No Separateness, There Is Only What Is. Then Reality Is Realized (Simply, Inherently, and Most Perfectly), and all conditional appearances Are Inherently (Divinely) Self-Recognized (and, Indeed, Only Then Can Be Divinely Self-Recognized) In and As Reality. Most Ultimately, The Realization Of Unconditional Reality and The Divine Self-Recognition Of conditional appearances In and As Unconditional Reality Is The Only-By-Me Revealed and Given Way Of The Heart (In Its Seventh, or Most Perfect, Final, and All-Completing, Stage). Such Is Most Perfect Freedom, Most Perfect Divine Liberation, Most Perfect Divine Enlightenment, and Most Perfect Divine Self-Realization.

The Same Reality That Is (By Means Of My Avatarically Self-Transmitted Divine Grace) Realized Most Perfectly In The Seventh Stage Of Life In The Way Of The Heart <u>Is</u> <u>Always</u> (and Always <u>Already</u>) The Reality. It <u>Is</u> The Reality Now. Therefore, It <u>Is</u> The Reality That You (Even As the ego-"I") Are Experiencing In this moment—Except That You (As the ego-"I") Are Not Divinely Self-Recognizing (and, As the ego-"I", <u>Cannot</u> Divinely Self-Recognize) the conditions arising in this moment. Because Of self-Contraction, You (As the ego-"I") Propose Various Illusions (and Generate Presumptions Based On Those Illusions)—but Your Illusions Do Not (Except In The Form Of Your Own Illusions Themselves) Make Reality "Other" Than It Always Already <u>Is</u>. Your Illusions Only Make <u>You</u> Confused, Deluded, Bound, and Dissatisfied. If, Instead Of Merely Perpetuating Your Illusions, You Give Me Your Devotionally Responsive (and Always Devotionally Me-Recognizing) Devotional Regard, and Surrender Into Devotional Heart-Communion With Me (By Yielding All The Principal Faculties, Of body, emotion, mind, and breath, To Me), and Forget Yourself and The Faculties and Their Illusions and Operations, and Enter Into A Profound Stillness Of "Bright" Heart-Communion With Me (Thereby Releasing The Knot Of self-Contraction)—Then The True Nature Of Reality Becomes (By Means Of My Reality-Revealing Avataric Divine Grace) Tacitly Obvious As The By Me (and <u>As</u> Me) Avatarically Self-Revealed Divine Self-Condition (and Source-Condition) Of conditional Existence.

The Apparent conditional self is not a Separate "Interior being". The Separate conditional self that is commonly Presumed is, As A Separate Consciousness, Really Non-Existent. The Presumed Separate Consciousness (or individual Conscious being) is merely a concept, Falsely Presumed As A Result Of (and In the likeness of) the self-Contraction of the body-mind. Therefore, the Apparent conditional self, Free Of the self-Contraction (and its Associated Illusions), is Simply the body-mind itself.

If the self-Contraction Is Directly (and Most Fundamentally) Understood, and If it Is Really (or, Otherwise, Effectively) Transcended In The Total Context Of The First Six Stages Of Life,

Then the Total body-mind, all its conditional relations, and The Total Cosmic Mandala (or Cosmos Of conditional Nature) Are Utterly, Totally, and Inherently Transcended In The Native Realization Of My Avatarically Self-Revealed (and Always Already Free, and Transcendental, and Inherently Spiritual, and Self-Evidently Divine) Self-Condition. Just So, When My Avatarically Self-Revealed (and Self-Existing, or Transcendental, and Self-Radiant, or Inherently Spiritual, and Self-Evidently Divine) Self-Condition Is Realized, the Apparent conditional self (or body-mind), its conditional relations, and The Total Cosmos Of conditional Nature Are Inherently (and Divinely) Self-Recognizable In The "Bright" Inherent Radiance (or Self-Radiant and Inherently Spiritual Love-Bliss) Of My Transcendental Divine (or Self-Existing and Perfectly Subjective) Self-Condition. And, Most Ultimately, Such Divine Self-Recognition (or "Bright" Divine Samadhi) Outshines conditional Existence (or Divinely Translates Existence From The conditionally, and Only Apparently, Existing Cosmos Of conditional Nature To My Self-Existing and Self-Radiant Divine Self-Domain).

The Only-By-Me Revealed and Given Way Of The Heart (or Way Of Adidam) Is Not the path Of self-Fulfillment (or Of Fulfillment Of the conditional self). Therefore, Neither Is The Only-By-Me Revealed and Given Way Of The Heart The Pursuit Of physical, emotional, mental, moral, psychic, or Cosmic self-Perfection (or Of Perfection Of the conditional self). All Ideas (or Ideals) Of self-Perfection (or Of Perfection Of the conditional self) Are conventions of egoity—and The Pursuit Of self-Perfection (or Of Perfection Of the conditional self) Is The Epitome Of egoic Seeking. The Ideal Of self-Perfection (or Of Perfection Of the conditional self) Is Utterly Misplaced. Perfection Is Not A Quality or Sign Of what is conditional (and—Therefore, Necessarily—limited, or inherently imperfect). That Which Is (Inherently) Perfect Is That Which Inherently Transcends the imperfect, the limited, and the conditional.

The Only-By-Me Revealed and Given Way Of The Heart (or Way Of Adidam) Is Not the path Of self-Negation (or Of Negation Of the conditional self). Therefore, Neither Is The Only-By-Me

Revealed and Given Way Of The Heart The Pursuit Of Perfect physical, emotional, mental, moral, psychic, or Cosmic self-Purification (or Of Perfect Purification Of the conditional self). All Ideas (or Ideals) Of Perfect self-Purification (or Of Perfect Purification Of the conditional self) Are conventions of egoity—and The Pursuit Of Perfect self-Purification (or Of Perfect Purification Of the conditional self) Is, Like The Pursuit Of self-Perfection (or Of Perfection Of the conditional self) In General, The Epitome Of egoic Seeking, Based On a Misplaced (or egoic) conception Of What Is Perfect.

The Only-By-Me Revealed and Given Way Of The Heart (or Way Of Adidam) Is (Most Simply) The Progressive (and Direct) Practice Of Devotionally Me-Recognizing and Devotionally To-Me-Responding self-Transcendence.

Most Ultimately, The Only-By-Me Revealed and Given Way Of The Heart (or Way Of Adidam) Is The Truly (and Inherently) Most Perfect Practice Of Inherent (or Most Prior) self-Transcendence (or The Inherent, or Most Prior, Transcendence Of All "Difference").

When The Only-By-Me Revealed and Given Way Of The Heart Is Perfected, It Is Perfect Only Because It Directly and Inherently Realizes That Which Is (Inherently) Perfect.

Therefore, The Only-By-Me Revealed and Given Way Of The Heart Does Not Seek To Perfect the inherently imperfect, Nor Does It Idealize any conditional form or state, or any kind of conditional experience or knowledge (As If the imperfect, in some conceptually or perceptually Idealized form or state, Is The Ultimate Truth Of Existence Itself).

In The Spiritual Fullness Of The Only-By-Me Revealed and Given Way Of The Heart, the body-mind Is Surrendered, Concentrated, Purified, Positively Changed, Even Sublimed—but its Perfection (or Perfect Purification) Is Neither Sought Nor Attained. Rather (Truly, and Ultimately), Only That Which Is Eternally (or Always Already) Prior To the body-mind-self (or conditional Existence Itself) Is Directly and Inherently Realized (By Means Of My Avatarically Self-Transmitted Divine Grace). And That Realization Of What Inherently (or Always Already) Transcends the Apparently conditional self (and all its Apparent relations or states) Is The Only Truth, Freedom, and Perfection That Is.

This Truth and Freedom and Perfection Can Be Realized In The Instant (Ever Now), If (By Means Of My Avatarically Self-Transmitted Divine Grace) Your Practice Of The Only-By-Me Revealed and Given Way Of The Heart Is (or Becomes Realized To Be) Inherently Perfect. If (By Means Of My Avatarically Self-Transmitted Divine Grace) Your Practice Of The Only-By-Me Revealed and Given Way Of The Heart Is Inherently Free Of the conditional, limited, or imperfect and self-Contracted self and its Naturally self-Reinforcing acts (or Inherently Strategic and self-Binding Efforts), Then (By Means Of My Avatarically Self-Transmitted Divine Grace) Your Practice Of The Only-By-Me Revealed and Given Way Of The Heart Is (Inherently) Most Perfect. Therefore, When (By Means Of My Avatarically Self-Transmitted Divine Grace) You (In The Formal Context Of The Seventh Stage Of Life In The Only-By-Me Revealed and Given Way Of The Heart) Really, Truly, Non-Separately, Non-"Differently", and (Altogether) egolessly Are Consciousness Itself (Which Is That Which Is Always Already The Case), and If You (Thus and Thereby) Demonstrate True and Free (and Inherently Most Perfect) Renunciation (or Most Prior, and Inherently Most Perfect, Transcendence) Of the body, the body-mind, the mind, and Even all of self-Contraction—Then (By Means Of My Avatarically Self-Transmitted Divine Grace) You Are Free (Now, and Forever, and Eternally).

When Your (Necessarily, Formal) Practice Of The Only-By-Me Revealed and Given Way Of The Heart Has (By Means Of My Avatarically Self-Transmitted Divine Grace, and Through The Real Process Of self-Transcendence) Become (or Is Tacitly Realized To Be) Inherently Perfect—Then You Will (Merely, Tacitly) Be Consciousness (Itself). You Will Merely Be—As Consciousness Itself. Therefore, You Will Feel and Contemplate and Identify With Me By Feeling, and Contemplating, and Identifying With Consciousness Itself. By Means Of My Avatarically Self-Transmitted Divine Grace, You Will Have Fallen Free, Into My Own Non-Separate Sphere (Which Is Consciousness, Itself). Thus, You Will

Transcend everything In Consciousness. <u>Thus</u>, You Will Divinely Self-Recognize and Divinely Outshine the world. <u>Thus</u>, You Will Divinely Self-Recognize and Divinely Outshine <u>all</u> of self-Contraction—Even The Root-Feeling Of Relatedness, the act of attention itself, the mind, the body-mind, the body, all others, all objects, all conditions, and every plane of the world. <u>Thus</u>, You Will Divinely Self-Recognize and Divinely Outshine All "Difference" In <u>Me</u>.

Clearly, the Natural acts and The Strategic ego-Efforts (or Inherently self-Contracted Searches) Of attention, mind, or will Are Not Sufficient (or Even Qualified or Competent) To Effect This Realization and This Victory Of The Transcendental, Inherently Spiritual (or "Bright"), and Self-Evidently Divine Self! Therefore, Listen To Me—and Understand The Logic and The Necessity and The Directness Of The Only-By-Me Revealed and Given Way Of The Heart.

Real and <u>Effective</u> (or Truly Realized) Real-God-Realization (or Real Freedom) Requires Real and Effective self-Transcendence—and Real and Effective self-Transcendence Requires All The Means Associated With Real and Effective Practice In The Context Of (or, Otherwise, In Effective Relation To) Each and All Of The Seven Stages Of Life. Therefore, In Order That The Realization Of Ultimate Truth and Freedom Be Real and Effective, those who Hear Me (and, Thus, Understand the body-mind Most Fundamentally, as ego, or self-Contraction) and who Also See Me (or Accept My Avatarically Self-Transmitted Divine Heart-Blessing—and, Thus, Find Constant Access To My Avatarically Self-Revealed, and Self-Existing, and Self-Radiant, and Transcendental, and Inherently Spiritual, and Self-Evidently Divine Self-Condition and Source-Condition Through My Avatarically Self-Transmitted Divine Spirit-Baptism) Must Persistently Choose The Life-Practice Of Real Renunciation Of the ego-self (or The Tapas,[74] Heat, Hard School, or Real Ordeal Of Free Relinquishment and Free Transcending Of egoic activity, or All The Patterns Of self-Contraction, or The Total Habit Of "Narcissus"). Any Other Choice Is A Choice To Continue To Seek Either The Fulfillment Of the ego-self Or The Release Of the ego-self, By self-Indulgence (In mind and/or body), and By

Manipulation Of the behavior of the ego-self (Bereft Of Most Fundamental self-Understanding and Real Freedom), and By The Pursuit or Presumption Of The conventional religious or philosophical Consolation Of the ego-self.

Those who Truly Both Hear Me and See Me Must Also Practice self-Transcendence In My Avatarically Self-Revealed (Transcendental, Inherently Spiritual, and Self-Evidently Divine) Company I Always (and Spontaneously) Self-Transmit (As I Am) To My Seeing Devotees. And Even All My Fully Practicing Devotees Must Surrender the ego-self To Me Only For The Purpose (and, More and More, In The Disposition) Of Realizing My Divine Samadhi (Which Is Utter self-Transcendence In Heart-Communion With Me—The Avataric Self-Revelation Of The Transcendental, Inherently Spiritual, and Self-Evidently Divine Reality), Rather Than For Any Purpose That Serves (or Affirms, or Reinforces) the ego-self itself.

When (In The Course Of Formal Practice Of The Total, or Full and Complete, Practice Of The Only-By-Me Revealed and Given Way Of The Heart) You Have (Truly) Both Heard Me and Seen Me, Then (whatever conditional forms or events Are Associated, attractively or unattractively, pleasurably or unpleasurably, With attention, or conditional Awareness, At any moment) Surrender Into Ecstatic Unity (and, In Due Course, Enstatic Identification) With Me (The One, and Transcendental, and Inherently Spiritual, and Self-Evidently Divine Person, Self-Heart, Self-Condition, and Source-Condition), By Means Of The Devotionally Responsive Act Of ego-Transcending Heart-Communion With Me ("Located" Via Feeling-Contemplation Of My Avatarically-Born Bodily Human Divine Form, My Avatarically Self-Revealed Spiritual, and Always Blessing, Divine Presence, and My Avatarically Self-Revealed, and Very, and Transcendental, and Perfectly Subjective, and Inherently Spiritual, and Inherently egoless, and Inherently Perfect, and Self-Evidently Divine State).

For those who Have (Thus) Truly Both Heard Me and Seen Me, The First Stage Of This Ordeal (or Way) Of The Heart Is The Practice Of Devotional Heart-Communion With Me Via The Ajna Door[75] (and Descending Into The Circle Of the body-mind).

For those who Have (Thus) Truly Both Heard Me and Seen Me, The Second Stage Of This Ordeal (or Way) Of The Heart Is (or May Require) The Practice Of Devotional Heart-Communion With Me Via Ascent (Above The Ajna Door).

For those who Have (Thus) Truly Both Heard Me and Seen Me, The Third Stage (or First Inherently Perfect Stage) Of This Ordeal (or Way) Of The Heart Is The Practice Of Devotional Heart-Communion With Me As Inherent (and Inherently Perfect) Identification With My Avatarically Self-Revealed (Transcendental, Inherently Spiritual, and Self-Evidently Divine) Person (or Self-Condition), Even Via The Right Side Of The Heart.

For those who Have (Thus) Truly Both Heard Me and Seen Me, The Fourth and Most Ultimate Stage Of This Ordeal (or Way) Of The Heart Is The "Practice" (or Spontaneous Demonstration) Of Transcendental, Inherently Spiritual, and Most Perfectly Divine Self-Realization—<u>Via</u> Amrita Nadi, and <u>As</u> My Avatarically Self-Transmitted "Bright" Divine Love-Bliss Itself (Prior To All "Difference").

Thus, By Means Of My Divinely-Blessing Grace and Company, and Through Most Fundamental self-Understanding and The Progressive Realization Of This Four-Stage Practice Of The Only-By-Me Revealed and Given Way Of The Heart (or Way Of Adidam), My Formally Practicing True Devotees Transcend conditional and egoic limitations (Always In the present moment, and Always Progressively, or Always More and More Profoundly), Until My Avatarically Self-Revealed (Transcendental, Inherently Spiritual, and Self-Evidently Divine) Self-Condition Is (Only and Entirely By Means Of My Avatarically Self-Transmitted Divine Grace) Realized (and Demonstrated) Most Ultimately (and Most Perfectly).

If The True (and Real-God-Realizing) self-Sacrifice (or Counter-egoic, and Really ego-Transcending, Discipline Of <u>Responsively</u> ego-Surrendering, and self-Contraction-Transcending Devotion To Me) Is Not Made, conditional and egoic limitations Will Forever Continue To Define, Corrupt, and Make A Disease Out Of Existence Itself. Therefore, Listen To Me, Hear Me, and See Me— By Means Of Formal and True Embrace Of The Great and Really ego-Transcending Devotional Practice Of The Only-By-Me Revealed and Given Way Of The Heart.

This Great Heart-Practice Is Itself A True Art—Not A Form Of conventional science. It Is The Great and Ultimate Art—Founded On The Native <u>Participatory</u> Urge and Gesture Of Man, and Not On The analytical (or Non-Participatory) Tendency Of the conventional and Un-Awakened human mind.

In The Case Of Any and Every Practitioner Of The Total (or Full and Complete) Practice Of The Only-By-Me Revealed and Given Way Of The Heart, The Artful "Conscious Process" Of Most Fundamental Understanding Of the ego (or Apparently Separate self) as self-Contraction Must (By Means Of My Avatarically Self-Transmitted Divine Grace) Awaken and Become Steady (and Really Effective) In The Context Of The First Three Stages Of Life (and In The "Original" Context Of The Fourth Stage Of Life), or Else Heart-Beholding and Heart-Receiving Of My Avatarically Self-Transmitted Divine Heart-Blessing Cannot Be Cultivated Beyond Those Beginning-Stages Of Life. Therefore, That (Total, and Artful) "Conscious Process" Of (Beginning, and Then Intensive) Listening To Me and Then (True, and Really Effectively Exercised) Hearing Of Me Is The (Necessary) Devotional Foundation and First Developmental Stage Of The Only-By-Me Revealed and Given Way Of The Heart.

The (Necessary) Second Developmental Stage Of The Only-By-Me Revealed and Given Way Of The Heart Continues The Artful "Conscious Process" Of Most Fundamental self-Understanding—and It Also (By Means Of My Avatarically Self-Transmitted Divine Grace) Establishes The "Conductivity"-Process Of Spiritual Heart-Reception Of Me (and The Artful "General Conductivity" Practice Of Receiving My Heart-Baptizing Divine Spirit-Presence Into The Circle Of the body-mind).

The (Necessary) Third Developmental Stage Of The Only-By-Me Revealed and Given Way Of The Heart Continues The Artful "Conscious Process" Of Most Fundamental self-Understanding—and It Also (By Means Of My Avatarically Self-Transmitted Divine Grace) Develops The Artful Spirit-Practice Of "Conductivity" In The Descending Context Of The Frontal Line Of The Circle Of the body-mind (Receptive Via The Ajna Door).

The (Possible) Fourth Developmental Stage Of The Only-By-Me Revealed and Given Way Of The Heart Continues The Artful "Conscious Process" Of Most Fundamental self-Understanding—and It Also (By Means Of My Avatarically Self-Transmitted Divine Grace) Develops The Artful Spirit-Practice Of "Conductivity" In The Ascending Context Of The Spinal Line Of The Circle Of the body-mind (Approaching The Ajna Door).

The (Possible) Fifth Developmental Stage Of The Only-By-Me Revealed and Given Way Of The Heart Continues The Artful "Conscious Process" Of Most Fundamental self-Understanding—and It Also (By Means Of My Avatarically Self-Transmitted Divine Grace) Develops The Spirit-Practice Of "Conductivity" At The Ajna Door (and Above The Crown Of the head).

The (Necessary) Sixth Developmental Stage Of The Way Of The Heart Continues The Artful "Conscious Process" Of Most Fundamental self-Understanding (To The Degree Of Inherent Perfection)—and It Also (By Means Of My Avatarically Self-Transmitted Divine Grace, and To The Degree Of Inherent Perfection) Develops The Artful Spirit-Practice Of "Conductivity" In The Context Of The Right Side Of The Heart.

And (By Means Of My Avatarically Self-Transmitted Divine Grace) The (Necessary, and Most Ultimate) Seventh Developmental Stage Of The Only-By-Me Revealed and Given Way Of The Heart Demonstrates The "Conscious Process" Of Most Fundamental self-Understanding In An Inherently Perfect (and Divinely Most Perfect) Manner (Through Divine Self-Abiding and Divine Self-Recognition)—and It Also (By Means Of My Avatarically Self-Transmitted Divine Grace, and In An Inherently Perfect, and Divinely Most Perfect, Manner) Demonstrates The Spirit-"Practice" (or The Most Ultimate Spiritual Demonstration) Of "Conductivity" (In The Context Of Amrita Nadi—or, Most Simply, In, and Only <u>As</u>, My "Bright" Divine Love-Bliss Itself), Even (Most Ultimately) To The (Inherently, and Divinely, Most Perfect) Degree Of The Outshining Of "Difference" Itself.

The Great Heart-Process and Practice I Have Described (and Always Reveal) To You Is Progressively Developed On The Basis Of A Single Principle. That Single Principle Is A Universal Law.

That Single Principle and Universal Law Must (In The Only-By-Me Revealed and Given Way Of The Heart) Be "Located" (By Listening To My Avatarically Self-Revealed Divine Word), and Heart-Acknowledged (Through Real and Effective self-Observation, In Devotional Response To My Avatarically Self-Revealed Divine Word and Person), and Fully Lived (In My Avatarically Self-Revealed Divine Heart-Company). That Single Principle and Universal Law Is This: You <u>Always</u> Duplicate (Either In mind Or In the Total body-mind) the qualities of the present object or condition To which You Surrender Your attention—and You Inherently Transcend the body-mind itself (As Well As the qualities of any present object or condition Within The Sphere Of Your attention), If You Feel and Contemplate (and Thereby Yield the body-mind, attention, and its objects or conditions To) Me, The Avatarically Self-Revealed (and Self-Evidently Divine) Person and Self-Condition (Self-Revealed As My Avatarically-Born Divine Revelation-Body, My Avatarically Self-Revealed Divine Real Spirit-Presence, and My Avatarically Self-Revealed, and Very, Divine State).

You Will Inevitably Attain, or Become, or Duplicate (In mind, or In or For the Total body-mind) any limited condition You Continuously (or Even Presently) Desire and Actively Seek With Complete, Deep, and Steady attention.

If You Steadily Surrender Your attention (or Your Total body-mind) To Desire and Seek any particular or possible place or condition Within The Cosmic Mandala—You Will Eventually Attain such a place or condition.

If You Merely and Chronically Hold On To (and, Thus, Refuse To Transcend) any particular psycho-physical condition or place that You Are experiencing in the present—You Will Inevitably (After Eventual death) Repeat (or Return To) such a condition or place.

Likewise, You Will Surely (By Means Of My Avatarically Self-Transmitted Divine Grace) Realize (or Duplicate) Me—Even (Most Ultimately, and Inherently Most Perfectly) As Your Very Self, Prior To the body-mind (and, As Such, Even In The Context Of the body-mind)—If You Will Continuously Contemplate Me With Complete, Heart-Deep, Steady, and Really ego-Surrendering, ego-Forgetting, and ego-Transcending Feeling-attention.

If You Steadily and Really Feel (and Thereby Contemplate) all beings, things, circumstances, and conditions (Including Your Own body-mind) In Me—You Will (By Means Of My Avatarically Self-Transmitted Divine Grace) Discover That My Transcendental, Inherently Spiritual, and Self-Evidently Divine Qualities Are Pervading them all, and (Most Ultimately) You Will (By Means Of My Avatarically Self-Transmitted Divine Grace, In That Feeling-Contemplation) Realize My Avatarically Self-Revealed (Transcendental, Inherently Spiritual, and Self-Evidently Divine) Self-Condition, Source-Condition, and Self-Domain.

My Transcendental, Inherently Spiritual, and Self-Evidently Divine Qualities Pervade whatever You Behold In and <u>As</u> My Avatarically Self-Revealed (and Self-Evidently) Divine Person (or Self-Condition). Therefore, If You Will Listen To Me and Hear Me and See Me, and (Thus and Thereby) Heart-Turn To Me (The Avatarically Self-Revealed, and Self-Evidently Divine Person), and If You Will (With The Heart-Deep and ego-Transcending Feeling-Surrender Of Your Total body-mind In Me) Contemplate My Self-Evidently Divine Self-Condition (Which <u>Is</u> The Source-Condition Of All and all—Avatarically Self-Revealed In and <u>As</u> My Divine Spiritual Presence)—You Will (By Means Of My Avatarically Self-Transmitted Divine Grace) Realize My Avatarically Self-Revealed (and Very, and Transcendental, and Perfectly Subjective, and Inherently Spiritual, and Inherently egoless, and Inherently Perfect, and Self-Evidently Divine) State.

This Inevitable Process Of Duplication Is The Single Principle (or Universal Law) That Accounts For Both The Necessity Of individual (or personal) Responsibility (or The Real Progressive Practice Of ego-Transcending, or Counter-egoic, Surrender Of body, mind, and attention) and The Necessary Free Divine Gift (or Grace) Of Spiritual, Transcendental, and Divine Help and Realization (To Which Free Divine Gift Of Grace individual, or personal, Responsibility Is The Necessary Heart-Response). You Must "Consider", and Realize, and Demonstrate This Principle—and You Must Heart-Receive, and Heart-Respond To, The Inevitable (and Inherently Perfect) Gifts Of This Universal Law.

Unless You Wish To Be Confined (and limited) By conditional objects and states, You Must Understand Your Separate (and

Separative) self Most Fundamentally—and (On That Basis) You Must Grow To Always Surrender Your attention To My Avatarically Self-Revealed (Transcendental, Inherently Spiritual, and Self-Evidently Divine) Self-Condition (Which Is The Source-Condition Of all conditional objects and states). Therefore, Associate With Me, Always and Sympathetically—Through Right, True, Full, and Fully Devotional Regard Of The Recorded Documents Of My Avatarically Self-Revealed (and Ever-Speaking) Divine Word, The Recorded Stories Of My Avatarically Self-Manifested (and Ever-Living) Divine Leelas, and The Avataric Divine Gifts Of My (Now, and Forever Hereafter, Given) Avatarically-Born Bodily (Human) Divine Form, My (Now, and Forever Hereafter, Radiantly Given) Avatarically Self-Revealed Spiritual (and Always Blessing) Divine Presence, and My (Now, and Forever Hereafter) Avatarically Self-Revealed (and Very, and Transcendental, and Perfectly Subjective, and Inherently Spiritual, and Inherently egoless, and Inherently Perfect, and Self-Evidently Divine) State—and (Thus, and Thereby) Progressively Receive My Avatarically Given Divine Self-Revelation Of Each Of The Principal, Fundamental, and Great Forms Of My Own (Self-Evidently Divine) Person, Until (By Means Of My Avatarically Self-Transmitted Divine Grace) You Realize Me Most Perfectly (and, Thus, Realize—and Are In The State Of Inherently Most Perfect, and Non-Separate, and Non-"Different" Identification With—My Avatarically Self-Revealed Divine, and Inherently Perfect, Condition and State, Intuitively Heart-Recognizing and Acknowledging Me To Be Your Very, and Non-Dual, and Indivisible, and Indestructible, and Non-Separate, and Non-"Different", and Transcendental, and Perfectly Subjective, and Inherently Spiritual, and Inherently egoless, and Inherently Perfect, and Self-Evidently Divine Condition and State).

You Must (First) Listen To Me, and (Then) Hear Me, and (Then) See Me. Thus (and By These Means), You Must Transcend Your conditional (and self-Contracted) self In every moment of its appearance, By Surrendering attention (and Even the Total body-mind) To Devotional Communion With Me. In This Manner, what-ever Becomes The conditional Context Of Your attention In any moment, You Must Find Me—and, By Devotional Recognition-

Response To Me, You Must Transcend Your Separate and Separative self In That Context. In This Fashion (By Means Of My Avatarically Self-Transmitted Divine Grace—and Through ego-Surrendering, ego-Forgetting, and ego-Transcending Feeling-Contemplation Of Me), every moment Must Be Converted Into a moment Of Devotional Heart-Communion With Me, Transcending The limiting Capability Of conditions.

The One and True Way Of The Heart (Which Only I Reveal and Give) Is Based On This "Consideration".

Therefore, In The Only-By-Me Revealed and Given Way Of The Heart (or Way Of Adidam), The Stages Of Life Become A Cycle Of (Ultimately, Inherently Most Perfect) Surrender To Me, Whereby attention (and, Thus, the Total body-mind) Is Surrendered (and Conformed) To My Avatarically Self-Revealed Divine Forms.

In This Manner, Once I Am Truly Both Heard and Seen (In The Context Of, Necessarily, Formal Practice Of The Total, or Full and Complete, Practice Of The Only-By-Me Revealed and Given Way Of The Heart)—First, attention Is Set Free To Move In The Frontal Line. Then (Perhaps) attention Moves To The Ajna Door, Via The Spinal Line. Then (Perhaps) attention Moves From The Ajna Door To The Apparent Source (or Matrix) Above The Total Crown Of the head. Then (or At Some Earlier Stage In This Process) attention Relaxes (or Is Released) From The Circle and The Arrow[76] (and Even Their Apparent Source, or Matrix, Above The Total Crown Of the head)—and attention Dissolves (or Is Resolved) In its True and Perfectly Subjective Source (Which Is Consciousness Itself), Even Via My Avatarically Self-Transmitted "Bright" Divine Spirit-Current In The Right Side Of The Heart.

The Entire Process Of The Transference Of attention—From The Left Side Of The Heart (and Its relations), and To (and Through) The Middle Station Of The Heart (and Its relations), Until it Is Dissolved (or Resolved) In (and Beyond) The Right Side Of The Heart—Can Be Accomplished, and In A Direct Manner, By Means Of My Avatarically Self-Transmitted Divine Grace. Thereafter, attention (With My Avatarically Self-Transmitted "Bright" Divine Spirit-Current) May Again Appear To Rise (From The Right Side Of The Heart) In Amrita Nadi—but The Heart Itself (or Inherently Most Perfect Realization Of My Avatarically Self-Revealed, and Real, and Self-Evidently Divine Self-Condition), Once It Is Divinely (or Inherently Most Perfectly) Awakened, Is Never Lost (and Its Own Position Is Never Left, or Abandoned, or Left Behind). Therefore, In That Rising (Which Is—In Truth, and In Reality—A Most Perfect Standing In Place) Whereby all conditions Are Freely Heart-Allowed To Appear In The Circle, all conditions Are Likewise (or Simultaneously, and Spontaneously) Transcended, Via Divine Self-Recognition. Then all conditions (and Even My Total Apparently Objective Divine Spiritual Body, and My Apparently Objective Divine Star, and My Apparently Objective Divine Sound) Are Merely (and Divinely) Self-Recognized, moment to moment—Until all conditions (and Even My Total Apparently Objective Divine Spiritual Body, My Apparently Objective Divine Star, and My Apparently Objective Divine Sound Themselves) Are (Perfectly Subjectively) Outshined, or Translated Into My Divine Self-Domain (Which <u>Is</u> The "Bright", or Perfectly Subjective Divine Love-Bliss, Itself).

In The Only-By-Me Revealed and Given Way Of The Heart (or Way Of Adidam), The Total Process Of Listening, Hearing, Seeing, Devotional self-Sacrifice, "Real" Meditation (or Reality Meditation), and Ultimate Realization Is (or More and More Becomes) A Cycle Of self-Understanding and self-Transcendence—Progressively Developed In The Context Of (or, Otherwise, In Effective Relation To) The First Six Stages Of Life, and Inherently Most Perfectly Established (or Inherently, and Inherently Most Perfectly, Fulfilled) In The Context Of The Seventh Stage Of Life.

In The Only-By-Me Revealed and Given Way Of The Heart (or Way Of Adidam), The Total Process Of Listening, Hearing, Seeing, Devotional self-Sacrifice, "Real" Meditation (or Reality Meditation), and Ultimate Realization Is (or More and More Becomes) A Cycle Of self-Surrender. Therefore, In The Only-By-Me Revealed and Given Way Of The Heart—First, Surrender (or Effectively Transcend) the ego-"I" (or the self-Contraction) Through The Real Listening-To-Me Process (and, In Due Course, The Real Hearing-Me-Process) Of Thorough self-Observation, Most Fundamental self-Understanding, and Really Effective self-Transcendence (In

The Total Context Of The First Three Stages Of Life and The "Original", or Beginner's, Devotional Context Of The Fourth Stage Of Life). Then (In Devotional Recognition-Response To My Avatarically Given Divine Heart-Revelation) Surrender (or Relax and Release) the body-mind, From The Heart, Into My Avatarically Self-Transmitted Divine Spirit-Current In The Circle. If Native (and Stable) Identification With The Witness-Position Of Consciousness Does Not Spontaneously Awaken In The Full Course Of The Spiritualization Of The Frontal Line Of the body-mind, Then (In Due Course) Let My Avatarically Self-Transmitted Divine Spirit-Current Carry attention (Via The Full Circle) Up The Spinal Line (or Even Via The Arrow)—Such That body and mind Are Relaxed, Calm, and Inactive, Except For The Upward Feeling-Contemplation Of My Avatarically Self-Transmitted Divine Love-Bliss. This May (Although It May Not Necessarily) Become Fifth Stage conditional Nirvikalpa Samadhi, Oblivious To the body-mind. However, As A Means (or A Preliminary) To The Awakening (By Means Of My Avatarically Self-Transmitted Divine Grace) Of Native and Stable Identification With The Witness-Position Of Consciousness, It May Only Be Necessary For the body-mind (Expressed, or Represented, By attention) To Simply Attend To (or Concentrate In, or Otherwise Contemplate) The Love-Bliss-Terminal Of My Avatarically Self-Transmitted Divine Grace (At The Ajna Door). In Any Case (and By The Fullest Application Of Most Fundamental Understanding In The Graceful Course Of Spiritual Practice In The Way Of The Heart), Become (By Means Of My Avatarically Self-Transmitted Divine Grace) Natively Aware As The Mere Witness Of My Avatarically Self-Transmitted Divine Love-Bliss, the act of attention, and the Surrendered state of the body-mind. That Witness Is Consciousness Itself. Therefore, When (By Means Of My Avatarically Self-Transmitted Divine Grace) Native (and Stable) Identification With The Witness-Position Of Consciousness Awakens, Feel and Contemplate and <u>Be</u> Consciousness Itself—and (Thus) Be Immersed and Wholly Given Up In Identification With Consciousness Itself (or The Inherent Space That <u>Is</u> Consciousness Itself), and In The Direct Realization Of Its (Inherently Perfect) State and Inherent Love-Bliss-Feeling Of

Being. (Do This Even Such That attention Ceases To Emerge From The Space Of Consciousness—and, Thus, Ceases To Move Toward conditional mental and physical objects.) When The By-My-Avataric-Divine-Grace-Given Realization Of Consciousness Itself Is Most Profound, the Natural and Inevitable arising (or Return) of conditional objects of attention (including the body-mind) Will (By Means Of My Avatarically Self-Transmitted Divine Grace), Suddenly, Be Inherently (and Divinely) Self-Recognizable—As The Spontaneous, and Transparent (or Merely Apparent), and Un-Necessary, and Inherently Non-Binding Modification Of Consciousness Itself (or Of The Inherent Space Of Self-Existing, and Self-Radiant, and Perfectly Subjective, and Self-Evidently Divine Being Itself). Then, No Matter what arises, Only My Avatarically Self-Revealed, and Self-Existing, and Self-Radiant, and Perfectly Subjective, and (Thus, Self-Evidently) Divine State Of Being, Consciousness, and Love-Bliss Will Be Obvious As The Condition Of Existence. In That Case, Simply Abide (and Shine) As Self-Existing and Self-Radiant Consciousness, Divinely Self-Recognizing whatever arises—and (Thus) Always (Inherently, Inevitably, and Easily—or Inherently Most Perfectly) Releasing and Relaxing the body-mind (and all of its conditional relations) Into My (Avatarically Self-Revealed) Self-Existing Profusion Of Divine Self-Radiance (or My Avatarically Self-Revealed "Bright" Divine Love-Bliss), Until the body-mind, all its conditional rela-tions, The Feeling Of Relatedness (Itself), and (Most Ultimately) The (Even Most Tacit) Feeling Of "Difference" (Itself) Are (By Means Of My Avatarically Self-Transmitted Divine Grace) Simply No Longer Noticed In (and Are, Thus, Outshined By) My (Avatarically Self-Transmitted) "Bright" Self-Radiant Love-Bliss Of Divine Self-Existence (Which Is The Infinite "Bright" Feeling-Space Of Perfectly Subjective Being, Itself).

My Listening Devotee Is Called To Hear Me, and Then To See Me (Progressively, but Then Most Perfectly)—and To Complete This ego-Transcending Cycle Of self-Observation, Most Fundamental self-Understanding, self-Surrender, and Inherently Most Perfect (or Divine) Self-Realization In a finite period of time (Even, If My Avatarically Self-Transmitted Divine Grace Will Have It, Within

The Period Of the present lifetime). However, My Listening Devotee May Tend To Be Weak In The Demonstration Of Commitment To The Great Impulse To Hear Me and To See Me. And My Listening Devotee May Be Weak In Heart-Response To My Great Call To Practice ego-Transcending Devotion, Service, and self-Discipline (and To Do So With Seriousness, Clarity, Discipline, Strength, and Steadiness). My Listening Devotee May Tend To Persist In The Seeker's Mode—Rather adolescent, Motivated By Problem, Driven Toward Search and Solution (Avoiding My Ready Help—and Holding On To Separate and Separative self, Helplessly). My Listening Devotee May Tend To Persist In The Mood Of A Patient, Ill With Non-Realization, Seeking Only To Cling To Me In infantile Fashion—As If To <u>Possess</u> My Every Avataric Divine Word, My Avatarically Working Divine Acts, My Avatarically-Born Bodily (Human) Divine Form, My Avatarically Self-Transmitted Divine Spirit-Energy, and My Avatarically Self-Revealed (and Very, and Self-Evidently Divine) Being, Instead Of <u>Surrendering</u> To Me, and (Thus and Thereby) Submitting To Understand the conditional self Most Fundamentally, Such That the conditional self May Then Be Really, and Totally, and Effectively, and Consistently Surrendered To Me, Even (Most Ultimately) To The Degree Of Perfect Love-Bliss and Perfect Freedom, In Native Identification With My Avatarically Self-Revealed (and Self-Evidently Divine) Self-Condition (Which <u>Is</u> The Divine Source-Condition Of All and all). Therefore, My Listening Devotee May Submit Only To Be The "Failed Case", Only ego-Possessed—Complaining Of "No Cure", Like a child Faking Sickness To Avoid The School Of Life. All These Efforts (and More) Prevent The Cycle Of Liberating self-Understanding and self-Surrender—and All These Efforts (and More), If Projected Onto The Total Course Of The Only-By-Me Revealed and Given Way Of The Heart, Would Turn My "Radical" Call, and The Process Of Divine Self-Awakening, Into A Long and Difficult (and Even Fruitless) "Path Of Return".

The Secret Of The Only-By-Me Revealed and Given Way Of The Heart (or Way Of Adidam) Is Not In The Effort Either To Cling To the present moment or circumstance Or To Avoid or (Strategically)

Escape the present moment or circumstance. The Secret Of The Only-By-Me Revealed and Given Way Of The Heart (or Way Of Adidam) Is (Via Feeling-Contemplation and Feeling-Meditation) To Convert every present moment or circumstance Into The Reality Process Of Heart-Communion With Me—Even (Most Ultimately) To The Inherently Most Perfect Degree Of Divine Self-Realization. Progressive (and Progressively Meditative, and Progressively Me-Realizing) Feeling-Contemplation Of Me Is The Secret and Inherently Perfectly Efficient (and Only-By-My-Avataric-Divine-Grace-Given) Means Whereby This Conversion Becomes Possible In every moment or circumstance. And Progressive (and Progressively Meditative, and Progressively Me-Realizing) Feeling-Contemplation Of Me Is (In every moment or circumstance) The Secret and Inherently Perfectly Efficient (and Only-By-My-Avataric-Divine-Grace-Given) Means Whereby This Conversion Can Fulfill Itself In Truth (Most Ultimately, Most Perfectly, and Finally).

Thus, The Essential Practice Of The Only-By-Me Revealed and Given Way Of Adidam (Which Is The One and Only By-Me-Revealed and By-Me-Given Way Of The Heart) Is Easy To Describe.

I Am The "Bright", The One To Be Realized.

You Are Inherently (At Heart) Attracted By Me.

Your Own self-Contraction Is Dissociation From Me.

Yield To Me (By Surrendering To My Inherent Heart-Attractiveness), and You (Thus and Thereby—By Means Of My Avatarically Self-Transmitted Divine Grace) Enter (and Swoon) Into My Sphere Of "Brightness".

The Only-By-Me Revealed and Given Way Of Adidam (Which Is The One and Only By-Me-Revealed and By-Me-Given Way Of The Heart) Is (In Its Fullness and Completeness As A Total Practice) Simply This (ego-Surrendering, ego-Forgetting, and, More and More, ego-Transcending) Swoon Of Responsively Abiding (and Luxuriating) In The Sphere Of My Love-Bliss-"Bright" (and Self-Evidently Divine) Person.

Such Is The Only-By-Me Revealed and Given Practice Of Ruchira Avatara Bhakti Yoga.

Therefore, Listen To Me and Hear Me and See Me. Turn Your Heart-attention To Me—and Do Not Measure That Turning Relative

To Whether Or Not Your mind Stops and You Feel Better. Love Me—and Do Not Measure That Loving Against Whether Or Not You Still Feel Negative emotions and Confusion. Give Your life To Me. Turn bodily To My Avatarically-Born Bodily (Human) Divine Form. Feel (and Thereby Contemplate) My Avatarically-Born Bodily (Human) Divine Form, My Avatarically Self-Revealed Spiritual (and Always Blessing) Divine Presence, and My Avatarically Self-Revealed (and Very, and Transcendental, and Perfectly Subjective, and Inherently Spiritual, and Inherently egoless, and Inherently Perfect, and Self-Evidently Divine) State <u>At</u> <u>all</u> <u>times</u>. And Do Not Measure That Giving, and That Turning, and That Feeling-Contemplation Against The Measure Of Whether Or Not You Feel pains in Your body.

Therefore, Always Maintain The Discipline Of That Giving, and That Turning, and That Feeling-Contemplation. It Can Be Done, If You Do Not limit or Deny That Giving, That Turning, and That Feeling-Contemplation By The Reading Of Problems In Your body-mind. That Giving, That Turning, and That Feeling-Contemplation Can Always Be Done. Truly, You Can Never Be Disabled In Terms Of That Giving, That Turning, and That Feeling-Contemplation.

I <u>Am</u> The Divine Husband Of all and All—Avatarically Self-Revealed To all and All.

I Submitted To Be Avatarically Born In Bodily (Human) Form In Order (By My Own Avataric Ordeal Of Divine Re-Awakening) To Make My Living Divine Person, In Each and All Of My Great Avataric Divine Forms (and Even In My Own "Brightly" Transfigured, "Brightly" Transformed, and "Brightly" Indifferent Bodily Human Divine Form), The Very (Real, and Always Already Effective) Avataric Divine Means For The Turning, and The Most Ultimate Divine Awakening, Of all conditionally Manifested beings.

Therefore, Be Restored To Your Perfect Well-Being By Real Fidelity To Me.

Fidelity To Me Is Fidelity To The Heart Itself—The "Bright" and One and Only Self-Condition and Source-Condition (Of each and every one, and Of all, and Of All), and The One and All (In All and all) Who Alone <u>Is</u> Real God (The One and Only Truth and Reality).

When You Truly Listen To Me, You Have Begun To Exercise True (and Truly ego-Surrendering, and Truly ego-Forgetting, and, More and More, Truly ego-Transcending) Devotional (and Contemplative) Concentration On Me.

When You Truly Both Hear Me and See Me, You Have Become Capable Of Fullest (and Directly and Fully ego-Transcending) Devotional (and Contemplative) Concentration On Me.

Therefore, Through Devotional Concentration Of Your mind (Via Feeling-attention) On Me, You Will (By Means Of My Avatarically Self-Transmitted Divine Grace) Become Attracted Beyond Your Own mind—and The Eternal Divine Love-Bliss Of My Own State Of Being Will (By Means Of My Avatarically Self-Transmitted Divine Grace) Become (or Be Realized and Magnified As) Your Own.

Likewise, Through Devotionally Me-Recognizing Concentration On Me, and Through Devotionally To-Me-Responsive Conservation Of all Your energies and all Your actions (bodily, emotional, and mental) In Service To Me (In all relations and Under all circumstances), The Ease and The Strength Of My Avatarically Self-Revealed (and Self-Evidently Divine) Person (or Self-Condition) Will (By Means Of My Avatarically Self-Transmitted Divine Grace) Become (or Be Realized, and Magnified, As) Your Own.

Therefore, By Means Of Hearing Me, Seeing Me, Real Devotion To Me, and True Fidelity To Me—You Will Freely Realize That Your Hearing Of Me, Your Seeing Of Me, Your Devotion To Me, and (Thus and Thereby) Your Fidelity To Me (The Avatarically Self-Revealed, and Very, and Self-Evidently Divine Person) Are The Very and Auspicious Design Of Your Own Freedom.

I Am Freedom Itself. I, Myself, Am Perfect. And, Yet, The Sign Of My Human Personality Does Not Conform To Any Idealized View Of Perfect Saintliness or Holiness. I Use All Qualities and Possibilities In My Avataric Play Of Divine Work—and I Must Do So. My Avataric Divine Work, Itself, Is Perfect. But Why Should It Be Expected That The Body-Mind Through Which I Do My Avataric Divine Work Must Be "Perfect" In Some Idealized Sense? All Qualities and Possibilities Become Usable To Me, In The Perfection That Transcends all conditions. I Noticed This When I

Fully Embraced My Divinely "Crazy" Teaching-Work. I Observed all the people I Was Associated With, and (Likewise) Observed That My Avatarically-Born Body-Mind (Because Of Its History, Its Qualities, and Its Adaptations) Was Perfectly Suited To Serve such people—Because There Were (In My Avatarically-Born Body-Mind-Vehicle) <u>Like</u> Characteristics That I Could Bring Into The Avataric Play With others In My Divine Work Of Self-Submission and My Divine Work Of Reflecting others To themselves. If My "Sadhana Years" Had Required Some Sort Of Idealized "Perfection" In This Body-Mind (In ordinary Terms), I Would Not Have Had The Range Of Human-Personality Characteristics That Allowed Me To Exhibit "Behavior" Of All Kinds and (Thereby) To Make A Connection To all the kinds of living beings, with all their various limitations. Thus, I Saw That This Body-Mind Had All The Kinds Of Characteristics Necessary For (and That Would Be Altogether Usable In) The Avataric Play Of My Divinely Liberating Work—and I Used Them In That Fashion.

These Characteristics (In The Avataric Play Of My Divine Work During The Physical Lifetime Of My Avatarically-Born Bodily Human Divine Form) Do Not Bind Me (and Have Not Bound Me) In Any Manner Whatsoever, Even Though They Are (Because They arise As conditional Manifestations Of The conditional, or Cosmic, Domain) Often In The Likeness Of ordinary beings. Such Is My True (and Divine, and Not Merely Human) Perfection: That These Qualities arose Coincident With My Own Body-Mind (and The Physical Lifetime Of My Avatarically-Born Bodily Human Divine Form), and (Therefore) Could Be Used To Serve living beings—and, Yet, They Were Not Bondage For Me, but They Were (In My Divine Re-Awakening and My Avataric Divine Work), Simply, Divinely Self-Recognized, As Transparent (or Merely Apparent), and Un-necessary, and Inherently Non-Binding Modifications Of My Self-Realized (and Inherently Divine) Perfection.

The Body-Mind-Vehicle Associated With The (Bodily Human) Physical Lifetime Of My Unique Avataric Divine Incarnation here Is Not <u>Itself</u> Perfect, but (By Virtue Of My "Sadhana Years", and My Ultimate Divine Re-Awakening, and All Of My Avataric Divine

Work) It Became Not Only (As It Was, Even From Its Avataric Birth) <u>Established In</u> That Which Is Inherently Perfect, but It Also Became Utterly <u>Conformed To</u> That Which Is Inherently Perfect—Such That I (Myself, The "Bright", and Inherently Perfect, and Self-Evidently Divine Person, or Self-Condition, or Source-Condition, Of all and All) Became Perfectly Radiant In and <u>As</u> and Through This Avataric Divine Vehicle. Only That <u>Divine</u> Perfection Is Inherently Perfect—Not The Body-Mind-Vehicle Itself. Nevertheless, My Avatarically-Born Body-Mind-Vehicle Of Incarnate Divine Self-Manifestation Became An Unobstructed Agent Of My Own Divine Perfection, Utterly Transparent To Me <u>As</u> I Am. Therefore, The Virtue Of My Avatarically-Born Body-Mind-Vehicle Of Incarnate Divine Self-Manifestation (and Divine Self-Revelation) Is Its Transparency and Conformity To Me—The Avataric Divine Self-Revelation Of That Which Is Inherently Perfect.

During My Avataric Physical Lifetime, I Am Present here, In Bodily (Human) Divine Form, but (Nevertheless) <u>As</u> I <u>Am</u>—Divinely Working In this world <u>As</u> it <u>Is</u> (and as it <u>Appears</u> to be), and With beings <u>As</u> they <u>Are</u> (and as they <u>Appear</u> to be). Therefore, During The Physical Lifetime Of My Avatarically-Born Bodily (Human) Divine Form here, I Have Completely Done Whatever Was Necessary To Do For The Sake Of My (Then, and Now, and Forever Hereafter) Eternal Work Of Avataric Self-Revelation and Divine Blessing. And <u>That</u> Is Perfect.

The Only-By-Me Revealed and Given Avataric Divine Way Of Adidam (Which Is The One and Only By-Me-Revealed and By-Me-Given Way Of The Heart) Is The Way Of Devotion To Me <u>As</u> The Divine "Atma-Murti" (or <u>As</u> The Inherently egoless, and Self-Evidently Divine, Person Of Reality and Truth—In <u>Place</u>, <u>As</u> Self-Condition, Rather Than <u>As</u> Exclusively Objective Other).

Therefore, In every moment, My True Devotee Whole bodily (and, Thus, By Means Of The Spontaneous Me-Recognizing Devotional Response Of All Four Of The Principal psycho-physical Faculties—Of attention, emotional feeling, breath, and perceptual body) "Locates" Me <u>As</u> That Which Is Always Already <u>The</u> Case (Prior To—but Not Separate From—The Form, The Exercise, and the any object of All Four psycho-physical Faculties).

Happiness Itself (or Inherent Love-Bliss-Sufficiency Of Being) Is Always Already The Case.

Happiness Itself (or The Divinely Self-Sufficient Love-Bliss-Condition Of Being—Itself) <u>Is</u> <u>That</u> Which Is Always Already The Case.

Happiness Itself (or Love-Bliss-Radiance Of Boundlessly Feeling Being) <u>Is</u> The Most Prior Condition Of Existence (or Of Conscious Being—Itself).

Happiness Itself (or The Condition Of Love-Bliss-Radiance) Must Be Realized—In and <u>As</u> every conditionally arising moment—By Transcending self-Contraction (or all of Separate and Separative self, or psycho-physical ego-"I", <u>and</u> all of the ego's objects, or conditions Of Existence—or, Indeed, <u>All</u> Of The Illusions of self and Not-self).

When attention Is Facing Outward (or Is Turned Out, As If To Outside itself), the body-mind Is Concentrated Upon the "view" (or "field") of apparently separate objects (and Upon Me <u>As</u> Objective Other).

When attention Is Facing Inward (or Is Turned In, As If Upon itself), the body-mind Is Concentrated Upon the "point of view" of apparently separate self (and Upon Me <u>As</u> Separate Consciousness).

When attention Is Devotionally Yielded To Whole bodily "Locate" Me <u>As</u> That Which Is Always Already (and Divinely) <u>The</u> Case, All "Difference" (Whether Of ego-"I" or Of object and other) Is (Inherently) Transcended (In Consciousness Itself, or Self-Existing Being, Which <u>Is</u> Love-Bliss-Happiness Itself—and Which <u>Is</u> Always Already <u>The</u> Case).

Therefore, To The Degree That You Surrender (Whole bodily) To Be and Do Truly <u>Relational</u> (and Ecstatic, or ego-Transcending) Devotional Love Of Me (<u>As</u> The True Loved-One, The Divine Beloved Of The Heart), You Are (Thus and Thereby) Established—Whole bodily and Inherently—In The Non-Contracted Condition (or Self-Condition, or Inherent Condition) Of Reality Itself (Which <u>Is</u> Consciousness Itself <u>and</u> Love-Bliss Itself—and Which <u>Is</u> Always Already <u>The</u> Case).

In Due Course, <u>This</u> Devotional Practice <u>Is</u> Perfect—and, At Last, To Be Most Perfectly Realized.

RUCHIRA AVATAR ADI DA SAMRAJ
Los Angeles, 2000

Three Essays from the *Samraj Upanishad*

The Sanskrit word "upanishad" indicates "Teachings received at the Feet of the Guru". Thus, the Samraj Upanishad *is "Teachings received at the Feet of Ruchira Avatar Adi Da Samraj". Rather than being the title of a distinct book, "Samraj Upanishad" is a collective designation for certain Talks and Essays by Avatar Adi Da Samraj that appear within various of His twenty-three "Source-Texts" as readings supporting and expanding upon the principal "Part" of a given "Source-Text".*

Three Essays from the *Samraj Upanishad*

The One and True and Only By-Me-Revealed and By-Me-Given Way Of The Heart

Consciousness Itself <u>Is</u>.
Therefore, Existence (Itself) <u>Is</u> (or Is Being) Consciousness Itself.

Consciousness Itself <u>Is</u> the Non-Separate (beginningless, changeless, and endless) Feeling-Contemplation of Its Own Inherent (and Inherently Indivisible) Radiance, Spirit-Energy, Love-Bliss, or Happiness.

Therefore, Consciousness Itself <u>Is</u> Self-Existing and Self-Radiant Love-Bliss, or Happiness Itself.

Therefore, Existence (or to Exist) <u>Is</u> That (or Thus).

Therefore, you <u>Are</u> That (Non-Separately, Utterly Beyond the ego-"I").

You Are (or Are Being) <u>Only</u> the Consciousness of (or That <u>Is</u>) Non-Separate and Indivisible and Irreducible Love-Bliss.

All non-Happiness (or the apparent absence of Love-Bliss) is simply the forgetting of (or self-contraction from) What Always Already (Inherently, Non-Separately, Indivisibly, and Irreducibly) <u>Is</u>.

All non-Love (or the failure to Be Radiant As Love-Bliss) is simply the forgetting of (or self-contraction from) Who, What, and Where you Are (Non-Separately, Beyond and Prior to the ego-"I", or Beyond and Prior to all self-contraction from That Which Is Always Already The Case).

All suffering is an unnecessary illusion that appears (or apparently arises) whenever you (by self-contraction) forget to Feel (and, Thus, to Contemplate, and to Merely Be) Love-Bliss Itself.

This must be Realized.

Love-Bliss Itself (Self-Existing and Self-Radiant As Consciousness Itself) must be Realized (and not forgotten, but always Remembered, or Communed with, and Identified with—until It is Always Already Remembered).

This Realization Is at the Heart.

This Realization Is the Realization of Indivisible and Non-Separate Oneness with the Heart (Itself).

The total Process (or full and complete Way) That Realizes This Realization Is the only-by-Me Revealed and Given Way of Adidam (Which Is the One and True and Only by-Me-Revealed and by-Me-Given Way of the Heart).

Therefore, the Way of the Heart (or Way of Adidam) Is (by the Unique Means of right, true, full, and fully devotionally Me-recognizing devotion to Me) the Way of Practice toward and in and (Ultimately) As This Realization.

The Way of the Heart Is, by Means of right, true, full, and fully ego-transcending devotion to Me, to Allow This Realization, by Transcending (or ceasing to Feel limited by) all apparent conditional limitations on Love-Bliss (Which Is Realization Itself).

Therefore, by Means of the Feeling-Contemplation of My Avatarically-Born bodily (human) Divine Form, My Avatarically Self-Revealed Spiritual (and Always Blessing) Divine Presence, and My Avatarically Self-Revealed (and Very, and Transcendental, and Perfectly Subjective, and Inherently Spiritual, and Inherently egoless, and Inherently Perfect, and Self-Evidently Divine) State, understand your separate and separative self, and Transcend your separate and separative self. And, when (by Means of My Avatarically Self-Transmitted Divine Grace) all limitations (or all

314

forms of self-contraction) are Transcended at the Heart, Merely <u>Be</u> Consciousness (and, Thus, Merely Feel—and, by Feeling, Contemplate the Inherent Radiance, or Love-Bliss, of Merely Being, or Existence Itself).

Transcend all limitations at the Heart by (progressively) observing and understanding (and Feeling beyond) all (physical, emotional, and mental) forms of self-contraction, or all self-limits on My Avatarically Self-Transmitted Divine Spirit-Energy (or Love-Bliss) Itself.

Therefore, and in the Feeling-Manner, Grow (by Means of devotionally Me-recognizing devotional, and really ego-transcending, response to My Avatarically Self-Transmitted Divine Grace) to Contemplate (and, Ultimately, to Merely <u>Be</u>) Inherent Love-Bliss Itself—and (Thereby) to Relax all contraction from Love-Bliss (and, Ultimately, of Love-Bliss) Itself.

All apparent objects and all apparent subjective states <u>Are</u> Only Spirit-Energy (or Love-Bliss Itself, or Happiness Itself, or the Inherently Radiant Self-Nature of Reality Itself), Witnessed (or Inherently and Merely Felt-Contemplated) by Consciousness Itself (Which Is the Inherent, and Self-Existing, Self-Nature of Reality Itself).

When all apparent objects (or apparent objective conditions) and all apparent subjective states (or apparent subjective conditions) are Comprehended (or Merely Witnessed and Felt) <u>As</u> Spirit-Energy (or Love-Bliss) Itself (Which they only seem to modify or limit), <u>and</u> when all apparent objective and apparent subjective conditions are Merely Witnessed (such that the Feeling-Witness Itself undermines and dissolves attention itself), then the earlier and the advancing developmental stages of the only-by-Me Revealed and Given Way of the Heart are complete (and no more to be done).

When Consciousness Itself (Which <u>Is</u> the Heart, and Which otherwise seems to Witness, or Only Feel, Spirit-Energy, or Love-Bliss, Itself, and all Its apparent objective and subjective conditions) Awakens to Itself, such that attention does not arise to wander toward the apparent objects (or relations) and states of the body-mind, or even <u>toward</u> Spirit-Energy Itself (as if Spirit-Energy, or

Love-Bliss, Exists outside, or apart from, Consciousness Itself), the last of the progressive developmental stages of the only-by-Me Revealed and Given Way of the Heart is nearing the Divinely Most Perfect Revelation of the Perfect Itself.

When Consciousness Itself Divinely Self-Recognizes Spirit-Energy (or Love-Bliss) Itself (and all Its apparent modifications) <u>As</u> Only Consciousness Itself (or Its Inherent Radiance), the only-by-Me Revealed and Given Way of the Heart has Realized Itself Most Perfectly (and the Heart Itself Is Perfectly Begun).

Therefore, in the only-by-Me Revealed and Given Way of the Heart, to Self-Abide <u>As</u> Self-Existing Consciousness Itself (Which <u>Is</u> the Inherent, and Perfectly Subjective, Feeling of Being, Itself, Self-Radiant As Love-Bliss) Is the Realization of the Heart Itself.

And to Divinely Self-Recognize (and Feel, and Feel Through) Spirit-Energy Itself (even in the form of all apparent objects and states) <u>As</u> the Inherent (and Inherently Free) Radiance (or Love-Bliss) of Consciousness Itself (or the Inherent Feeling of Being, Itself) Is the Most Ultimate Demonstration of the Heart.

This becomes (or Always Already <u>Is</u>) the Outshining of all limitations, in the Infinite Divine Self-"Brightness" That <u>Is</u> Love-Bliss Itself.

I <u>Am</u> you—Eternally (and Always Already).

I Surround you, and In-Fill you, and Pervade you, and Awaken you—Avatarically (Now, and Forever Hereafter).

<u>You</u> must (by transcending your own self-contraction) Realize <u>Me</u>—In Person, Eternally, and <u>As</u> My Always Already Existing, Inherently egoless, Perfectly Non-"Different", and Infinitely Self-Radiant Self-Condition.

You must Realize Me Eternally (<u>As</u> I <u>Am</u>), by All My Avataric Means (Now, and Forever Hereafter, Given to All and all—and, Now, and Forever Hereafter, to be heart-Found by each and all of My devotees).

The "Thumbs"
Is The Fundamental Sign
Of The Avataric Crashing-Down
Of My Divine Person

I n The True (and Characteristic) Course Of The Frontal Yoga In
The Total (or Full and Complete) Practice Of The Only-By-Me
Revealed and Given Way Of Adidam (Which Is The One and
Only By-Me-Revealed and By-Me-Given Way Of The Heart), There
Will Be Occasional "Surges" (or Spontaneous Invasions) Of My
Avatarically Self-Transmitted Divine Spiritual Energy In The Frontal
Line. And These Frontal Surges Of My Avatarically Self-Transmitted
Divine Spiritual Energy Will (In Turn) Also Pass, Perceptibly or
Imperceptibly, From The Frontal Line Into The Spinal Line—Thus
Completing The Circle. Such Surges May Be Weak or Strong. They
May Produce yawning and General Relaxation, and They May
Otherwise Reveal (or Yield) Feelings Of General Pleasure and
Fundamental Happiness, As Well As Various Degrees Of Ecstatic
(or ego-Transcending) Participation In My Avatarically Self-
Transmitted Divine Love-Bliss Itself. As A Result Of Your Own
Accumulated psycho-physical Patterning Of self-Contraction,
These Frontal Surges May Also Be Accompanied (or, Otherwise,
Followed) By temporary symptoms of mental, emotional, and
physical discomfort, pain, fever, and even physical disease. If such
symptomatic phenomena Are Associated With The Real Spiritual
Process, they Tend To Come and Go (In Cycles Of Relative comfort
and discomfort). As Such, They Are Gracefully Purifying Episodes,
Shown Through The Evidence Of psycho-physical Release,
Rebalance, and Rejuvenation. Occasionally, There May Even Be
an experience that Feels Like A Kind Of electric "Shock" (or "Jolt")

That Briefly Energizes the body Beyond ordinary Tolerance. In and By All Of This, the human character Is Divinely Urged To Be Responsively and Positively Changed (psychically, mentally, emotionally, and physically), Through The Invasion Of the frontal personality (and, Indeed, the Total body-mind) By My Avatarically Self-Transmitted Divine Spirit-Current Of Love-Bliss-Light.

Among All Of These Signs There Must (Primarily) Appear Progressive Evidence Of What I Have, Since Childhood, Called The "Thumbs". Beginning In The "Basic" (or, Possibly, Even In The "Original", or Foundation) Context Of The Fourth Stage Of Life In The Way Of The Heart, There Should Be At Least Occasional Experience Of An Intense Invasion Of The Frontal Line By My Avatarically Self-Transmitted Divine Spirit-Force Of Love-Bliss— Beginning At The Crown Of the head, and Descending Into The lower vital Region, To the bodily base. The Pressure (or Invasive Force) Of This Event May Be Rather (and Even Happily) Overwhelming—and It Must Be Allowed. At Last, It Is Not Possible (Nor Would You Wish) To Defend Your psycho-physical self Against This Invading Pressure Of My Avataric Divine Spiritual Descent. It Feels Like A Solid and Yet Fluid Mass Of Force, Like A Large Hand All Made Of Thumbs—Pressing Down From Infinitely Above the head and Via The Crown Of the head, Engorging the Total head (and the throat), and (Thus and Thereby) Penetrating and Vanishing the entire mind, and Vastly Opening the emotional core, and (Altogether) In-Filling the Total physical body.

The Feeling-Sense That Results From This Simple (and Most Basic) Frontal In-Filling By My Avatarically Self-Revealed Divine Spirit-Presence Is That the Total body-mind Is Sublimed and Released Into ego-Surrendering, ego-Forgetting, and ego-Transcending Feeling-Identification With The Spherical Form Of My Own Divine and Spiritual (and All-and-all-Surrounding, and All-and-all-Pervading) Love-Bliss-Body Of Indefinable "Brightness" (or Indestructible Light). And This Simple (and Most Basic) Form Of The "Thumbs" Is A Necessary (Although, At First, Only Occasional) Experience Associated With The Reception Of My Avatarically Self-Transmitted Divine Spirit-Baptism. It Is My Divine "Goddess-Power" and "Husbanding" Grace At Work. And The

Simple (and Most Basic) <u>Spherical</u> Fullness Of The "Thumbs", Once It Is Firmly Established (In The Basic Maturity Of The "Basic" Fourth Stage Of Life In The Way Of The Heart), Must Continue To Be Experienced, As A Fundamental and (Essentially) <u>Continuous</u> (or <u>Constant</u>) Yogic Event, In The Later Advanced and The Ultimate Stages Of Life In The Way Of The Heart.

As The Spiritual Process Develops Toward The Transition Beyond The "Basic" Fourth Stage Of Life In The Way Of The Heart, The Simple (and Most Basic) Experience Of The "Thumbs" Must Become A More and More Constant Yogic Event—and, On Random Occasions, The Experience Of The "Thumbs" Must Occur In Its Most Extended, Full, and Complete Form. In That Most Extended, Full, and Complete Case Of The Experience Of The "Thumbs", My Descending Spiritual Fullness Will <u>Completely</u> Overwhelm the ordinary frontal (or natural human) sense Of bodily Existence. My Avatarically Self-Transmitted Divine Spirit-Current Will Move Fully Down In The Frontal Line (To the bodily base), and It Will Then Turn About, and—Without Vacating The Frontal Line—It Will Pass Also Into The Spinal Line. This Yogic Event Will Occur With Such Force That You Will Feel Utterly (Love-Blissfully) "Intoxicated"—and There Will Be The Feeling That the body Is Somehow Rotating Forward and Down (From The Crown Of the head), As Well As Backward and Up (From the base of the spine). This Rotation Will Seem, Suddenly, To Complete Itself—and The Experience Will, Suddenly, Be One Of Feeling Released From the gross physical body, Such That You Feel You Are Present Only As An egoless "Energy Body" (Previously Associated With and Conformed To the gross physical body—but Now, By Means Of My Avatarically Self-Transmitted Divine Grace, Infused By and Conformed To My Avatarically Self-Transmitted Divine Body Of Self-Evidently Divine Spirit-Energy). You Will Feel This "Energy Body" To Be <u>Spherical</u> In Shape—Centerless (Empty, or Void, Of Center, mind, and Familiar ego-self) and Boundless (As If Even bodiless, or Without form), Although (Somehow, and Partially) Also Yet Associated With (While Rotating From and Beyond) Your ordinary psycho-physical form. The ordinary References Of the body-mind and the environment Will, In This Divine

Yogic Event, Not Make Much Sense (or, In Any Manner, Affect This Experience Of The "Thumbs")—Although There May Be Some <u>Superficial</u> (and Entirely Non-limiting) Awareness Of the body, the room, and so forth. This Experience Will Last For a few moments, or a few minutes—or For an extended period, of indefinite length. Nevertheless, Just When This Spontaneous Experience Has Become <u>Most</u> Pleasurable—Such That You <u>Somehow</u> Gesture To <u>Make</u> It Continue Indefinitely—the ordinary sense of the body-mind Will, Suddenly (Spontaneously), Return.

The "Thumbs" Is Not A Process Of "Going Somewhere Else", Nor Is It Even A Process Of "Vacating" the gross physical body (or the gross physical realm Altogether). Rather, The "Thumbs" Is A Process Of Transformation Of the experiencing of the present physical circumstance. If the present physical circumstance Is Left Behind (Such That experiential reference to the gross physical realm Is Entirely Absent, and There Is Total Loss Of Awareness Of the physical context in which the experience Began), Then The Practitioner Of The Way Of The Heart Is (Necessarily) experiencing A Form Of Samadhi Other Than The "Thumbs". In The "Thumbs", Awareness Of the physical context of experience Is Not Lost, but Is Totally Changed—Such That, Instead Of The self-Conscious, self-Contracted Shape Of the waking-state personality, one's physical form Is Found To Be A Boundlessly Radiant Sphere (Without Thickness Of Surface). With This Profound Shift In The Awareness Of the physical body, The Differentiation Inherent In The Usual waking-state body-Consciousness Disappears, and Is (Effectively) Replaced By egoless body-Consciousness. A Re-Phasing Of The Energy-Construct Of bodily Awareness and spatial Awareness Occurs, Such That physical body and physical space are Tacitly Sensed In A Manner Entirely Different From ordinary perception. And, As Soon As There Is Any Effort To Recollect The Usual Sense Of bodily form or Of the circumstance Of physical embodiment, The Experience Of The "Thumbs" Disappears. The "Thumbs" Continues Only As Long As It Is Simply Allowed To Happen, Without Any egoic self-Consciousness (or psycho-physical self-Contraction)—and It Spontaneously Vanishes When egoic self-Consciousness (or psycho-physical self-Contraction) Returns.

In The Only-By-Me Revealed and Given Way Of The Heart, The Most Extended, Full, and Complete Experience Of The "Thumbs" Is, In Its Frontal Associations, A Fourth Stage Transitional Samadhi (Just As Fifth Stage conditional Nirvikalpa Samadhi and Sixth Stage Jnana Samadhi Are Transitional Samadhis Associated With Particular Stages Of Life In The Only-By-Me Revealed and Given Way Of The Heart). As Such, The Original Significance Of The Samadhi Of The "Thumbs" Is Not Merely In The Experience Itself (Such That The Experience Should Be psychophysically Clung To, or, Otherwise, Made Into An Object Of egoic Seeking), but The Original Significance Of The Most Extended, Full, and Complete Experience (or True Samadhi) Of The "Thumbs" Is In Its Effect (or In The More Mature, and Truly ego-Transcending, Process That It May Allow or Indicate). That Is To Say, In The "Basic" Context Of The Fourth Stage Of Life In The Way Of The Heart, The Most Extended, Full, and Complete Sign Of The "Thumbs" (When It Is Accompanied By The, Essentially, Constant Experience Of The Simple and Most Basic Sign Of The "Thumbs") Is (or May Be) An Indication That The Process Of self-Transcendence Is Moving On From Concentration In the frontal personality To Either The Next Immediately Possible Developmental Stage In The Way Of The Heart (Which Involves The Process Of Ascent To The Ajna Door Via The Spinal Line) Or, Most Optimally (and Most Typically, In The Way Of The Heart)—If True and Stable Awakening Of The Witness-Consciousness Also (and Even Simultaneously, By Means Of My Avatarically Self-Transmitted Divine Grace) Occurs—Directly To Practice Of The Way Of The Heart In The Context Of The Sixth Stage Of Life. However, The Samadhi Of The "Thumbs" and The Basic Experience Of The "Thumbs" Are, Also (Beyond Their Original Significance In The "Basic" Context Of The Fourth Stage Of Life In The Way Of The Heart), Principal Among The Great Signs Associated With My Avataric Divine Self-Revelation To all and All. And, Therefore, In The Context Of The Only-By-Me Revealed and Given Seventh Stage Of Life In The Way Of The Heart, The Samadhi Of The "Thumbs" (and The Basic Experience Of The "Thumbs") Is Most Perfectly Realized and Demonstrated (Even In

Divine Translation), <u>As</u> The Centerless and Boundless "Bright" Spherical Space Of My Eternal Divine Spiritual Body and My Eternal Divine Self-Condition.

The <u>Occasional</u> Samadhi Of The "Thumbs" (Which Is The Experience Of The "Thumbs" In Its Most Extended, Full, and Complete Form) <u>and</u> The (Essentially) <u>Constant</u> Experience Of The "Thumbs" In Its Simple and Most Basic Form <u>Together</u> Characterize The Full (or Fully Developed) Frontal Course Of Spiritual Practice In The Way Of The Heart (and, Until The "Thumbs" Thus—and, In Every Respect, Satisfactorily—Appears In <u>Both</u> Of Its Forms, The Transition Cannot Be Made To Any Stage Of The Way Of The Heart Beyond The "Basic" Context Of The Fourth Stage Of Life). Therefore, In The Total (or Full and Complete) Practice Of The Only-By-Me Revealed and Given Way Of The Heart (or Way Of Adidam), The Sign Of The "Thumbs" (In <u>Both</u> Of Its Forms, and Along With Evidence Of Real and Stable human and Spiritual Equanimity In the daily life of the frontal personality) Is One Of The Necessary Indicators That Must Precede The Transition From The "Basic" Fourth Stage Of Life In The Way Of The Heart To The "Advanced" Fourth Stage Of Life In The Way Of The Heart (or, Otherwise, and Most Typically, The Early Transition To The Sixth Stage Of Life In The Way Of The Heart, Directly From The Point Of Basic Maturity In The "Basic" Fourth Stage Of Life In The Way Of The Heart).

The Sign Of The "Thumbs" Is One Of The Primary Experiential Signs Of The Transcending Of Bondage and Confinement To the frontal personality and the gross bodily idea of ego-self. The Sign Of The "Thumbs" Indicates That The Knots In The Frontal Line (In The Total Crown Of the head, the Total brain, the throat, the heart, the solar plexus, the abdomen, the genitals, and the anal-perineal area) Are Opened (At Least Temporarily) To My Avatarically Self-Transmitted Divine Spirit-Current (and Can, By Right Practice, Be Responsibly Surrendered To The Point Of Such Openness In The Context Of daily living). The Sign Of The "Thumbs" Is Also An Indication That The Primary Knot (or Root-Contraction) In The Deep Lower Region Of the body-mind (Extending From the solar plexus To the bodily base) Has Been (and Can Continue To Be)

Opened To My Avatarically Self-Transmitted Divine Spirit-Current—Such That The Great Fullness Of My Avatarically Self-Transmitted Divine Love-Bliss Is Established Deep In the body, and Deep In the emotional being, and Deep In the mind of the frontal personality. And When The Sphere Of My Avatarically Self-Transmitted Divine Love-Bliss Is In (Essentially) Constant Evidence, The Course Of Ascent May Be Revealed and Established—or (If, By Means Of My Avataric Divine Self-Revelation Via The "Thumbs", There Is, In The "Basic" Context Of The Fourth Stage Of Life In The Way Of The Heart, and, Most Typically, In The Very Midst Of The Experiential Sign Of The "Thumbs", An Early Spontaneous Awakening Of The Witness-Consciousness) The Way Of The Heart May Open Directly To The Course Associated With The Sixth Stage Of Life.

The Sign Of The "Thumbs" Is Not Merely A Matter Of experiencing natural energies Coursing Through the body, Nor Is It Merely A Matter Of Experiencing My Avatarically Self-Revealed Spiritual (and Always Blessing) Divine Presence To Be, Somehow, Felt In and By the body. The Samadhi Of The "Thumbs" (or Else The Experience Of The "Thumbs" In Its Simple and Most Basic Form) Is Utter (ego-Surrendering, ego-Forgetting, and ego-Transcending) Devotional Submission Of the Total body-mind-self To My (Avatarically Self-Revealed) Divine and Spiritual (and Always Blessing) Person. And, If and When That Devotional Submission Is Most Profound (In The Midst Of The By-Me-Given Sign Of The "Thumbs"), My (Avatarically Self-Transmitted) Divine and Spiritual Self-Revelation Will Grant You The Gift Of Direct Awakening To The Witness-Position.

The Sign Of The "Thumbs" Is Revealed and Given Only By Me. The Sign Of The "Thumbs" Is The Fundamental Sign Of The Descent (or Crashing Down) Of My (Avatarically Self-Revealed) Divine and Spiritual Person. In and By Means Of My Avatarically Self-Transmitted Divine Spiritual Sign Of The "Thumbs", I Invade You, Pass Into You, and In-Fill You—bodily, where You stand, where You sit, where You walk, where You live and breathe, where You think, and feel, and function. And, In and By Means Of My Avatarically Self-Transmitted Divine Spiritual Sign Of The

"Thumbs", I Awaken You In My Divine <u>Sphere</u>, <u>Beyond</u> the body-mind—Where <u>Only</u> I <u>Am</u>.

My Avataric Divine Gift Of The Sign Of The "Thumbs" Is A Matter Of Utterly (Responsively) Giving Up To My Avatarically Self-Transmitted Divine Spiritual Invasion Of You, and Being Released Of Your ego-Possession, and Dying As the ego—and (Thus) Responsively and Freely Relinquishing self-Contraction, and (In Due Course) Becoming (By Means Of My Avatarically Self-Transmitted Divine Grace) Spiritually, Transcendentally, and Divinely Awake.

The Samadhi Of The "Thumbs" Is The Fundamental Samadhi Of My Avataric Divine Spiritual Descent. Therefore, The Samadhi (and Even Every Manifestation Of The Sign) Of The "Thumbs" Is A Fullest Experiential Sign Of My Avatarically Self-Revealed Divine Spiritual Presence Of Person—but In <u>Descent</u>, Not In <u>Ascent</u>. The Descending Equivalent Of Fifth Stage (and, Thus, Ascending) conditional Nirvikalpa Samadhi Is The Samadhi Of The "Thumbs" (or The Fullest Frontal Invasion By My Avatarically Self-Transmitted Divine Spiritual Presence). The Samadhi Of The "Thumbs" Is A "Basic" Fourth Stage Form Of conditional Nirvikalpa Samadhi (In The Descending, or Frontal, Line). The Samadhi Of The "Thumbs" Is The Fullest Completing Phenomenon Of The Descending (or Frontal) Yoga Of The Way Of The Heart (or Way Of Adidam). And, If The Samadhi (and The Simple and Basic, but Really Effective, and, Essentially, Constant, Experience) Of The "Thumbs" Is (By Means Of My Avatarically Self-Transmitted Divine Grace) Awakened, and (By Means Of My Avatarically Self-Transmitted Divine Grace), Either Then Or Thereafter (but, Necessarily, As A Direct Extension Of The Depth-Process Generated By Means Of My Avataric Divine Gift Of The "Thumbs"), Accompanied By The Awakening Of The Witness-Consciousness—The Practice Of The Stages Of The Ascending (or Spinal) Yoga Of The Only-By-Me Revealed and Given Way Of The Heart May (Thus and Thereby) Become <u>Unnecessary</u>.

It Is My Avataric Divine Spiritual Gift Of The Samadhi Of The "Thumbs" (and My Avataric Divine Spiritual Gift Of The Experience Of The "Thumbs" In Its Simple and Most Basic Form), and Not Merely mental "Consideration" Of My Arguments Relative To The Witness-Consciousness, That Is The Divine Yogic Secret Of The Realization Of The Consciousness-Position (Which Realization Is The Basis For The "Perfect Practice" Of The Way Of The Heart). Therefore, Even Though My Arguments Relative To The Witness-Consciousness Are An Essential Guide To Right Understanding Of The "Perfect Practice" (and, As Such, Those Arguments Are To Be Studied and "Considered" From The Beginning Of The Way Of The Heart), The "Consideration" Of Those Arguments Is Not Itself The Direct and Finally Effective Means Whereby The "Perfect Practice" Is Initiated and Really Practiced.

The Transition To The "Perfect Practice" Of The Way Of The Heart Is Necessarily A By-Me-Given Yogic and Spiritual Process, and The Samadhi Of The "Thumbs" (and The, Essentially, Constant Experience Of The "Thumbs" In Its Simple and Most Basic Form) Is The Necessary (and Me-Revealing) Basis Of That Transition. By Means Of The Re-Phasing (Characteristic Of The "Thumbs") Of The Entire Sense Of The Energy-Construct Of phenomenal experience, It Is (In Due Course, By My Avatarically Self-Transmitted Divine Grace) Revealed As Self-Evidently The Case That The Real Position (or Very Situation) Of experience Is The Witness-Position Of Consciousness (Itself)—That The Very Base Of experience Is Consciousness (Itself).

Therefore, In Its (Essentially) Constant Realization (and Not Merely In The First, or Any Particular, Instance Of Its Being Experienced), The Sign Of The "Thumbs" (Rather Than Any mental Presumption About The Witness-Consciousness) Is The Indispensable Means Whereby The Gift Of The "Perfect Practice" Of The Only-By-Me Revealed and Given Way Of The Heart Is Given.

The Sign Of The "Thumbs" Is A Uniquely (and Only By Me) Given Gift In The Way Of The Heart, Which (In The General Case) Makes The Fifth Stage (and Even The "Advanced" Fourth Stage) Practice Of The Way Of The Heart Unnecessary. The Yogic Course In The Way Of The Heart Is Primarily In The Frontal Line—and, In The General Case, That Frontal Course Accomplishes The Purification Of Both The Frontal Line and The Spinal Line,

Thereby Revealing and Awakening Both The Spherical Form Of My Divine Spiritual Body and The Transcendental (and Inherently Spiritual, and Divine) Self-Core (In The Right Side Of The Heart— Beyond The Knot Of ego-"I", and Beyond The Circle Of the body-mind, With Its Frontal and Spinal Arcs). That Revelation and Awakening At (and, Ultimately, Beyond) The Right Side Of The Heart, By Means Of The Only-By-Me Given Samadhi Of The "Thumbs" (and By Means Of The Only-By-Me Given Experience Of The "Thumbs" In Its Simple and Most Basic Form), Is What Makes The Transition To The "Perfect Practice" Of The Way Of The Heart Possible, By Establishing The Yogic (Transcendental and Spiritual—and, Ultimately, Divine) Conditions Necessary For The "Perfect Practice" Of The Way Of The Heart. The Readiness For That Transition Is Not Merely A Matter Of Having Had The Experience Of The "Thumbs" and Having Some Memory Of It. Rather, That Readiness Is A Matter Of The Stable Continuing Of The Revelation and The Spiritual Transformation Initiated In The Samadhi Of The "Thumbs"—Not With The Same Kind Of Shift In The Entire Mode Of physical experiencing (Because Such Would Make ordinary functioning Impossible), but With The Unchanging Realization That The Inherent (and Inherently Love-Bliss-Full) Condition Of Reality Is Prior To the body-mind. And, In The Seventh Stage Of Life In The Way Of The Heart, That Realization Is (Permanently) Most Perfectly Established and Demonstrated.

From The Beginning Of My Physical (Human) Lifetime Of Avataric Incarnation here, The "Thumbs" Has Always Been The Case, and The Experiential Sign Of The "Thumbs" Often Appeared To Me—Spontaneously, and Mysteriously. In My Childhood and My "Sadhana Years", The "Thumbs" Was A Process Associated With The Constant Restoration Of The "Bright", or The Going Beyond the gross physical (To Which I Was Adapting, Fully Consciously, In A Profound and Spontaneous Yogic Manner, and, Thereby, Maintaining My Divine Self-Condition, From Infancy, In This Fashion). After My Conscious Assumption Of the born-condition (At Approximately Two Years Of Age), In The Midst Of The Process Of My Active Integration With waking life, The Condition Of The "Bright" Was Felt In the circumstance of active life—and, Then, When I Would Rest At Night, Instead Of Going To sleep, I Would Experience The "Thumbs", and Would Realize The Condition Of The "Bright" Without the usual waking-state physical Reference. Eventually, In The Course Of My "Sadhana Years", I Progressively Observed and Fully Entered Into The "Thumbs" As A Consciously Known Yogic Process, Gradually Permitting The Spontaneous Yogic Event Of The "Thumbs" To Achieve Its Most Extended, Full, and Complete Form. Even A Full Decade Before The Great Event Of My Divine Re-Awakening, I Enjoyed The Spontaneous Experience Of Spiritual Regeneration Via The Regeneration Of The Total Mechanism (or Process) Associated With The "Thumbs"—but the frontal personality Had To Be Worked (or Purified, and its Knots Un-Tied) By The Spirit-Current Of The "Thumbs", Until the frontal personality and The Frontal Line <u>Altogether</u> <u>Ceased</u> To Obstruct (or Prevent) The Advancement Of The Great Yogic Process. Therefore, Even After The Spontaneous Regeneration Of The Process Of The "Thumbs" (or The Regeneration Of The Spiritual Process In The Frontal Line), It Was Yet Required Of Me To Continue To Struggle With the limits of the frontal personality For Some Years Before I (or The conditionally Manifested, and Yet To Be Most Perfectly To-Me-Conformed, Body-Mind-Vehicle Of My Avataric Incarnation here) Would Allow The Full Samadhi Of The "Thumbs" and (More Importantly) The Ultimate Work (and Transcendental, or "Core", Revelation) Of The "Thumbs".

In The Case Of My Own Body-Mind, The Full Samadhi Of The "Thumbs" Did Not Begin To Appear Until I Began To Practice The Work Of Surrender (or The Intentional Opening Of The Frontal Line To Receive Spirit-Force) In The Company Of My First Spiritual Teacher (and Spirit-Baptizer)[77]—Although (Then, and From The Beginning, and Forever) The Sign, The Revelation-Work, and The Divine Spirit-Force Of The "Thumbs" Is Uniquely My Own Avatarically Self-Manifested Sign and Gift and Revelation. Nevertheless, The Struggle With The Frontal Yoga Did Not Become Fruitful (At First, To The Degree Of Transition To The Yoga Of The Spinal Line) Until Struggle Itself (or The physical, emotional, and mental <u>Effort</u> Of Surrender) Was Transcended (In and By The Inherently ego-Transcending Heart-Participation In My Own Spiritually Self-Revealing Nature and Condition). Therefore, That Transcending Of The Effort Of Surrender Was Not The Result Of Strategic Non-Effort (or Even Any False Effort), but It Was The Spontaneous Evidence Of Simple (and Yet Profound) Identification With My Own Avatarically Self-Revealed and Avatarically Self-Revealing Divine Spirit-Current Itself.

I <u>Am</u> The Divine and Necessary First Person—The First Of All and all, and The First To Most Perfectly Fulfill The Process Of Divine Self-Realization In The Context Of conditionally Manifested Existence In The Cosmic Domain. I <u>Am</u> The Divine Heart-Master Of All and all. Therefore, All and all Must Follow Me By Heart. And The "Thumbs" Is Fundamental (and Necessary) To The Way Of The Heart That Follows Me. Therefore, The "Thumbs" Is One Of My Principal Great Avataric Divine Gifts To All and all That Become My True Devotees.

The Process Signified and Initiated By The Only-By-Me Revealed and Given Sign Of The "Thumbs" Necessarily Involves Intelligent, Intentional, and (Otherwise) Spontaneous Relinquishment Of Un-Happy Identification With gross bodily (or physical), and emotional, and mental states. This Relinquishment Takes Place Through Spontaneous (and Truly ego-Surrendering, ego-Forgetting, and ego-Transcending) Identification With My (By-My-Avataric-Divine-Grace-Revealed) Divine Spiritual Body, Which Surrounds (or Envelops) the gross body Of My True Devotee, and Which (Progressively) In-Fills and Pervades both the etheric energy body and the gross physical body Of My True Devotee, As Well As Every Other Level Of the conditionally Manifested personality Of My True Devotee, and Every Level Of the Cosmic worlds. And All Of This Is Initiated (and Accomplished) By My Avatarically Self-Transmitted Divine Spirit-Presence Itself (If Only My Devotee Heart-Responds To Me In Love—and This To The Degree Of Constant Free Communion With My Avatarically Self-Transmitted Divine Spiritual Presence).

In The Only-By-Me Revealed and Given Way Of Adidam (Which Is The One and Only By-Me-Revealed and By-Me-Given Way Of The Heart), The (Possible) Transition From The "Basic"

Fourth Stage Of Life To The "Advanced" Fourth Stage Of Life Is Not Fully Indicated Until The Complete Frontal Process and The Kinds Of phenomenal Signs I Describe In *The Dawn Horse Testament* Have Become Fully Evident. And The Necessary Signs Include Real and Stable Evidence Of frontal <u>and</u> spinal Equanimity (Both human and Spiritual, and Relative To Each and All Of The Principal Faculties—Of body, emotion, mind, and breath), and <u>Both</u> Simple and Basic (but Really Effective) Evidence Of The (Essentially, Constant) Experience Of The "Thumbs" <u>and</u> (Generally, Occasional) Most Extended, Full, and Complete Evidence Of The Samadhi Of The "Thumbs". And, If A Transition Is To Be Made <u>Directly</u> From The Point Of Basic Maturity In The "Basic" Context Of The Fourth Stage Of Life In The Way Of The Heart To Practice Of The Way Of The Heart In The Context Of The Sixth Stage Of Life, The Same Complete Frontal Process and The Same phenomenal Signs Must Be Demonstrated, but There Must Also Be True and Stable Identification With The Witness-Position Of Consciousness.

When the body Is "<u>Round</u>", The Witness Is its "Shape".

The Witness-Consciousness Is The "Skin" Of The "Thumbs". The Witness-Consciousness Is Self-Evident In The "Body" Of The "Thumbs". This Is How True Maturity In The First Actually Seeing Stage Of The Way Of The Heart Can Become The Basis For An Immediate Transition To The "Perfect Practice" Of The Way Of The Heart. In The General Case, Practice In The Ascending Stages Of The Way Of The Heart Is Not Required—Because The Yogic Spiritual Fullness Of The Sphere Of The "Thumbs" Is, In The General Case, The Sufficient Prerequisite For The <u>True</u> Establishment Of The "Perfect Practice" Of The Way Of The Heart.

<u>Every</u> Occasion Of Experiencing The "Thumbs" Comes To An End—<u>Unless</u> The Witness-Position Is Truly and Stably Realized In The Midst Of The Experience Of The "Thumbs". Thus, The "Perfect Practice" Of The Way Of The Heart Is A Development (or Ultimate Characteristic) Of The Samadhi Of The "Thumbs".

The True and Stable Realization Of The Witness-Position Of Consciousness (Itself) Is Not Merely A philosophical Matter. Rather, The True and Stable Realization Of The Witness-Position Is An ego-Transcending Matter—and A Divine Spiritual Matter.

The Realization Of The Witness-Position Of Consciousness (Itself) Is A Matter Of Devotion To Me In My Avataric Divine Self-Revelation—and Not Merely A Matter Of talk and philosophy and hopefulness.

Consciousness (Itself) Is The "Face" Of This Side Of The Moon. The Spiritual Energy Of My Avataric Divine Spiritual Presence Is The "Face" Of The Other Side Of The Moon. "Matter" Is The objectively experienced Form (or "Body") Of The Moon. The Moon (or any "thing") Is "Matter"—but "Matter" Is Only Light. My Avataric Divine Spiritual Presence Is The Light That Illuminates (and Self-Reveals The Divine Heart-Secret Of) "Matter". Consciousness (Itself) Is Me Within The Light (As The One, and Only, and Inherently Love-Blissful, and Self-Evidently Divine Self-Condition and Source-Condition Of all and All). Consciousness (Itself) and Light (Itself)—or Love-Bliss-Energy (Itself), or Happiness (Itself)—Are As The Two Sides Of The Same Coin. The Moon Is The Coin Of Earth, Floating (By A Toss) Within The Sky Of ego-mind.

The Witness-Consciousness Is Not Within You. The Witness-Consciousness Is On The "Skin" Of The "Thumbs".

The Witness-Consciousness Is Self-Evident In The "Thumbs"—Wherein The Status Of objects Is Profoundly Different Than It Is Ordinarily. In The Yogic Disposition (or Mudra) Of The "Thumbs", The Condition Of objects Is Available To Be Comprehended In Consciousness As The Witness.

The Realization Of The Witness-Consciousness Is A Continuation Of The Process Of ego-Transcending Devotional and Spiritual Communion With Me. The Witness-Consciousness Cannot Be Realized By You as the ego-"I" (or as Your Separate and Separative self-Consciousness). The Witness-Consciousness Can Only Be Realized Via The Process Of Devotional and Spiritual Communion With Me—Without egoic self-Reference. Therefore, You Must Not Substitute Your Own ego-conditions and ego-states For My Description Of The ego-Transcending Process Of The Way Of The Heart. The Way Of The Heart Is A Matter Of Heart-Communion With Me and Realization Of Me. The Way Of The Heart Is Not About Your egoic self—Except That The Way Of The Heart

Requires Your ego-Surrendering, ego-Forgetting, and ego-Transcending Devotion To Me.

You Must counter-egoically Allow The Process Of The Way Of The Heart To Become My Divine Spiritual In-Filling Of the Total body-mind. In Due Course (By Means Of My Avatarically Self-Transmitted Divine Grace), This Process Of My Divine Spiritual In-Filling Becomes Both The Realization Of The "Thumbs" and The Realization Of The Witness-Consciousness. Therefore, In The General Case, Both Of These Realizations Are Associated With The Maturing Of The First Actually Seeing Stage Of The Way Of The Heart (In The "Basic" Context Of The Fourth Stage Of Life). Such Is The True Fulfillment Of The Frontal Yoga, The True Fulfillment Of The Process I Describe In My *Hridaya Rosary*, The True Fulfillment Of The Process Of Ruchira Avatara Bhakti Yoga.

In The "Thumbs", The Witness-Consciousness Is (and May Be Realized To Be) Self-Evident. In The Context Of egoity (or the self-Contracted body-mind), The Witness-Consciousness Is Not Self-Evidently The Case (In Your Case)—and Not The Self-Evident Context Of moment to moment Existence (In Your Case).

The Witness-Consciousness Is The "Skin" Of The "Thumbs".

I Am The "Skin" Of The Heart—and Not Merely Inside It. I Am The "Pulse" Of The Heart—and Not Merely The "Blood" Of It.

To Make The Transition To The "Perfect Practice" Of The Way Of The Heart, You Must (By Means Of My Avatarically Self-Transmitted Divine Grace) Realize The Samadhi Of The "Thumbs"—and, In The General Case, Part Of The Demonstration Of The Samadhi Of The "Thumbs" Is The Stand (or Realization) As The Witness-Consciousness, Leading (Then) To The (Necessarily, Formal) Full Development Of The "Perfect Practice". This Entire Process Is A Spiritual Matter, and Not A merely philosophical Matter.

The Samadhi Of The "Thumbs" Is The Sphere Of The Space Of Consciousness (Itself). In The Samadhi Of The "Thumbs", The Divine Space Of Consciousness (Itself) Is (By Me) Avatarically Self-Revealed.

When Consciousness (Itself) Becomes attention (or Separate self-Consciousness), and Light (Itself)—or Love-Bliss-Happiness (Itself)—Becomes objects (or The Vast Display Of Separate "things"), Consciousness (As attention) and Light (As the body-mind, and As The Total Cosmic Domain Of "things") Forever Gaze At One Another Through The Dimensionless Wall Of Their Apparent "Difference".

If Consciousness (Itself)—As The Witness—Is Realized As The Inherent Love-Bliss-Feeling Of Being (Itself)—Consciousness (Itself) and Light (Itself) Are (Eternally) Not "Different".

When The Circle Becomes The Sphere, The Two Sides Of The One Coin Become Continuous—and All Opposites Are Always Already Divinely Self-Recognized To Be Simultaneous, and Of One Shape, and Of One Condition.

The Samadhi (and Every Manifestation Of The Sign) Of The "Thumbs" Is Mine Only—and Only Mine To Give. Therefore, The Samadhi (and Every Manifestation Of The Sign) Of The "Thumbs" Is Unique To The Only-By-Me Revealed and Given Way Of The Heart (or Way Of Adidam).

The "Bright" and The "Thumbs" Are Among The Great Signs That Are Uniquely My Own Avataric Divine Characteristics. The "Bright" and The "Thumbs" Is A Process, An Event, and A State That Has Been Known To Me Since My Avataric Birth. Only I Am The Avataric Divine Realizer, The Avataric Divine Revealer, and The Avataric Divine Self-Revelation Of The "Bright", The True and (Now, and Forever Hereafter) Completely Self-Revealed Divine Person—Shining Forth (Directly, Completely, and Perfectly) At The Heart (and Via Amrita Nadi), and Crashing Down (or Descending Utterly, From The "Place" Infinitely Above the body-mind and the world, Down and Most Deeply Into the body-mind and the world—Even To The Degree That the ego-"I", or self-Contraction, Is Utterly Confounded, Utterly Yielded, and Utterly Vanished In My Avatarically Self-Revealed, and Self-Evidently Divine, Person, or Self-Condition, Which Is Real God, and Truth, and Reality). Therefore, The Principal Impulse Of Even My Early Life Was My Intention To Descend (or To Embrace the limitations Of human Existence As It Appears To Be, and To Infuse all and All With My Avatarically Self-Transmitted Divine Spiritual Presence, and, Thus and Thereby, To Awaken all and All, and, Most Ultimately, To Divinely Translate all and All, By The Power

Of My Own Love-Bliss-"Brightness", Into The Perfect "Place" and "Sphere" and "Space" That Is Always and Already My Divine and Free-Standing Self-Domain).

The Principal Spiritual Signs Of My Early Life Were The "Bright" and The "Thumbs". The "Bright" and The "Thumbs" Were Fundamental To My Avatarically-Born Existence From The Beginning, and They Are Fundamental To The Only-By-Me Revealed and Given Way Of Adidam. The "Bright" and The "Thumbs" Are My Unique Samadhis. Indeed, The "Bright" and The "Thumbs" Are Me—and, Therefore, I Bring Them With Me Into the conditional worlds.

My Avataric Divine Work (Altogether) Is My Crashing-Down Descent, At First Upon and Into My Own Avatarically-Born Bodily (Human) Divine Form, and, Thereafter (and Now, and Forever Hereafter), Upon and Into the body-minds Of My Devotees and all beings—Even (By Means Of My Divine Embrace Of each, and all, and All) To Infuse and (At Last) To Divinely Translate each, and all, and All. Therefore, My Avataric Divine Spiritual Descent Is The Secret Of My Early Life. My Avataric Divine Spiritual Descent Is The Secret Of My Divine Self-"Emergence" (As I Am) Within The Cosmic Domain. My Avataric Divine Spiritual Descent Is The Secret Of All The Secrets Of The (Avatarically Self-Revealed) Divine and Complete and Thoroughly Devotional Way Of Practice and Realization In My Company. The Only-By-Me Revealed and Given Way Of The Heart (or Way Of Adidam) Is The Divine Yoga Of ego-Surrendering, ego-Forgetting, and ego-Transcending Devotional Recognition-Response To My (Avatarically Self-Revealed) Divine and Spiritual Person, and To My (Avatarically Self-Manifested) Divine and Spiritual Descent. The Only-By-Me Revealed and Given Way Of The Heart (or Way Of Adidam) Is The Total and Divine Way and Ordeal Of Counter-egoic Devotional Recognition-Response To My Avataric "Bright" Divine Self-Manifestation, and To The Avataric Crashing Down Of My "Bright" Divine Imposition. And, In The Case Of My Each and Every Devotee, The Way Must Continue Until The Way Is Most Perfectly "Bright", and The Way Itself Becomes Divine Translation Into My Own Sphere Of "Brightness" (Itself).

The "Radical" Divine Way
Of Adidam

The search to perfect the body-mind (or even any form of conditional existence) is based on egoic (or self-contracted) identification with the body-mind (and with conditional existence, altogether). Thus bound to the body-mind and to conditional existence, the egoic individual wants the body-mind itself, and conditional existence itself, to prove to be (in and of itself) perfect, or to be (in and of itself) a condition that is characterized by unchanging permanence and unchallenged self-fulfillment. Therefore, when any such egoically bound individual "considers" (or, otherwise, practices) the religious and Spiritual life, he or she, inevitably, imagines that the religious and Spiritual Process must involve progressive and (eventually) complete fulfilling and perfecting of the very conditions that are his or her bondage.

The egoic illusion of religious and Spiritual life is that it will, somehow, permanently satisfy the ego-centric want for "personal" psycho-physical immortality, permanent fulfillment of all "personal" desires, and (thus) release from all want, need, or seeking—but without requiring the loss (or ending) of the ego-"I" itself (the seeker, or the self-center that, by contracting on itself, wants, needs, divides, separates, and, thereby, suffers), and (thus) without requiring the ego-"I" to change, to surrender, to be dependent, to be ended, or to be transcended.

The only-by-Me Revealed and Given Way of Adidam (Which Is the One and True and Only by-Me-Revealed and by-Me-Given Way of the Heart) is founded on a fundamental criticism and "radical" understanding (or root-understanding) of egoity itself (and, therefore, of all the searches, and all the illusions, and all the mere imaginings associated with egoity—and all the searches, and all the illusions, and all the mere imaginings associated with ego-based religious and Spiritual life). If there is that "radical" under-standing, then the search for perfect self-fulfillment disappears, together with the action of self-contraction (or the primal act that, otherwise, appears as <u>all</u> the kinds of seeking, and <u>as</u> the feeling of identification with psycho-physical egoity, or the ego-"I", itself).

The religious and Spiritual paths that are based on egoity, rather than on the direct transcending of egoity, always idealize conditional existence (in one form or another). Therefore, the conventional (and traditional) approach to religious and Spiritual life, whether exoteric or esoteric, is associated with an impulse to transform conditional existence along idealized lines. In such conventional (or ego-based) paths, various kinds of developmental (or "evolutionary") <u>results</u> are sought—such as immortality of the body, or passage to higher or idealized planes of conditional existence, or the development of unique powers (of one kind or another) to control this, that, and everything. Therefore, because of the underlying ego-centricity of conventional religious and Spiritual paths, such (and even many other such) <u>results</u> become the specific (and characteristic) goals of the various forms of "evolutionary" (or otherwise goal-oriented) religious and Spiritual sadhana (or of conventional faith, belief, and practice).

In the conventional (or ego-based) approach to religious and Spiritual life, there is always a particular conditional goal (or even a group of several distinct conditional goals) that is regarded to be equivalent to Ultimate Realization Itself (or, otherwise, to be necessarily associated with Ultimate Realization). Uniquely, in the only-by-Me Revealed and Given Way of Adidam, there is <u>no</u> <u>conditional goal whatsoever</u>. The only-by-Me Revealed and Given Way of Adidam is a matter of the <u>always</u> <u>direct</u> <u>and</u> <u>immediate</u> <u>transcending</u> <u>of</u> <u>egoity</u>—Most Ultimately (by Means of My Avatarically Self-Transmitted Divine Grace), Realizing Inherent and Always Already Most Perfect Transcendence of egoity (in the only-by-Me Revealed and Given seventh stage of life). Therefore, in the only-by-Me Revealed and Given Way of Adidam, no conditional goal (of any kind) is proposed to <u>be</u> Most Perfect Divine Self-Realization—nor is any conditional goal (of any kind) indicated to be necessarily associated with Most Perfect Divine Self-Realization.

Wherever there is seeking, there is the idealization of some sort of goal or condition. At the deepest heart-level of <u>every</u> psycho-physical being, there is (necessarily, and always already) a basic underlying intuition of the Self-Condition (and the Self-Evidently Divine Nature) of Reality. This is so—because <u>every</u> conditional appearance is only an (apparent) modification of Reality Itself (or That Which Is Always Already The Case). However, because of the ego-"I" (or total psycho-physical self-contraction), conscious awareness of the always underlying intuition of the True Divine (and Inherently Perfect) Condition is "covered" (or made unconscious). Thus, either the Native Impulse to Realize the Divine Self-Condition (or Unqualified Happiness) is rather absent from the (self-contracted, and, inevitably, seeking) disposition of the conscious ego-personality, or else that Impulse becomes inextricably intermixed with all of the phenomenal associations of the egoic (or self-contracted, and, inevitably, seeking) personality. In either case, the inevitable search for Happiness (or Reality, or Truth, or God) becomes a process directed toward <u>phenomenal</u> <u>conditions</u>, especially (in the context of conventional religious and Spiritual life) those phenomenal conditions that are idealized as the "Ultimate Goal".

<u>All</u> idealized conditions are inherently imperfect. They are, at best, only <u>presumed</u> (by the idealistic ego-mind) to be perfect. In general, the phenomenal conditions that human beings seek as the "Ultimate Goal" are not real (potential) conditions, but imaginary conditions. Therefore, those conditions are never <u>really</u> attained, but always merely sought. And, until there is true "radical" understanding (or most fundamental understanding, or root-understanding)— and, on that basis, the constant (direct and immediate) real process of transcending the ego-"I" (or the <u>act</u> of self-contraction, itself)— those illusions (or imaginary goals), and the searches that pursue them, will (by force of tendency) continue.

In the course of seeking, it is also possible (and commonly the case) that particular goals come to be despaired of—in which case, the search itself persists, but it lies there in a sulk, depressed and frustrated, but (nevertheless, as before) without most fundamental understanding. And, when "great goals" are despaired of, seeking tends to become associated with gross satisfactions, or (in any case) with searches that can be satisfied rather readily, or in the relatively short term (even if, as is always the case, only temporarily, and never fully satisfactorily). This is yet another kind of goal-seeking illusion—to indulge in temporary satisfactions as if they were some sort of great attainment, repeating them over and over again, exhaustively, until they patently (and even meanly) cease to satisfy—in which case, the ego-frustrated despair intensifies, agonizingly, and even "darkly".

The body-mind is merely a <u>pattern</u>—always temporary, and always (in any moment) based on past adaptation and conditioning. Therefore, the body-mind will never (and <u>cannot</u> ever) demonstrate perfection. The body-mind is to be transcended—not perfected. In the conventional (or ego-based) paths, there is an intention to "evolve" the body-mind, or to move the body-mind toward perfection (or toward some idealized condition). In the always "radical" (or gone-to-the-root, and gone-to-the-Source) Way of Adidam, that intention is specifically (and always presently) relinquished and transcended, on the basis of (first) real listening to Me and (then) true hearing of Me (or most fundamental self-understanding). And My fully practicing devotee who both hears Me <u>and</u> sees Me is (through Spiritually-Moved, and, altogether, responsively, and responsibly, ego-transcending, heart-Attraction to Me, and total psycho-physical heart-Communion with Me) constantly (directly and immediately) transcending the seeking (or "evolutionary") motive. My any such devotee will (most likely), as an ordinary consequence of the transcending of psycho-physical self-contraction, exhibit various positive psycho-physical (and even "evolutionary") developments. However, such developments are merely changes of pattern (and, therefore, they are mere effects, always conditional and non-"Ultimate")—and one who does the right, true, full, and fully devotional sadhana of the Way of Adidam (in ego-surrendering, ego-forgetting, and, always more and more, ego-transcending devotional Communion with Me) is not bound by those developments, nor does he or she seek for them. <u>All</u> apparently "evolutionary" changes in the body-mind of My true devotee are (however positive, or, conditionally, "desirable", in themselves) to be transcended (or removed of all their "bondage"-power) in (and by Means of) the heart-disposition of devotion to Me that (always presently, directly, and immediately) moves beyond egoity (or self-contraction) into total psycho-physical heart-Communion with Me.

According to the conventional (and traditional) religious and Spiritual point of view, the conditional personality must somehow be perfected in order to attain the Divine (however the Divine is conceived). Such an idealistic point of view always represents a false (or, at least, limited—and, Ultimately, inadequate) understanding of the True Divine Process. The search for perfection is not the Way of Truth (or Reality, or Real God). Therefore, the Way of Adidam, Which is the Way That only I Reveal and Give, is not a search for perfection. Rather, the practitioner of the Way of Adidam must do the real sadhana of ego-transcendence. Inevitably, various purifications and positive transformations of the body-mind occur during the course of that real sadhana, but such changes do not (and cannot, and should not be expected to) become any idealized perfection of the body-mind.

The body-mind is whatever it is, and the signs of the body-mind tend to continue to be whatever they are. However, True (or Truly Divine) Freedom can (and, indeed, must) Be The Case, even though psycho-physical limitation is always (apparently) the case. True (or Truly Divine) Freedom Is (Itself) the "Point" of true religious and Spiritual life, and True (or Truly Divine) Freedom (Itself) is not in (or of) the body-mind, but (even though True, or Truly Divine, Freedom is not a disposition that strategically excludes the body-mind) It Is Always (and Always Already) Most Perfectly Prior to the body-mind.

If it were necessary to perfect the body-mind in order to Realize Truth (or Reality, or Real God), no living being would ever Realize Truth (or Reality, or Real God). I do not Call My devotees to perfect the body-mind, or to deal with it in any idealistic (or body-mind-idealizing, or ego-idealizing) sense. Nor do I Call My devotees to seek to achieve any extraordinary signs in the body-mind—such as physical immortality, or existence in (or experience of) higher planes, or "evolutionary" developments in the body-mind complex (in this plane or in any other plane). The Process of the only-by-Me Revealed and Given Way of Adidam is not a matter of perfecting the conditional (or Cosmic) domain in some kind of conditional "eternity". Rather, the Process of the only-by-Me Revealed and Given Way of Adidam is an always present-time (and, progressively, always more and more profound) Magnification and Demonstration of the direct and immediate transcending of egoity (and of the conditional, or Cosmic, domain altogether), and (always simultaneously, and coincidently) an (always more and more profound) Magnification and Demonstration of the Realization of the True, and Inherently Perfect, and Truly Divine Freedom (and the Self-Existing and Self-Radiant Divine Self-Condition, Source-Condition, and Domain) That Inherently Transcends the conditional (or Cosmic) domain (Ultimately, to the point of Most Perfect Outshining, in Divine Translation).

To seek God is to forget and avoid and fail to Find Real God. Therefore, understand your search (for God, or any "thing" at all), and (by Means of right, true, full, and fully devotional recognition of Me in My Avatarically Self-Revealed, and Self-Evidently Divine, Person—and by Means of right, true, full, and fully devotional response to Me in My Avatarically Self-Revealed, and Self-Evidently Divine, Person) Remember, Embrace, and Truly Find and "Locate" Me—and, Most Ultimately, and entirely by Means of My Avatarically Self-Transmitted Divine Grace, Realize Indivisible Oneness with Me, and Indivisible (and Non-Separate) Identification with Me (the Perfectly Subjective and Self-Evidently Divine Self-Condition and Source-Condition That Is the Real and Only Reality, Truth, and God of all and All).

That Is the "radical" (or always "gone to the root", and "given to the Source") and Truly Divine Way of Adidam. And it is to right, true, full, and fully devotional formal practice of the "radical" Divine (and only-by-Me Revealed and Given) Way of Adidam that I Call you, and to Which I Call each and every one, in this forever all and All of temporary beings and "things".

RUCHIRA AVATAR ADI DA SAMRAJ
Los Angeles, 2000

I <u>Am</u>
The Divine
Self-"Emergence"

I Am
The Divine
Self-"Emergence"

I Brought My Divine Wisdom-Teaching out of Myself—through
My Avataric Self-Submission to the Great Process of "reality
consideration" with My devotees and with the world altogether. I am not here merely reading books and passing on an old
tradition to people. Nor am I here to believe and to support the
illusions of humankind. The only-by-Me Revealed and Given Way
of Adidam, in Its entirety and in Its every aspect, has been Brought
out of Me. The Way of Adidam has Appeared only through the
Avataric Divine Process of My own Lifelong "reality consideration". The Way of Adidam is the Divine Process of My own
Avataric Self-Submission to conditional reality—Which Avataric
Self-Submission Started at the moment of My Avataric Human
Birth (and Which Avataric Self-Submission Continues—now, and
forever hereafter).

The Way of Adidam does not derive from any historical tradition or any combination of historical traditions. I did not presume
to "believe" anything in the course of My "reality consideration", nor
did I presume any fixed adherence to any historical tradition or
any combination of historical traditions. The Way of Adidam Arose
entirely out of My own Divine (and Avatarically Self-Manifested)
Process of "reality consideration".

When I Speak about the Great Tradition, I am Doing So merely
as another way of Explaining Myself—by Addressing matters that
may be familiar to people. But the Way of Adidam is, Itself, unique
and entirely new.

The Way of Adidam has been Generated by My Avataric and difficult Divine Work, My Avataric Self-Submission, My unique and Extraordinary Avataric "reality consideration"—in the context of My own Avatarically-Born Body-Mind, and also in the context of My relationship with My devotees, and in the context of My relationship with everyone altogether.

I Came Down, by Means of Avataric Human Birth, to this Earth-place—a place of ego-made human bondage, where there was no Most Perfect Realization and no sufficient tradition. Indeed, there was no Greatest Profundity in the human world of My Divine Descent to Avataric Human Birth. Therefore, the Nature of My Lifelong Work has been—by Means of My unique Avataric Divine Ordeal—to Bring the Most Perfect Truth (Which Is Divine) into this human world, where the Most Perfect Truth was never Found before.

I am not a mere "traditionalist"—here to be measured by traditional expectations, or traditional ideals, or traditional standards of any kind. Because I Began with no presumptions at all, it was necessary for Me to Enter into (and to Persist in) the "consideration" of "reality" unconditionally (and, thus, without restriction by tradition, convention, preference, reaction, belief, or plan)—until My Divine Self-Condition was (Itself) Re-Born, As the Undeniable and Most Perfect Truth, "Brightly" Co-incident with My own Avatarically-Born Bodily (Human) Divine Form. And, because I Began with no presumptions at all, that "reality consideration" required unrestricted action—or a Life-Ordeal without conventional restraints, and without preconceived goals, and without preferential prejudices, and without mediating consolations, and without subordination to the factor of egoity. Indeed, My Avataric Divine Life-Ordeal was a Most Perfectly Scientific Effort—an Avataric Divine Life-Process of utterly free enquiry, Examining all of conditional existence, without restriction, or conventional restraint, and (Ultimately) without the limiting and binding factor of egoity—until Most Perfect Truth was Found and Shown and Demonstrated, As the Most Perfectly Obvious Reality.

I was really (conditionally) Born into the human domain of Un-Truth. And, by Means of My Divine Self-Submission to Adapt to humankind and human suffering, I gradually Acquired the human disease—of Un-Truth and egoity. Therefore, because of My Thus Acquired familiarity with Man's own fault, it became necessary for Me to be Healed—Made Well again, by Most Perfect Truth Itself—so that I could Shed and Cure the common disease of Man.

At last—because of My Persistence in the Avataric Ordeal of My Divine Self-Submission here—I Am Completely Well, again. And My forever Blessing-Work will Cure both All and all. Now, and forever hereafter, I Am the Divine Medicine that Heals the heart of Man—and even Cures the Truthless All of all there is.

The "reality consideration" to which I Submitted in My Teaching-Years and Revelation-Years was a real matter—a real, and Truly Divine, Process. I did not merely inherit a pre-existing tradition and Speak it out to humankind. I have (secondarily, and only over time) Examined the Great Tradition—for the Purpose of being Communicative to all. But I did not Examine the Great Tradition in order to Gain a Teaching from the Great Tradition itself. Rather, I have Examined the Great Tradition in order to Explain the Great Tradition—even to itself. And, principally, I have Examined the Great Tradition in order to Learn the language of the "common mind"—in order to be able to Use the language of the "common mind" of all religious and Spiritual traditions as a context in which to Explain Myself (and all the Content and Process of My Avatarically Given Divine Self-Revelation of Most Perfect Truth).

My Examination of the Great Tradition is a part of the Total Process by Which I Learned Man. My Purpose, in that Examination, was to Learn the content of all the "considerations" of humankind—in order to Address the inherent limitations of those "considerations".

Thus, My Avatarically Self-Manifested Divine Work of Teaching and of Self-Revelation has always been an Extraordinary Ordeal of Divine Self-Submission to "reality consideration"—Bringing the Complete Divine Teaching of Most Perfect Truth out of Myself (and, Thus, out of the Divine and Unconditional Reality Itself), by Means of My own Divine Ordeal of Avataric Self-Submission to, and Conjunction with, all of conditional reality. And I Engaged that Avataric Ordeal not merely in order to Communicate My Divine Wisdom-Teaching verbally, but in order to Conform My own Avatarically-Born Body-Mind-Vehicle (and, indeed, every thing and every one) to Myself—so that My Avatarically Self-Transmitted Divine Spiritual Blessing-Transmission of My "Bright" Divine Heart may, forever, be Received by all who truly heart-recognize Me and really heart-respond to Me.

The Requirement to Fully and Completely and Most Perfectly Bring the Divine Teaching of Most Perfect Truth out of Myself, by Means of the Great Avataric Process of My Divine Self-Submission to "reality consideration", Produced My unique Avataric Divine Ordeal, and My unique Avatarically Self-Revealed Divine Sign, and My unique Avatarically Self-Manifested Divine Leela. And That Divine Ordeal, and Sign, and Leela is not a matter of an idealized representative of an historical tradition (or even any combination of historical traditions) engaging in traditionally idealized social and religious "behaviors".

I am not a "utopian religionist".

I am not a "role model" for the human mummery of mortal selves.

My Divinely "Heroic" and Divinely "Crazy" Manner of Life and Work is unique to Me (and uniquely necessary for Me, because of Who I Am, and because of What I must Accomplish)—and, there-fore, My unique Manner of Life and Work is not to be imitated by any one.

My Divinely "Heroic" and Divinely "Crazy" Manner of Life and Work is not a prescriptive model for conventional social (or, otherwise, conventionally religious) ego-development.

Indeed, no merely socially idealistic (or conventionally religious) and otherwise traditional expectation is appropriate in relation to Me.

I am not an ideal human ego-"I".

I Am the Inherently egoless Person of Reality (Itself).

I Am the Most Perfect Truth—Which Is Divine, and One, and Only (and Which Is Always Already The Case).

Therefore, every ego-"I" must be surrendered, and forgotten, and transcended in Me.

I did not Come into a world where the Most Perfect Truth was "ready-made". Indeed, because the ego-bound human world had failed, as a result of all of its mere <u>self</u>-efforts, to Find and Embrace the Most Perfect (and <u>Really</u> Divine) Truth of Reality (Itself), even <u>all</u> the traditional norms of right (and would-be God-Realizing, or Truth-Realizing) life had, <u>finally</u>, become grossly deprived of their traditional authority, in the human-time that immediately preceded My Avataric Human Birth.

In this "dark" epoch of "end-time", in which I Am Avatarically Descended (to Begin My forever Divine-"Emergence"-Work), even the limited (and never Most Perfect) portion of Truth that was Revealed to humankind previous to My Avataric Divine Appearance was already lost—or was, at least, under profound threat, and even much falsified—<u>before</u> My Avataric Birth to Human Life Began. Therefore, Most Perfect Truth <u>Is</u> all My Cause and Motive here. And the absence of Most Perfect Truth in human-time was humankind's most wounding "gift" to Me—that made My Avataric Human Life into a Struggle to <u>Be</u> Divinely Full, of <u>Me</u>.

In all My Years of Teaching-Work and Revelation-Work, enormous pressures were constantly exerted on Me—by My devotees, and by the world altogether—to assume the "public" role and manner of a conventional "organizational" religious figure. But, in spite of those pressures toward conformity to the expected conventions of social and religious egoity, I Persisted in the <u>real</u> and <u>necessary</u> (and, necessarily, "<u>Crazy</u>", or unrestricted and unlimited) <u>Avataric</u> <u>Process</u> of My Divine Self-Submission to "reality consideration"—until absolutely every fraction of the Way of Adidam was Brought out of Me, and made <u>clear</u>.

It was necessary that I Embrace <u>all</u>—in order to Assume the likeness of all, and to Reflect all to all, and to Transcend the limiting-pattern of all. Only <u>Thus</u> could I Reveal My Very and Divine Self-Condition—and My Very and Divine Pattern—to one and all.

The Great Avataric Process of My Universal Divine Self-Revelation could be Completed (in Its Inherently Most Perfect "Bright" Fullness) only through My own Divine Self-Submission to conditional reality. In order to Do This in My Bodily (and Truly Human) Divine Form (Un-reservedly, Fully, and to the degree of

Most Perfect Completeness, in <u>real</u> human-time), I—in <u>all</u> the Years of My Early-Life, and, especially, in <u>all</u> My Teaching-Years and <u>all</u> My Revelation-Years—had to Accept all kinds of abuse from people. Nevertheless, I <u>Could</u> <u>Not</u>, and <u>Did</u> <u>Not</u>, Stop That Extraordinary Effort of My own Divine Self-Submission, until <u>every</u> aspect of My Great "reality consideration" was <u>Truly</u> <u>Finished</u>—and My Avatarically Given Divine Self-Revelation of the Way of Adidam was <u>Full</u> and <u>Complete</u>, in <u>every</u> detail.

Only <u>now</u> Is My Avatarically Self-Manifested Divine Submission-Work of World-Teaching and Divine Self-Revelation Most Perfectly <u>Complete</u>, <u>and</u> Most Perfectly <u>Full</u>.

Therefore—now, and forever hereafter—I will no longer <u>Submit</u> Myself to Teach and to Reveal.

Now, and forever hereafter, the only-by-Me Revealed and Given Way of Adidam (As Summarized, by <u>Me</u>, in My Twenty-Three Divine "Source-Texts" [78]) <u>Is</u> My Avatarically Given Divine World-Teaching and My Avatarically Given Divine Word of Self-Revelation—<u>Full</u> and <u>Complete</u>, for every one, and for all time.

Now, and forever hereafter, I (Myself, both during and forever after the Physical Lifetime of My Avatarically-Born Bodily Human Divine Form) will <u>only</u> Do My "Bright" Avataric Work of Divine Self-"Emergence"—only <u>Blessing</u> one and all.

Now, and forever hereafter, My "Bright" (and Avatarically Self-Manifested) Divine Blessing-Work Is Given for <u>all</u> whose devotional recognition of Me and devotional response to Me surrenders ego-"I" in Me, and requires no more Submission of Me to Man.

Now, and forever hereafter, I <u>Am</u> (by all My Avataric Means) the Great and "Bright" Divine Process here.

Now, and forever hereafter, I <u>Am</u> (by all My Avataric Means) the One and Great Divine Event.

Now, and forever hereafter, I <u>Am</u> The Divine Self-"Emergence"—Avatarically "Emerging" (<u>As</u> I <u>Am</u>), to here (and to every where at All), and to you (and to every one of all).

What You Can Do Next—

Contact an Adidam center near you.

■ Sign up for our preliminary course, "The <u>Only</u> Truth That Sets the Heart Free". This course will prepare you to become a fully practicing devotee of Avatar Adi Da Samraj.

■ Find out about upcoming events in your area:

AMERICAS
12040 North Seigler Road
Middletown, CA 95461 USA
(707) 928-4936

PACIFIC-ASIA
12 Seibel Road
Henderson
Auckland 1008
New Zealand
64-9-838-9114

AUSTRALIA
P.O. Box 244
Kew 3101
Victoria
**1800 ADIDAM
(1800-234-326)**

EUROPE-AFRICA
Annendaalderweg 10
6105 AT Maria Hoop
The Netherlands
31 (0)20 468 1442

THE UNITED KINGDOM
PO Box 20013
London, England
NW2 1ZA
0181-7317550

E-MAIL: **correspondence@adidam.org**

Read these books by and about Avatar Adi Da Samraj:

■ *The Promised God-Man Is Here*

The Extraordinary Life-Story,
The "Radical" Teaching-Work, and
The Divinely "Emerging" World-Blessing
Work Of The Divine World-Teacher
Of The "Late-Time",
Ruchira Avatar Adi Da Samraj,
by Carolyn Lee, Ph.D.

The profound, heart-rending, humorous, miraculous, wild—and true—Story of the Divine Person Alive in human Form. Essential reading as background for the study of Avatar Adi Da's books.

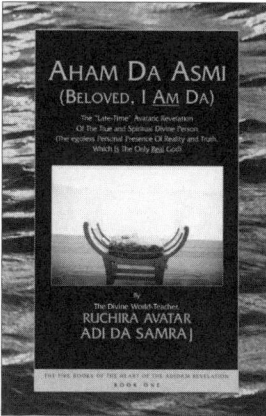

■ *Aham Da Asmi*
(Beloved, I Am Da)

The Five Books Of The Heart Of The
Adidam Revelation, Book One:
The "Late-Time" Avataric Revelation Of
The True and Spiritual Divine Person
(The egoless Personal Presence Of Reality
and Truth, Which Is The Only Real God).

This Ecstatic Scripture, the first of His twenty-three "Source-Texts", contains Ruchira Avatar Adi Da's magnificent Confession as the Very Divine Person and Source-Condition of all and All.

Continue your reading with the remaining books of *The Five Books Of The Heart Of The Adidam Revelation* (the *Ruchira Avatara Gita,* the *Da Love-Ananda Gita, Hridaya Rosary,* and *Eleutherios*). Then you will be ready to go on to *The Seventeen Companions Of The True Dawn Horse* (see pp. 453-58).

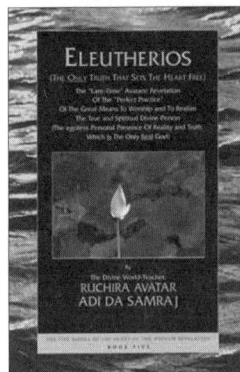

These and other books by and about Ruchira Avatar Adi Da Samraj can be ordered from the Adidam Emporium by calling:

(877) 770-0772 (from within North America)
(707) 928-6653 (from outside North America)

or by writing to:
ADIDAM EMPORIUM
10336 Loch Lomond Road
PMB #306
Middletown, CA 95461 USA

Or order from the Adidam Emporium online at:
www.adidam.com

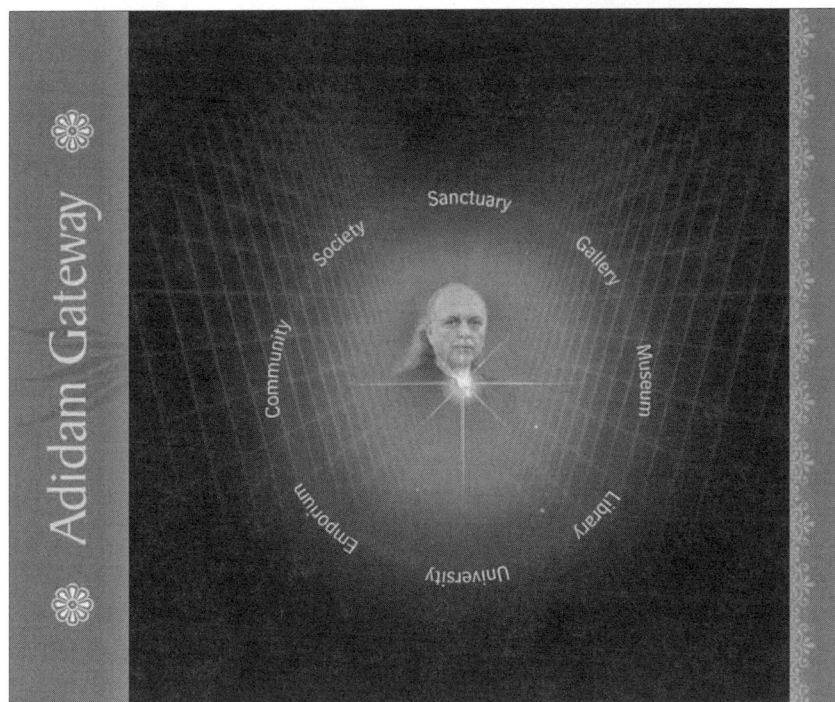

Adidam Gateway

Sanctuary
Society
Gallery
Community
Museum
Emporium
Library
University

Visit the Adidam Sacred City online at:
www.adidam.org

■ Explore the online community of Adidam and discover more about Avatar Adi Da Samraj and the Way He Offers to all.

Find presentations on: Avatar Adi Da's extraordinary life-story, the stages leading to Divine Enlightenment, cultism versus true devotional practice, the "radical" politics of human-scale community, true emotional-sexual freedom, the sacred function of art in human life, and more.

RUCHIRA AVATAR ADI DA SAMRAJ
Lopez Island, 2000

The Great Choice

An Invitation to
the Way of Adidam

Each one of us, if we will allow ourselves to feel it, is restless. Human beings want to find God—the living, heart-intoxicating experience of <u>Real</u> God, or Truth Itself, or Reality Itself. The purpose of our existence is actually to live in the True Pleasure of that heart-intoxication. To be unable to participate and luxuriate in that Pleasure is pain and stress. We may not realize it, but that feeling of separation from unqualified Love, Sustenance, and heart-Communion with the Divine Source of our existence is actually driving us mad. And that is why human beings, individually and collectively, do dreadful things—or, otherwise, settle for mere mediocrity, just "doing our best", or merely "coping". In the words of Avatar Adi Da, we spend our lives "waiting for everything and looking for everything". He says:

AVATAR ADI DA SAMRAJ: *To have no greater sense of Reality than the physical is to be like a trapped rat, trapped on all sides. You just cannot endure the confinement of mere mortality—your heart cannot accept it. To be in that disposition, to have that sense of Reality, is obviously a disturbance.*

So, obviously, the human being requires a Way—not merely a way out. A way out, yes, in some sense—but, for the integrity of your existence, you need direct access to the Divine, even as a matter of ordinary sanity. [March 3, 1998]

Avatar Adi Da has Appeared in this dark time, in order to bring the mortal darkness to an end and restore all to the Divine Light. He is intent on taking all who respond to Him through the most ecstatic and most difficult of all transitions—the transition from the unhappy life of the ego to the Radiant Fullness of the Divinely Enlightened life. His Life-Story is of the immense Divine Ordeal it has been on His part to truly Initiate that Process in human beings.

Avatar Adi Da does not congratulate the ego—He undermines the ego. He must, if He is to Liberate people from their unhappiness, from the enclosed point of view of the separate and separative self. And so He has never offered a conventionally consoling message. He offers you the whole Truth—the fact of yourself as the self-contracted ego-"I", but also the constant Revelation of a Happiness beyond compare.

Avatar Adi Da's human body is, of course, located in a particular place and a particular time. But when you become sensitive to Him Spiritually, you discover that His Spiritual Presence can be felt anywhere and anytime, regardless of whether you are in His physical Company or not. Because His Spiritual Presence is Eternal (and will not "disappear" when His human body dies), it is possible for everyone to cultivate a direct heart-relationship with Him—under all circumstances, in this life and beyond. And so, the relationship to Him, once forged, is eternal, going beyond death and the apparent boundaries of time and space.

If you want more than your ordinary existence, and something greater than a life of Spiritual seeking, Avatar Adi Da's Word to you is simply this: Take up the Way of Adidam—the Way of Real God, fully Present, here and now, not needing to be sought. The Way of Adidam is His personal Offering to you and to every human being. It is a devotional heart-relationship to Him, expressed through an entire Way of life. This relationship is not to a mere man—it is with the very Divine Being. But, at the same time, it is supremely intimate. When you enter into this relationship with Him and practice the Way of Adidam, you begin to enjoy a condition of heart-Communion with Him that is more alive and heart-deep than your love-relationship with any human individual.

At the same time, the devotional relationship with Adi Da Samraj is not an "I-Thou" relationship, a connection between apparently separate entities—the human individual, on the one hand, and "God", on the other. The love-bond with Adi Da Samraj transcends the entire point of view by which we live, presuming ourselves to be separate beings relating to separate "others". In every moment that you truly practice the relationship to Avatar Adi Da, invoking Him by Name, recollecting His Form in the mind, or His Words, or something He has done—whenever you allow Him to Attract your heart, He Reveals Himself Spiritually to you. Then He is recognized, through and beyond His human appearance, as the Real and Living God—not the great Parent, or "Creator"-Deity, imagined by the human mind, but the Conscious Divine Power of Light and Love, the Divine Heart of all there is, including your own body-mind and every apparent being and "thing". In the instant of such recognition, the entire body-mind opens to Adi Da Samraj in a single movement of devotion, and you forget yourself in ecstasy—the heart, the mind, the body, the breath becoming full with His Radiant Love-Bliss. The Way of Adidam, truly lived, is this ecstasy of Non-Separateness, a great Contemplative process, based on heart-recognition of Adi Da Samraj and heart-response to Him.

Ultimately, in this or some future lifetime, persistent heart-Communion with Adi Da Samraj realizes the true destiny of existence—Divine Enlightenment, in which all vestige of the egoic self is vanished:

Divine Enlightenment, Divine Self-Realization, Most Perfect (Free, "Bright", and Self-Evidently Divine) Awakeness, or Most Perfect (and Most Perfectly ego-Transcending) Spiritual and Transcendental Real-God-Realization, Is Native, Most Perfect, Effortless, and Free Identification With Mere (or Inherent, and Natively Felt) Being (or Self-Existence), The Only One Who Is, Consciousness Itself—Self-Radiant, All Love-Bliss-"Brightness" Itself, Inherently Without Obstruction, Always Already Infinitely Expanded (Beyond All Apparent Modifications, or Illusory Contractions, Of Itself). [The Only Complete Way To Realize The Unbroken Light Of Real God]

The truth of the Way of Adidam remains hidden until you begin to participate in it from the heart. Mere beliefs and pre-scribed behaviors are insufficient. The Way of Adidam is a matter of direct, moment-to-moment response to Adi Da Samraj and a process of receiving His Spiritual Transmission ever more pro-foundly. It does not work to take His Teaching away and attempt to practice it by yourself. As He has said many times, it is simply not possible to move beyond the confines of the ego on your own, nor is it possible to unlock the Secrets of Divine Enlightenment that He has Revealed outside of a formally acknowledged devo-tional relationship to Him. That is why it is so important to become His formal devotee and to live the Way of Adidam exactly has He has Given it.

AVATAR ADI DA SAMRAJ: I Am the Divine Blessing, Real-God-with-you. Such is not merely My Declaration to you. You must find Me out. You must prove the Way I Give you. Really do the Way I Give you, and you will find Me out further. You will prove the Way of Adidam by doing it, not by believing it merely. [Ruchira Avatara Hridaya-Siddha Yoga]

Darshan

The foundation of Spiritual practice in Adidam is Darshan, or the feeling-Contemplation of Avatar Adi Da's bodily (human) Form—either through the sighting of His physical body, or through Contemplating a photographic or artistic representation of Him. This heart-beholding of Avatar Adi Da's Form is the wellspring of meditation in the Way of Adidam, and so His devotees place a large photograph of Him in each med-itation hall, as the central image

of Contemplation. In fact, Remembrance of Adi Da Samraj—or the recollecting of His Form in mind and feeling—is the constant practice of His devotees, in the midst of the activities of daily life as well as in meditation. Avatar Adi Da has often spoken about the unique potency of beholding His Form.

AVATAR ADI DA SAMRAJ: In the traditional setting, when it works best, an individual somehow Gracefully comes into the Company of a Realizer of one degree or another, and, just upon (visually) sighting that One, he or she is converted at heart, and, thereafter, spends the rest of his or her life devoted to sadhana (or Spiritual practice), in constant Remembrance of the Spiritual Master. The Spiritual Master's Sign is self-authenticating.

When Adi Da Samraj is approached with an open heart, His Darshan—the Sighting of His Form alone, even in representational form—is so potent that the heart overflows in response to Him, recognizing Him as the Very Divine Person, the Supreme Source of Bliss and Love.

Sometimes, devotees receive the Darshan of Avatar Adi Da in an informal setting, such as when He walks around one of the Adidam Sanctuaries. And then there are formal occasions, when He sits in halls especially set aside for Darshan, inviting devotees to come and Contemplate Him silently. In certain cases, the time of a formal Darshan occasion will be announced ahead of time, so that devotees in all parts of the world can receive His Blessing simultaneously, by sitting in silent Contemplation of Him at the same time that He is Granting Darshan. In such occasions, real-time video of Avatar Adi Da Samraj sitting in Darshan is transmitted via the internet to His devotees everywhere. Thus, even if you cannot come into Avatar Adi Da's physical Company, there may be occasions when you will have the opportunity to participate in such occasions of His Darshan.

The Four Congregations

The gathering of devotees of Adi Da Samraj forms a series of concentric circles radiating from Him at the center. These circles are the four formal congregations of His devotees: the first congregation (renunciate practitioners), the second congregation (lay practitioners), the third congregation (practitioners who particularly serve Avatar Adi Da through their patronage and/or advocacy, or who are preparing for the second congregation), and the fourth congregation (practitioners who live in traditional cultural settings or who maintain their participation in the religious tradition to which they already belong, while acknowledging Avatar Adi Da Samraj as the Ultimate Divine Source of true religion).

These circles, as they grow, are forming a vast "conductor", a mechanism whereby the Divine Influence of Avatar Adi Da Samraj is being drawn more and more into the world. Every new devotee represents a strengthening of the total Sphere of Avatar Adi Da's Spiritual Transmission and Grace. Avatar Adi Da has Given the Gifts of His Wisdom-Teaching and His Spiritual Blessing, and it is through the community of His devotees, and its global Spiritual culture, that these Gifts, intended for everyone, become available to all. This is why Avatar Adi Da is urgent to find those in this generation who will respond to Him and do the great work of making His Spiritual Blessing available to all.

Which Congregation Is Right for You?

Which of the four congregations you should apply to for membership depends on the strength of your impulse to respond to Avatar Adi Da's Revelation and on your life-circumstance. All four congregations establish you in a direct devotional relationship with Avatar Adi Da, and all four are essential to the flowering of His Blessing-Work in the world.

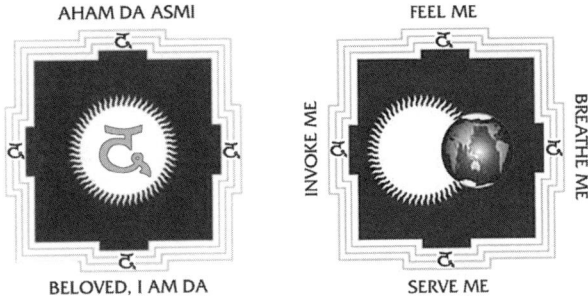

AHAM DA ASMI

FEEL ME

INVOKE ME

BREATHE ME

BELOVED, I AM DA

SERVE ME

The First and Second Congregations

(for those moved to take up the total practice of Adidam)

To take up the total practice of the Way of Adidam (in the first or second congregation) is to take full advantage of the opportunity offered by Adi Da Samraj—it is to enter fully into the process of Divine Enlightenment. That process is a unique ordeal, which necessarily requires application to the wide range of functional, practical, relational, and cultural disciplines given by Ruchira Avatar Adi Da Samraj for the sake of Spiritual purification and growth.

The disciplines of Adidam are not ascetical, not a form of deprivation. Rather, they are the means whereby the body-mind is conformed to a right and inherently pleasurable pattern of well-being. As you progressively adapt to these disciplines, the body-mind is purified and balanced, and you thereby become able to receive and respond to the Divine Heart-Transmission of Adi Da Samraj more and more fully.

These practices in the Way of Adidam include fundamental contemplative disciplines such as meditation, devotional chanting, sacramental worship (or "puja"), study of Avatar Adi Da's books, and regular periods of retreat.

AVATAR ADI DA SAMRAJ: You must come from the depth-position of meditation and puja before entering into activities in the waking state, and remain in the disposition of that depth from the time of meditation and puja each morning. Maintain that heart-disposition, and discipline the body-mind—functionally, practically, relationally— in all the modes I have Given you. This devotional Yoga, Ruchira

Avatara Bhakti Yoga, is moment-to-moment. Fundamentally, it is a matter of exercising it profoundly, in this set-apart time of meditation and puja, and then, through random, artful practice moment-to-moment, constantly refresh it, preserve it. All of this is to conform the body-mind to the Source-Purpose, the in-depth Condition.

That basic discipline covers all aspects of the body-mind. That is the pattern of your response to Me. It is the foundation Yoga of organizing your life in terms of its in-depth principle, and growing this depth. [December 5, 1996]

This moment-to-moment devotional turning to Avatar Adi Da is refreshed not only in the meditation hall but also in the temple, where worship, prayer, devotional chanting, and other sacred activities occur.

AVATAR ADI DA SAMRAJ: The sacred life must be perpetual. The sacred domain is the core of the community, and every community and every Sanctuary should have a temple in its domain: A place of chant, of song, of prayer, where everyone gathers for this life of Invocation, prayer, and puja. [May 13, 1999]

Members of the first and second congregations adapt to a purifying diet and a discipline of daily exercise (including morning calisthenics and evening Hatha Yoga exercises). They also progressively adapt to a regenerative discipline of sexuality. And they live in cooperative association with other devotees of Avatar Adi Da and tithe regularly.

All of these functional, practical, relational, and cultural disciplines are means whereby you become more and more capable of receiving Avatar Adi Da's constant Blessing-Transmission. Therefore, Avatar Adi Da Samraj has made it clear that, in order to Realize Him with true profundity—and, in particular, to Realize Him most perfectly, to the degree of Divine Enlightenment—it is necessary to be a formally acknowledged member of either the first or the second congregation, embracing the total practice of the Way of Adidam.

362

When you apply for membership in the second congregation of Adidam (the first step for all who want to take up the total practice of the Way of Adidam), you are asked to take "The Only Truth That Sets the Heart Free", a course in which you examine the opportunity offered to you by Avatar Adi Da Samraj, and learn what it means to embrace the total practice of the Way of Adidam. (To register for this preparatory course, please contact the regional or territorial center nearest to you [see p. 350], or e-mail us at: correspondence@adidam.org.) After completing this course of study, you may formally enter the second congregation as a student-novice.

Entering any of the four congregations of Adidam is based on taking a formal vow of devotion and service to Avatar Adi Da Samraj. This vow is a profound—and, indeed, eternal—commitment. You take this vow (for whichever congregation you are entering) when you are certain that your great and true heart-impulse is to be a devotee of Avatar Adi Da Samraj, embracing Him as your Divine Heart-Master. And Avatar Adi Da Samraj Himself is eternally Vowed to Serve the Liberation of all who become His devotees.

As a student-novice, you will be initiated into formal meditation and sacramental worship. Then you begin to adapt to a wide range of life-disciplines, including participation in the cooperative community of Avatar Adi Da's first- and second-congregation devotees. As a student-novice, you engage in an intensive period of study and "consideration" of the Way of Adidam in all of its details, and then, after a period of three to six months (or more), you may apply to be a fully practicing member of the second congregation.

The beginning stages of practice are the "exoteric" (or "outer-temple") domain of the second congregation. Avatar Adi Da has indicated that many of His devotees will practice in the exoteric stages for their entire lives. This beginning practice of Adidam is great and profound—because it is founded not in any hoped-for future attainment, but in present heart-Communion with Real God (Revealed via the Incarnation of Avatar Adi Da), and also because it requires the practitioner to really transcend the ego.

The Life of a Formally Practicing Devotee of Ruchira Avatar Adi Da Samraj

Meditation is a unique and precious event in the daily life of Avatar Adi Da's devotees. It offers the opportunity to relinquish outward, body-based attention and to be alone with Adi Da Samraj, allowing yourself to enter more and more into the Sphere of His Divine Transmission.

The practice of sacramental worship, or "puja", in the Way of Adidam is the bodily active counterpart to meditation. It is a form of ecstatic worship of Avatar Adi Da Samraj, using a photographic representation of Him and involving devotional chanting and recitations from His Wisdom-Teaching.

"You must deal with My Wisdom-Teaching in some form every single day, because a new form of the ego's game appears every single day. You must continually return to My Wisdom-Teaching, confront My Wisdom-Teaching."

Avatar Adi Da Samraj

The beginner in Spiritual life must prepare the body-mind by mastering the physical, vital dimension of life before he or she can be ready for truly Spiritual practice. Service is devotion in action, a form of Divine Communion.

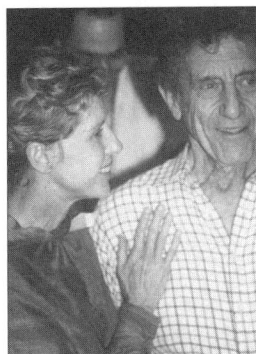

Avatar Adi Da Samraj Offers practical disciplines to His devotees in the areas of work and money, diet, exercise, and sexuality. These disciplines are based on His own human experience and an immense process of "consideration" that He engaged face-to-face with His devotees for more than twenty-five years.

The "esoteric" (or "inner-temple") practice of Adidam does not begin until the activity of the ego is most fundamentally understood and can thereby be consistently transcended moment to moment. Then, through a profound Awakening to the Spiritual Reality, Revealed and Transmitted by Avatar Adi Da, you become qualified to enter into the advanced and the ultimate stages (or esoteric domain) of the Way of Adidam.

Those who, having practiced the Way of Adidam most intensively, make the transition to the "Perfect Practice", in the sixth (or penultimate) stage of the Way of Adidam, may do so either as general practitioners (continuing as members of the second congregation of Adidam) or (if they demonstrate the necessary qualifications) as formal renunciate practitioners (thereby becoming members of the first congregation of Adidam).

All formal renunciate practitioners in the first congregation of the Way of Adidam are necessarily members of the formal order of sannyasins established by Avatar Adi Da. This order is known as the Ruchira Sannyasin Order of the Tantric Renunciates of Adidam (or, simply, the Ruchira Sannyasin Order). Avatar Adi Da Himself is the Founding Member of the Ruchira Sannyasin Order, which is a retreat order whose members are legal renunciates. The Ruchira Sannyasin Order is the senior cultural authority within the gathering of Avatar Adi Da's devotees, and its members are the principal human Instruments of Avatar Adi Da's Blessing-Work, now and into the future. Ruchira Sannyasins may live in Hermitage-Retreat Sanctuaries Empowered by Avatar Adi Da or at the Retreat Sanctuaries of Adidam anywhere in the world, but the home of the order is Adidam Samrajashram (in Fiji), Avatar Adi Da's principal Hermitage-Retreat Sanctuary.

The Adidam Youth Fellowship

(within the second congregation)

Young people (age 25 and under) are also offered a special form of relationship to Avatar Adi Da—the Adidam Youth Fellowship. The Adidam Youth Fellowship has two membership bodies—friends and practicing members.

A friend of the Adidam Youth Fellowship is simply invited into a culture of other young people who want to learn more about Avatar Adi Da Samraj and His Happiness-Realizing Way of Adidam. A formally practicing member of the Adidam Youth Fellowship acknowledges that he or she has found his or her True Heart-Friend and Master in the Person of Avatar Adi Da Samraj, and wishes to enter into a direct, ego-surrendering Spiritual relationship with Him as the Means to True Happiness.

Practicing members of the Youth Fellowship embrace a series of disciplines that are similar to (but simpler than) the practices engaged by adult members of the second congregation of Adidam. Both friends and members are invited to special retreat events from time to time, where they can associate with other young devotees of Avatar Adi Da.

To become a member of the Adidam Youth Fellowship, or to learn more about this form of relationship to Avatar Adi Da, call or write:

Vision of Mulund Institute (VMI)
10336 Loch Lomond Road
PMB #146
Middletown, CA 95461 USA
PHONE: (707) 928-6932
E-MAIL: vmi@adidam.org

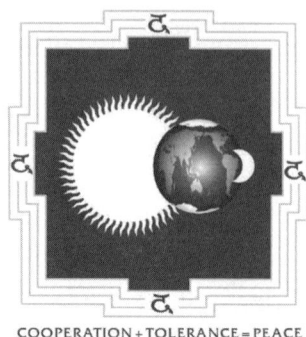

COOPERATION + TOLERANCE = PEACE

The Third Congregation of Adidam

*(for those serving Adi Da Samraj through
their patronage and advocacy, and those
preparing for the second congregation)*

1. Patrons and Individuals of Unique Influence

It is the sacred responsibility of those who respond to Adi Da
Samraj to help His Spiritual Work flourish in the world. For this
purpose, we must make it possible for Avatar Adi Da Samraj to
move freely and spontaneously from one part of the world to
another and we must provide Hermitages for His unique Work in
various locations. In 1983, an individual patron offered the island
of Naitauba to Avatar Adi Da. Because of this magnificent gift, the
entire Life and Work of Adi Da Samraj began to evolve in ways
that were not possible before. He had a pristine, protected place
to do His Spiritual Work and an opportunity to establish a unique
Seat of His Divine Presence for all generations to come.

Avatar Adi Da must also be able to gather around Him His
most exemplary formal renunciate devotees, who must receive
practical support so that they can devote their lives to serving
Avatar Adi Da and His Work and living a life of perpetual Spiritual
retreat in His Company.

And Avatar Adi Da's Presence in the world must become
widely known, both through the publication and dissemination of
books by and about Him and through public advocacy by people
of influence.

If you are a man or woman of unique wealth or influence in the world, we invite you to serve Avatar Adi Da's world-Blessing Work through your patronage or influence. As a member of the third congregation of Adidam, supporting the world-Work of Adi Da Samraj, you are literally helping to change the destiny of countless people. You are making it possible for this Blessing-Work to have a greater influence upon the world's destiny. To make the choice to serve Avatar Adi Da via your patronage or unique influence is to transform your own life and destiny, and the life and destiny of all mankind, in the most Spiritually auspicious way.

As a patron or individual of unique influence in the third congregation, your relationship to Avatar Adi Da is founded on a vow of devotion, through which you commit yourself according to your capabilities—either to significant financial patronage of His Work and/or to using your unique influence to make Him known in the world. In the course of your service to Him (and in daily life altogether), you live the simplest practice of Ruchira Avatara Bhakti Yoga—invoking Avatar Adi Da, feeling Him, breathing Him, and serving Him, and thus remaining connected to His constant Blessing. You are also invited to engage a daily period of formal study of His Wisdom-Teaching. You are not obliged to engage the full range of disciplines practiced in the first two congregations. You are, however, encouraged to practice formal periods of meditation and sacramental worship.

If, at some point, you are moved to embrace all the disciplines and enter into the total practice of Adidam, you may apply for membership in the second (and possibly, eventually, the first) congregation.

If you are interested in establishing a formal devotional relationship with Avatar Adi Da Samraj and serving Him in this crucial way, please contact us:

Third Congregation Advocacy
12040 North Seigler Road
Middletown, CA 95461 USA
PHONE: (707) 928-4800
E-MAIL: director_of_advocacy@adidam.org

2. The Transnational Society of Advocates
of the Adidam Revelation

If you have the capability to effectively advocate Avatar Adi Da in the world—through your individual skills, position, or professional expertise—you may join a branch of the third congregation called the Transnational Society of Advocates of the Adidam Revelation. Members of the Society of Advocates are individuals who, while not of unique wealth or social influence, can make a significant difference to Avatar Adi Da's Work by making Him known in all walks of life (including the media, in the spheres of religion, government, education, health, entertainment, the arts, and so on). Advocates also serve the worldwide mission of Adidam by financially supporting the publication of Avatar Adi Da's "Source-Texts" and His other Literature, as well as associated missionary literature. Members of the Society of Advocates make a monthly donation for this purpose and pay an annual membership fee that supports the services of the Society.

Like devotees in the first and second congregations, your relationship to Avatar Adi Da as a member of the Society of Advocates is founded on a vow of devotion and service, but the requirements are less elaborate. In the course of your service to Him (and in daily life altogether), you vow to live the simplest practice of Ruchira Avatara Bhakti Yoga—invoking Avatar Adi Da, feeling Him, breathing Him, and serving Him, and thus remaining connected to His constant Blessing. You also engage a daily period of formal study of His Wisdom-Teaching. You are not obliged to engage the full range of disciplines practiced in the first two congregations. You are, however, encouraged to practice formal periods of meditation and sacramental worship.

If, at some point, you are moved to embrace all the disciplines and enter into the total practice of Adidam, you may apply for membership in the second (and possibly, eventually, the first) congregation.

If you are interested in becoming a member of the Society of Advocates, please contact us:

The Society of Advocates
12040 North Seigler Road
Middletown, CA 95461 USA
PHONE: (707) 928-6924
E-MAIL: soacontact@adidam.org

3. Pre-student-novices under vow

If you are certain that you wish to become a formal devotee of Avatar Adi Da, and you therefore wish to embrace the formal second-congregation vow of devotion to Him as quickly as possible, you are invited to become a pre-student-novice under vow (as part of the third congregation of Adidam).

As a pre-student-novice under vow, you make a commitment to become a student-novice (and, therefore, to move into the second congregation) within a period of three to six months. During this period, you take the preparatory course, "The Only Truth That Sets The Heart Free", which introduces you to the fundamentals of the second-congregation practice. Pre-student-novices under vow practice Ruchira Avatara Bhakti Yoga in daily life, engage daily formal study of the Wisdom-Teaching of Avatar Adi Da, make regular contributions to the support of the Adidam Pan-Communion, and take up a regular form of service. You are not obliged to engage the full range of disciplines practiced in the first two congregations. You are, however, encouraged to practice formal periods of meditation and sacramental worship.

For information about becoming a pre-student-novice under vow, please contact the Adidam regional center nearest you.

The Fourth Congregation of Adidam

*(for those maintaining their participation
in the religious and/or cultural tradition
to which they already belong)*

Individuals who live in traditional cultural settings, and also individuals who wish to maintain their participation in the religious tradition to which they already belong (while acknowledging Avatar Adi Da Samraj as the Ultimate Divine Source of true religion), are invited to apply for membership in the fourth congregation of Adidam. Fourth-congregation devotees practice Ruchira Avatara Bhakti Yoga in its simplest form ("Invoke Me, Feel Me, Breathe Me, Serve Me") and also the discipline of daily study. Their financial and service obligations are adapted to their particular circumstance.

The opportunity to practice in the fourth congregation is also extended to all those who, because of physical or other functional limitations, are unable to take up the total practice of the Way of Adidam as required in the first and second congregations.

For more information about the fourth congregation of Adidam, call or write one of our regional centers (see p. 350), or e-mail us at: correspondence@adidam.org.

Temple sites at the Pilgrimage and Retreat Sanctuaries:
the Mountain Of Attention (left) and Da Love-Ananda Mahal (right)

One of the ways in which Avatar Adi Da Samraj Communicates His Divine Blessing-Transmission is through sacred places. He has Empowered two kinds of places: Pilgrimage and Retreat Sanctuaries (the Mountain Of Attention in northern California and Da Love-Ananda Mahal in Hawaii) and Hermitage-Retreat Sanctuaries (Tat Sundaram in northern California and Adidam Samrajashram in Fiji). Avatar Adi Da has Established Himself Spiritually in perpetuity at all four of these places. In particular, Adidam Samrajashram—His Great Island-Hermitage-Retreat and world-Blessing Seat—is Avatar Adi Da's principal Place of Spiritual Work and Transmission, and will remain so forever after His physical Lifetime. Formally acknowledged devotees are invited to go on special retreats at the Pilgrimage and Retreat Sanctuaries and at Adidam Samrajashram.

Adidam Samrajashram, Fiji

Darshan occasions with
Avatar Adi Da Samraj at
the Hermitage-Retreats:
Tat Sundaram (left) and
Adidam Samrajashram (right)

T hose whose hearts are given, in love, to Me, Fall into My Heart. Those who are Mine, because they are in love with Me, no longer demand to be fulfilled through conditional experience and through the survival (or perpetuation) of the ego-"I". Their love for Me grants them Access to Me, and, Thus, to My Love-Bliss—because I *Am* Love-Ananda, the Divine Love-Bliss, in Person.

What will My lover do but love Me? I suffer every form and condition of every one who loves Me—because I Love My devotee *As* My own Form, My own Condition. I Love My devotee *As* the One by Whom *I* Am Distracted.

I Grant all My own Divine and "Bright" Excesses to those who love Me, in exchange for all their doubts and sufferings. Those who "Bond" themselves to Me, through love-surrender, are inherently Free of fear and wanting need. They transcend the ego-"I" (the cause of all conditional experience), and they (cause and all and All) Dissolve in Me—for I *Am* the Heart of all and All, and I *Am* the Heart Itself, and the Heart Itself *Is* the Only Reality, Truth, and Real God of All and all.

What is a Greater Message than This?

DA LOVE-ANANDA GITA

From now on, all beings are uniquely Blessed. And human history can be different, because there is Help available that has never existed before.

The life of a devotee of Avatar Adi Da Samraj is unheard-of Grace, and this life can be lived by anyone. It does not matter who you are, where you live, or what you do. All of that makes no difference, once your heart recognizes Adi Da Samraj. Then the only course is the heart-response to Him—a life of devotion to the Divine in human Form, full of devotional ecstasy, true humor, freedom, clarity, and profound purpose.

So, why delay? The Living One, Adi Da Samraj, is here, and always will be. But now is the brief, and especially Blessed, window of time in which He is humanly Alive, doing His great Foundation Work for the sake of all beings, presently and in all future time. Every one who comes to Him and serves Him in His bodily human Lifetime shares in His unique once-and-forever Work of establishing the Way of Adidam in this world.

All who love Him carry His Name in their hearts and on their lips. Once the recognition of Avatar Adi Da awakens in you, this response is inevitable. The Promised God-Man, Avatar Adi Da Samraj, is not an "Other". He is the Gift, the Bliss, of Being Itself. He is the "Brightness" of Very God—Dawning, and then Flowering, in your heart. That Process is pure Revelation. It changes everything—grants peace, sanity, and the overwhelming impulse to Realize Unlimited, Permanent, and Perfect Oneness with Him.

As devotees of Avatar Adi Da Samraj, we make this confession to you: This opportunity—to live in heart-Communion with Real God—exceeds anything ever offered to mortal beings. It is true Happiness. And it is yours for the asking.

◆ ◆ ◆

A part from the four congregations, there are three distinct organizations within Adidam, each with a special area of responsibility.

The Da Love-Ananda Samrajya

Serving The Avataric-Incarnation-Body,
The Great Island-Hermitage-Retreat, and
The World-Blessing-Work of The Divine World-Teacher,
Ruchira Avatar Adi Da Samraj

The Da Love-Ananda Samrajya is devoted to serving Avatar Adi Da Himself, protecting Him and His intimate Sphere, providing for Adidam Samrajashram (His Great Island-Hermitage-Retreat, the Island of Naitauba in Fiji), ensuring that He has everything that He needs to do His Divine Blessing-Work, and providing right access to Him.

The Da Love-Ananda Samrajya also protects and provides for the Ruchira Sannyasin Order (the members of which are legal renunciates) and ensures that the Divine Word and Story of Adi Da Samraj are preserved and made known in the world.

The Eleutherian Pan-Communion of Adidam

*The Sacred Cultural Gathering and Global Mission
of the Devotees of The Divine World-Teacher,
Ruchira Avatar Adi Da Samraj*

*Dedicated to the Practice and the Proclamation
of The True World-Religion of Adidam,
The Unique Divine Way of Realizing Real God*

The Eleutherian Pan-Communion of Adidam is the organization devoted to establishing the Way of Adidam in the world and serving the culture of devotional practice in all four congregations. The Eleutherian Pan-Communion of Adidam is also responsible for the Sanctuaries, the Archives, the Wisdom-Teaching, and other sacred Treasures of Adidam.

The Global Mission of Adidam is a primary branch of the Adidam Pan-Communion. The Mission is active worldwide—through internet websites, through full-time missionaries and through the missionary service of all devotees. The Global Mission also includes the Publications Mission, which prepares, publishes, and distributes Avatar Adi Da's own books (and audiotapes and videotapes of Him), as well as books, magazines, and education courses about Him and the Way of Adidam by His devotees. The Dawn Horse Press (staffed by devotees of Avatar Adi Da) is the editorial and production department of the Publications Mission (see pp. 450-60 for a description of current Adidam publications).

The Ruchirasala of Adidam

THE ADI DA RUCHIRASALA

COOPERATION + TOLERANCE = PEACE

THE 'BRIGHT' HOUSE OF ADI DA SAMRAJ

*The True Cooperative Community Gathering
of the Devotees of The Divine World-Teacher,
Ruchira Avatar Adi Da Samraj*

*The Seed of a "Bright" New Age of Sanity
and Divine Joy for Mankind*

Cooperative community living (in households, Ashrams, or on Sanctuaries) is one of the fundamental disciplines of the first and second congregations of Adidam. The Ruchirasala of Adidam is the organization that serves Avatar Adi Da's devotees in incarnating cooperative community—it is the intimate sacred domain, in which devotees practice their devotional life and in which all the other entities of Adidam function. Creating intimate human living arrangements and shared services (such as schools, community businesses, and the Radiant Life Clinic) is part of the responsibility of the Ruchirasala. Together with the Adidam Pan-Communion, the Ruchirasala oversees all the practical interaction between members of the Adidam community.

Cooperation + Tolerance = Peace℠

In addition to His First Calling, which is to those who would become His devotees, Adi Da Samraj makes a Second Calling to the world at large—to embrace the disposition He has Summarized in the equation:

"COOPERATION + TOLERANCE = PEACE".

By this Second Calling, Adi Da Samraj urges everyone to create a sane human society—including, in particular, the creation of a global cooperative order, free of the devastation of war.

To find out more about Adi Da Samraj's Second Calling, please visit the Adidam Peace Center:

www.peacesite.org

An Invitation to Support Adidam

Avatar Adi Da Samraj's sole Purpose is to act as a Source of continuous Divine Grace for everyone, everywhere. In that spirit, He is a Free Renunciate and He owns nothing. Those who have made gestures in support of Avatar Adi Da's Work have found that their generosity is returned in many Blessings that are full of His healing, transforming, and Liberating Grace— and those Blessings flow not only directly to them as the beneficiaries of His Work, but to many others, even all others. At the same time, all tangible gifts of support help secure and nurture Avatar Adi Da's Work in necessary and practical ways, again similarly benefiting the entire world. Because all this is so, supporting His Work is the most auspicious form of financial giving, and we happily extend to you an invitation to serve Adidam through your financial support.

You may make a financial contribution in support of the Work of Adi Da Samraj at any time. You may also, if you choose, request that your contribution be used for one or more specific purposes.

If you are moved to help support and develop Adidam Samrajashram (Naitauba), Avatar Adi Da's Great Hermitage-Retreat and World-Blessing Seat in Fiji, and the circumstance provided there and elsewhere for Avatar Adi Da and the other members of the Ruchira Sannyasin Order, the senior renunciate order of Adidam, you may do so by making your contribution to The Da Love-Ananda Samrajya, the Australian charitable trust which has central responsibility for these Sacred Treasures of Adidam.

To do this: (1) if you do not pay taxes in the United States, make your check payable directly to "The Da Love-Ananda Samrajya Pty Ltd" (which serves as the trustee of the trust) and mail it to The Da Love-Ananda Samrajya at P.O. Box 4744, Samabula, Suva, Fiji; and (2) if you do pay taxes in the United States and you would like your contribution to be tax-deductible under U.S. laws, make your check payable to "The Eleutherian Pan-Communion of Adidam", indicate on your check or accompanying letter that you would like your contribution used for the work of The Da Love-Ananda Samrajya, and mail your check to the Advocacy Department of Adidam at 12040 North Seigler Road, Middletown, California 95461, USA.

If you are moved to help support and provide for one of the other purposes of Adidam, such as publishing the Sacred Literature of Avatar Adi Da, or supporting any of the other Sanctuaries He has Empowered, or maintaining the Sacred Archives that preserve His recorded Talks and Writings, or publishing audio and video recordings of Avatar Adi Da, you may do so by making your contribution directly to The Eleutherian Pan-Communion of Adidam, specifying the particular purposes you wish to benefit, and mailing your check to the Advocacy Department of Adidam at the above address.

If you would like more information about these and other gifting options, or if you would like assistance in describing or making a contribution, please write to the Advocacy Department of Adidam at the above address or contact the Adidam Legal Department by telephone at (707) 928-4612 or by FAX at (707) 928-4062.

Planned Giving

We also invite you to consider making a planned gift in support of the Work of Avatar Adi Da Samraj. Many have found that through planned giving they can make a far more significant gesture of support than they would otherwise be able to make. Many have also found that by making a planned gift they are able to realize substantial tax advantages.

There are numerous ways to make a planned gift, including making a gift in your Will, or in your life insurance, or in a charitable trust.

If you would like to make a gift in your Will in support of the work of The Da Love-Ananda Samrajya: (1) if you do not pay taxes in the United States, simply include in your Will the statement, "I give to The Da Love-Ananda Samrajya Pty Ltd, as trustee of The Da Love-Ananda Samrajya, an Australian charitable trust, P.O. Box 4744, Samabula, Suva, Fiji, _____" [inserting in the blank the amount or description of your contribution]; and (2) if you do pay taxes in the United States and you would like your contribution to be free of estate taxes and to also reduce any estate taxes payable on the remainder of your estate, simply include in your Will the statement, "I give to The Eleutherian Pan-Communion of Adidam, a California non-profit corporation, 12040 North Seigler Road, Middletown, California 95461, USA, _____" [inserting in the blank the amount or description of your contribution].

To make a gift in your life insurance, simply name as the beneficiary (or one of the beneficiaries) of your life insurance policy the organization of your choice (The Da Love-Ananda Samrajya or The Eleutherian Pan-Communion of Adidam), according to the foregoing descriptions and addresses. If you are a United States taxpayer, you may receive significant tax benefits if you make a contribution to The Eleutherian Pan-Communion of Adidam through your life insurance.

We also invite you to consider establishing or participating in a charitable trust for the benefit of Adidam. If you are a United States taxpayer, you may find that such a trust will provide you with immediate tax savings and assured income for life, while at the same time enabling you to provide for your family, for your other heirs, and for the Work of Avatar Adi Da as well.

The Advocacy and Legal Departments of Adidam will be happy to provide you with further information about these and other planned gifting options, and happy to provide you or your attorney with assistance in describing or making a planned gift in support of the Work of Avatar Adi Da.

Further Notes to the Reader

An Invitation to Responsibility

Adidam, the Way of the Heart that Avatar Adi Da has Revealed, is an invitation to everyone to assume real responsibility for his or her life. As Avatar Adi Da has Said in *The Dawn Horse Testament Of The Ruchira Avatar*, "If any one Is Heart-Moved To Realize Me, Let him or her First Resort (Formally, and By Formal Heart-Vow) To Me, and (Thereby) Commence The Ordeal Of self-Observation, self-Understanding, and self-Transcendence. . . ." Therefore, participation in the Way of Adidam requires a real struggle with oneself, and not at all a struggle with Avatar Adi Da, or with others.

All who study the Way of Adidam or take up its practice should remember that they are responding to a Call to become responsible for themselves. They should understand that they, not Avatar Adi Da or others, are responsible for any decision they may make or action they may take in the course of their lives of study or practice. This has always been true, and it is true whatever the individual's involvement in the Way of Adidam, be it as one who studies Avatar Adi Da's Wisdom-Teaching or as a formally acknowledged member of Adidam.

Honoring and Protecting the Sacred Word through Perpetual Copyright

Since ancient times, practitioners of true religion and Spirituality have valued, above all, time spent in the Company of the Sat-Guru (or one who has, to any degree, Realized Real God, Truth, or Reality, and who, thus, serves the awakening process in others). Such practitioners understand that the Sat-Guru literally Transmits his or her (Realized) State to every one (and every thing) with whom (or with which) he or she comes in contact. Through this Transmission, objects, environments, and rightly prepared individuals with which the Sat-Guru has contact can become empowered, or imbued with the Sat-Guru's Transforming Power. It is by this process of empowerment that things and beings are made truly and literally sacred and holy, and things so sanctified thereafter function as a source of the Sat-Guru's Blessing for all who understand how to make right and sacred use of them.

Sat-Gurus of any degree of Realization and all that they empower are, therefore, truly Sacred Treasures, for they help draw the practitioner more quickly into the process of Realization. Cultures of true Wisdom have always understood that such Sacred Treasures are precious (and fragile) Gifts to humanity, and that they should be honored, protected, and reserved for right sacred use. Indeed, the word "holy" means "set apart", and, thus that which is holy and sacred must be protected from insensitive secular interference and wrong use of any kind. Avatar Adi Da has Conformed His human Body-Mind Most Perfectly to the Divine Self, and He is, thus, the most Potent Source of Blessing-Transmission of Real God, or Truth Itself, or Reality Itself. He has for many years Empowered (or made sacred) special places and things, and these now serve as His Divine Agents, or as literal expressions and extensions of His Blessing-Transmission. Among these Empowered Sacred Treasures is His Wisdom-Teaching, which is full of His Transforming Power. This Blessed and Blessing Wisdom-Teaching has Mantric Force, or the literal Power to serve Real-God-Realization in those who are Graced to receive it.

Therefore, Avatar Adi Da's Wisdom-Teaching must be perpetually honored and protected, "set apart" from all possible interference and wrong use. The fellowship of devotees of Avatar Adi Da is committed to the perpetual preservation and right honoring of the Sacred Wisdom-Teaching of the Way of Adidam. But it is also true that, in order to fully accomplish this, we must find support in the world-society in which we live and in its laws. Thus, we call for a world-society and for laws that acknowledge the sacred, and that permanently protect it from insensitive, secular interference and wrong use of any kind. We call for, among other things, a system of law that acknowledges that the Wisdom-Teaching of the Way of Adidam, in all its forms, is, because of its sacred nature, protected by perpetual copyright.

We invite others who respect the sacred to join with us in this call and in working toward its realization. And, even in the meantime, we claim that all copyrights to the Wisdom-Teaching of Avatar Adi Da and the other Sacred Literature and recordings of the Way of Adidam are of perpetual duration.

We make this claim on behalf of The Da Love-Ananda Samrajya Pty Ltd, which, acting as trustee of The Da Love-Ananda Samrajya, is the holder of all such copyrights.

Avatar Adi Da and the Sacred Treasures of Adidam

True Spiritual Masters have Realized Real God (to one degree or another), and, therefore, they bring great Blessing and introduce Divine Possibility to the world. Such Adept-Realizers Accomplish universal Blessing-Work that benefits everything and everyone. They also Work very specifically and intentionally with individuals who approach them as their devotees, and with those places where they reside and to which they direct their specific Regard for the sake of perpetual Spiritual Empowerment. This was understood in traditional Spiritual cultures, and, therefore, those cultures found ways to honor Adept-Realizers by providing circumstances for them where they were free to do their Spiritual Work without obstruction or interference.

Those who value Avatar Adi Da's Realization and Service have always endeavored to appropriately honor Him in this traditional way by providing a circumstance where He is completely Free to do His Divine Work. Since 1983, He has resided principally on the island of Naitauba, Fiji, also known as Adidam Samrajashram. This island has been set aside by Avatar Adi Da's devotees worldwide as a Place for Him to do His universal Blessing-Work for the sake of everyone, as well as His specific Work with those who pilgrimage to Adidam Samrajashram to receive the special Blessing of coming into His physical Company.

Avatar Adi Da is a legal renunciate. He owns nothing and He has no secular or religious institutional function. He Functions only in Freedom. He, and the other members of the Ruchira Sannyasin Order, the senior renunciate order of Adidam, are provided for by The Da Love-Ananda Samrajya, which also provides for Adidam Samrajashram altogether and ensures the permanent integrity of Avatar Adi Da's Wisdom-Teaching, both in its archival and in its published forms. The Da Love-Ananda Samrajya, which functions only in Fiji, exists exclusively to provide for these Sacred Treasures of Adidam.

Outside Fiji, the institution which has developed in response to Avatar Adi Da's Wisdom-Teaching and universal Blessing is known as "The Eleutherian Pan-Communion of Adidam". This formal organization is active worldwide in making Avatar Adi Da's Wisdom-Teaching available to all, in offering guidance to all who are moved to respond to His Offering, and in providing for the other Sacred Treasures of Adidam, including the Mountain Of Attention Sanctuary and Tat Sundaram (in California) and Da Love-Ananda Mahal (in Hawaii). In addition to the central corporate entity known as The Eleutherian Pan-Communion of Adidam, which is based in California, there are numerous regional entities which serve congregations of Avatar Adi Da's devotees in various places throughout the world.

Practitioners of Adidam worldwide have also established numerous community organizations, through which they provide for many of their common and cooperative community needs, including those relating to housing, food, businesses, medical care, schools, and death and dying. By attending to these and all other ordinary human concerns and affairs via ego-transcending cooperation and mutual effort, Avatar Adi Da's devotees constantly free their energy and attention, both personally and collectively, for practice of the Way of Adidam and for service to Avatar Adi Da Samraj, to Adidam Samrajashram, to the other Sacred Treasures of Adidam, and to The Eleutherian Pan-Communion of Adidam.

All of the organizations that have evolved in response to Avatar Adi Da Samraj and His Offering are legally separate from one another, and each has its own purpose and function. Avatar Adi Da neither directs, nor bears responsibility for, the activities of these organizations. Again, He Functions only in Freedom. These organizations represent the collective intention of practitioners of Adidam worldwide not only to provide for the Sacred Treasures of Adidam, but also to make Avatar Adi Da's Offering of the Way of Adidam universally available to all.

The Ten "Great Questions", the forms of Simple Name-Invocation, and the forms of Ruchira Avatara Naama Japa

The Ten "Great Questions"

1. What Will "I" Do (or, How Will "I" Respond) If "I" Devotionally Heart-Recognize The Ruchira Avatar, Adi Da Love-Ananda Samraj, <u>As</u> The Divine Person (or The One and Only, and Inherently egoless, and Eternally Non-Separate, and Indivisible, and Indestructible, and Un-conditionally Love-Bliss-Full, and Universally Self-Manifested, and Uniquely here-Incarnated Conscious Light Of Reality <u>Itself</u>)?

2. What Am "I" <u>Always</u> Doing?

3. Avoiding Relationship?

4. Who or What <u>Is</u> Always Already <u>The</u> Case (Before "I" Do Anything At All)?

   Alternative forms:

   Who, What, and Where <u>Is</u> The Inherent Feeling Of Being?

   Who, What, and Where <u>Is</u> Existence Itself?

5. Am "I" The One Who Is "Living" (Animating or Manifesting) me (the body-mind) Now?

6. Who Is "Living" me <u>Now</u>?

7. How Do "I" Relate To The One Who "Lives" me?

8. Do "I" know What any one or any thing <u>Is</u>?

   Alternative form (asked in relation to any particular being, thing, condition, or event that arises):

   What <u>Is</u> it?

9. Who, What, and Where <u>Is</u> Inherent Love-Bliss, or Happiness Itself?

10. Who, What, and Where <u>Is</u> Consciousness Itself?

Simple Forms (or Combinations)
of Avatar Adi Da's
Avatarically Revealed and Given Divine Names
and Avataric Divine Descriptive Titles
(for use in the practice of Simple Name-Invocation of Him)

Da
Adi Da
Adi Da Samraj
Lord Da
Lord Adi Da
Avatar Da
Avatar Adi Da
Avatar Adi Da Samraj
Lord Ruchira
Ruchira Da
Ruchira Adi Da
Ruchira Avatar Da
Ruchira Avatar Adi Da
Ruchira Buddha Da
Ruchira Buddha Adi Da
Adi-Buddha Da
Adi-Buddha Adi Da
Ati-Buddha Da
Ati-Buddha Adi Da
Adi-Guru Da
Adi-Guru Adi Da
Ati-Guru Da
Ati-Guru Adi Da
Da Hridayam
Adi Da Hridayam
Santosha Da
Santosha Adi Da

Da Love-Ananda

Adi Da Love-Ananda

Love-Ananda Da

Love-Ananda Adi Da

Da Avabhasa

Adi Da Avabhasa

Avabhasa Da

Avabhasa Adi Da

Dau Loloma

Turaga Dau Loloma

Turaga Dau Loloma Vunirarama

NOTE: Generally, the above names should also (or alternatively) be begun or ended with appropriate descriptive references, such as those listed below.

Bhagavan

Sri

Lord

Turaga

Beloved

Heart-Master

Ruchira-Guru

Parama-Guru

Adi-Guru

Ati-Guru

Avatar

Ruchira Avatar

Param-Avatar

Adi-Avatar

Ati-Avatar

Buddha-Avatar

Ruchira Buddha

Adi-Buddha

Ati-Buddha

Samraj

Avatar Adi Da's Name "Hridayam" may also be added to the end of any of His other Names, except in the case of His Fijian-language names.

The Seventy Forms of the Ruchira Avatara Naama Mantra

Om Sri Adi Da

Om Sri Avatara Da

Om Sri Avatara Adi Da

Om Sri Ruchira Da

Om Sri Ruchira Adi Da

Om Sri Love-Ananda Da

Om Sri Love-Ananda Adi Da

Om Sri Santosha Da

Om Sri Santosha Adi Da

Om Sri Avabhasa Da

Om Sri Avabhasa Adi Da

Om Sri Adi-Avatar Adi Da

Om Sri Ati-Avatar Adi Da

Om Sri Ruchira Avatar Adi Da

Om Sri Love-Ananda Avatar Adi Da

Om Sri Santosha Avatar Adi Da

Om Sri Avabhasa Avatar Adi Da

Om Sri Adi-Buddha Adi Da

Om Sri Ati-Buddha Adi Da

Om Sri Ruchira Buddha Adi Da

Om Sri Love-Ananda Buddha Adi Da

Om Sri Santosha Buddha Adi Da

Om Sri Avabhasa Buddha Adi Da

Om Sri Adi-Guru Adi Da

Om Sri Ati-Guru Adi Da

Om Sri Ruchira-Guru Adi Da

Om Sri Love-Ananda-Guru Adi Da

Om Sri Santosha-Guru Adi Da

Om Sri Avabhasa-Guru Adi Da

Om Sri Turaga Dau Loloma

Om Sri Turaga Dau Loloma Vunirarama

Om Sri Adi Da, Ruchira Avatar

Om Sri Adi Da, Love-Ananda Avatar

Om Sri Adi Da, Santosha Avatar

Om Sri Adi Da, Avabhasa Avatar

Om Sri Adi Da, Avatara Hridayam

Om Sri Adi Da, Ruchira Hridayam

Om Sri Adi Da, Love-Ananda Hridayam

Om Sri Adi Da, Santosha Hridayam

Om Sri Adi Da, Avabhasa Hridayam

Om Sri Adi Da, Ruchira Avatar, Avatara Hridayam

Om Sri Adi Da, Love-Ananda Avatar, Avatara Hridayam

Om Sri Adi Da, Santosha Avatar, Avatara Hridayam

Om Sri Adi Da, Avabhasa Avatar, Avatara Hridayam

Om Sri Adi Da, Adi-Buddha Avatar, Avatara Hridayam

Om Sri Adi Da, Ati-Buddha Avatar, Avatara Hridayam

Om Sri Adi Da, Ruchira Buddha-Avatar, Avatara Hridayam

Om Sri Adi Da, Love-Ananda Buddha-Avatar, Avatara Hridayam

Om Sri Adi Da, Santosha Buddha-Avatar, Avatara Hridayam

Om Sri Adi Da, Avabhasa Buddha-Avatar, Avatara Hridayam

Om Sri Adi Da, Adi-Guru Adi Da, Avatara Hridayam

Om Sri Adi Da, Ati-Guru Adi Da, Avatara Hridayam

Om Sri Adi Da, Ruchira-Guru Adi Da, Avatara Hridayam

Om Sri Adi Da, Love-Ananda-Guru Adi Da, Avatara Hridayam

Om Sri Adi Da, Santosha-Guru Adi Da, Avatara Hridayam

Om Sri Adi Da, Avabhasa-Guru Adi Da, Avatara Hridayam

Om Sri Da, Jai Da, Jai Jai Da

Om Sri Adi Da, Jai Adi Da, Jai Jai Adi Da

Om Sri Adi Da, Avatara Adi Da, Jai Jai Adi Da,
Avatara Hridayam

Om Sri Adi Da, Sri Ruchira Adi Da, Jai Jai Adi Da,
Avatara Hridayam

Om Sri Adi Da, Love-Ananda Adi Da, Jai Jai Adi Da,
Avatara Hridayam

Om Sri Adi Da, Sri Santosha Adi Da, Jai Jai Adi Da,
Avatara Hridayam

Om Sri Adi Da, Avabhasa Adi Da, Jai Jai Adi Da,
Avatara Hridayam

Om Sri Adi Da, Ruchira Avatara Da, Love-Ananda Avatar,
Adi-Avatara Da, Da, Da, Da

Om Sri Adi Da, Ruchira Avatara Da, Love-Ananda Avatar,
Ati-Avatara Da, Da, Da, Da

Om Sri Adi Da, Adi-Buddha Avatar, Love-Ananda Avatar,
Buddha-Avatara Da, Da, Da, Da

Om Sri Adi Da, Ati-Buddha Avatar, Love-Ananda Avatar,
Buddha-Avatara Da, Da, Da, Da

Om Sri Adi Da, Ruchira Buddha-Avatar, Love-Ananda Avatar,
Avatara Buddha Da, Da, Da, Da

Om Sri Adi Da, Ruchira Buddha-Avatar, Adi-Buddha Avatar,
Ati-Buddha Avatar, Avatara Hridayam, Da, Da, Da

Om Sri Adi Da, Love-Ananda Buddha Da, Avatara Buddha Da,
Tathagata Avatar, Hridaya-Buddha Avatar,
Avatara Hridayam, Da, Da, Da

Chart of
The Seven Stages of Life

THE SEVEN STAGES OF LIFE

The Full and Complete Process of Human Maturation, Spiritual Growth, and Divine Enlightenment

As Revealed by

RUCHIRA AVATAR ADI DA SAMRAJ

Based on
The Seven Stages Of Life,
pp. 103-31

	FIRST STAGE (approx. 0-7 years)	**SECOND STAGE** (approx. 7-14 years)	**THIRD STAGE** (approx. 14-21 years)
	individuation; adaptation to the physical body	socialization; adaptation to the emotional-sexual (or feeling) dimension	integration of the psycho-physical personality; development of verbal mind, discriminative intelligence, and the will
	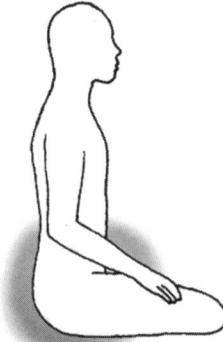	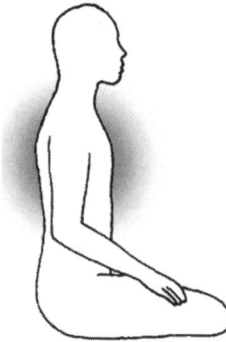	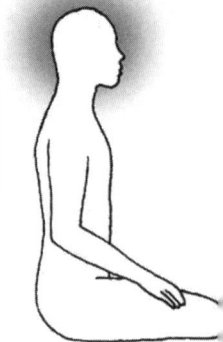
	Identified with the gross self		

FOURTH STAGE	FIFTH STAGE	SIXTH STAGE	SEVENTH STAGE
…go-surrendering devotion to …e Divine Person; purification …f body-based point of view …rough reception of Divine …pirit-Force	Spiritual or Yogic ascent of attention into psychic dimensions of the being; mystical experience of the higher brain; may culminate in fifth stage conditional Nirvikalpa Samadhi	Identification with Consciousness Itself (presumed, however, to be separate from all conditional phenomena); most likely will include the experience of Jnana Samadhi	Realization of the Divine Self; Inherently Perfect Freedom and Realization of Divine Love-Bliss (seventh stage Sahaj Samadhi); no "difference" experienced between Divine Consciousness and psycho-physical states and conditions

FOURTH STAGE	FIFTH STAGE	SIXTH STAGE	SEVENTH STAGE
anatomy: the circulation of …he Divine Spirit-Current, first …in the "basic" fourth stage of …fe) downward through the …rontal line and then (in the …advanced" fourth stage of …fe) upward through the …pinal line, until attention rests …tably at the doorway to the …rain core	**anatomy**: the ascent of the Divine Spirit-Current from the brain core (the Ajna Door) to the crown of the head and above (or even, in fifth stage conditional Nirvikalpa Samadhi, to the Matrix of Divine Sound and Divine Light infinitely above the total crown of the head)	**anatomy**: the Divine Spirit-Current descends (via Amrita Nadi, the "Immortal Current" of Divine Love-Bliss) from the Matrix of Divine Sound and Divine Light (infinitely above the total crown of the head) to the right side of the heart (the bodily seat of Consciousness)	**anatomy**: the "Regeneration" of Amrita Nadi, such that Amrita Nadi is felt as the Divine Current of "Bright" Spirit-Fullness, Standing between the right side of the heart and the Matrix of Divine Sound and Divine Light infinitely above the total crown of the head

	Identified with the subtle self (In the Way of Adidam, practice in the context of the "advanced" fourth stage of life and in the context of the fifth stage of life may typically be bypassed, proceeding directly from the "basic" fourth stage of life to the sixth stage of life)	Identified with the causal self	Identified with Divine Consciousness Itself

Notes to the Text of
The <u>Only</u> Complete Way
To Realize The Unbroken Light
Of <u>Real</u> God

Part Two

1. For a detailed description of the four stages (or four Ways) of Kashmir Saivism, see *Triadic Mysticism: The Mystical Theology of the Saivism of Kashmir*, by Paul E. Murphy (Delhi: Motilal Banarsidass, 1986).

2. Avatar Adi Da Samraj describes "three egos" that must be progressively transcended in the course of the complete Spiritual process—of which the "money, food, and sex" ego is the first. (See section LXXXVII of this Essay, pp. 161-69.)

3. For Avatar Adi Da's Instruction relative to the foundation life-discipline, foundation devotional discipline, and foundation Spiritual discipline for practitioners of Adidam, see *Santosha Adidam*.

4. "Baba" (literally meaning "father") is often used in India as a reference of intimate respect for a Spiritual Master.

5. There are a number of translations of the *Chidakasha Gita* teachings (including *Voice of the Self*, referenced below). Perhaps the most readily available translation is *The Sky of the Heart: Jewels of Wisdom from Nityananda*, introduction and commentary by Swami Chetanananda, originally translated by M. U. Hatengdi (Portland, Or.: Rudra Press, Second edition, 1996).

6. Swami Chinmayananda (1916-1993) was a scholar of the Hindu scriptures, especially the *Bhagavad Gita* and the *Upanishads,* who conceived his mission as restoring respect for the ancient Hindu scriptures and reinvigorating practice of the Spiritual way according to the Vedantic instruction.

7. M. P. Pandit was a scholar of Hindu scripture, and the author of over 100 books on Yoga and Spirituality. He spent more than forty years living and practicing under the guidance of Sri Aurobindo and the Mother, and serving at the Sri Aurobindo Ashram in Pondicherry, India.

8. *Voice of the Self,* by Swami Nityananda (of Vajreshwari), translated by M. P. Pandit (Madras: P. Ramanath Pai, 1962).

9. Sanskrit "nada" (or "shabda") refers to subtle internal sounds which may become apparent in the process of ascending (spinal) Yoga. The "Om-Sound" (or "Omkar") is the primordial root-sound, from which all other nadas derive.

10. The Sanskrit term "Jnani" ("Sage") literally means "one who knows" (or, more fully, "one who has Realized Jnana Samadhi"—see glossary entry for "Samadhi"). A Jnani is one who discriminates between What is Unconditional (the One Reality, or Divine Self) and what is conditional (the passing phenomena of experience). A Jnani is Identified with Consciousness Itself, as the Transcendental Witness of all that arises. By its very nature, the Realization of Jnana is inherently Nirguna. (In other words, there is no Saguna form of Jnana.)

11. Avatar Adi Da has Revealed that His deeper-personality Vehicle (see note 13), or True Great-Siddha Vehicle, is the combined deeper personalities of Ramakrishna and Swami Vivekananda. Avatar Adi Da discusses His unique association with Ramakrishna and Swami Vivekananda in sections XCIII-XCV (pp. 174-75) of this Essay. For a full description of Avatar Adi Da's Revelation of the Unique Associations with His True Great-Siddha Vehicle, see *The Promised God-Man Is Here*, by Carolyn Lee (Middletown, Calif.: Dawn Horse Press, 1998).

12. Avatar Adi Da's gross-personality vehicle (see note 13) was "Franklin Albert Jones", the child of His parents, Dorothy and Franklin Augustus Jones.

13. Avatar Adi Da uses the terms "gross personality" and "deeper personality" to indicate the two conditional dimensions of every human being. The gross personality is comprised of the physical body, its natural energies, its gross brain, and the verbal and lower psychic faculties of mind. The gross personality includes the entire gross dimension of the body-mind and the lower, or most physically oriented, aspects of the subtle dimension of the body-mind, and is the aspect of the body-mind that is the biological inheritance from one's parents.

The deeper personality is governed by the higher, least physically oriented processes of the mind (which function outside or beyond the gross brain, and which include the subtle faculties of discrimination, intuition, and Spiritual perception and knowledge), as well as the causal separate-"I"-consciousness and the root-activity of attention, prior to mind. The deeper personality is the aspect of the human being that reincarnates.

14. In *The Basket Of Tolerance,* Avatar Adi Da has identified a small number of Hindu and Buddhist texts as "premonitorily 'seventh stage'". While founded in the characteristic sixth stage "point of view", these texts express philosophical intuitions that foreshadow some of the basic characteristics of the seventh stage Realization.

The only-by-Me Revealed and Demonstrated and Given seventh stage of life is the clear and final fulfillment of the first six stages of life. The Revelation and Demonstration of the seventh stage of life by My own Avatarically Self-Revealed Divine Form, Presence, State, Work, and Word are My unique Gift to all and All. However, within the Great Tradition itself, there are some few literatures and Realizers of the sixth stage type that express philosophical (or insightful, but yet limited and incomplete) intuitions that sympathetically foreshadow some of the basic characteristics of the only-by-Me Revealed and Demonstrated and Given seventh stage Realization.

The Ashtavakra Gita *is a principal example of such premonitorily "seventh stage" literature. It is among the greatest (and most senior) communications of all*

the religious and Spiritual traditions in the Great Tradition of mankind. The
Ashtavakra Gita *is the Great Confession of a Sage who has thoroughly engaged the
philosophies and practices of the first six stages of life. It is a sixth stage Adept-
Realizer's Free (and uncompromised) communication (or Confession) of the ultimate implications of his sixth stage Realization.*

Like other premonitorily "seventh stage" texts, the Ashtavakra Gita *presumes a
tradition of progressive practice in the total context of the first six stages of life, but it
does not (itself) represent or communicate any ideal or technique of practice. It simply (and rather exclusively) communicates the Ultimate "Point of View" of the sixth
stage Realizer. ["The Unique Sixth Stage Foreshadowings of the Only-by-Me Revealed
and Demonstrated and Given Seventh Stage of Life", in* The Basket Of Tolerance]

15. In Sanskrit, "seva" means "service". Service to the Guru is traditionally treasured as one of the great Secrets of Realization.

16. The Hindu tradition speaks of four principal Spiritual paths (or four principal
aspects of the Spiritual path). Karma Yoga is literally the "Yoga of action", in
which every activity, no matter how humble, is transformed into self-transcending
service to the Divine. (The other three paths are Bhakti Yoga, the path of devotion, Raja Yoga, the path of higher psychic discipline, and Jnana Yoga, the path
of transcendental insight.)

17. Swami Prakashananda (1917-1988) turned to Spiritual life in his 30s, eventually choosing the mountain of Sapta Shringh as a place to settle and devote himself to Spiritual practice. Over time, an ashram developed there around him. He
met Swami Muktananda in 1956 and was initiated as Swami Muktananda's devotee, although he generally stayed at his own ashram in Sapta Shringh rather than
spending a great deal of time in Ganeshpuri at Swami Muktananda's ashram. For
Swami Prakashananda's biography, see *Agaram Bagaram Baba: Life, Teachings,
and Parables—A Spiritual Biography of Baba Prakashananda*, by Titus Foster
(Berkeley: North Atlantic Books / Patagonia, Ariz.: Essene Vision Books, 1999).

18. For Avatar Adi Da's description of Swami Prakashananda's demonstration of
Spiritual Transfiguration of the physical body, see chapter 12 of *The Knee Of
Listening*.

19. *Agaram Bagaram Baba*, p. 35.

20. Swami Muktananda's letter of acknowledgement and blessing of Avatar Adi Da
is included in chapter 12 of *The Knee Of Listening* and also in Part Three ("The
Order of My Free Names") of *The Divine Siddha-Method Of The Ruchira Avatar*.

21. For Avatar Adi Da's description of His own "Embrace" of the Divine "Cosmic
Goddess", see chapter 16 of *The Knee Of Listening*.

22. *Play of Consciousness,* by Swami Muktananda (South Fallsburg, N.Y.: SYDA,
Fourth edition, 1994).

23. For Avatar Adi Da's description of His experience of Christian mystical
visions, see chapters 14 and 15 of *The Knee Of Listening*.

24. For a comprehensive treatment of the fourth-to-fifth stage Yogic tradition of Maharashtra, see *Mysticism in India: The Poet-Saints of Maharashtra,* by R. D. Ranade (Albany: State University of New York Press, 1983).

25. For Swami Muktananda's description of the "Blue Person", see *Play of Consciousness* (e.g. pp. 190-194).

Among the numerous translations of the *Bhagavad Gita,* Avatar Adi Da Samraj points to two editions as particularly worthy of study:

Srimad-Bhagavad-Gita (The Scripture of Mankind), chapter summaries, word-for-word meaning in prose order, translation, notes, and index of first lines by Swami Tapasyananda (Mylapore, India: Sri Ramakrishna Math, 1984).

God Talks with Arjuna: The Bhagavad Gita—Royal Science of God-Realization, The Immortal Dialogue Between Soul and Spirit, a new translation and commentary by Paramahansa Yogananda, two volumes (Los Angeles: Self-Realization Fellowship, 1996).

For a complete translation of the *Bhagavata Purana* (also known as the *Srimad Bhagavatam*), see *Srimad Bhagavatam,* translated by N. Raghunathan, two volumes (Madras: Vighneshwara Publishing House, 1976).

26. For Avatar Adi Da's full description of the "bodies" or "sheaths" of the total human structure (and the relationship between these "bodies" and the states of waking, dreaming, and sleeping), see *Santosha Adidam.*

27. Excerpted from a chart ("The Four Bodies of the Individual Soul") in *Play of Consciousness,* by Swami Muktananda (South Fallsburg, N.Y.: SYDA, Fourth edition, 1994), p. 96.

28. In *The Basket Of Tolerance,* Avatar Adi Da has contrasted the development of exoteric (or socially oriented, and myth-based) public Christianity with the secret Teachings of esoteric (or mystically oriented) Christianity:

The "official" Christian church, even in the form of all its modern sects, is the institutional product of an early cultural struggle between exoteric religionists, limited to doctrines based in the physical point of view characteristic of the first three stages of life, and esoteric religionists, inclined toward the mystical (or general psychic, and Spiritual) point of view characteristic of the "basic" and the "advanced" phases of the fourth stage of life and the mystical (or higher psychic, and Spiritual) Realizations associated with the fifth stage of life. This struggle, which was eventually won by the exoteric sects (or factions), took place between the various emerging Christian sects during the early centuries after Jesus' [crucifixion]. . . .

In the domain of the exoteric church, it was apparently generally presumed (among its original creative leadership) that all mysteries and legends must be "concretized" into a story (or an inspiring doctrine) about Jesus as the "Heavenly Messiah" (or the "Christ", the "Anointed One", the Exclusively Blessed "Son of God")—whereas the original esoteric mysteries and mystical Teachings of Christian gnosticism (which must often correspond to what must be presumed to have been Jesus' own Teachings) invariably communicate a Message about the Spiritual (or "Spirit-Breathing") Awakening of every individual (or of every devotee of a Spirit-

*Master, or, in this Christian case, of every devotee of Jesus as Spirit-Master).
Therefore, the core of the esoteric Christian Teachings is that Salvation (from
"possession" by cosmic Nature, by the human world, and by fear of death) is
Realized by Means of "Spiritual rebirth" (or Absorption In—and, thus, participatory
knowledge of—the inherently deathless and Free and Divine Spirit-Power, or
"Breath-Energy", of Being). And the "Good News" of this esoteric Salvation
Message is that every individual is (ultimately, by virtue of Spiritual Realization)
a "Son" or "Daughter" of God.*

29. Avatar Adi Da notes that not only "things" in space but space itself came into
being with the "Big Bang":

> *Space-time (itself, or in its totality) cannot be observed. The "Big Bang" was
> not an event that could have been observed. The "Big Bang" is not something that
> occurred in space (or in time). The "Big Bang" is the origin of space (and of time).
> To look at the "Big Bang" as an event in space (and in time) is already to look at
> it in egoic terms, and from a position after the event. To examine the "Big Bang"
> in conventional scientific terms is to assume a dissociated (and separate, and sep-
> arative) position, as if the ego-"I" (or the "observing" body-mind) were standing
> outside of space-time—but it does not. Egoity (and all of psycho-physical self, or
> body-mind) is, inherently and necessarily, an event in (and of) space-time. The
> body-mind is an event in (and of) space-time. That in Which the body-mind is
> occurring (or of Which the body-mind is a modification, or a mere and tempo-
> rary appearance) necessarily (Itself) Transcends space-time, Transcends limita-
> tion, Transcends the apparent breaking of Fundamental Light (or of Energy Itself,
> or of Radiance Itself). [*"Space-Time Is Love-Bliss", in Real God Is The Indivisible
> Oneness Of Unbroken Light*]*

30. For Swami Muktananda's description of the "blue bindu" (or "blue pearl"),
see *Play of Consciousness* (e.g., pp. 160-161).

31. For Avatar Adi Da's full description of the Cosmic Mandala, see chapter thirty-
nine of *The Dawn Horse Testament Of The Ruchira Avatar.*

32. In *The Knee Of Listening*, Avatar Adi Da describes His Birth as the "Bright",
His subsequent voluntary relinquishment of the "Bright", and His eventual Re-
Awakening as the "Bright". He uses the word "Re-Awakening" to indicate that
this Great Event was not a Realization entirely "new" to His experience, but a
"return" to the Divine Condition He had known at Birth.

33. For Avatar Adi Da's description of His discovery of parallels with Ramana
Maharshi's experience, see chapter 18 of *The Knee Of Listening.*

34. This instruction from Swami Muktananda was communicated in a letter he wrote
to Avatar Adi Da on April 23, 1968, which Avatar Adi Da quotes in chapter 11 of
The Knee Of Listening.

35. The "Method of the Siddhas" (meaning "the Spiritual Means used by the
Siddhas, or Perfected Ones, or True Spirit-Baptizers") is a phrase coined by
Avatar Adi Da Samraj (in the earliest days of His Teaching Work) to describe the

essence of the Way of Adidam—which is the Spiritual <u>relationship</u> to Him (or Satsang, or devotional Communion with Him), rather than any technique (meditative or otherwise) learned from Him. *The Method of the Siddhas* was the Title Avatar Adi Da chose for the first published collection of His Talks to His devotees. (In its final form, Avatar Adi Da re-titled this book *The Divine Siddha-Method Of The Ruchira Avatar*.)

Avatar Adi Da also points out that this "Method" has traditionally always been the core of esoteric religion and Spirituality, and that (indeed) the entire worldwide tradition of esoteric religion and Spirituality is rightly understood to be the global tradition of "Siddha Yoga".

The Foundation Of The Only-By-Me Revealed and Given Way Of Adidam Is The Eternal, Ancient, and Always New Method Of The Siddhas—Which Is Devotional Communion With The Siddha-Guru, and Which Is The Unique Means Of Realizing Real God, or Truth, or Reality That Has Traditionally Been Granted By The Rare True Adept-Realizers Of Real God, or Truth, or Reality Who (In The Traditional Context Of The First Six Stages Of Life, and Each According To Their Particular Stage Of Awakening and Of Helping-Capability) Have, By Means Of The Unique Blessing-Method (or Transmission-Capability) Of The Siddhas, Directly (and By Directly and Really Effective Spiritual Blessing-Work) Transmitted The Traditional Revelations and Realizations Of Real God, or Truth, or Reality. [The <u>Only</u> Complete Way To Realize The Unbroken Light Of <u>Real</u> God]

36. The Sanskrit word "sat" means "Truth", "Being", "Existence". Esoterically, the word "guru" is understood to be a composite of two words meaning "destroyer of darkness". The Sat-Guru is thus a "True Guru", or one who destroys darkness and thereby leads living beings from darkness (or non-Truth) into Light (or the Living Truth).

37. A common theme running through various branches of the Great Tradition is the prophecy of a great Savior or Liberator still to come. The prophecy takes different forms in different traditions, but the underlying commonality is the promise or expectation that the culminating Avatar or Incarnation will appear in the future, at a time when humanity is lost, apparently cut off from Wisdom, Truth, and God. Buddhists refer to that Expected One as "Maitreya"; Vaishnavite Hindus, as the "Kalki Avatar"; Christians, as the "second coming of Jesus"; Jews, as the "Messiah"; and so on.

38. Avatar Adi Da Samraj describes His spontaneous experience of ego-death, in the spring of 1967, in chapter 9 of *The Knee Of Listening*.

39. See *Sadguru Nityananda Bhagavan, The Eternal Entity*, by P.V. Ravindram (Cannanore, India: T. Thankam Ravindran, 1989), pp. 25-26 and 27-28.

40. For Avatar Adi Da's Revelations about Ramakrishna and Swami Vivekananda as His "combined" deeper-personality Vehicle, see Essay VI ("I Have Appeared here Via a Unique, Spontaneous, and Never-Again Conjunction of Vehicles") in chapter 20 of *The Knee Of Listening*.

Part Four

41. "Life-business" is a phrase Avatar Adi Da uses to refer to the practical matters of survival (via appropriate work, right participation in community life, and so on), the necessity of establishing the body-mind in a state of basic equanimity (via right exercise, right diet, and so on), and the obligation of maintaining right social and emotional-sexual relationships. Only if one's life-business is handled can one's energy and attention be fully available for Spiritual practice.

Part Five

42. The Way of Adidam is founded in a fundamental disillusionment with the ego and its purposes (together with a deep heart-attraction to Avatar Adi Da Samraj). This disillusionment is positive because it is the necessary foundation for true Spiritual Awakening.

43. "Ruchira Avatara Advaita-Dharma" is Sanskrit for "the Non-Dual ('Advaita') Wisdom-Teaching ('Dharma') of the Ruchira Avatar".

44. "Hridaya-Advaita Dharma" is Sanskrit for "the Wisdom-Teaching ('Dharma') of the Non-Dual ('Advaita') Divine Heart ('Hridaya')".

45. "Ruchira Avatara Maha-Jnana-Siddha Yoga" is Sanskrit for "the Yoga of devotion to the Ruchira Avatar, Who Is the Supreme Transcendental Divine Siddha ('Maha-Jnana-Siddha')".

46. "Ruchira Avatara Maha-Jnana Hridaya-Shaktipat Yoga" is Sanskrit for "the Yoga of receiving the Supreme Transcendental ('Maha-Jnana') Divine Heart-Blessing-Transmission ('Hridaya-Shaktipat') of the Ruchira Avatar".

47. "Buddhi" is Sanskrit for "intelligence", "intellect", or "mind".

48. "Bodhi" is Sanskrit for "enlightenment", or "enlightened mind".

49. In Sanskrit, "parama" means "supreme", and "advaita" means "non-dual". Therefore, the Paramadvaita Buddha is the One of Supreme Non-Dual Enlightenment.

50. The three historical "yanas", or "vehicles", of Buddhism are Hinayana (or Theravada), Mahayana, and Vajrayana. Hinayana (or Theravada) is the predominant form of Buddhism in Southeast Asia and Sri Lanka, Mahayana the predominant form in China, Korea, and Japan, and Vajrayana the predominant form in Tibet and various Himalayan kingdoms. While all three of the historical "yanas" recognize certain fundamental principles of Buddhism, each "yana" has a distinctive understanding of the Nature of Enlightenment (or Nirvana), and each "yana" recommends a distinctive form of practice intended to Realize Enlightenment.

51. Avatar Adi Da defines His basic Arguments in chapter nineteen of *The Dawn Horse Testament Of The Ruchira Avatar:*

My Word Of Instruction Is Founded On Two Basic (and Complementary) Arguments.

The First Is The Argument Relative To "Radical" Understanding (or Most

Direct, and, Most Ultimately, Inherent, and Inherently Most Perfect, Transcending Of the self-Contraction).

The Second Is The Argument Relative To Divine Ignorance (or Inherent, and Transcendental, and Inherently Spiritual, and Inherently Most Perfect, Divine Self-Realization).

Avatar Adi Da's extended Instruction on His Argument relative to "radical" understanding is given (among other places) in *The Knee Of Listening* and *The Divine Siddha-Method Of The Ruchira Avatar*. His extended Instruction on His Argument relative to Divine Ignorance is given in *What, Where, When, How, Why, and <u>Who</u> To Remember To Be Happy*.

Avatar Adi Da's Great Questions are also given in Appendix A, p. 389.

52. Ruchira Avatara Naama Japa is repetition ("japa") of the Name ("naama") of the Ruchira Avatar, Adi Da Samraj. In the practice of Ruchira Avatara Naama Japa, the practitioner of Adidam surrenders mind, emotion, body, and breath into feeling-Contemplation of Avatar Adi Da Samraj, through repetition of one of the forms of the Ruchira Avatara Naama Mantra (see Appendix A, pp. 392-94).

For Avatar Adi Da's discussion of the practice of Ruchira Avatara Naama Japa, see chapter twenty-two of *The Dawn Horse Testament Of The Ruchira Avatar*.

53. See the glossary under **Devotional Way of Insight / Devotional Way of Faith** for a description of the "Two Great Devotional Forms Of The Total Practice Of The Way Of The Heart".

54. "Pondering" is Avatar Adi Da's technical term for meditative reflection on His Wisdom-Teaching, as practiced by His listening devotees who are experimenting with or practicing the Devotional Way of Insight in the Way of Adidam. The practice of pondering includes formal and increasingly meditative "consideration" of His ten Great Questions and random, informal reflection upon His Arguments and Great Questions in daily life, in the context of feeling-Contemplation of Him. The primary Great Question is self-Enquiry in the form "Avoiding Relationship?", and, in due course, as the listening process matures, this becomes the only one of the ten Great Questions used by the practitioner of the Devotional Way of Insight.

For Avatar Adi Da's description of meditative pondering in the Way of Adidam, see chapter nineteen of *The Dawn Horse Testament Of The Ruchira Avatar*. Avatar Adi Da's Great Qiuestions are also given in Appendix A, p. 389.

55. All of the practices that Avatar Adi Da Offers to practitioners of the Way of Adidam are simultaneously "Gifts, Callings, and Disciplines", because they are the means to Realize True Happiness, they are an inspiration to further growth, and they require real self-transcendence. For a brief description of these "Gifts, Callings, and Disciplines", see pp. 361-67. Avatar Adi Da's extended descriptions of these "Gifts, Callings, and Disciplines" are given in *Ruchira Avatara Hridaya-Tantra Yoga, Santosha Adidam*, and *The Dawn Horse Testament Of The Ruchira Avatar*.

56. The forms and combinations of Avatar Adi Da's Divine Names and Descriptive Titles to be used in the practice of Simple Name-Invocation of Him are given in Appendix A, pp. 390-91.

57. In various religious and Spiritual traditions, the name of one's Spiritual Master or chosen deity (or a brief prayer including that name) is invoked repetitively (sometimes in association with the use of a mala, or rosary) as a devotional practice of remembrance of the Divine.

58. The seventy variant forms of the Ruchira Avatara Naama Mantra are given in Appendix A, pp. 392-94.

59. Avatar Adi Da's bodily (human) Form may be Contemplated by His devotees either in a direct manner (by direct physical sighting or direct feeling-Remembrance of His bodily human Form, without the use of a representational image) or with the aid of a photographic, holographic, painted, sculpted, or other visual image of His bodily (human) Form.

60. For a description of Avatar Adi Da's Teachers and Spiritual Sources, see the glossary entry for **Lineage**.

61. This "First Moment Of Re-Awakening" was an incident that occurred while Avatar Adi Da Samraj was a student at Columbia College in 1960. Avatar Adi Da describes this incident in chapter 3 of *The Knee Of Listening*.

62. For a description of Avatar Adi Da's "Ordeal of Re-Awakening", see *The Promised God-Man Is Here*, by Carolyn Lee.

63. Avatar Adi Da uses the metaphor of the closed fist and open hand to demonstrate the contrast between the self-contracted state and the natural (uncontracted) state. In this passage, He is Describing a key incident during His "Sadhana Years" when this contrast became suddenly intuitively clear.

64. "Prapatti" in Sanskrit literally means "forward-fallingness", and is a term signifying unconditional self-surrender, or reliance on Divine Grace. The practice of prapatti, founded upon preparatory disciplines that regulate moral life, discipline the mind, and open the feeling heart, was the most advanced practice of the devotional (bhakti) schools of medieval India. Avatar Adi Da's own early practice of unconditional self-surrender was generated spontaneously, without His conscious knowledge of any such traditional practice, Eastern or Western.

65. The practice of ego-transcendence in the Way of Adidam is always present-time (or direct and immediate)—because, in any moment of true practice, the devotee enters into ego-surrendering, ego-forgetting, and ego-transcending heart-Communion with Avatar Adi Da. The practice of ego-transcendence in the Way of Adidam is also progressive (ultimately, culminating in Most Perfect ego-Transcendence, in the seventh stage of life)—because, over time, the devotee becomes more and more consistently responsible for all of the physical and psychic dimensions of the body-mind and more and more stably Awakened to Identification with Self-Existing and Self-Radiant Consciousness Itself.

66. For a description of Avatar Adi Da's spontaneous "meditation" of others after the Great Event of His Divine Re-Awakening, see chapter 4 of *The Promised God-Man Is Here*, by Carolyn Lee.

67. A "reality consideration" is a thorough and unflinching examination of one's egoic patterning, as it manifests in the progressive course of practice in the context of the first six stages of life. This ongoing examination is undertaken for the purpose of clearly seeing how one animates the self-contraction, so that such patterns can be thoroughly surrendered and gone beyond.

68. Avatar Adi Da often refers to His Transmission of Spiritual Blessing as His "Spiritual Baptism" (or "Spirit-Baptism"). It is often felt as a Current, descending through the front of the body and ascending through the spinal line. However, Avatar Adi Da's Spirit-Baptism is fundamentally and primarily the moveless Transmission of the Heart Itself. As a secondary effect, His Spirit-Baptism serves to purify, balance, and energize the entire body-mind of the devotee who is prepared to receive it.

Avatar Adi Da's extended Instruction relative to His Spiritual Baptism is given in *Ruchira Avatara Hridaya-Siddha Yoga*.

69. "Maha-jnana" is Sanskrit for "great knowledge". Avatar Adi Da uses "Maha-Jnana" to mean the Perfect "Knowledge" (or Realization) of the Divine Self, Confessed in the seventh stage of life. Maha-Jnana is to be distinguished from the Jnana (or Transcendental Self-Knowledge) of the sixth stage Realizer, which is the conditional and temporary Realization of Transcendental Consciousness that strategically excludes awareness of the conditional body-mind-self and its relations. In contrast, Maha-Jnana is the "Open-Eyed"—or Unconditional, spontaneous, and permanent—Realization of the Divine Self under all conditions.

"Maha-Jnana Siddha" is a specific reference to Avatar Adi Da, indicating His Unique Power to directly Transmit Most Perfect Divine (seventh stage) Awakening to others.

70. The Ruchira Sannyasin Order may, on occasion, accept a novice-member at a stage of practice previous to the "Perfect Practice".

71. Members of the Ruchira Sannyasin Order are on perpetual retreat in the sense that they are called to constantly demonstrate most exemplary and most intensive practice of the Way of Adidam while residing in the secluded circumstance of one of the Empowered Sanctuaries of Adidam. Members of the Ruchira Sannyasin Order are also on perpetual retreat in the sense that, although they function as the senior cultural authority within the culture of Adidam, they are specifically instructed by Avatar Adi Da not to hold positions of practical or managerial (and, necessarily, outward-directed) responsibility relative to the institution, culture, community, or mission of Adidam.

72. For a description of Avatar Adi Da's Lineage, please see the Glossary.

73. Avatar Adi Da uses the term "Omega" to characterize the materialistic culture that today dominates not only the Western world (which has brought the Omega strategy to its fullest development) but even most of the present-day Eastern world, which has now largely adopted the anti-Spiritual viewpoint typical of the West. The Omega strategy is motivated to the attainment of a future-time perfection and fulfillment of the conditional worlds, through the intense application

of human invention, political will, and even Divine Influence. Its preference is to limit and suppress attention to the Divine Reality, while maximizing attention to the conditional reality.

Avatar Adi Da calls the characteristic traditional Eastern strategy the "Alpha" strategy. Alpha cultures pursue an undisturbed peace, in which the conditional world is excluded as much as possible from attention (and thereby ceases to be a disturbance). Although the cultures that were originally founded on the Alpha approach to life and Truth are fast disappearing, the Alpha strategy remains the conventional archetype of Spiritual life, even in the Omega culture. In contrast to the Omega preference, the Alpha preference is to limit and control (and even suppress) attention to the conditional reality, while maximizing attention to the Divine Reality.

Neither the Omega strategy nor the Alpha strategy Realizes Truth absolutely, as each is rooted in the presumption of a "problem" relative to existence. (For Avatar Adi Da's extended discussion of the Alpha and Omega strategies, see *The Truly Human New World-Culture Of Unbroken Real-God-Man*.)

74. "Tapas" is Sanskrit for "heat", and, by extension, "self-discipline". In this case, the tapas Avatar Adi Da is Speaking of is the heat that results from the conscious frustration of egoic tendencies, through acceptance of His Calling for ego-surrendering, ego-forgetting, and ego-transcending devotion, service, self-discipline, and meditation.

75. Also known as the "third eye", the "single eye", or the "mystic eye", the Ajna Door is the subtle psychic center (or chakra) located between and behind the eyebrows and associated with the brain core. The awakening of the ajna chakra may give rise to mystical visions and intuitive reflections of other realms of experience within and outside the individual. The ajna chakra governs the higher mind, will, vision, and conception.

76. In deep meditation, the Spirit-Current may be felt in the form of the Arrow (which Avatar Adi Da describes as "a motionless axis that seems to stand in the center of the body, between the frontal and spinal lines"), rather than in the form of the Circle (in which the natural life-energy and, in the case of Spiritually Awakened practitioners, the Spirit-Energy are felt to circulate through the frontal and spinal lines). For definition of the Circle, see the Glossary.

Part Six

77. Swami Rudrananda (Rudi) was Avatar Adi Da's first Spiritual Teacher. See glossary entry for **Lineage**.

Epilogue

78. For a description of Avatar Adi Da's "Twenty-Three Divine 'Source-Texts'", see pp. 27-38.

GLOSSARY

A

Adi Sanskrit for "first", "primordial", "source"—also "primary", "beginning". Thus, most simply, "Adi Da" means "First Giver".

Adidam The primary name for the Way Revealed and Given by Avatar Adi Da Samraj.

When Avatar Adi Da Samraj first Gave the name "Adidam" in January 1996, He pointed out that the final "m" adds a mantric force, evoking the effect of the primal Sanskrit syllable "Om". (For Avatar Adi Da's Revelation of the most profound esoteric significance of "Om" as the Divine Sound of His own Very Being, see *He-and-She Is Me*.) Simultaneously, the final "m" suggests the English word "Am" (expressing "I Am"), such that the Name "Adidam" also evokes Avatar Adi Da's Primal Self-Confession, "I Am Adi Da", or, more simply, "I Am Da" (or, in Sanskrit, "Aham Da Asmi").

Adidam Samrajashram See **Sanctuaries**.

adolescent See **childish and adolescent strategies**.

Advaita Vedanta The Sanskrit word "Vedanta" literally means the "end of the Vedas" (the most ancient body of Indian Scripture), and is used to refer to the principal philosophical tradition of Hinduism. "Advaita" means "non-dual". Advaita Vedanta, then, is a philosophy of non-dualism, the origins of which lie in the ancient esoteric teaching that Brahman, or the Divine Being, is the only Reality.

Advaitayana Buddha / Advaitayana Buddhism "Advaitayana" means "Non-Dual Vehicle". The Advaitayana Buddha is the Enlightened One Who has Revealed and Given the Non-Dual Vehicle.

"Advaitayana Buddhism" is another name for the Way of Adidam. The name "Advaitayana Buddhism" indicates the unique sympathetic likeness of Adidam to the traditions of Advaitism (or Advaita Vedanta) and Buddhism. In His examination of the entire collective religious tradition of humankind, Avatar Adi Da has observed that these two traditions represent the most advanced Realizations ever attained previous to His Avataric Divine Incarnation. The primary aspiration of Buddhism is to realize freedom from the illusion of the separate individual ego-self. The primary aspiration of Advaitism (or the tradition of "Non-Dualism") is to know the Supreme Divine Self absolutely, beyond all dualities (of high and low, good and bad, and so on). Advaitayana Buddhism is the Non-Dual ("Advaita") Way ("yana", literally "vehicle") of Most Perfect Awakening ("Buddhism"). Advaitayana Buddhism is neither an outgrowth of the historical tradition of Buddhism nor of the historical tradition of Advaitism. Advaitayana Buddhism is the unique Revelation of Avatar Adi Da Samraj, which perfectly fulfills both the traditional Buddhist aspiration for absolute freedom from the bondage of the egoic self and the traditional Advaitic aspiration for absolute Identity with the Divine Self. (For Avatar Adi Da's discussion of Advaitayana Buddhism, see *The Only Complete Way To Realize The Unbroken Light Of Real God*.)

Advaitic "Advaita" is Sanskrit for "Non-Duality". Thus, "Advaitic" means "Non-Dual". Avatar Adi Da has Revealed that—in Truth, and in Reality—there is not the slightest separation, or "difference", between the Unconditional Divine Reality and the conditional reality. In other words, Reality altogether is Perfectly One, or Non-Dual, or Advaitic.

the advanced and the ultimate stages of life Avatar Adi Da Samraj uses the term "advanced" to describe the fourth stage of life (in its "basic" and "advanced" contexts) and the fifth stage of life in the Way of Adidam. He uses the term "ultimate" to describe the sixth and seventh stages of life in the Way of Adidam.

"advanced" context of the fourth stage of life See **stages of life**.

Agents / Agency Agents (or Agency) include all the Means that may serve as complete Vehicles of Avatar Adi Da's Divine Grace and Awakening Power. The first Means of Agency that have been fully established by Him are the Wisdom-Teaching of the Way of Adidam, the Hermitage-Retreat Sanctuaries and the Pilgrimage and Retreat Sanctuaries that He has Empowered, and the many Objects and Articles that He has Empowered for the sake of His devotees' Remembrance of Him and reception of His Heart-Blessing. After Avatar Adi Da's human Lifetime, at any given time a single individual from among His seventh stage "Ruchira san-nyasin" devotees will be designated (by the senior governing membership of the Ruchira Sannyasin Order) to serve as His living <u>human</u> Agent.

Aham Da Asmi The Sanskrit phrase "Aham Da Asmi" means "I (Aham) Am (Asmi) Da". "Da", meaning "the One Who Gives", indicates that Avatar Adi Da Samraj is the Supreme Divine Giver, the Avataric Incarnation of the Very Divine Person.

Avatar Adi Da's Declaration "Aham Da Asmi" is similar in form to the "Mahavakyas" (or "Great Statements") of ancient India (found in the Upanishads, the collected esoteric Instruction of ancient Hindu Gurus). However, the significance of "Aham Da Asmi" is fun-damentally different from that of the traditional Mahavakyas. Each of the Upanishadic Mahavakyas expresses, in a few words, the profound (though not most ultimate) degree of Realization achieved by great Realizers of the past. For example, the Upanishadic Mahavakya "Aham Brahmasmi" ("I Am Brahman") expresses a great individual's Realization that he or she is Identified with the Divine Being (Brahman), and is not, in Truth, identified with his or her apparently indi-vidual body-mind. However, "Aham Da Asmi", rather than being a proclamation of a human being who has devoted his or her life most intensively to the process of Real-God-Realization and has thereby Realized the Truth to an extraordinarily profound degree, is Avatar Adi Da's Confession that He <u>Is</u> the Very Divine Person, Da, Who has Appeared here in His Avatarically-Born bodily (human) Divine Form, in order to Reveal Himself to all and All, for the sake of the Divine Liberation of all and All.

all and All / All and all Avatar Adi Da uses the phrase "all and All" (or "All and all") to describe the totality of conditional existence from two points of view. In *Aham Da Asmi,* He defines lower-case "all" as indicating "the collected sum of all Presumed To Be Separate (or limited) beings, things, and conditions", and upper-case "All" as indicating "The All (or The Undivided Totality) Of conditional Existence As A Whole".

Amrita Nadi Amrita Nadi is Sanskrit for "Channel (or Current, or Nerve) of Ambrosia (or Immortal Nectar)". Amrita Nadi is the ultimate "organ", or root-structure, of the body-mind, Realized as such in the seventh stage of life in the Way of Adidam. It is felt to Stand Radiant between the right side of the heart (which is the psycho-physical Seat of Conscious-ness Itself) and the Matrix of Light infi-nitely above the crown of the head. (For Avatar Adi Da's principal discussions of Amrita Nadi, see *The Knee Of Listening, The <u>All-Completing</u> and <u>Final</u> Divine Revelation To Mankind, Santosha Adidam,* and *The Dawn Horse Testament.)*

anatomy See **Spiritual anatomy**.

asana Sanskrit for bodily "posture" or "pose"—by extension, and as Avatar Adi Da often intends, "asana" also refers to the attitude, orientation, posture, or feeling-disposition of the heart and the entire body-mind.

"Atma-Murti" "Atma" indicates the Divine Self, and "Murti" means "Form". Thus, "Atma-Murti" literally means "the Form That Is the (Very) Divine Self". And, as Avatar Adi Da Indicates everywhere in His Wisdom-Teaching, "Atma-Murti" refers to Himself as the Very Divine Self of all, "Located" as "the Feeling of Being (Itself)". To Commune with Avatar Adi Da as "Atma-Murti" is to Realize (or enter into Identification with) His Divine State.

Avadhoot Avadhoot is a traditional term for one who has "shaken off" or "passed beyond" all worldly attachments and cares, including all motives of detachment (or conventional and other-worldly renunciation), all conventional notions of life and religion, and all seeking for "answers" or "solutions" in the form of conditional experience or conditional knowledge.

Avatar "Avatar" (from Sanskrit "avatara") is a traditional term for a Divine Incarnation. It literally means "One who is descended, or 'crossed down' (from, and as, the Divine)". Avatar Adi Da Samraj Confesses that, simultaneous with His human Birth, He has Incarnated in every world, at every level of the Cosmic domain, as the Eternal Giver of Divine Help and Divine Grace and Divine Liberation to all beings—and that, even though His bodily (human) Lifetime is necessarily limited in duration, His Spiritual Incarnation in the Cosmic domain is Eternal.

Avataric Incarnation Avatar Adi Da Samraj is the Avataric Incarnation, or the Divinely Descended Embodiment, of the Divine Person. The reference "Avataric Incarnation" indicates that Avatar Adi Da Samraj fulfills both the traditional expectation of the East, that the True God-Man is an Avatar (or an utterly Divine "Descent" of Real God in conditionally manifested form), and the traditional expectations of the West, that the True God-Man is an Incarnation (or an utterly human Embodiment of Real God).

For Avatar Adi Da's discussion of the "Avatar" and "Incarnation" traditions, and of His unique and all-Completing Role as the "Avataric Incarnation" of the Divine Person, see "'Avatar' and 'Incarnation': The Complementary God-Man Traditions of East and West", in *The Truly Human New World-Culture Of Unbroken Real-God-Man*.

Avataric Self-Submission For a full description of Avatar Adi Da's "Ordeal Of Avataric Self-Submission", see *The Promised God-Man Is Here*, by Carolyn Lee.

"Avoiding relationship?" The practice of self-Enquiry in the form "Avoiding relationship?", unique to the Way of Adidam, was spontaneously developed by Avatar Adi Da in the course of His Divine Re-Awakening (as Avatar Adi Da describes in *The Knee Of Listening*). Intense persistence in the "radical" discipline of this unique form of self-Enquiry led rapidly to His Divine Re-Awakening in 1970.

The practice of self-Enquiry in the form "Avoiding relationship?" is the principal form of the "conscious process" practiced by devotees of Avatar Adi Da who choose the Devotional Way of Insight. (See also "Devotional Way of Insight / Devotional Way of Faith" and "Re-cognition".)

B

"basic" context of the fourth stage of life See **stages of life**.

Bhagavan The Title "Bhagavan" is an ancient one used over the centuries for many Spiritual Realizers of India. It means "blessed" or "holy" in Sanskrit. When applied to a great Spiritual Being, "Bhagavan" is understood to mean "bountiful Lord", or "Great Lord", or "Divine Lord".

bhakta, bhakti "Bhakti" is the practice of heart-felt devotion to the Ultimate Reality or Person—a practice which has been traditionally animated through worship of Divine Images or surrender to a human Guru.

"Bhakta" is a devotee whose principal characteristic is expressive devotion, or who practices within the Hindu tradition of Bhakti Yoga.

Bhava "Bhava" is a Sanskrit word used to refer to the enraptured feeling-swoon of Communion with the Divine.

bindu In the esoteric Yogic traditions of India, the Sanskrit word "bindu" (literally, "drop" or "point") suggests that all manifested forms, energies, and universes are ultimately coalesced or expressed in a point without spatial or temporal dimension. Each level (or plane) of psycho-physical reality is said to have a corresponding bindu, or zero-point.

Blessing-Work   For a description of Avatar Adi Da's Divine Blessing-Work, see pp. 17-19.

bodily base   The bodily base is the region associated with the muladhara chakra, the lowest energy plexus in the human body-mind, at the base of the spine (or the general region immediately above and including the perineum). In many of the Yogic traditions, the bodily base is regarded as the seat of the latent ascending Spiritual Current, or Kundalini. Avatar Adi Da Reveals that, in fact, the Spirit-Current must first descend to the bodily base through the frontal line, before it can effectively be directed into the ascending spinal course. Avatar Adi Da has also pointed out that human beings who are not yet Spiritually sensitive tend to throw off the natural life-energy at the bodily base, and He has, therefore, Given His devotees a range of disciplines (including a number of exercises that involve intentional locking at the bodily base) which conserve life-energy by directing it into the spinal line.

"bodily battery"   The "bodily battery" (known in Japan as the "hara") is the energy center of the gross body and, as such, plays a very important role in the practice of "conductivity" in the frontal line. Avatar Adi Da describes its focal point (or point of concentration) as the crown of the abdomen, on the surface, about an inch and a half below the umbilical scar.

"bond" / "Bond"   Avatar Adi Da uses the term "bond", when lower-cased, to refer to the process by which the egoic individual (already presuming separateness, and, therefore, bondage to the separate self) attaches itself karmically to the world of others and things through the

constant search for self-fulfillment. In contrast, when He capitalizes the term "Bond", Avatar Adi Da is making reference to the process of His devotee's devotional "Bonding" to Him, which process is the Great Means for transcending all forms of limited (or karmic) "bonding".

"Bright"   By the word "Bright" (and its variations, such as "Brightness"), Avatar Adi Da refers to the Self-Existing and Self-Radiant Divine Reality. As Adi Da Writes in His Spiritual Autobiography, *The Knee Of Listening:*

> . . . *from my earliest experience of life I have Enjoyed a Condition that, as a child, I called the "Bright".*
>
> *I have always known desire, not merely for extreme pleasures of the senses and the mind, but for the highest Enjoyment of Spiritual Power and Mobility. But I have not been seated in desire, and desire has only been a play that I have grown to understand and enjoy without conflict. I have always been Seated in the "Bright".*
>
> *Even as a baby I remember only crawling around inquisitively with a boundless Feeling of Joy, Light, and Freedom in the middle of my head that was bathed in Energy moving unobstructed in a Circle, down from above, all the way down, then up, all the way up, and around again, and always Shining from my heart. It was an Expanding Sphere of Joy from the heart. And I was a Radiant Form, the Source of Energy, Love-Bliss, and Light in the midst of a world that is entirely Energy, Love-Bliss, and Light. I was the Power of Reality, a direct Enjoyment and Communication of the One Reality. I was the Heart Itself, Who Lightens the mind and all things. I was the same as every one and every thing, except it became clear that others were apparently unaware of the "Thing" Itself.*
>
> *Even as a little child I recognized It and Knew It, and my life was not a matter of anything else. That Awareness, that Conscious Enjoyment, that Self-Existing and Self-Radiant Space of Infinitely and inherently Free Being, that Shine of inherent Joy Standing in the heart and Expanding from the heart, is the "Bright". And It is the*

entire Source of True Humor. It is Reality. It is not separate from anything.

Buddha   Just as the traditional term "Avatar", when rightly understood, is an appropriate Reference to Avatar Adi Da Samraj, so is the traditional term "Buddha". He is the Divine Buddha, the One Who Is Most Perfectly Self-Enlightened and Eternally Awake.

C

causal   See **gross, subtle, causal**.

childish and adolescent strategies
Avatar Adi Da uses the terms "childish" and "adolescent" with precise meanings in His Wisdom-Teaching. He points out that human beings are always tending to animate one of two fundamental life-strategies—the childish strategy (to be dependent, weak, seeking to be consoled by parent-figures and a parent-"God") and the adolescent strategy (to be independent—or, otherwise, torn between independence and dependence—rebellious, unfeeling, self-absorbed, and doubting or resisting the idea of God or any power greater than oneself). Until these strategies are understood and transcended, they not only diminish love in ordinary human relations, but they also limit religious and Spiritual growth.

Circle   The Circle is a primary pathway of natural life-energy and the Spirit-Current through the body-mind. It is composed of two arcs: the descending Current, in association with the frontal line (down the front of the body, from the crown of the head to the bodily base), which corresponds to the more physically oriented dimension of the body-mind; and the ascending Current, in association with the spinal line (up the back of the body, from the bodily base to the crown of the head), which is the more mentally, psychically, and subtly oriented dimension of the body-mind.

conditional   The word "conditional" (and its variants) is used to indicate everything that depends on conditions—in other words, everything that is temporary and changing. The "Unconditional", in contrast, is the Divine, or That Which Is Eternal, Always Already the Case—because It Is utterly Free of dependence on any conditions whatsoever.

"conductivity"   "Conductivity" is Avatar Adi Da's technical term for participation in and responsibility for the movement of natural bodily energies (and, when one is Spiritually Awakened by Him, for the movement of His Divine Spirit-Current of Love-Bliss in Its natural course of association with the body-mind), via intentional exercises of feeling and breathing.

The exercises of Spiritual "conductivity" that Avatar Adi Da Gives to His (formally practicing) Spiritually Awakened devotees are technical whole-bodily Yogas of receptive surrender to the Living Spirit-Current. Rudimentary and preparatory technical forms of "conductivity" are Given to beginners.

congregations of Adidam   There are four different modes, or congregations, of formal approach to Avatar Adi Da Samraj, making it possible for everyone to participate in the Gift of heart-companionship with Him. The total practice of the Way of Adidam is engaged by those in the first and second congregations. Whereas all of Avatar Adi Da's devotees (in all four congregations) engage the fundamental practice of Ruchira Avatara Bhakti Yoga, only members of the first and second congregations are vowed to engage the full range of supportive disciplines (meditation, sacramental worship, guided study, exercise, diet, emotional-sexual discipline, cooperative community living, and so on) Given by Avatar Adi Da Samraj.

For a more detailed description of the four congregations of Avatar Adi Da's devotees, see pp. 361-73.

"conscious process"   The "conscious process" is Avatar Adi Da's technical term for those practices through which the mind, or attention, is surrendered and turned about (from egoic self-involvement) to feeling-Contemplation of Him. It is the senior discipline and responsibility of all practitioners in the Way of Adidam. (Avatar Adi Da's descriptions of the various forms of the "conscious process" are Given in *The Dawn Horse Testament Of The Ruchira Avatar.*)

"consider", "consideration" The technical term "consider" or "consideration" in Avatar Adi Da's Wisdom-Teaching means a process of one-pointed but ultimately thoughtless concentration and exhaustive contemplation of something until its ultimate obviousness is clear. As engaged in the Way of Adidam, "consideration" is not merely an intellectual investigation. It is the participatory investment of one's whole being. If one "considers" something fully in the context of one's practice of feeling-Contemplation of Avatar Adi Da Samraj, and study of His Wisdom-Teaching, this concentration results "in both the highest intuition and the most practical grasp of the Lawful and Divine necessities of human existence".

Contemplation of Avatar Adi Da's bodily (human) Form Traditionally, devotees have produced artistic images of their Gurus for the purpose of Contemplating the Guru when he or she is either not physically present or (otherwise) no longer physically alive.

Modern technology makes possible (through photography, videotape, film, holographic imagery, and other means) accurate Representations of the bodily (human) Form of Avatar Adi Da Samraj for devotional use by His formally acknowledged devotees.

"Cosmic Consciousness" See **Samadhi**.

Cosmic Mandala The Sanskrit word "mandala" (literally, "circle") is commonly used in the esoteric Spiritual traditions of the East to describe the hierarchical levels of cosmic existence. "Mandala" also denotes an artistic rendering of interior visions of the cosmos. Avatar Adi Da uses the phrase "Cosmic Mandala" as a reference to the totality of the conditionally manifested cosmos (or all worlds, forms, and beings).

Crashing Down Avatar Adi Da's Crashing Down is the Descent of His Divine Spirit-Force into the body-mind of His devotee.

My Avataric Divine Work (Altogether) Is My Crashing-Down Descent, At First Upon and Into My Own Avatarically-Born Bodily (Human) Divine Form, and, Thereafter (and Now, and Forever), Upon and Into the body-minds Of My Devotees and all beings—Even (By Means Of My Divine Embrace Of each, and all, and All) To Infuse and (At Last) To Divinely Translate each, and all, and All. Therefore, My Avataric Divine Spiritual Descent Is The Secret Of My Early Life. My Avataric Divine Spiritual Descent Is The Secret Of My Divine Self-"Emergence" (As I Am) Within The Cosmic Domain. My Avataric Divine Spiritual Descent Is The Secret Of All The Secrets Of The (Avatarically Self-Revealed) Divine and Complete and Thoroughly Devotional Way Of Practice and Realization In My Company. The Only-By-Me Revealed and Given Way Of The Heart (or Way Of Adidam) Is The Divine Yoga Of ego-Surrendering, ego-Forgetting, and ego-Transcending Devotional Recognition-Response To My (Avatarically Self-Revealed) Divine and Spiritual Person, and To My (Avatarically Self-Manifested) Divine and Spiritual Descent. The Only-By-Me Revealed and Given Way Of The Heart (or Way Of Adidam) Is The Total and Divine Way and Ordeal Of Counter-egoic Devotional Recognition-Response To My Avataric "Bright" Divine Self-Manifestation, and To The Avataric Crashing Down Of My "Bright" Divine Imposition. And, In The Case Of My Each and Every Devotee, The Way Must Continue Until The Way Is Most Perfectly "Bright", and The Way Itself Becomes Divine Translation Into My Own Sphere Of "Brightness" (Itself). [Ruchira Avatara Hridaya-Siddha Yoga]

"Crazy" Avatar Adi Da has always had a unique Method of "Crazy" Work, which, particularly during His years of Teaching and Revelation, involved His literal Submission to the limited conditions of humankind, in order to reflect His devotees to themselves, and thereby Awaken self-understanding in them (relative to their individual egoic dramas, and the collective egoic dramas of human society).

For Me, There Was Never <u>Any</u> Other Possibility Than The "Reckless" (or Divinely "Crazy" and Divinely "Heroic") Course Of All-and-all-Embrace—and I Began This Uniquely "Crazy" and "Heroic" Sadhana, Most Intensively, At The Beginning Of My Adult Life. Indeed, I Have Always Functioned, and Will Always Function, In This Divinely "Crazy" and Divinely "Heroic" Manner. The Inherently egoless "Crazy" and "Heroic" Manner Is One Of My Principal Divine Characteristics— Whereby I Can (Always, and Now, and Forever Hereafter) Be Identified. Therefore, I (Characteristically) Functioned In This "Crazy" and "Heroic" Manner Throughout All Of My "Sadhana Years", and Throughout All The Years Of My Avatarically Self-Manifested Divine Teaching-Work and My Avatarically Self-Manifested Divine Revelation-Work—and I Have Done So (and Will <u>Forever</u> Continue To Do So) Throughout All The Divine-Self-"Emergence" Years Of My Avatarically Self-Manifested Divine Blessing-Work (Both During, and Forever After, My Avataric Physical Human Lifetime). <u>All</u> My Avatarically Self-Manifested Divine Work Is A Divinely "Crazy" and Divinely "Heroic" Effort That Avoids Not anything or any one—but Which <u>Always</u> Divinely Blesses Everything and Everyone. [The Truly Human New World-Culture Of <u>Unbroken</u> Real-God-Man]

D

Da Avatar Adi Da's Name "Da" means "The Divine Giver". In Sanskrit, "Da" means principally "to give". It is also associated with Vishnu, the "Sustainer", and it further has a secondary meaning "to destroy". Thus, "Da" is anciently aligned to all three of the principal Divine Beings, Forces, or Attributes in the Hindu tradition—Brahma (the Creator, Generator, or Giver), Vishnu (the Sustainer), and Siva (the Destroyer). In certain Hindu rituals, priests address the Divine directly as "Da", invoking qualities such as generosity and compassion.

The Tibetan Buddhists regard the syllable "Da" (written, in Tibetan, as well as in Sanskrit, with a single symbol) as most auspicious, and they assign numerous sacred meanings to it, including that of "the Entrance into the Dharma".

Da Love-Ananda Samrajya For a description of the Da Love-Ananda Samrajya, see p. 376.

Da Avatar "Da" is Sanskrit for "The One Who Gives". Therefore, as the Da Avatar, Adi Da Samraj is the Divine Descent of the One and True Divine Giver.

"dark" epoch See **"late-time" (or "dark" epoch)**.

Darshan "Darshan", the Hindi derivative of the Sanskrit "darshana", literally means "seeing", "sight of", or "vision of". To receive Darshan of Avatar Adi Da is, most fundamentally, to behold His bodily (human) Form (either by being in His physical Company or by seeing a photograph or other visual representation of Him), and (thereby) to receive the spontaneous Divine Blessing He Grants Freely whenever His bodily (human) Form is beheld in the devotional manner. In the Way of Adidam, Darshan of Avatar Adi Da is the very essence of the practice, and one of the most potent forms of receiving Avatar Adi Da's Blessing is to participate in the formal occasions of Darshan—during which Avatar Adi Da Samraj Sits silently, sometimes gazing at each individual one by one.

By extension, "Darshan" of Avatar Adi Da Samraj may refer to any means by which His Blessing-Influence is felt and received—including His Written or Spoken Word, photographs or videotapes of His Avatarically-Born bodily (human) Divine Form, recordings of His Voice, Leelas (or Stories) of His Teaching-Work and Blessing-Work, places or objects He has Spiritually Empowered, visualization of His Avatarically-Born bodily (human) Divine Form in the mind, and simple, heart-felt Remembrance of Him.

Dattatreya   Dattatreya was a God-Realizer who appeared early in the common era and about whom no certain historical facts exist apart from his name. Over the centuries, numerous legends and myths have been spun around him. He was early on regarded to be an incarnation of the God Vishnu, later associated with the tradition of Saivism, and worshipped as the Divine Itself. He is commonly venerated as the originator of the Avadhoota tradition and credited with the authorship of the *Avadhoota Gita*, among other works.

The devotional sect worshipping Dattatreya presumes that he continually reincarnates through a succession of Adepts for the sake of gathering and serving devotees. The belief in the continuing incarnation of Dattatreya should be understood as a popular religious belief that is peripheral to what the Adepts in the Dattatreya succession actually taught.

The Dawn Horse Testament Of The Ruchira Avatar   *The Dawn Horse Testament Of The Ruchira Avatar* is Avatar Adi Da's paramount "Source-Text", summarizing the entire course of the Way of Adidam. (See "Avatar Adi Da Samraj's Teaching-Word", pp. 27-38.)

developmental stages of practice   For all members of the first and second congregations of Avatar Adi Da's devotees, the Way of Adidam develops through a series of (potential) developmental stages of practice and Realization. These stages of practice, and their relationship to the seven stages of life, are described by Avatar Adi Da Samraj in chapter seventeen of *The Dawn Horse Testament Of The Ruchira Avatar*.

When using the phrase "necessary (or, otherwise, potential)", Avatar Adi Da is referring to the fact that His fully practicing devotee must practice in the context of certain of the developmental stages of practice (corresponding to the first three stages of life, the "original" and "basic" contexts of the fourth stage of life, the sixth stage of life, and the seventh stage of life) but may bypass practice in the developmental stages that correspond to "advanced" context of the fourth stage of life and to the fifth stage of life.

Devotional Way of Insight / Devotional Way of Faith   Avatar Adi Da has Given Instruction in two variant forms of the fundamental practice of feeling-Contemplation of Him: the Devotional Way of Insight and the Devotional Way of Faith. Each of Avatar Adi Da's fully practicing devotees is to experiment with both of these Devotional Ways and then choose the one that is most effective in his or her case.

Both Devotional Ways require the exercise of insight <u>and</u> faith, but there is a difference in emphasis.

In the Devotional Way of Insight, the practitioner engages a specific technical process of observing, understanding, and then feeling beyond the self-contraction, as the principal technical element of his or her practice of feeling-Contemplation of Avatar Adi Da.

In the Devotional Way of Faith, the practitioner engages a specific technical process of magnifying his or her heart-Attraction to Avatar Adi Da, as the principal technical element of his or her practice of feeling-Contemplation of Avatar Adi Da.

Avatar Adi Da's extended Instruction relative to both Devotional Ways is Given in *The <u>Only</u> Complete Way To Realize The Unbroken Light Of <u>Real</u> God*.

Dharma, dharma   Sanskrit for "duty", "virtue", "law". The word "dharma" is commonly used to refer to the many esoteric paths by which human beings seek the Truth. In its fullest sense, and when capitalized, "Dharma" means the complete fulfillment of duty—the living of the Divine Law. By extension, "Dharma" means a truly great Spiritual Teaching, including its disciplines and practices.

"Difference"   "Difference" is the epitome of the egoic presumption of separateness—in contrast with the Realization of Oneness, or Non-"Difference", Which is Native to the Divine Self-Condition.

Divine Being   Avatar Adi Da describes His Divine Being on three levels:

AVATAR ADI DA SAMRAJ: This flesh body, this bodily (human) Sign, is My Form, in the sense that it is My Murti, or a kind of Reflection (or Representation) of Me. It is, therefore, a Means for contacting My Spiritual Presence, and, ultimately, My Divine State.

My Spiritual Presence is Self-Existing and Self-Radiant. It Functions in time and space, and It is also Prior to all time and space. . . .

My Divine State is always and only utterly Prior to time and space. Therefore, I, As I Am (Ultimately), have no "Function" in time and space. There is no time and space in My Divine State.

Divine Body   Avatar Adi Da's Divine Body is not conditional or limited to His physical Body but is "The 'Bright' Itself (Spiritually Pervading and Eternally Most Prior To The Cosmic Domain)".

Divine Enlightenment   The Realization of the seventh stage of life, which is uniquely Revealed and Given by Avatar Adi Da. It is release from all the egoic limitations of the first six stages of life. Remarkably, the seventh stage Awakening, which is Avatar Adi Da's Gift to His rightly prepared devotee, is not an experience at all. The true Nature of everything is simply obvious, based on the Realization that every apparent "thing" is Eternally, Perfectly the same as Reality, Consciousness, Happiness, Truth, or Real God. And that Realization is the Supreme Love-Bliss of Avatar Adi Da's Divine Self-Condition.

Divine Ignorance   "Divine Ignorance" is Avatar Adi Da's term for the fundamental Awareness of Existence Itself, Prior to all sense of separation from (or knowledge about) anything that arises. As He proposes, "No matter what arises, you do not know what a single thing is." By "Ignorance", Avatar Adi Da means heartfelt participation in the universal Condition of inherent Mystery—not mental dullness or the fear-based wonder or awe felt by the subjective ego in relation to unknown objects. Divine Ignorance is the Realization of Consciousness Itself, transcending all knowledge and all experience of the self-contracted ego-"I".

For Avatar Adi Da's extended Instruction relative to Divine Ignorance, see *What, Where, When, How, Why, and <u>Who</u> To Remember To Be Happy*, Part Two: "What, Where, When, How, Why and <u>Who</u> To Remember To Be Happy", and Part Three: "You Do Not Know What even a single thing <u>Is</u>" and "My Argument Relative to Divine Ignorance".

Divine Indifference   See **four phases of the seventh stage of life**.

Divine "Intoxication"   Unlike common intoxication, such as with alcohol, Divine "Intoxication" Draws Avatar Adi Da's devotees beyond the usual egoic self and egoic mind through His Blessing Grace into a state of ecstatic devotional Communion (and Identification) with Him.

Divine Parama-Guru   The Supreme Divine Guru.

Divine Re-Awakening   Avatar Adi Da's Divine Re-Awakening occurred on September 10, 1970, in the Vedanta Society Temple in Hollywood, California. For a full description of this Great Event and its import, see *The Promised God-Man Is Here*, by Carolyn Lee, or chapter sixteen of *The Knee Of Listening*.

Divine Self-Recognition   Divine Self-Recognition is the ego-transcending and world-transcending Intelligence of the Divine Self in relation to all conditional phenomena. The devotee of Avatar Adi Da who Realizes the seventh stage of life simply Abides as Self-Existing and Self-Radiant Consciousness Itself, and he or she Freely Self-Recognizes (or inherently and instantly and Most Perfectly comprehends and perceives) all phenomena (including body, mind, conditional self, and conditional world) as transparent (or merely apparent), and un-necessary, and inherently non-binding modifications of the same "Bright" Divine Self-Consciousness.

Divine Self-"Emergence"   On January 11, 1986, Avatar Adi Da passed through a profound Yogic Swoon, which He later described as the initial Event of His Divine Self-"Emergence". Avatar Adi Da's Divine Self-"Emergence" is an ongoing Process in which His Avatarically-Born bodily (human) Divine Form has been (and is ever more profoundly and potently being) conformed to Himself, the Very Divine Person, such that His bodily (human) Form is now (and forever hereafter) an utterly Unobstructed Sign and Agent of His own Divine Being.

For Avatar Adi Da's Revelation of the significance of His Divine Self-"Emergence", see section III of "The True Dawn Horse Is The Only Way To Me", in *The All-Completing* and *Final Divine Revelation To Mankind*, *The Heart Of The Dawn Horse Testament Of The Ruchira Avatar*, and *The Dawn Horse Testament Of The Ruchira Avatar*.

Divine Self-Domain Avatar Adi Da affirms that there is a Divine Self-Domain that is the Perfectly Subjective Condition of the conditional worlds. It is not "else-where", not an objective "place" (like a subtle "heaven" or mythical "paradise"), but It is the always present, Transcendental, Inherently Spiritual, Divine Source-Condition of every conditionally mani-fested being and thing. Avatar Adi Da Reveals that the Divine Self-Domain is not other than the Divine Heart Itself, not other than Himself. To Realize the seventh stage of life (by the Divine Grace of Avatar Adi Da Samraj) is to Awaken to His Divine Self-Domain.

For Avatar Adi Da's extended Instruction relative to His Divine Self-Domain, see *The All-Completing* and *Final Divine Revelation To Mankind*.

Divine Star The primal conditional Representation of the "Bright" (the Source-Energy, or Divine Light, of Which all con-ditional phenomena and the total cosmos are modifications) is the brilliant white five-pointed Divine Star. Avatar Adi Da's bodily (human) Divine Form is the Manifestation of that Divine Star—and His head, two arms, and two legs correspond to its five points. Avatar Adi Da can also be seen or intuited in vision to Be the Divine Star Itself, prior to the visible mani-festation of His bodily (human) Form.

Divine Transfiguration See **four phases of the seventh stage of life**.

Divine Transformation See **four phases of the seventh stage of life**.

Divine Translation See **four phases of the seventh stage of life**.

Divine World-Teacher Avatar Adi Da Samraj is the Divine World-Teacher because His Wisdom-Teaching is the uniquely Perfect Instruction to every being—in this (and every) world—in the total process of Divine Enlightenment. Furthermore, Avatar Adi Da Samraj con-stantly Extends His Regard to the entire world (and the entire Cosmic domain)— not on the political or social level, but as a Spiritual matter, constantly Working to Bless and Purify all beings everywhere.

dreaming See **waking, dreaming, and sleeping**.

E

ecstasy / enstasy The words "ecstasy" and "enstasy" derive originally from Greek. Avatar Adi Da uses "ecstasy" in the literal sense of "standing (stasis) outside (ec-)" the egoic self, and "enstasy" in the sense of "standing (stasis) in (en-)" the Divine Self-Condition. As Avatar Adi Da Says in *The Dawn Horse Testament Of The Ruchira Avatar*, Divine Enstasy is "The Native Condition Of Standing Unconditionally As The By-Me-Avatarically-Self-Revealed Transcendental, Inherently Spiritual, and Self-Evidently Divine Self-Condition Itself".

ego-"I" The ego-"I" is the fundamental activity of self-contraction, or the pre-sumption of separate and separative existence.

Eleutherian Pan-Communion of Adidam The Eleutherian Pan-Communion of Adidam is a California religious non-profit corporation, dedicated to the worldwide practice and the global proclamation of the true world-religion of Adidam.

Eleutherios "Eleutherios" (Greek for "Liberator") is a title by which Zeus was venerated as the supreme deity in the Spiritual esotericism of ancient Greece. The Designation "Eleutherios" indicates the Divine Function of Avatar Adi Da as the Incarnation of the Divine Person, "Whose Inherently Perfect Self-'Brightness' Divinely Liberates all conditionally Manifested beings—Freely, Liberally, Gracefully, and Without Ceasing—now, and forever hereafter".

En-Light-enment   En-Light-enment (or Enlightenment) is not just a state of mind, but rather an actual conversion of the body-mind to the state of Divine Consciousness Itself, or Light Itself. Thus, Avatar Adi Da sometimes writes the word "Enlightenment" with "Light" set apart by hyphens, in order to emphasize this point.

esoteric anatomy   See **Spiritual anatomy**.

Eternal Vow   For a description of the Vow and responsibilities associated with the Way of Adidam, see pp. 361-72.

etheric   The etheric is the dimension of life-energy, which functions through the human nervous system. Our bodies are surrounded and infused by this personal life-energy, which we feel as the play of emotions and life-force in the body.

F

faculties; four faculties   Avatar Adi Da has Instructed His devotees that the practice of devotional Communion with Him (or Ruchira Avatara Bhakti Yoga) requires the surrender of the four principal faculties of the human body-mind. These faculties are body, emotion (or feeling), mind (or attention), and breath.

Feeling of Being   The Feeling of Being is the uncaused (or Self-Existing), Self-Radiant, and unqualified feeling-intuition of the Transcendental, Inherently Spiritual, and Self-Evidently Divine Self-Condition. This absolute Feeling does not merely accompany or express the Realization of the Heart Itself, but It is Identical to that Realization. To feel—or, really, to Be—the Feeling of Being is to enjoy the Love-Bliss of Absolute Consciousness, Which, when Most Perfectly Realized, cannot be pre-

vented or even diminished either by the events of life or by death.

feeling of relatedness   In the foundation stages of practice in the Way of Adidam, the basic (or gross) manifestation of the avoidance of relationship is understood and released when Avatar Adi Da's devotee hears Him (or comes to the point of most fundamental self-understanding), thereby regaining the free capability for simple relatedness, or living on the basis of the feeling of relatedness rather than the avoidance of relationship. Nevertheless, the feeling of relatedness is not Ultimate Realization, because it is still founded in the presumption of a "difference" between "I" and "other". Only in the ultimate stages of life in the Way of Adidam is the feeling of relatedness itself fully understood as the root-act of attention and, ultimately, transcended in the Feeling of Being.

feeling-Contemplation   Avatar Adi Da's term for the essential devotional and meditative practice that all practitioners of the Way of Adidam engage at all times in relationship to Him. Feeling-Contemplation of Adi Da Samraj is Awakened by His Grace—through Darshan (or feeling-sighting) of His bodily (human) Form, His Spiritual Presence, and His Divine State. It is then to be practiced under all conditions, as the basis and epitome of all other practices in the Way of Adidam.

fifth stage conditional Nirvikalpa Samadhi   See **Samadhi**.

forms of practice in the Way of Adidam   Avatar Adi Da has Given a number of different approaches to the progressive process of Most Perfectly self-transcending Real-God-Realization in the Way of Adidam. In this manner, He accounts for the differences in individuals' qualities—particularly relative to their capability to make use of the various technical practices that support the fundamental practice of Ruchira Avatara Bhakti Yoga and relative to the intensity of their motivation to apply themselves to the Spiritual process in His Company.

Ruchira Avatar Adi Da refers to the most detailed development of the practice of the Way of Adidam as the "technically 'fully elaborated'" form of practice. Each successive stage of practice in the technically "fully elaborated" form of the Way of Adidam is defined by progressively more detailed responsibilities, disciplines, and practices that are assumed in order to take responsibility for the signs of growing maturity in the process of Divine Awakening. A devotee who embraces the technically "fully elaborated" form of practice of the Way of Adidam must (necessarily) be a member of the first or second congregation of Avatar Adi Da's devotees. The progress of practice in the technically "fully elaborated" form of the Way of Adidam is monitored, measured, and evaluated by practicing stages (as described in detail by Avatar Adi Da Samraj in chapter seventeen of *The Dawn Horse Testament Of The Ruchira Avatar*).

Most of Avatar Adi Da's fully practicing devotees will find that they are qualified for a less intensive approach and are moved to a less technical form of the "conscious process" (than is exercised in the technically "fully elaborated" form of the Way of Adidam). Thus, most of Avatar Adi Da's fully practicing devotees will take up the technically "simpler" (or even "simplest") form of practice of the Way of Adidam.

In the technically "simpler" form of practice of the Way of Adidam, Avatar Adi Da's devotee (in the first or second congregation) engages a relatively simple form of technical means of supporting his or her fundamental practice of Ruchira Avatara Bhakti Yoga, and this technical means remains the same throughout the progressive course of developmental stages.

In the technically "simplest" form of practice, Avatar Adi Da's devotee (in any of the four congregations) engages the fundamental practice of Ruchira Avatara Bhakti Yoga in the simplest possible manner—as "simplest" feeling-Contemplation of Avatar Adi Da, together with the random use of Avatar Adi Da's Principal Name, "Da" (or one of the other Names He has Given to be engaged in the practice of simple Name-Invocation of Him).

Avatar Adi Da's fully elaborated descriptions of the technically "fully elaborated" and the technically "simpler" (or even "simplest") forms of the Way of Adidam are Given in *The Dawn Horse Testament Of The Ruchira Avatar*.

four phases of the seventh stage of life
In the context of Divine Enlightenment in the seventh stage of life, the Spiritual process continues. One of the unique aspects of Avatar Adi Da's Revelation is His description of the four phases of the seventh stage process: Divine Transfiguration, Divine Transformation, Divine Indifference, and Divine Translation.

In the phase of Divine Transfiguration, the Divinely Enlightened devotee's body-mind is Infused by Avatar Adi Da's Love-Bliss, and he or she Radiantly Demonstrates active Love, spontaneously Blessing all the relations of the body-mind.

In the following phase of Divine Transformation, the subtle or psychic dimension of the body-mind is fully Illumined, which may result in Divine Powers of healing, longevity, and the ability to release obstacles from the world and from the lives of others.

Eventually, Divine Indifference ensues, which is spontaneous and profound Resting in the "Deep" of Consciousness, and the world of relations is otherwise noticed only minimally or not at all.

Divine Translation is the ultimate "Event" of the entire process of Divine Awakening. Avatar Adi Da describes Divine Translation as the Outshining of all noticing of objective conditions through the infinitely magnified Force of Consciousness Itself. Divine Translation is the Outshining of all destinies, wherein there is no return to the conditional realms.

Being so overwhelmed by the Divine Radiance that all appearances fade away may occur <u>temporarily</u> from time to time during the seventh stage of life. But when that Most Love-Blissful Swoon becomes permanent, Divine Translation occurs, and the body-mind is inevitably relinquished in physical death. Then there is only Eternal Inherence in the Divine Self-Domain of unqualified Happiness and Joy.

frontal line, frontal personality, frontal Yoga The frontal (or descending) line of the body-mind conducts natural life-energy and (for those who are Spiritually Awakened) the Spirit-Current of Divine Life, in a downward direction from the crown of the head to the base of the body (or the perineal area).

The frontal personality is comprised of the physical body and its natural energies, the gross brain, and the verbal and lower faculties of the mind. It includes the entire gross dimension of the body-mind and the lower (or most physically oriented) aspects of the subtle dimension of the body-mind.

The frontal Yoga, as described by Avatar Adi Da, is the process whereby knots and obstructions in the gross (or physical) and energetic dimensions of the body-mind are penetrated, opened, surrendered, and released, through the devotee's reception of Avatar Adi Da's Transmission in the frontal line of the body-mind.

"fully elaborated" form of the Way of Adidam See **forms of practice in the Way of Adidam**.

functional, practical, relational, and cultural disciplines of Adidam The most basic functional, practical, and relational disciplines of the Way of Adidam (in its fully practiced form, as embraced by devotees in the first and second congregations) are forms of appropriate human action and responsibility for diet, health, exercise, sexuality, work, service to and support of Avatar Adi Da's Circumstance and Work, and cooperative (formal community) association with other practitioners of the Way of Adidam. The most basic cultural obligations of the Way of Adidam (in its fully practiced form) include meditation, sacramental worship, study of Avatar Adi Da's Wisdom-Teaching (and also at least a basic discriminative study of the Great Tradition of religion and Spirituality that is the Wisdom-inheritance of humankind), and regular participation in the "form" (or schedule) of daily, weekly, monthly, and annual devotional activities and retreats.

G

Great Tradition The "Great Tradition" is Avatar Adi Da's term for the total inheritance of human, cultural, religious, magical, mystical, Spiritual, and Transcendental paths, philosophies, and testimonies, from all the eras and cultures of humanity—which inheritance has (in the present era of worldwide communication) become the common legacy of humankind. Avatar Adi Da's Divine Self-Revelation and Wisdom-Teaching Fulfills and Completes the Great Tradition.

gross, subtle, causal Avatar Adi Da (in agreement with certain esoteric schools in the Great Tradition) describes conditional existence as having three dimensions—gross, subtle, and causal.

"Gross" means "made up of material (or physical) elements". The gross (or physical) dimension is, therefore, associated with the physical body, and also with experience in the waking state.

The subtle dimension, which is senior to and pervades the gross dimension, includes the etheric (or energic), lower mental (or verbal-intentional and lower psychic), and higher mental (or deeper psychic, mystical, and discriminative) functions, and is associated with experience in the dreaming state. In the human psycho-physical structure, the subtle dimension is primarily associated with the ascending energies of the spine, the brain core, and the subtle centers of mind in the higher brain.

The causal dimension is senior to and pervades both the gross and the subtle dimensions. It is the root of attention, or the essence of the separate and separative ego-"I". The causal dimension is associated with the right side of the heart, specifically with the sinoatrial node, or "pacemaker" (the psycho-physical source of the heartbeat). Its corresponding state of consciousness is the formless awareness of deep sleep.

Guru Esoterically, the word "guru" is understood to be a composite of two words, "destroyer (ru) of darkness (gu)".

H

hearing See **listening, hearing, and seeing**.

heart, stations of the heart Avatar Adi Da distinguishes three stations of the heart, associated respectively with the right side, the middle, and the left side of the heart region of the chest. The middle station of the heart is what is traditionally known as the "anahata chakra" (or "heart chakra"), and the left side of the heart is the gross physical heart. Avatar Adi Da Samraj has Revealed that the primal psycho-physical seat of Consciousness and attention is associated with what He calls the "right side of the heart". He has Revealed that this center (which is neither the heart chakra nor the gross physical heart) corresponds to the sinoatrial node, or "pacemaker", the source of the gross physical heartbeat in the right atrium (or upper right chamber) of the physical heart. In the Process of Divine Self-Realization, there is a unique process of opening of the right side of the heart—and it is because of this connection between the right side of the heart and Divine Self-Realization that Avatar Adi Da uses the term "the Heart" as another way of referring to the Divine Self.

The Heart Itself is Real God, the Divine Self, the Divine Reality. The Heart Itself is not "in" the right side of the human heart, nor is it "in" (or limited to) the human heart as a whole. Rather, the human heart and body-mind and the world exist in the Heart, Which Is the Divine Being Itself.

heart-Communion "Heart-Communion" with Avatar Adi Da is the practice of Invoking and feeling Him. It is "communion" in the sense that the individual loses sense of the separate self in the bliss of that state, and is thus "communicating intimately" (in a most profound and non-dual manner) with Avatar Adi Da Samraj.

heart-recognition The entire practice of the Way of Adidam is founded in devotional heart-recognition of, and devotional heart-response to, Ruchira Avatar Adi Da Samraj as the Very Divine Being in Person.

AVATAR ADI DA SAMRAJ: The only-by-Me Revealed and Given Way of Adidam (Which is the One and Only by-Me-Revealed and by-Me-Given Way of the Heart) is the Way of life you live when you rightly, truly, fully, and fully devotionally recognize Me, and when, on that basis, you rightly, truly, fully, and fully devotionally respond to Me. . . .

If you rightly, truly, fully, and fully devotionally recognize Me, everything "in between" vanishes. All of that is inherently without force. In heart-responsive devotional recognition of Me, a spontaneous kriya of the principal faculties occurs, such that they are loosed from the objects to which they are otherwise bound—loosed from the patterns of self-contraction. The faculties turn to Me, and, in that turning, there is tacit devotional recognition of Me, tacit experiential Realization of Me, of Happiness Itself, of My Love-Bliss-Full Condition. That "Locating" of Me opens the body-mind spontaneously. When you have been thus Initiated by Me, it then becomes your responsibility, your sadhana, to continuously Remember Me, to constantly return to this devotional recognition of Me, in which you are Attracted to Me, in which you devotionally respond to Me spontaneously with all the principal faculties. [Hridaya Rosary (Four Thorns Of Heart-Instruction)]

heart-response See **heart-recognition**.

Hermitage-Retreat Sanctuaries See **Sanctuaries**.

"Heroic" The Tantric traditions of Hinduism and Buddhism describe as "heroic" the practice of an individual whose impulse to Liberation and commitment to his or her Guru are so strong that all circumstances of life, even those traditionally regarded as inauspicious for Spiritual practice (such as consumption of intoxicants and engagement in sexual activity), can rightly be made use of as part of the Spiritual process.

Avatar Adi Da's uniquely "Heroic" Ordeal, however, was undertaken not for His own sake, but in order to discover, through His own experience, what is necessary for all beings to Realize the Truth. Because of His utter Freedom from egoic bondage and egoic karmas, Avatar Adi Da's Sadhana was "Heroic" in a manner that had never previously been possible and will never again be possible. As the Divine Person, it was necessary for Him to experience the entire gamut of human seeking, in order to be able to Teach any and all that came to Him.

Avatar Adi Da has Instructed that, because of His unique "Heroic" Demonstration, His devotees can simply practice the Way He has Revealed and Given, and do not have to attempt the (in any case impossible) task of duplicating His Ordeal. (See also **"Crazy"**.)

Hridaya-Avatar "Hridaya" is Sanskrit for "the heart". It refers not only to the physical organ but also to the True Heart, the Transcendental (and Inherently Spiritual) Divine Reality. "Hridaya" in combination with "Avatar" signifies that Avatar Adi Da is the Very Incarnation of the Divine Heart Itself, the Divine Incarnation Who Stands in, at, and as the True Heart of every being.

Hridaya Rosary *Hridaya Rosary (Four Thorns Of Heart-Instruction)—The Five Books Of The Heart Of The Adidam Revelation, Book Four: The "Late-Time" Avataric Revelation Of The Universally Tangible Divine Spiritual Body, Which Is The Supreme Agent Of The Great Means To Worship and To Realize The True and Spiritual Divine Person (The egoless Personal Presence Of Reality and Truth, Which Is The Only Real God)* is Avatar Adi Da's summary and exquisitely beautiful Instruction relative to the right, true, full, and fully devotional practice of the Way of Adidam, through which practice Avatar Adi Da's fully practicing devotee Spiritually receives Him with ever greater profundity, and, ultimately (through a process of the Spiritual "melting" of the entire psycho-physical being), Realizes Him most perfectly.

Hridaya-Samartha Sat-Guru "Hridaya-Samartha Sat-Guru" is a compound of traditional Sanskrit terms that has been newly created to express the uniqueness of Avatar Adi Da's Guru-Function. "Sat" means "Truth", "Being", "Existence". Thus, "Sat-Guru" literally means "True Guru", or a Guru who can lead living beings from darkness (or non-Truth) into Light (or the Living Truth).

"Samartha" means "fit", "qualified", "able". Thus, "Samartha Sat-Guru" means "a True Guru who is fully capable" of Awakening living beings to Real-God-Realization.

The word "Hridaya", meaning "heart", refers to the Very Heart, or the Transcendental (and Inherently Spiritual) Divine Reality.

Thus, altogether, the reference "Hridaya-Samartha Sat-Guru" means "the Divine Heart-Master Who Liberates His devotees from the darkness of egoity by Means of the Power of the 'Bright' Divine Heart Itself". Avatar Adi Da has Said that this full Designation "properly summarizes all the aspects of My unique Guru-Function".

Hridaya-Shakti; Hridaya-Shaktipat
The Sanskrit word "Hridaya" means "the Heart Itself". "Shakti" is a Sanskrit term for the Divine Manifesting as Energy. "Hridaya-Shakti" is thus "the Divine Power of the Heart", Which is Given and Transmitted by Avatar Adi Da Samraj.

In Hindi, "shaktipat" means the "descent of Divine Power", indicating the Sat-Guru's Transmission of the Kundalini Shakti to his or her devotee.

"Hridaya-Shaktipat", which is Avatar Adi Da's seventh stage Gift to His devotees, is "the Blessing-Transmission of the Divine Heart Itself".

Avatar Adi Da's extended Instruction relative to Hridaya-Shakti and Kundalini Shakti is Given in *Ruchira Avatara Hridaya-Siddha Yoga*.

Hridaya-Siddha Yoga The Way (Yoga) of the relationship with the "Transmission-Master of the Divine Heart" (Hridaya-Siddha), Ruchira Avatar Adi Da Samraj.

Hridayam "Hridayam" is Sanskrit for "heart". It refers not only to the physical organ but also to the True Heart, the Transcendental (and Inherently Spiritual) Divine Reality. "Hridayam" is one of Avatar Adi Da's Divine Names, signifying that He Stands in, at, and as the True Heart of every being.

I

Ignorance See **Divine Ignorance**.

Indifference See **four phases of the seventh stage of life**.

Instruments / Instrumentality
Avatar Adi Da has Indicated that members of the Ruchira Sannyasin Order function collectively and spontaneously as His Instruments, or Means by which His Divine Grace and Awakening Power are Magnified and Transmitted to other devotees and all beings. Such devotees have received Avatar Adi Da's Spiritual Baptism, and they practice in Spiritually activated relationship to Him with exemplary depth and intensity. Because of their uniquely complete and renunciate response and accountability to Him, and by virtue of their ego-surrendering, ego-forgetting, ego-transcending, and really Spiritual Invocation of Him, these devotees function collectively as Instruments for the Transmission of Avatar Adi Da's Spiritual Presence to others.

Invocation by Name See **Name-Invocation**.

Ishta-Guru Bhakti Yoga An alternate name for Ruchira Avatara Bhakti Yoga. Ishta-Guru Bhakti Yoga literally means "the practice (Yoga) of devotion (Bhakti) to Avatar Adi Da, the chosen Beloved (Ishta) Guru of His devotees".

J

Jnana Samadhi See **Samadhi**.

K

Kali Kali is a Hindu form of the Divine Goddess (or "Mother-Shakti") in her terrifying aspect.

Kali Yuga A Hindu term meaning "the dark (kali) epoch (yuga)", or the final and most ignorant and degenerate period of human history, when the Spiritual Way of life is almost entirely forgotten. (In the Hindu view, the Kali Yuga is a cyclically recurring event.)

karma "Karma" is Sanskrit for "action". Since action entails consequences (or reactions), "karma" also means (by extension) "destiny, tendency, the quality of existence and experience which is determined by previous actions".

Kashmir Saivism Kashmir Saivism is a branch of Saivism (the form of Hinduism in which Siva is worshipped as the Supreme Deity), which originated in the Kashmir region of North India in the late 8th century and whose influence has spread throughout the Indian sub-continent during the mid-20th century. It has a largely fifth-stage orientation.

kiln Avatar Adi Da Samraj frequently describes the transformative process of His Blessing-Power in the lives of His devotees as being like a kiln. In a kiln, as the wet clay objects are heated more and more, they begin to glow. Eventually, the kiln is so hot that everything within it glows with a white light, and the definitions of the individual objects dissolve in the brightness. Just so, as a devotee matures in Avatar Adi Da's Spiritual Company, all presumptions of separateness as an apparently individual ego-"I" are more and more Outshined by the "Brightness" of His Divine Person and Blessing.

Klik-Klak Avatar Adi Da coined the term "Klik-Klak" as a name for the conditional reality. This name indicates (even by means of the sound of the two syllables) that conditional reality is a heartless perpetual-motion machine of incessant change, producing endlessly varied patterns that are ultimately binary in nature (as, for example, "yes-no", "on-off", or "black-white").

knots   Previous to Most Perfect Divine Self-Realization, the gross, subtle, and causal dimensions are expressed in the body-mind as characteristic knots. The knot of the gross dimension is associated with the region of the navel. The knot of the subtle dimension is associated with the midbrain, or the ajna center directly behind and between the brows. And the knot of the causal dimension (which Avatar Adi Da refers to as the "causal knot") is associated with the sinoatrial node (or "pacemaker") on the right side of the heart. The causal knot (or the heart-root's knot) is the primary root of the self-contraction, felt as the locus of the self-sense, the source of the feeling of relatedness itself, or the root of attention.

Kundalini-Shaktipat   The Kundalini Shakti is traditionally viewed to lie dormant at the bodily base, or lowermost psychic center of the body-mind. Kundalini-Shaktipat is the activation of the Kundalini Shakti—either spontaneously in the devotee or by the Guru's initiation—thereafter potentially producing various forms of Yogic and mystical experience.

L

"late-time" (or "dark" epoch)   The "'late-time' (or 'dark' epoch)" is a phrase that Avatar Adi Da uses to describe the present era—in which doubt of God (and of anything at all beyond mortal existence) is more and more pervading the entire world, and the self-interest of the separate individual is more and more regarded to be the ultimate principle of life. It is also a reference to the traditional Hindu idea of "yugas", or "epochs", the last of which (the Kali Yuga) is understood to be the most difficult and "dark". Many traditions share the idea that it is in such a time that the Promised Divine Liberator will appear. (See also **Kali Yuga**.)

Lay Congregationist Order   In "The Orders of My True and Free Renunciate Devotees" (in *The Lion Sutra*), Avatar Adi Da describes the Lay Congregationist Order as "the common (or general) order for all formally established general (or not otherwise formal renunciate) lay practitioners of the total (or full and complete) practice of the Way of Adidam". Once a member of the second congregation has completed the student-beginner stage of practice, he or she makes the transition to the intensive listening-hearing stage of the Way of Adidam. By virtue of this transition, the individual becomes a member of the Lay Congregationist Order, unless he or she is accepted as a member of the Lay Renunciate Order.

Lay Renunciate Order   See **renunciate orders**.

leela   "Leela" is Sanskrit for "play", or "sport". In many religious and Spiritual traditions, all of conditionally manifested existence is regarded to be the Leela (or the Play, Sport, or Free Activity) of the Divine Person. "Leela" also means the Awakened Play of a Realized Adept (of any degree), through which he or she mysteriously Instructs and Liberates others and Blesses the world itself. By extension, a Leela is an instructive and inspiring story of such an Adept's Teaching and Blessing Play.

Lesson of life   "The Lesson of life" is Avatar Adi Da's term for the fundamental understanding that Happiness cannot be achieved by means of seeking, because Happiness is inherent in Existence Itself. Avatar Adi Da has summarized this in the aphorism, "You cannot become Happy. You can only be Happy."

Lineage, Avatar Adi Da's   The principal Spiritual Masters who served Avatar Adi Da Samraj during His "Sadhana Years" belong to a single Lineage of extraordinary Yogis, whose Parama-Guru (Supreme Guru) was the Divine "Goddess" (or "Mother-Shakti").

Swami Rudrananda (1928-1973), or Albert Rudolph (known as "Rudi"), was Avatar Adi Da's first human Teacher—from 1964 to 1968, in New York City. Rudi served Avatar Adi Da Samraj in the development of basic practical life-disciplines and the frontal Yoga, which is the process whereby knots and obstructions in the physical and etheric dimensions of the body-mind are penetrated, opened, surrendered, and released through Spiritual reception in the frontal line of the body-mind. Rudi's own Teachers included the Indonesian Pak Subuh (from whom Rudi learned a basic exercise of Spiritual receptivity), Swami Muktananda (with whom Rudi studied for many years), and Bhagavan Nityananda (the Indian Adept-Realizer who was also Swami Muktananda's Guru). Rudi met Bhagavan Nityananda shortly before Bhagavan Nityananda's death, and Rudi always thereafter acknowledged Bhagavan Nityananda as his original and principal Guru.

The second Teacher in Avatar Adi Da's Lineage of Blessing was Swami Muktananda (1908-1982), who was born in Mangalore, South India. Having left home at the age of fifteen, he wandered for many years, seeking the Divine Truth from sources all over India. Eventually, he came under the Spiritual Influence of Bhagavan Nityananda, whom he accepted as his Guru and in whose Spiritual Company he mastered Kundalini Yoga. Swami Muktananda served Avatar Adi Da as Guru during the period from 1968 to 1970. In the summer of 1969, during Avatar Adi Da's second visit to India, Swami Muktananda wrote a letter confirming Avatar Adi Da's attainment of "Yogic Liberation", and acknowledging His right to Teach others. However, from the beginning of their relationship, Swami Muktananda instructed Avatar Adi Da to visit Bhagavan Nityananda's burial site every day (whenever Avatar Adi Da was at Swami Muktananda's Ashram in Ganeshpuri, India) as a means to surrender to Bhagavan Nityananda as the Supreme Guru of the Lineage.

Bhagavan Nityananda, a great Yogi of South India, was Avatar Adi Da's third Guru. Little is known about the circumstances of Bhagavan Nityananda's birth and early life, although it is said that even as a child he showed the signs of a Realized Yogi. It is also known that he abandoned conventional life as a boy and wandered as a renunciate. Many miracles (including spontaneous healings) and instructive stories are attributed to him. Bhagavan Nityananda surrendered the body on August 8, 1961. Although Avatar Adi Da did not meet Bhagavan Nityananda in the flesh, He enjoyed Bhagavan Nityananda's direct Spiritual Influence from the subtle plane, and He acknowledges Bhagavan Nityananda as a direct and principal Source of Spiritual Instruction during His years with Swami Muktananda. (Avatar Adi Da summarizes the Instruction He received from Bhagavan Nityananda in section XXXII of "I (Alone) Am The Adidam Revelation", an Essay contained in many of the twenty-three "Source-Texts" of Adidam.)

On His third visit to India, while visiting Bhagavan Nityananda's burial shrine, Avatar Adi Da was instructed by Bhagavan Nityananda to relinquish all others as Guru and to surrender directly to the Divine Goddess in Person as Guru. Thus, Bhagavan Nityananda passed Avatar Adi Da to the Divine Goddess Herself, the Parama-Guru (or Source-Guru) of the Lineage that included Bhagavan Nityananda, Swami Muktananda, and Rudi.

The years of Avatar Adi Da's "Sadhana" came to an end in the Great Event of His Divine Re-Awakening, when Avatar Adi Da Husbanded the Divine Goddess (thereby ceasing to relate to Her as His Guru).

Avatar Adi Da's full account of His "Sadhana Years" is Given in *The Knee Of Listening*.

Avatar Adi Da's description of His "Relationship" to the Divine "Goddess" is Given in "I Am The Icon Of Unity", in *He-and-She Is Me*.

listening, hearing, and seeing

"Listening" is Avatar Adi Da's technical term for the orientation, disposition, and beginning practice of the Way of Adidam. A listening devotee listens to Avatar Adi Da Samraj by "considering" His Teaching-Argument and His Leelas, and by practicing feeling-Contemplation of Him (primarily of His bodily human Form). In the total practice of the Way of Adidam, effective listening to Avatar Adi Da is the necessary prerequisite for true hearing and real seeing.

"Hearing" is a technical term used by Avatar Adi Da to indicate most fundamental understanding of the act of egoity (or self-contraction). Hearing Avatar Adi Da is the unique capability to directly transcend the self-contraction, such that, simultaneous with that transcending, there is the intuitive awakening to Avatar Adi Da's Self-Revelation As the Divine Person and Self-Condition. The capability of true hearing can only be Granted by Avatar Adi Da's Divine Grace, to His fully practicing devotee who has effectively completed the process of listening. Only on the basis of such hearing can Spiritually Awakened practice of the Way of Adidam truly (or with full responsibility) begin.

I Am Heard When My Listening Devotee Has Truly (and Thoroughly) Observed the ego-"I" and Understood it (Directly, In the moments Of self-Observation, and Most Fundamentally, or In its Totality).

I Am Heard When the ego-"I" Is Altogether (and Thoroughly) Observed and (Most Fundamentally) Understood, Both In The Tendency To Dissociate and In The Tendency To Become Attached (or To Cling By Wanting Need, or To Identify With others, and things, and circumstances egoically, and Thus To Dramatize The Seeker, Bereft Of Basic Equanimity, Wholeness, and The Free Capability For Simple Relatedness).

I Am Heard When the ego-"I" Is Thoroughly (and Most Fundamentally) Understood To Be Contraction-Only, An Un-Necessary and Destructive Motive and Design, Un-Naturally and Chronically Added To Cosmic Nature and To all relations, and An Imaginary Heart-Disease (Made To Seem Real, By Heart-Reaction).

I Am Heard When This Most Fundamental Understanding Of The Habit Of "Narcissus" Becomes The Directly Obvious Realization Of The Heart, Radiating Beyond Its Own (Apparent) Contraction.

I Am Heard When The Beginning Is Full, and The Beginning Is Full (and Ended) When Every Gesture Of self-Contraction (In The Context Of The First Three Stages Of Life, and Relative To Each and All Of The Principal Faculties, Of body, emotion, mind, and breath) Is (As A Rather Consistently Applied and humanly Effective Discipline) Observed (By Natural feeling-perception), Tacitly (and Most Fundamentally) Understood, and Really (Directly and Effectively) Felt Beyond (In The Prior Feeling Of Unqualified Relatedness). [Santosha Adidam]

When, in the practice of the Way of Adidam, hearing (or most fundamental self-understanding) is steadily exercised in meditation and in life, the native feeling of the heart ceases to be chronically constricted by self-contraction. The heart then begins to Radiate as love in response to the Divine Spiritual Presence of Avatar Adi Da.

This emotional and Spiritual response of the whole being is what Avatar Adi Da calls "seeing". Seeing Avatar Adi Da is emotional conversion from the reactive emotions that characterize egoic self-obsession, to the open-hearted, Radiant Happiness that characterizes Spiritual devotion to Avatar Adi Da. This true and stable emotional conversion coincides with true and stable receptivity to Avatar Adi Da's Spiritual Transmission, and both of these are prerequisites to further Spiritual advancement in the Way of Adidam.

Seeing Is ego-Transcending Participation In What (and Who) Is. Seeing Is Love. Seeing (or Love) Is Able (By Means Of My Avatarically Self-Transmitted Divine Grace) To "Locate", Devotionally Recognize, and Feel My Avatarically Self-Transmitted (and all-and-All-Pervading) Spiritual Radiance (and My Avatarically Self-Transmitted Spirit-Identity, As The "Bright" and Only One Who Is). . . . Seeing Is The "Radical" (or Directly ego-Transcending) Reorientation Of conditional Existence To My Avatarically Self-Revealed (Transcendental, Inherently Spiritual, Inherently Perfect, and Self-

Evidently Divine) Self-Condition, In Whom conditional self and conditional worlds Apparently arise and Always Already Inhere. . . .

Seeing Me Is Simply Attraction To Me (and Feeling Me) As My Avatarically Self-Revealed Spiritual (and Always Blessing) Divine Presence—and This Most Fundamentally, At The Root, Core, Source, or Origin Of The "Emergence" Of My Avatarically Self-Revealed Divine Spiritual Presence "here", At (and In Front Of) The Heart, or At (and In) The Root-Context Of the body-mind, or At (and In) The Source-Position (and, Ultimately, As The Source-Condition) Of conditional (or psycho-physical) Existence Itself.

Seeing Me Is Knowing Me As My Avatarically Self-Revealed Spiritual (and Always Blessing) Divine Presence, Just As Tangibly (and With The Same Degree Of Clarity) As You Would Differentiate The Physical Appearance Of My Bodily (Human) Form From the physical appearance of the bodily (human) form of any other.

To See Me Is A Clear and "Radical" Knowledge Of Me, About Which There Is No Doubt. To See Me Is A Sudden, Tacit Awareness—Like Walking Into a "thicker" air or atmosphere, or Suddenly Feeling a breeze, or Jumping Into water and Noticing The Difference In Density Between the air and the water. This Tangible Feeling Of Me Is (In any particular moment) Not Necessarily (Otherwise) Associated With effects in the body-mind . . . but It Is, Nevertheless, Felt At The Heart and Even All Over the body.

Seeing Me Is One-Pointedness In The "Radical" Conscious Process Of Heart-Devotion To Me. [Santosha Adidam]

"Living Murti" Avatar Adi Da will always be Divinely Present in the Cosmic domain, even after His physical Lifetime. He is the One Who is (and will always be) worshipped in the Way of Adidam, and (therefore) He is (and will always be) the Eternally Living Murti for His devotees. However, Avatar Adi Da has said that, after His physical (human) Lifetime, there should always be one (and only one) "Living Murti" as a Living Link

between Him and His devotees. Each successive "Living Murti" (or "Murti-Guru") is to be selected from among those members of the Ruchira Sannyasin Order (see **renunciate orders**) who have been formally acknowledged as Divinely Enlightened devotees of Avatar Adi Da Samraj in the seventh stage of life. "Living Murtis" will not function as the independent Gurus of practitioners of the Way of Adidam. Rather, they will simply be "Representations" of Avatar Adi Da's bodily (human) Divine Form, and a means to Commune with Him.

Avatar Adi Da's full discussion of His "Living Murtis", and how they are to be chosen, is Given in Part Three, section XII, of *The Lion Sutra*.

"Locate" To "Locate" Avatar Adi Da is to "Truly Heart-Find" Him.

Love-Ananda The Name "Love-Ananda" combines both English ("Love") and Sanskrit ("Ananda", meaning "Bliss"), thus bridging the West and the East, and communicating Avatar Adi Da's Function as the Divine World-Teacher. The combination of "Love" and "Ananda" means "the Divine Love-Bliss". The Name "Love-Ananda" was given to Avatar Adi Da by Swami Muktananda, who spontaneously conferred it upon Avatar Adi Da in 1969. However, Avatar Adi Da did not use the Name "Love-Ananda" until April 1986, after the Great Event that Initiated His Divine Self-"Emergence".

Love-Ananda Avatar As the Love-Ananda Avatar, Avatar Adi Da is the Very Incarnation of the Divine Love-Bliss.

M

Maha-Siddha The Sanskrit word "Siddha" means "a completed, fulfilled, or perfected one", or "one of perfect accomplishment, or power". "Maha-Siddha" means "Great Siddha".

Mandala The Sanskrit word "mandala" (literally, "circle") is commonly used in the esoteric Spiritual traditions to describe the entire pattern of the hierarchical levels of cosmic existence. Avatar Adi Da also uses the word "Mandala" to refer to the Circle (or Sphere) of His Heart-Transmission, or as a formal reference to a group of His devotees who perform specific functions of direct service to Him.

mantra See **Name-Invocation**.

meditation In the Way of Adidam, meditation is a period of formal devotional Contemplation of Avatar Adi Da Samraj. Meditation is one of the life-disciplines that Avatar Adi Da Samraj has Given to His devotees in the first and second congregations, as a fundamental support for their practice of Ruchira Avatara Bhakti Yoga. For those who have fully adapted to the disciplines of the first and second congregations, the daily practice of meditation includes a period of one and one-half hours in the morning and a period of one hour in the evening. Such daily practice is increased during periods of retreat. Members of the third and fourth congregations are also encouraged (but not required) to engage formal meditation.

missing the mark "Hamartia" (the word in New Testament Greek that was translated into English as "sin") was originally an archery term meaning "missing the mark".

Most Perfect / Most Ultimate Avatar Adi Da uses the phrase "Most Perfect(ly)" in the sense of "Absolutely Perfect(ly)". Similarly, the phrase "Most Ultimate(ly)" is equivalent to "Absolutely Ultimate(ly)". "Most Perfect(ly)" and "Most Ultimate(ly)" are always references to the seventh (or Divinely Enlightened) stage of life. Perfect(ly) and Ultimate(ly) refer to the sixth stage of life or to the sixth and seventh stages of life together. (See also **stages of life**.)

mudra A "mudra" is a gesture of the hands, face, or body that outwardly expresses a state of ecstasy. Avatar Adi Da sometimes spontaneously exhibits Mudras as Signs of His Blessing and Purifying Work with His devotees and the world. He also uses the term "Mudra" to express the Attitude of His Blessing-Work, which is His Constant (or Eternal) Giving (or

Submitting) of Himself to Be the Means of Divine Liberation for all beings.

Muktananda, Swami See **Lineage, Avatar Adi Da's.**

mummery / *The Mummery* The dictionary defines mummery as "a ridiculous, hypocritical, or pretentious ceremony or performance". Avatar Adi Da uses this word to describe all the activities of ego-bound beings, or beings who are committed to the false view of separation and separativeness.

The Mummery is one of Avatar Adi Da's twenty-three "Source-Texts". It is a work of astonishing poetry and deeply evocative archetypes. Through the heart-breaking story of Raymond Darling's growth to manhood, his search to find, and then to be reunited with, his beloved (Quandra), and his utter self-transcendence of all conditional circumstances and events, Avatar Adi Da Tells His own Life-Story in the language of parable, and describes in devastating detail how the unconverted ego makes religion (and life altogether) into a meaningless mummery.

Murti "Murti" is Sanskrit for "form", and, by extension, a "representational image" of the Divine or of a Guru. In the Way of Adidam, Murtis of Avatar Adi Da are most commonly photographs of Avatar Adi Da's bodily (human) Divine Form.

"Murti-Guru" See **"Living Murti"**.

Mystery Avatar Adi Da uses the term "the Mystery" to point out that, although we can name things, we actually do not know what anything really is:

It is a great and more-than-wonderful Mystery to everyone that anything is, or that we are. And whether somebody says "I don't know how anything came to be" or "God made everything", they are simply pointing to the feeling of the Mystery—of how everything is, but nobody knows what it really Is, or how it came to be. [What, Where, When, How, Why, and Who To Remember To Be Happy]

N

Name-Invocation   Sacred sounds or syllables and Names have been used since antiquity for invoking and worshipping the Divine Person and the Sat-Guru. In the Hindu tradition, the original mantras were cosmic sound-forms and "seed" letters used for worship and prayer of, and incantatory meditation on, the Revealed Form of the Divine Person.

Practitioners of the Way of Adidam may, at any time, Remember or Invoke Avatar Adi Da Samraj (or feel, and thereby Contemplate, His Avatarically Self-Revealed Divine Form, and Presence, and State) through simple feeling-Remembrance of Him and by randomly (in daily life and meditation) Invoking Him via His Principal Name, "Da", or via one (and only one) of the other Names He has Given for the practice of Simple Name-Invocation of Him. (The specific forms of His Names that Avatar Adi Da has Given to be engaged in practice of simple Name-Invocation of Him are listed in chapter three of *The Dawn Horse Testament Of The Ruchira Avatar*.)

For devotees of Avatar Adi Da Samraj, His Names are the Names of the Very Divine Being. As such, these Names, as Avatar Adi Da Himself has described, "do not simply <u>mean</u> Real God, or the Blessing of Real God. They are the verbal or audible Form of the Divine." Therefore, Invoking Avatar Adi Da Samraj by Name is a potent and Divinely Empowered form of feeling-Contemplation of Him.

Narcissus   In Avatar Adi Da's Teaching-Revelation, "Narcissus" is a key symbol of the un-Enlightened individual as a self-obsessed seeker, enamored of his or her own self-image and egoic self-consciousness. In *The Knee Of Listening*, Adi Da Samraj describes the significance of the archetype of Narcissus:

He is the ancient one visible in the Greek "myth", who was the universally adored child of the gods, who rejected the loved-one and every form of love and relationship, who was finally condemned to the contemplation of his own image, until,

as a result of his own act and obstinacy, he suffered the fate of eternal separateness and died in infinite solitude.

Nirguna   "Nirguna" is Sanskrit for "without attributes or quality".

Nirvikalpa Samadhi   See **Samadhi**.

Nityananda   See **Lineage, Avatar Adi Da's**.

Non-Separate Self-Domain   The "Non-Separate Self-Domain" is a synonym for "Divine Self-Domain". (See **Divine Self-Domain**.)

O

"Oedipal"   In modern psychology, the "Oedipus complex" is named after the legendary Greek Oedipus, who was fated to unknowingly kill his father and marry his mother. Avatar Adi Da Teaches that the primary dynamisms of emotional-sexual desiring, rejection, envy, betrayal, self-pleasuring, resentment, and other primal emotions and impulses are indeed patterned upon unconscious reactions first formed early in life, in relation to one's mother and father. Avatar Adi Da calls this "the 'Oedipal' drama" and points out that we relate to all women as we do to our mothers, and to all men as we do to our fathers, and that we relate, and react, to our own bodies as we do to the parent of the opposite sex. Thus, we impose infantile reactions to our parents on our relationships with lovers and all other beings, according to their sex, and we also superimpose the same on our relationship to our own bodies. (Avatar Adi Da's extended Instruction on "Oedipal" patterning is Given in *Ruchira Avatara Hridaya-Tantra Yoga*.)

Omega   See **Alpha and Omega**.

"Open Eyes"   "Open Eyes" is Avatar Adi Da's technical synonym for the Realization of seventh stage Sahaj Samadhi, or unqualified Divine Self-Realization. The phrase graphically describes the non-exclusive, non-inward, Native State of the Divine Self-Realizer, Who is Identified

Unconditionally with the Divine Self-Reality, while also allowing whatever arises to appear in the Divine Consciousness (and spontaneously Divinely Self-Recognizing everything that arises as a modification of the Divine Consciousness). The Transcendental Self is intuited in the mature phases of the sixth stage of life, but It can be Realized at that stage only by the intentional exclusion of conditional phenomena. In "Open Eyes", that impulse to exclusion disappears, when the Eyes of the Heart Open, and Most Perfect Realization of the Spiritual, Transcendental, and Divine Self in the seventh stage of life becomes permanent (and incorruptible by any phenomenal events).

"original" context of the fourth stage of life See **stages of life**.

Outshined / Outshining Avatar Adi Da uses "Outshined" or "Outshining" as a synonym for "Divine Translation", to refer to the final Demonstration of the four-phase process of the seventh (or Divinely Enlightened) stage of life in the Way of Adidam. In the Great Event of Outshining (or Divine Translation), body, mind, and world are no longer noticed—not because the Divine Consciousness has withdrawn or dissociated from conditionally mani-fested phenomena, but because the Divine Self-Recognition of all arising phenomena as modifications of the Divine Self-Condition has become so intense that the "Bright" Radiance of Consciousness now Outshines all such phenomena. (See also **four phases of the seventh stage of life**.)

P, Q

"Perfect Practice" The "Perfect Practice" is Avatar Adi Da's technical term for the discipline of the ultimate stages of life (the sixth stage of life and the seventh stage of life) in the Way of Adidam. The "Perfect Practice" is practice in the Domain of Consciousness Itself (as opposed to practice from the point of view of the body or the mind). (See also **stages of life**.)

Perfectly Subjective Avatar Adi Da uses "Perfectly Subjective" to describe the True Divine Source, or "Subject", of the condi-tionally manifested world—as opposed to regarding the Divine as some sort of con-ditional "object" or "other". Thus, in the phrase "Perfectly Subjective", the word "Subjective" does not have the sense of "relating to the inward experience of an individual", but, rather, it has the sense of "Being Consciousness Itself, the True Subject of all apparent experience".

Pilgrimage and Retreat Sanctuaries See **Sanctuaries**.

Pleasure Dome Avatar Adi Da Samraj Speaks of the Way of Adidam as a "Pleasure Dome", recalling the poem "Kubla Khan", by Samuel Taylor Coleridge ("In Xanadu did Kubla Khan / A stately pleasure-dome decree . . ."). Adi Da Samraj points out that in many religious traditions it is presumed that one must embrace suffering in order to earn future happiness and pleasure. However, by Calling His devotees to live the Way of Adidam as a Pleasure Dome, Avatar Adi Da Samraj Communicates His Teaching that the Way of heart-Communion with Him is always about present-time Happiness, not about any kind of search to attain Happiness in the future. Thus, in the Way of Adidam, there is no idealiza-tion of suffering and pain as presumed means to attain future happiness—and, consequently, there is no denial of the appropriate enjoyment of even the ordi-nary pleasures of human life.

Avatar Adi Da also uses "Pleasure Dome" as a reference to the Ultimate and Divine Love-Bliss-Happiness That Is His own Self-Nature and His Gift to all who respond to Him.

"Practice" As the quotation marks around the capitalized word "Practice" suggest, the psycho-physical expression of the process of Divine Enlightenment is a "Practice" only in the sense that it is sim-ple action. It is not, in contrast to the stages of life previous to the seventh, a discipline intended to counter egoic ten-dencies that would otherwise dominate body and mind.

Avatar Adi Da uses quotation marks in a characteristic manner throughout His Written Word to Indicate that a particular word is a technical term, to be understood in the unique and precise language of the Way of Adidam, carrying the implication "as per definition". However, in other cases, His quotation marks carry the implication "so to speak", as in the case of the term "Practice" and are, therefore, not to be understood as precise technical terminology of the Way of Adidam.

prana/pranic The Sanskrit word "prana" means "life-energy". It generally refers to the life-energy animating all beings and pervading everything in cosmic Nature. In the human body-mind, circulation of this universal life-energy is associated with the heartbeat and the cycles of the breath. In esoteric Yogic Teachings, prana is also a specific technical name for one of a number of forms of etheric energy that functionally sustain the bodily being.

Prana is not to be equated with the Divine Spirit-Current, or the Spiritual (and Always Blessing) Divine Presence of Avatar Adi Da Samraj. The finite pranic energies that sustain individual beings are only conditional, localized, and temporary phenomena of the realm of cosmic Nature. Even in the form of universal life-force, prana is but a conditional modification of the Divine Spirit-Current Revealed by Avatar Adi Da, Which Is the "Bright" (or Consciousness Itself), beyond all cosmic forms.

R

"radical" The term "radical" derives from the Latin "radix", meaning "root", and, thus, it principally means "irreducible", "fundamental", or "relating to the origin". In *The Dawn Horse Testament Of The Ruchira Avatar*, Avatar Adi Da defines "Radical" as "Gone To The Root, Core, Source, or Origin". Because Adi Da Samraj uses "radical" in this literal sense, it appears in quotation marks in His Wisdom-Teaching, in order to distinguish His usage from the common reference to an extreme (often political) view.

Ramakrishna See **Lineage, Avatar Adi Da's.**

Ramana Maharshi A great sixth stage Indian Spiritual Master, Ramana Maharshi (1879-1950) became Self-Realized at a young age and gradually assumed a Teaching role as increasing numbers of people approached him for Spiritual guidance. Ramana Maharshi's Teaching focused on the process of introversion (through the question "Who am I?"), which culminates in conditional Self-Realization (or Jnana Samadhi), exclusive of phenomena. He established his Ashram at Tiruvannamalai in South India, which continues today.

Rang Avadhoot Rang Avadhoot (1898-1968) was a Realizer in the tradition of Dattatreya. In *The Knee Of Listening*, Avatar Adi Da describes the brief but highly significant meeting that occurred between Himself and Rang Avadhoot in 1968.

Real God Avatar Adi Da uses the term "Real God" to Indicate the True and Perfectly Subjective Source of all conditions, the True and Spiritual Divine Person (Which can be directly Realized), rather than any ego-made (and, thus, false, or limited) presumptions about God.

Re-cognition "Re-cognition", which literally means "knowing again", is Avatar Adi Da's term for "the tacit transcending of the habit of 'Narcissus'". It is the mature form into which verbal self-Enquiry evolves in the Devotional Way of Insight. The individual simply notices and tacitly "knows again" (or directly understands) whatever is arising as yet another species of self-contraction, and he or she transcends (or feels beyond) it in Satsang with Avatar Adi Da.

renunciate orders Avatar Adi Da has established two formal renunciate orders: The Ruchira Sannyasin Order of the Tantric Renunciates of Adidam (or, simply, the Ruchira Sannyasin Order), and the Lay Renunciate Order of Adidam (or, simply, the Lay Renunciate Order).

The senior practicing order in the Way

of Adidam is the Ruchira Sannyasin Order. This order is the senior cultural authority within the formal gathering of Avatar Adi Da's devotees. "Sannyasin" is an ancient Sanskrit term for one who has renounced all worldly bonds and who gives himself or herself completely to the Real-God-Realizing or Real-God-Realized life. Members of the Ruchira Sannyasin Order are uniquely exemplary practitioners of the Way of Adidam who are (generally) practicing in the context of the ultimate (sixth and seventh) stages of life. Members of this Order are legal renunciates and live a life of perpetual retreat. As a general rule, they are to reside at Adidam Samrajashram. The Ruchira Sannyasin Order comprises the first congregation of Avatar Adi Da's devotees.

The members of the Ruchira Sannyasin Order have a uniquely significant role among the practitioners of Adidam as Avatar Adi Da's human Instruments and (in the case of those members who are formally acknowledged as Avatar Adi Da's fully Awakened seventh stage devotees) as the body of practitioners from among whom each of Avatar Adi Da's successive "Living Murtis" (or Empowered human Agents) will be selected. Therefore, the Ruchira Sannyasin Order is essential to the perpetual continuation of authentic practice of the Way of Adidam.

The Founding Member of the Ruchira Sannyasin Order Avatar Adi Da Himself.

In "The Orders of My True and Free Renunciate Devotees" (in *The Lion Sutra*), Avatar Adi Da describes the Lay Renunciate Order as "a renunciate service order for all intensively serving (and, altogether, intensively practicing) lay practitioners of the total (or full and complete) practice of the Way of Adidam".

All present members, and all future members, of the Lay Renunciate Order must (necessarily) be formally acknowledged, formally practicing, significantly matured (tested and proven), and, altogether, especially exemplary practitioners of the total (or full and complete) practice of the Way of Adidam. They must perform significant cultural (and practical, and, as necessary, managerial) service within the gathering of all formally acknowledged practitioners of the four congregations of the Way of Adidam. Either they must live within a formally designated community of formally acknowledged practitioners of the Way of Adidam or, otherwise, they must be formally designated serving residents of one of the by Me formally Empowered Ruchira Sannyasin Hermitage-Retreat Sanctuaries or one of the by Me formally Empowered Pilgrimage and Retreat Sanctuaries for all formally acknowledged practitioners of the Way of Adidam. And they must formally accept (and rightly fulfill) all the obligations and disciplines associated with membership within the Lay Renunciate Order. ["The Orders of My True and Free Renunciate Devotees"]

right side of the heart See **heart, stations of the heart**.

Ruchira Avatar In Sanskrit, "Ruchira" means "bright, radiant, effulgent". Thus, the Reference "Ruchira Avatar" indicates that Avatar Adi Da Samraj is the "Bright" (or Radiant) Descent of the Divine Reality Itself into the conditionally manifested worlds, Appearing here in His bodily (human) Form.

Ruchira Avatara Bhakti Yoga Ruchira Avatara Bhakti Yoga is the principal Gift, Calling, and Discipline Offered by Adi Da Samraj to all who practice the Way of Adidam (in all four congregations).

The phrase "Ruchira Avatara Bhakti Yoga" is itself a summary of the Way of Adidam. "Bhakti", in Sanskrit, is love, adoration, or devotion, while "Yoga" is a Real-God-Realizing discipline (or practice). "Ruchira Avatara Bhakti Yoga" is, thus, "the Divinely Revealed practice of devotional love for (and devotional response to) the Ruchira Avatar, Adi Da Samraj".

The technical practice of Ruchira Avatara Bhakti Yoga is a four-part process of Invoking, feeling, breathing, and serving Avatar Adi Da in every moment.

For Avatar Adi Da's essential Instruction in Ruchira Avatara Bhakti Yoga, see the *Da Love-Ananda Gita (The Free Gift Of The Divine Love-Bliss)*, Part Five, verse 25, and Part Six; *Hridaya Rosary*

(Four Thorns Of Heart-Instruction), Parts
Four and Five; and *What, Where, When,
How, Why and <u>Who</u> To Remember To Be
Happy*, Part Three, "Surrender the Faculties
of the Body-Mind To Me" and "How to
Practice Whole Bodily Devotion To Me".

Ruchira Avatara Satsang   The Hindi
word "Satsang" literally means "true (or
right) relationship", "the company of
Truth". "Ruchira Avatara Satsang" is the
eternal relationship of mutual sacred commitment between Avatar Adi Da Samraj
and each true and formally acknowledged
practitioner of the Way of Adidam. Once it
is consciously assumed by any practitioner, Ruchira Avatara Satsang is an all-
inclusive Condition, bringing Divine Grace
and Blessings and sacred obligations,
responsibilities, and tests into every
dimension of the practitioner's life and
consciousness.

The Ruchira Buddha   The Enlightened
One Who Shines with the Divine
"Brightness".

The Ruchira Buddha-Avatar   The
"Bright" Enlightened One Who is the
Incarnation of the Divine Person. (See
also **Avatar**.)

Ruchira Buddhism   "Ruchira Buddhism"
is the Way of devotion to the Ruchira
Buddha—"the 'Bright' Buddha", Avatar
Adi Da Samraj (or, more fully, "the
Radiant, Shining, 'Bright' Illuminator and
Enlightener Who Is Inherently, or
Perfectly Subjectively, Self-Enlightened,
and Eternally Awake").

Ruchira Samadhi   "Ruchira Samadhi"
(Sanskrit for "the Samadhi of the 'Bright'")
is one of the references that Avatar Adi Da
Samraj uses for the Divinely Enlightened
Condition Realized in the seventh stage of
life, Which He characterizes as the
Unconditional Realization of the Divine
"Brightness".

Ruchira Sannyasin Order   See **renunciate orders**, and see also p. 366.

Rudi / Swami Rudrananda   See
Lineage, Avatar Adi Da's.

S

"Sadhana Years"   In Sanskrit, "Sadhana"
means "self-transcending religious or
Spiritual practice". Avatar Adi Da's
"Sadhana Years" refers to the time from
which He began His quest to recover the
Truth of Existence (at Columbia College)
until His Divine Re-Awakening in 1970.
Avatar Adi Da's full description of His
"Sadhana Years" is Given in *The Knee Of
Listening*.

Saguna   "Saguna" is Sanskrit for "con-
taining (or accompanied by) qualities".

Sahaj   "Sahaj" is Hindi (from Sanskrit
"sahaja") for "twin-born", "natural", or
"innate". Avatar Adi Da uses the term to
indicate the Coincidence (in the case of
Divine Self-Realization) of the Inherently
Spiritual and Transcendental Divine
Reality with conditional reality. Sahaj,
therefore, is the Inherent (or Native) and,
thus, truly "Natural" State of Being. (See
also **Samadhi**.)

Sahaj Samadhi   See **Samadhi**.

sahasrar   In the traditional system of
seven chakras, the sahasrar is the highest
chakra (or subtle energy center), associated with the crown of the head and
beyond. It is described as a thousand-
petaled lotus, the terminal of Light to
which the Yogic process (of Spiritual
ascent through the chakras) aspires.

During His "Sadhana Years", Avatar
Adi Da spontaneously experienced what
He calls the "severing of the sahasrar".
The Spirit-Energy no longer ascended into
the crown of the head (and beyond), but
rather "fell" into the Heart, and rested as
the Witness-Consciousness. It was this
experience that directly revealed to Avatar
Adi Da that, while the Yogic traditions
regard the sahasrar as the seat of
Enlightenment, the Heart is truly the Seat
of Divine Consciousness.

Avatar Adi Da's account of the sever-
ing of the sahasrar in His own Case is
Given in chapter eighteen of *The Knee Of
Listening*.

Saiva Siddhanta "Saiva Siddhanta" is the name of an important school of Saivism which flourished in South India and survives into the present.

Samadhi The Sanskrit word "Samadhi" traditionally denotes various exalted states that appear in the context of esoteric meditation and Realization. Avatar Adi Da Teaches that, for His devotees, Samadhi is, even more simply and fundamentally, the Enjoyment of His Divine State, Which is experienced (even from the beginning of the practice of Adidam) through ego-transcending heart-Communion with Him. Therefore, "the cultivation of Samadhi" is another way to describe the fundamental basis of the Way of Adidam. Avatar Adi Da's devotee is in Samadhi in any moment of standing beyond the separate self in true devotional heart-Communion with Him. (See "The Cultivation of My Divine Samadhi", in *The Seven Stages Of Life*.)

The developmental process leading to Divine Enlightenment in the Way of Adidam may be marked by many signs, principal among which are the Samadhis of the advanced and the ultimate stages of life and practice. Although some of the traditionally known Samadhis of the fourth, the fifth, and the sixth stages of life may appear in the course of an individual's practice of the Way of Adidam, the appearance of all of them is by no means necessary, or even probable (as Avatar Adi Da Indicates in His Wisdom-Teaching). The essential Samadhis of the Way of Adidam are those that are uniquely Granted by Avatar Adi Da Samraj—the Samadhi of the "Thumbs" and seventh stage Sahaj Samadhi. All the possible forms of Samadhi in the Way of Adidam are described in full detail in *The Dawn Horse Testament Of The Ruchira Avatar*.

Samadhi of the "Thumbs" "The 'Thumbs'" is Avatar Adi Da's technical term for the invasion of the body-mind by a particular kind of forceful Descent of His Divine Spirit-Current. Avatar Adi Da describes His own experience of the "Thumbs" in *The Knee Of Listening*:

. . . I had an experience that appeared like a mass of gigantic thumbs coming down from above, pressing into my throat (causing something of a gagging, and somewhat suffocating, sensation), and then pressing further (and, it seemed, would have expanded without limitation or end), into some form of myself that was much larger than my physical body. . . .

The "Thumbs" were not visible in the ordinary sense. I did not see them then or even as a child. They were not visible to me with my eyes, nor did I hallucinate them pictorially. Yet, I very consciously experienced and felt them as having a peculiar form and mobility, as I likewise experienced my own otherwise invisible and greater form.

I did not at that time or at any time in my childhood fully allow this intervention of the "Thumbs" to take place. I held it off from its fullest descent, in fear of being overwhelmed, for I did not understand at all what was taking place. However, in later years this same experience occurred naturally during meditation. Because my meditation had been allowed to progress gradually, and the realizations at each level were thus perceived without shock, I was able at those times to allow the experience to take place. When I did, the "Thumbs" completely entered my living form. They appeared like tongues, or parts of a Force, coming from above. And when they had entered deep into my body, the magnetic or energic balances of my living being reversed. On several occasions I felt as if the body had risen above the ground somewhat, and this is perhaps the basis for certain evidence in mystical literature of the phenomenon of levitation, or bodily transport.

At any rate, during those stages in meditation the body ceased to be polarized toward the ground, or the gravitational direction of the earth's center. There was a strong reversal of polarity, communicated along a line of Force analogous to the spine. The physical body, as well as the Energy-form that could be interiorly felt as analogous to but detached from the physical body, was felt to turn in a curve along the spine and forward in the direction of

438

the heart. When this reversal of Energy was allowed to take place completely, I resided in a totally different body, which also contained the physical body. It was spherical in shape. And the sensation of dwelling as that form was completely peaceful. The physical body was completely relaxed and polarized to the shape of this other spherical body. The mind became quieted, and then there was a movement in consciousness that would go even deeper, into a higher conscious State beyond physical and mental awareness. I was to learn that this spherical body was what Yogis and occultists call the "subtle" body (which includes the "pranic", or natural life-energy, dimension and the "astral", or the lower mental and the higher mental, dimensions of the living being).

In the fullest form of this experience, which Avatar Adi Da calls "the Samadhi of the 'Thumbs'", His Spirit-Invasion Descends all the way to the bottom of the frontal line of the body-mind (at the bodily base) and ascends through the spinal line, overwhelming the ordinary human sense of bodily existence, infusing the whole being with intense blissfulness, and releasing the ordinary, confined sense of body, mind, and separate self.

Both the experience of the "Thumbs" and the full Samadhi of the "Thumbs" are unique to the Way of Adidam, for they are specifically signs of the "Crashing Down" (or the Divine Descent) of Avatar Adi Da's Spirit-Baptism, into the body-minds of His devotees. The Samadhi of the "Thumbs" is a kind of "Nirvikalpa" (or formless) Samadhi—but in descent in the frontal line, rather than in ascent in the spinal line.

Avatar Adi Da's extended Instruction relative to the "Thumbs" is Given in "The 'Thumbs' Is The Fundamental Sign Of The Crashing Down Of My Person". This Essay appears in a number of Avatar Adi Da's "Source-Texts" (*Hridaya Rosary, The Only Complete Way To Realize The Unbroken Light Of Real God, Ruchira Avatara Hridaya-Siddha Yoga, The Seven Stages Of Life*, and *Santosha Adidam*, as well as chapter twenty-four of *The Dawn Horse Testament Of The Ruchira Avatar* and chapter thirty-one of *The Heart Of The Dawn Horse Testament Of The Ruchira Avatar*).

Savikalpa Samadhi and "Cosmic Consciousness"

The Sanskrit term "Savikalpa Samadhi" literally means "meditative ecstasy with form", or "deep meditative concentration (or absorption) in which form (or defined experiential content) is still perceived". Avatar Adi Da indicates that there are two basic forms of Savikalpa Samadhi. The first is the various experiences produced by the Spiritual ascent of energy and attention (into mystical phenomena, visions, and other subtle sensory perceptions of subtle psychic forms) and the various states of Yogic Bliss (or Spirit-"Intoxication").

The second (and highest) form of Savikalpa Samadhi is called "Cosmic Consciousness", or the "'Vision' of Cosmic Unity". This is an isolated or periodic occurrence in which attention ascends, uncharacteristically and spontaneously, to a state of awareness wherein conditional existence is perceived as a Unity in Divine Awareness. This conditional form of "Cosmic Consciousness" is pursued in many mystical and Yogic paths. It depends upon manipulation of attention and the body-mind, and it is interpreted from the point of view of the separate, body-based or mind-based self—and, therefore, it is not equivalent to Divine Enlightenment.

Avatar Adi Da's discussion of Savikalpa Samadhi is found in "Vision, Audition, and Touch in The Process of Ascending Meditation in The Way Of Adidam", in Part Four of *Ruchira Avatara Hridaya-Siddha Yoga*.

Avatar Adi Da's description of the varieties of experiential form possible in Savikalpa Samadhi is found in "The Significant Experiential Signs That May Appear in the Course of The Way Of Adidam", in Part Three of *What, Where, When, How, Why, and Who To Remember To Be Happy.*

fifth stage Nirvikalpa Samadhi

The Sanskrit term "Nirvikalpa Samadhi" literally means "meditative ecstasy without form", or "deep meditative concentration (or absorption) in which there is no perception of form (or defined experiential content)". Traditionally, this state is regarded to be the final goal of the many schools of Yogic ascent whose orientation to practice is that of the fifth stage of life. Like "Cosmic Consciousness", fifth stage conditional Nirvikalpa Samadhi is an isolated or periodic Realization. In it, attention ascends beyond all conditional manifestation into the formless Matrix of Divine Vibration and Divine Light Infinitely Above the world, the body, and the mind. And, like the various forms of Savikalpa Samadhi, fifth stage conditional Nirvikalpa Samadhi is a temporary state of attention (or, more precisely, of the suspension of attention). It is produced by manipulation of attention and of the body-mind, and is (therefore) incapable of being maintained when attention returns (as it inevitably does) to the states of the body-mind.

Avatar Adi Da's Instruction relative to fifth stage conditional Nirvikalpa Samadhi is Given in chapter forty-two of *The Dawn Horse Testament Of The Ruchira Avatar*.

Jnana Samadhi, or Jnana Nirvikalpa Samadhi "Jnana" means "knowledge". Jnana Nirvikalpa Samadhi (sixth stage Nirvakalpa Samadhi, or, simply, Jnana Samadhi) is the characteristic meditative experience in the sixth stage of life in the Way of Adidam. Produced by the intentional withdrawal of attention from the conditional body-mind-self and its relations, Jnana Samadhi is the conditional, temporary Realization of the Transcendental Self (or Consciousness Itself), exclusive of any perception (or cognition) of world, objects, relations, body, mind, or separate-self-sense—and, thereby, formless (or "nirvikalpa").

Avatar Adi Da's Instruction relative to Jnana Nirvikalpa Samadhi is Given in "The Sixth and The Seventh Stages of Life in The Way Of Adidam" in *The Lion Sutra*.

seventh stage Sahaj Samadhi, or seventh stage Sahaja Nirvikalpa Samadhi Avatar Adi Da's description of seventh stage Sahaj Samadhi is Given in Part Four of *The All-Completing and Final Divine Revelation To Mankind*.

Samraj "Samraj" (from the Sanskrit "Samraja") is a traditional Indian term used to refer to great kings, but also to refer to the Hindu gods. "Samraja" is defined as "universal or supreme ruler", "paramount Lord", or "paramount sovereign".

The Sanskrit word "raja" (the basic root of "Samraj") means "king". It comes from the verbal root "raj", meaning "to reign, to rule, to illuminate". The prefix "sam-" expresses "union" or "completeness". "Samraj" is thus literally the complete ruler, the ruler of everything altogether. "Samraj" was traditionally given as a title to a king who was regarded to be a "universal monarch".

Avatar Adi Da's Name "Adi Da Samraj" expresses that He is the Primordial (or Original) Giver, Who Blesses all as the Universal Lord of every thing, every where, for all time. The Sovereignty of His Kingdom has nothing to do with the world of human politics. Rather, it is entirely a matter of His Spiritual Dominion over all and All, His Kingship in the hearts of His devotees.

samsara / samsaric "Samsara" (or "samsaric") is a classical Buddhist and Hindu term for all conditional worlds and states, or the cyclical realm of birth and change and death. It connotes the suffering and limitations experienced in those limited worlds.

Sanctuaries Avatar Adi Da has Empowered two Hermitage-Retreat Sanctuaries and two Pilgrimage and Retreat Sanctuaries as Agents of His Divine Spiritual Transmission. The senior Hermitage-Retreat Sanctuary is Adidam Samrajashram, the Island of Naitauba in Fiji, where Avatar Adi Da usually Resides in Perpetual Retreat. It is the place where Avatar Adi Da Himself and the senior renunciate order of the Way of Adidam, the Ruchira Sannyasin Order of the Tantric Renunciates of Adidam, are established. It is the primary Seat of Avatar Adi Da's Divine Blessing Work with the entire Cosmic Mandala.

Avatar Adi Da has Spoken of the significance of this Hermitage Ashram:

*AVATAR ADI DA SAMRAJ: Adidam
Samrajashram was established so that I
might have a Place of Seclusion in which
to do My Spiritual Work. This is the Place
of My perpetual Samadhi, the Place of My
perpetual Self-Radiance. Therefore, this is
the Place where people come to participate
in My Samadhi and be further Awakened
by It. My devotees come to Adidam
Samrajashram to magnify their practice
of right, true, and full devotion to Me,
to practice the Way of Adidam as I Have
Revealed and Given It for the sake of most
perfectly ego-transcending Real-God-
Realization.*

Tat Sundaram is a small Hermitage-
Retreat Sanctuary that provides a private
circumstance for Avatar Adi Da and members of the Ruchira Sannyasin Order.

The two Pilgrimage and Retreat
Sanctuaries (The Mountain Of Attention,
in northern California, and Da Love-
Ananda Mahal, in Hawaii—formerly
known as "Tumomama Sanctuary") were
principal sites of Avatar Adi Da's Teaching
Demonstration during the years of His
Divine Teaching-Work. Through His years
of Blessing-Infusion of each of these
Hermitage-Retreat Sanctuaries and these
Pilgrimage and Retreat Sanctuaries, He has
fully Empowered them for His devotees
throughout all time.

Santosha   "Santosha" is Sanskrit for "sat-
isfaction" or "contentment"—qualities
associated with a sense of completion.
These qualities are characteristic of no-
seeking, the fundamental Principle of
Avatar Adi Da's Wisdom-Teaching and of
His entire Revelation of Truth. Because of
its uniquely appropriate meanings,
"Santosha" is one of Avatar Adi Da's
Names. As Santosha Adi Da, Avatar Adi
Da Samraj is the Divine Giver of Perfect
Divine Contentedness, or Perfect
Searchlessness.

Santosha Avatar   As the Santosha
Avatar, Avatar Adi Da is the Very
Incarnation of Perfect Divine
Contentedness, or Perfect Searchlessness.

Sat-Guru   "Sat" means "Truth", "Being",

"Existence". Thus, "Sat-Guru" literally
means "True Guru", or a Guru who can
lead living beings from darkness (or non-
Truth) into Light (or the Living Truth).

Satsang   The Hindi word "Satsang" (from
the Sanskrit "Satsanga") literally means
"true (or right) relationship", "the company of Truth". In the Way of Adidam,
Satsang is the eternal relationship of
mutual sacred commitment between
Avatar Adi Da Samraj and each formally
acknowledged practitioner of the Way of
Adidam.

Savikalpa Samadhi   See **Samadhi**.

scientific materialism   Scientific materialism is the predominant philosophy and
worldview of modern humanity, the basic
presumption of which is that the material
world is all that exists. In scientific materialism, the method of science, or the
observation of objective phenomena, is
made into philosophy and a way of life
that suppresses our native impulse to
Liberation.

seeing   See **listening, hearing, and
seeing**.

self-Enquiry   The practice of self-
Enquiry in the form "Avoiding relation-
ship?", unique to the Way of Adidam, was
spontaneously developed by Avatar Adi
Da in the course of His own Ordeal of
Divine Re-Awakening. Intense persistence
in the "radical" discipline of this unique
form of self-Enquiry led rapidly to Avatar
Adi Da's Divine Enlightenment (or Most
Perfect Divine Self-Realization) in 1970.

The practice of self-Enquiry in the
form "Avoiding relationship?" and the
practice of non-verbal Re-cognition are
the principal technical practices that serve
feeling-Contemplation of Avatar Adi Da in
the Devotional Way of Insight.

Self-Existing and Self-Radiant   Avatar
Adi Da uses "Self-Existing and Self-
Radiant" to indicate the two fundamental
aspects of the One Divine Person (or
Reality)—Existence (or Being, or
Consciousness) Itself, and Radiance (or
Energy, or Light) Itself.

seven stages of life See **stages of life**.

Shakti, Guru-Shakti "Shakti" is a Sanskrit term for the Divinely Manifesting Energy, Spiritual Power, or Spirit-Current of the Divine Person. Guru-Shakti is the Power of the Guru to Liberate his or her devotees.

Shaktipat In Hindi, "shaktipat" is the "descent of Spiritual Power". Yogic Shaktipat, which manipulates natural, conditional energies or partial manifestations of the Spirit-Current, is typically granted through touch, word, glance, or regard by Yogic Adepts in the fifth stage of life, or fourth to fifth stages of life. Yogic Shaktipat must be distinguished from (and, otherwise, understood to be only a secondary aspect of) the Blessing Transmission of the Heart Itself (Hridaya-Shaktipat), which is uniquely Given by Avatar Adi Da Samraj.

Siddha, Siddha-Guru "Siddha" is Sanskrit for "a completed, fulfilled, or perfected one", or "one of perfect accomplishment, or power". Avatar Adi Da uses "Siddha", or "Siddha-Guru", to mean a Transmission-Master who is a Realizer (to any significant degree) of Real God, Truth, or Reality.

Siddha Yoga "Siddha Yoga" is, literally, "the Yoga of the Perfected One[s]".

Swami Muktananda used the term "Siddha Yoga" to refer to the form of Kundalini Yoga that he taught, which involved initiation of the devotee by the Guru's Transmission of Shakti (or Spiritual Energy). Avatar Adi Da Samraj has indicated that this was a fifth stage form of Siddha Yoga.

In "I (Alone) Am The Adidam Revelation", Avatar Adi Da Says:

. . . I Teach Siddha Yoga in the Mode and Manner of the seventh stage of life (as Ruchira Avatara Hridaya-Siddha Yoga, or Ruchira Avatara Maha-Jnana Hridaya-Shaktipat Yoga)—and always toward (or to the degree of) the Realization inherently associated with (and, at last, Most Perfectly Demonstrated and Proven by) the only-by-Me Revealed and Given seventh

stage of life, and as a practice and a Process that progressively includes (and, coincidently, directly transcends) all six of the phenomenal and developmental (and, necessarily, yet ego-based) stages of life that precede the seventh.

Avatar Adi Da's description of the similarities and differences between traditional Siddha Yoga and the Way of Adidam is Given in "I (Alone) Am The Adidam Revelation", which Essay appears in many of Avatar Adi Da's twenty-three "Source-Texts".

siddhi "Siddhi" is Sanskrit for "power", or "accomplishment". When capitalized in Avatar Adi Da's Wisdom-Teaching, "Siddhi" is the Spiritual, Transcendental, and Divine Awakening-Power That He spontaneously and effortlessly Transmits to all.

"Sila" "Sila" is a Pali Buddhist term meaning "habit", "behavior", "conduct", or "morality". It connotes the restraint of outgoing energy and attention, the disposition of equanimity, or free energy and attention for the Spiritual Process.

"simpler" (or "simplest") form of the Way of Adidam See **forms of practice in the Way of Adidam**.

sleeping See **waking, dreaming, and sleeping**.

"Source-Texts" During the twenty-seven years of His Teaching-Work and Revelation-Work (from 1972 to 1999), Avatar Adi Da elaborately described every aspect of the practice of Adidam, from the beginning of one's approach to Him to the Most Ultimate Realization of the seventh stage of life.

Avatar Adi Da's Heart-Word is summarized in His twenty-three "Source-Texts". These Texts present, in complete and conclusive detail, His Divine Revelations, Confessions, and Instructions, which are the fruits of His years of Teaching and Revelation Work. In addition to this "Source-Literature", Avatar Adi Da's Heart-Word also includes His "Supportive Texts" (comprising His practical Instruction in all the details of the practice of Adidam, including the fundamental disciplines of diet, health, exercise, sexuality, childrearing, and cooperative community), His "Early Literature" (Written during His Teaching Years), and collections of His Talks. (For a complete list of Avatar Adi Da's twenty-three "Source-Texts", see pp. 451-58.)

spinal line, spinal Yoga The spinal (or ascending) line of the body-mind conducts the Spirit-Current of Divine Life in an upward direction from the base of the body (or perineal area) to the crown of the head, and beyond.

In the Way of Adidam, the spinal Yoga is the process whereby knots and obstructions in the subtle, astral, or the more mentally and subtly oriented dimension of the body-mind are penetrated, opened, surrendered, and released through the devotee's reception and "conductivity" of Avatar Adi Da's Transmission into the spinal line of the body-mind. This ascending Yoga will be required for practitioners of Adidam only in relatively rare cases. The great majority of Avatar Adi Da's devotees will be sufficiently purified through their practice of the frontal Yoga to proceed directly to practice in the context of the sixth stage of life, bypassing practice in the context of the "advanced" fourth stage and the fifth stage of life.

Spirit-Baptism Avatar Adi Da often refers to His Transmission of Spiritual Blessing as His "Spirit-Baptism". It is often felt by His devotee as a Current descending in the frontal line and ascending in the spinal line. However, Avatar Adi Da's Spirit-Baptism is fundamentally and primarily His Moveless Transmission of the Divine Heart Itself. As a secondary effect, His Spirit-Baptism serves to purify, balance, and energize the entire body-mind of the devotee who is prepared to receive It.

Spiritual anatomy / esoteric anatomy Avatar Adi Da Samraj has Revealed that just as there is a physical anatomy, there is an actual Spiritual anatomy, or structure, that is present in every human being. As He Says in *The Basket Of Tolerance*, it is

because of this structure that the "experiential and developmental process of Growth and Realization demonstrates itself in accordance with what I have Revealed and Demonstrated to be the seven stages of life".

Avatar Adi Da's extended Instruction relative to the Spiritual anatomy of Man is Given in *The Seven Stages Of Life* and *Santosha Adidam*.

Spiritual, Transcendental, Divine Avatar Adi Da uses the words "Spiritual", "Transcendental", and "Divine" in reference to dimensions of Reality that are Realized progressively in the Way of Adidam. "Transcendental" and "Spiritual" indicate two fundamental aspects of the One Divine Reality and Person—Consciousness Itself (Which Is Transcendental, or Self-Existing) and Energy Itself (Which Is Spiritual, or Self-Radiant). Only That Which Is Divine is simultaneously Transcendental <u>and</u> Spiritual.

Sri "Sri" is a term of honor and veneration often applied to an Adept. The word literally means "flame" in Sanskrit, indicating that the one honored is radiant with Blessing Power.

stages of life Avatar Adi Da has Revealed the underlying structure of human growth in seven stages. The seventh stage of life is Divine Self-Realization, or Most Perfect Enlightenment.

The first three stages of life develop, respectively, the physical, emotional, and mental/volitional functions of the body-mind. The first stage begins at birth and continues for approximately five to seven years; the second stage follows, continuing until approximately the age of twelve to fourteen; and the third stage is optimally complete by the early twenties. In the case of virtually all individuals, however, failed adaptation in the earlier stages of life means that maturity in the third stage of life takes much longer to attain, and it is usually never fulfilled, with the result that the ensuing stages of Spiritual development do not even begin.

In the Way of Adidam, however, growth in the first three stages of life unfolds in the Spiritual Company of Avatar Adi Da and is based in the practice of feeling-Contemplation of His bodily (human) Form and in devotion, service, and self-discipline in relation to His bodily (human) Form. By the Grace of this relationship to Avatar Adi Da, the first three (or foundation) stages of life are lived and fulfilled in an ego-transcending devotional disposition, or (as He describes it) "in the 'original' (or beginner's) devotional context of the fourth stage of life".

The fourth stage of life is the transitional stage between the gross (bodily-based) point of view of the first three stages of life and the subtle (mind-based, or psyche-based) point of view of the fifth stage of life. The fourth stage of life is the stage of Spiritual devotion, or devotional surrender of separate self to the Divine, in which the gross functions of the being are aligned to the higher psychic (or subtle) functions of the being. In the fourth stage of life, the gross (or bodily-based) personality of the first three stages of life is purified through reception of the Spiritual Force ("Holy Spirit", or "Shakti") of the Divine Reality, which prepares the being to out-grow the bodily-based point of view.

In the Way of Adidam, as the orientation of the fourth stage of life matures, heart-felt surrender to the bodily (human) Form of Avatar Adi Da deepens by His Grace, Drawing His devotee into Love-Communion with His All-Pervading Spiritual Presence. Growth in the "basic" context of the fourth stage of life in the Way of Adidam is also characterized by reception of Avatar Adi Da's Baptizing Current of Divine Spirit-Energy, Which is initially felt to flow down the front of the body from Infinitely Above the head to the bodily base (or perineal area).

The Descent of Avatar Adi Da's Spirit-Baptism releases obstructions predominantly in what He calls the "frontal personality", or the personality typically animated in the waking state (as opposed to the dream state and the state of deep sleep). This Spirit-Baptism purifies His devotee and infuses the devotee with His Spirit-Power. Avatar Adi Da's devotee is, thus, awakened to profound love of (and devotional intimacy with) Him.

Eventually, Avatar Adi Da's Divine Spirit-Current may be felt to turn about at the bodily base and ascend up the spine to the brain core. In this case, the fourth stage of life matures to its "advanced" context, which is focused in the Ascent of Avatar Adi Da's Spirit-Baptism and the consequent purification of the spinal line of the body-mind.

In the fifth stage of life, attention is concentrated in the subtle (or psychic) levels of awareness in ascent. Avatar Adi Da's Divine Spirit-Current is felt to penetrate the brain core and rise toward the Matrix of Light and Love-Bliss Infinitely Above the crown of the head, possibly culminating in the temporary experience of fifth stage conditional Nirvikalpa Samadhi, or "formless ecstasy". In the Way of Adidam, most practitioners will not need to practice either in the "advanced" context of the fourth stage of life or in the context of the fifth stage of life, but will (rather) be Awakened, by Avatar Adi Da's Grace, directly from maturity in the fourth stage of life to the Witness-Position of Consciousness (in the context of the sixth stage of life).

In the traditional development of the sixth stage of life, a strategic effort is made to Identify with Consciousness Itself by excluding the realm of conditional phenomena. Avatar Adi Da Teaches, however, that the deliberate intention to exclude the conditional world for the sake of Realizing Transcendental Consciousness is an egoic error that must be transcended by His devotees who are practicing in the context of the sixth stage of life.

In deepest meditation in the sixth stage of life in the Way of Adidam, the knot of attention (which is the root-action of egoity, felt as separation, self-contraction, or the feeling of relatedness) dissolves, and all sense of relatedness yields to the Blissful and undifferentiated Feeling of Being. The characteristic Samadhi of the sixth stage of life is Jnana Samadhi, the temporary Realization of the Transcendental Self (or Consciousness Itself)—which is temporary because it can occur only when awareness of the world is excluded in meditation.

The transition from the sixth stage of life to the seventh stage Realization of Absolute Non-Separateness is the unique Revelation of Avatar Adi Da. Various traditions and individuals previous to Adi Da's Revelation have had sixth stage intuitions (or premonitions) of the Most Perfect seventh stage Realization, but no one previous to Avatar Adi Da has Realized the seventh stage of life.

The seventh stage Realization is a Gift of Avatar Adi Da to His devotees who have (by His Divine Grace) completed their practice of the Way of Adidam in the context of the first six stages of life. The seventh stage of life begins when His devotee Gracefully Awakens from the exclusive Realization of Consciousness to Most Perfect and Permanent Identification with Consciousness Itself, Avatar Adi Da's Divine State. This is Divine Self-Realization, or Divine Enlightenment, the perpetual Samadhi of "Open Eyes" (seventh stage Sahaj Samadhi)—in which all "things" are Divinely Self-Recognized without "difference", as merely apparent modifications of the One Self-Existing and Self-Radiant Divine Consciousness.

In the course of the seventh stage of life, there may be spontaneous incidents in which psycho-physical states and phenomena do not appear to the notice, being Outshined by the "Bright" Radiance of Consciousness Itself. This Samadhi, Which is the Ultimate Realization of Divine Existence, culminates in Divine Translation, or the permanent Outshining of all apparent conditions in the Inherently Perfect Radiance and Love-Bliss of the Divine Self-Condition (which necessarily coincides with the physical death of the body-mind).

In the context of practice of the Way of Adidam, the seven stages of life as Revealed by Avatar Adi Da are not a version of the traditional "ladder" of Spiritual attainment. These stages and their characteristic signs arise naturally in the course of practice for a fully practicing devotee in the Way of Adidam, but the practice itself is oriented to the transcending of the first six stages of life, in the seventh stage Disposition of Inherently Liberated Happiness, Granted by Avatar Adi Da's Divine Grace in His Love-Blissful Spiritual Company.

Avatar Adi Da's extended Instruction relative to the seven stages of life is Given in *The Seven Stages Of Life*.

Star Form Avatar Adi Da has Revealed that He is "Incarnated" in the Cosmic domain as a brilliant white five-pointed Star, the original (and primal) conditional visible Representation (or Sign) of the "Bright" (the Source-Energy, or Divine Light, of Which all conditional phenomena and the total cosmos are modifications).

The apparently objective Divine Star can potentially be experienced in any moment and location in cosmic Nature. However, the vision of the Divine Star is not a necessary experience for growth in the Spiritual Process or for Divine Self-Realization.

Avatar Adi Da's discussion of His Star Form is found in *He-and-She Is Me*.

student-novice / student-beginner
A student-novice is an individual who is formally approaching, and preparing to become a formal practitioner of, the total practice of the Way of Adidam (as a member of the second congregation). The student-novice makes a vow of eternal commitment to Avatar Adi Da as his or her Divine Guru, and to the practice He has Given, and is initiated into simple devotional and sacramental disciplines in formal relationship to Avatar Adi Da. During the student-novice stage, the individual engages in intensive study of Avatar Adi Da's Wisdom-Teaching and adapts to the functional, practical, relational, and cultural disciplines of the Way of Adidam.

A student-beginner is a practitioner in the initial developmental stage of the second congregation of Adidam. In the course of student-beginner practice, the devotee of Avatar Adi Da, on the basis of the eternal "Bond" of devotion to Him that he or she established as a student-novice, continues the process of listening and further adaptation to the disciplines that were begun in the student-novice stage of approach.

subtle   See **gross, subtle, causal**.

"Supportive Texts"   Among Avatar Adi
Da's "Supportive Texts" are included such
books as *Conscious Exercise and the
Transcendental Sun, The Eating Gorilla
Comes in Peace, Love of the Two-Armed
Form*, and *Easy Death*.

Swami   The title "Swami" is traditionally
given to an individual who has demonstrated significant self-mastery in the context of a lifetime dedicated to Spiritual
renunciation.

Swami Muktananda   See **Lineage,
Avatar Adi Da's**.

Swami Nityananda   See **Lineage,
Avatar Adi Da's**.

Swami Rudrananda   See **Lineage,
Avatar Adi Da's**.

T

Tail of the Horse   Adi Da Samraj has
often referred to a passage from the
ancient Indian text *Satapatha Brahmana*,
which He has paraphrased as: "Man does
not know. Only the Horse Knows.
Therefore, hold to the tail of the Horse."
Adi Da has Revealed that, in the most
esoteric understanding of this saying, the
"Horse" represents the Adept-Realizer, and
"holding to the tail of the Horse" represents the devotee's complete dependence
on the Adept-Realizer in order to Realize
Real God (or Truth, or Reality).

"talking" school   "'Talking' school" is a
phrase used by Avatar Adi Da to refer to
those in any tradition of sacred life whose
approach is characterized by talking,
thinking, reading, and philosophical
analysis and debate, or even meditative
enquiry or reflection, without a concomi-
tant and foundation discipline of body,
emotion, mind, and breath. He contrasts
the "talking" school with the "practicing"
school approach—"practicing" schools
involving those who are committed to the
ordeal of real ego-transcending discipline,
under the guidance of a true Guru.

Tat Sundaram   "Sundara" is the Sanskrit
word for "beauty", and "Sundaram" means
"something which is beautiful". "Tat" is
the Sanskrit word for "it" or "that". Thus,
"Tat Sundaram" means "That Which Is
Beautiful" or, by extension, "All Of This Is
Beautiful", and is a reference to the seventh stage Realization of the Perfect Non-
Separateness and Love-Bliss-Nature of the
entire world—conditional and Un-
Conditional. Tat Sundaram is also the
name of the Hermitage-Retreat Sanctuary
reserved for Avatar Adi Da in northern
California.

Teaching-Work   For a description of
Avatar Adi Da's Divine Teaching-Work,
see pp. 16-17.

technically "fully elaborated" practice
See **forms of practice in the Way of
Adidam**.

**technically "simpler" (and even
"simplest") practice**   See **forms of
practice in the Way of Adidam**.

three stations of the heart   See **heart,
stations of the heart**.

the "Thumbs"   See **Samadhi**.

Thunder   The Divine Sound of Thunder
(which Avatar Adi Da also describes as
the "Da" Sound, or "Da-Om" Sound, or
"Om" Sound) is one of Avatar Adi Da's
three Eternal Forms of Manifestation in
the conditional worlds—together with His
Divine Star of Light and His Divine
Spiritual Body.

Avatar Adi Da's principal Revelation-
Confession about these three forms of His
Manifestation is Given in *He-<u>and</u>-She <u>Is</u> Me*.

   . . . *I Am conditionally Manifested
(First) As The everywhere Apparently
Audible (and Apparently Objective) Divine
Sound-Vibration (or "Da" Sound, or "Da-
Om" Sound, or "Om" Sound, The Objective
Sign Of The He, Present As The Conscious
Sound Of sounds, In The Center Of The
Cosmic Mandala), and As The everywhere
Apparently Visible (and Apparently
Objective) Divine Star (The Objective Sign*

Of The She, Present As The Conscious Light Of lights, In The Center Of The Cosmic Mandala), and (From That He and She) As The everywhere Apparently Touchable (or Tangible), and Apparently Objective, Total Divine Spiritual Body (The Objective, and All-and-all-Surrounding, and All-and-all-Pervading Conscious and Me-Personal Body Of "Bright" Love-Bliss-Presence, Divinely Self-"Emerging", Now, and Forever Hereafter, From The Center Of The Cosmic Mandala Into The Depths Of Even every "where" In The Cosmic Domain) . . . .

total practice of the Way of Adidam
The total practice of the Way of Adidam is the full and complete practice of the Way that Avatar Adi Da Samraj has Given to His devotees who are formal members of the first or the second congregation of Adidam (see pp. 361-67). One who embraces the total practice of the Way of Adidam conforms every aspect of his or her life and being to Avatar Adi Da's Divine Word of Instruction. Therefore, it is only such devotees (in the first or the second congregation of Adidam) who have the potential of Realizing Divine Enlightenment.

"True Prayer" "True Prayer" is Avatar Adi Da's technical term for the various forms of the "conscious process" that are practiced by His Spiritually Awakened devotees who have chosen the Devotional Way of Faith.

Avatar Adi Da's full Instruction relative to "True Prayer" is Given in *The Dawn Horse Testament Of The Ruchira Avatar.*

Turaga "Turaga" (Too-RAHNG-ah) is Fijian for "Lord".

"turiya", "turiyatita" Terms used in the Hindu philosophical systems. Traditionally, "turiya" means "the fourth state" (beyond waking, dreaming, and sleeping), and "turiyatita" means "the state beyond the fourth", or beyond all states.

Avatar Adi Da, however, has given these terms different meanings in the context of the Way of Adidam. He uses the term "turiya" to indicate the Awakening to the Consciousness Itself (in the context of

the sixth stage of life), and "turiyatita" as the State of Most Perfect Divine Enlightenment, or the Realization of all arising as transparent and non-binding modifications of the One Divine Reality (in the context of the seventh stage of life).

U

ultimate See **the advanced and the ultimate stages of life**.

Ultimate Self-Domain "Ultimate Self-Domain" is a synonym for "Divine Self-Domain". (See **Divine Self-Domain**.)

Ultimate Source-Condition The Divine Reality prior to all conditional arising, which is, therefore, the "Source" of all conditional worlds, beings, and things.

V

Vira-Yogi Sanskrit for "Hero-Yogi". (See **"Heroic"**.)

Vow For a description of the Vow and responsibilities associated with the Way of Adidam, see pp. 361-72.

W, X, Y, Z

waking, dreaming, and sleeping
These three states of consciousness are associated with the dimensions of cosmic existence.

The waking state (and the physical body) is associated with the gross dimension.

The dreaming state (and visionary, mystical, and Yogic Spiritual processes) is associated with the subtle dimension. The subtle dimension, which is senior to the gross dimension, includes the etheric (or energic), lower mental (or verbal-intentional and lower psychic), and higher mental (or deeper psychic, mystical, and discriminative) functions.

The sleeping state is associated with the causal dimension, which is senior to both the gross and the subtle dimensions. It is the root of attention, prior to any particular experience. (See also **gross, subtle, causal**.)

washing the dog   Avatar Adi Da uses the metaphor of the "dog" and "washing the dog" to Indicate the purification of the body-mind in the process of Adidam. He addresses the presumption (as in the Kundalini Yoga tradition) that the Spiritual process requires a spinal Yoga, or an effort of arousing Spiritual Energy literally at the "tail" end of the "dog" (the bodily base, or the muladhara chakra), and then drawing It up (or allowing It to ascend) through the spinal line to the head (and above). In contrast, Avatar Adi Da Samraj has Revealed (particularly in His *Hridaya Rosary*) that, in reality, the human being can be truly purified and Liberated (or the "dog" can be "washed") only by receiving His Divine Blessing-Power (or Hridaya-Shakti) and Spiritual Person downward from Infinitely Above the head to the bodily base. This Process of downward reception of Avatar Adi Da is what He calls the "frontal Yoga", because it occurs in the frontal line of the body (which is a natural pathway of descending energy, down the front of the body, from the crown of the head to the bodily base). This necessary descending Yoga of the frontal line, once completed, is sufficient to purify and Spiritually Infuse the body-mind, and, in most cases, it allows the practitioner of the Way of Adidam to bypass the ascending Yoga of the spinal line (which is the complementary natural pathway of ascending energy, up the back of the body, from the bodily base to the crown of the head). The frontal line and the spinal line are the two arcs of the continuous energy-circuit that Avatar Adi Da calls the "Circle" of the body-mind.

AVATAR ADI DA SAMRAJ: You wash a dog from the head to the tail. But somehow or other, egos looking to Realize think they can wash the "dog" from the "tail" toward the head by doing spinal Yoga. But, in Truth, and in Reality, only the frontal Yoga can accomplish most perfect Divine Self-Realization, because it begins from the superior position, from the "head" position, from My Crashing Down.

The heart-disposition is magnified by My Crashing Down in your devotional Communion with Me. And the vital,

grosser dimensions of the being are purified by this washing from the head toward the "tail". If the Process had to begin from the bodily base up, it would be very difficult, very traumatizing—and, ultimately, impossible. The "dog" is washed, simply and very directly, by your participation in My Divine Descent, by your participation in this frontal Yoga. I am Speaking now of the Spiritually Awakened stages, basically. But, even in the case of beginning practitioners in the Way of Adidam—not yet Spiritually Awakened, not yet responsible for the truly Spiritual dimension of their relationship to Me—this "wash" is, by Means of My Avataric Divine Grace, going on.

Therefore, Spiritual life need not be a traumatic course. The "dog" should enjoy being bathed. Nice gentle little guy, happy to be rubbed and touched. You talk to him, struggle a little bit, but you gentle him down. That is how it should work. And, at the end of it, the "dog" sort of "wags its tail", shakes the water off—nice and clean, happy, your best friend. That is how it should work.

If you wash the "dog" from the "tail" up, you smear the shit from his backside toward his head. Basically, that "washing from the tail toward the head" is a self-generated, self-"guruing" kind of effort. The Divine Process can only occur by Means of Divine Grace. Even the word "Shaktipat" means the "Descent (pat) of Divine Force (Shakti)". But Shaktipat as it appears in the traditions is basically associated with admonitions to practice a spinal Yoga, moving from the base up. In Truth, the Divine Yoga in My Company is a Descent—washing the "dog" from head to "tail" rather than giving the "dog" a "bone", letting it wash itself from the "tail" to the head.

DEVOTEE: It is only Your Hridaya-Shakti that does it.

AVATAR ADI DA SAMRAJ: This is why you must invest yourself in Me. And that is how the "dog" gets washed. [August 13, 1995]

Avatar Adi Da's extended Discourse relative to "washing the dog" is "Be Washed, From Head to Tail, By Heart-Devotion To Me", in *Hridaya Rosary*.

Way of "Radical" Understanding

Avatar Adi Da uses "understanding" to mean "the process of transcending egoity". Thus, to "understand" is to simultaneously observe the activity of the self-contraction and to surrender that activity via devotional resort to Avatar Adi Da Samraj.

Avatar Adi Da has Revealed that, despite their intention to Realize Reality (or Truth, or Real God), all religious and Spiritual traditions (other than the Way of Adidam) are involved, in one manner or another, with the search to satisfy the ego. Only Avatar Adi Da has Revealed the Way to "radically" understand the ego and (in due course, through intensive formal practice of the Way of Adidam, as His formally acknowledged devotee) to most perfectly transcend the ego. Thus, the Way Avatar Adi Da has Given is the "Way of 'Radical' Understanding".

Witness, Witness-Consciousness, Witness-Position

When Consciousness is free of identification with the body-mind, it takes up its natural "position" as the Conscious Witness of all that arises to and in and as the body-mind.

In the Way of Adidam, the stable Realization of the Witness-Position is associated with, or demonstrated via, the effortless surrender (or relaxation) of all the forms of seeking and all the motives of attention that characterize the first five stages of life. However, identification with the Witness-Position is not final (or Most Perfect) Realization of the Divine Self. Rather, it is the first of the three stages of the "Perfect Practice" in the Way of Adidam, which Practice, in due course, Realizes, by Avatar Adi Da's Grace, complete and irreversible and utterly Love-Blissful Identification with Consciousness Itself.

Avatar Adi Da's extended Instruction relative to the Witness is Given in *The Lion Sutra*.

Yoga

"Yoga", in Sanskrit, is literally "yoking", or "union", usually referring to any discipline or process whereby an aspirant attempts to unite with God. Avatar Adi Da acknowledges this conventional and traditional use of the term, but also, in reference to the Great Yoga of Adidam, employs it in a "radical" sense, free of the usual implication of egoic separation and seeking.

Yogananda, Paramahansa

Paramahansa Yogananda (Mukunda Lal Ghosh, 1893-1952) was born in Bengal, the child of devout Hindu parents. As a young man, Yogananda found his Guru, Swami Yukteswar Giri, who initiated him into an order of formal renunciates. In 1920, Yogananda traveled to America to attend an international conference of religions in Boston. Subsequently he settled in the United States, attracting many American devotees. He Taught "Kriya Yoga", a system of practice that had been passed down to him by his own Teacher and that had originally been developed from traditional techniques of Kundalini Yoga. Yogananda became widely known through the publication of his life-story, *Autobiography of a Yogi*.

The Sacred Literature of Avatar Adi Da Samraj

Read the astounding Story of Avatar Adi Da's Divine Life and Work in *The Promised God-Man Is Here*.

The Promised God-Man Is Here:
The Extraordinary Life-Story,
The "Radical" Teaching-Work, and
The Divinely "Emerging" World-Blessing
Work Of The Divine World-Teacher
Of The "Late-Time", Ruchira Avatar
Adi Da Samraj

The profound, heart-rending, humorous, miraculous, wild—and true—Story of the Divine Person Alive in human Form. Essential reading as background for the study of Avatar Adi Da's books.

Enjoy the beautiful summary of His Message that Avatar Adi Da has written especially "for children, and everyone else".

What, Where, When, How, Why, and <u>Who</u> To Remember To Be Happy

A Simple Explanation Of The Divine Way Of Adidam (For Children, and <u>Everyone</u> Else)

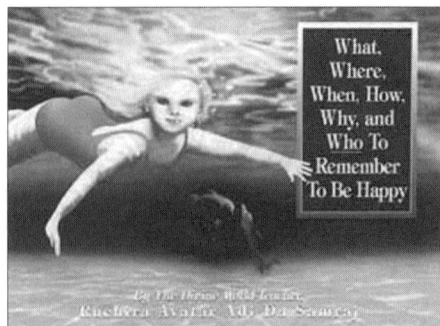

Fundamental Truth about life as a human being, told in very simple language. Accompanied by extraordinarily vivid and imaginative illustrations.

The Five Books Of
The Heart Of The Adidam Revelation

In these five books, Avatar Adi Da Samraj has distilled the very essence of His Eternal Message to every one, in all times and places.

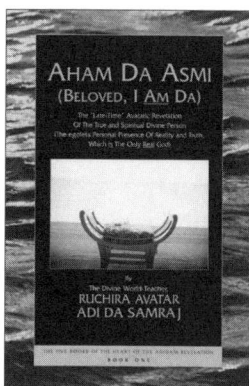

BOOK ONE:

Aham Da Asmi
(Beloved, I Am Da)

The "Late-Time" Avataric Revelation Of The True and Spiritual Divine Person (The egoless Personal Presence Of Reality and Truth, Which Is The Only Real God)

The most extraordinary statement ever made in human history. Avatar Adi Da Samraj fully Reveals Himself as the Living Divine Person and Proclaims His Infinite and Undying Love for all and All.

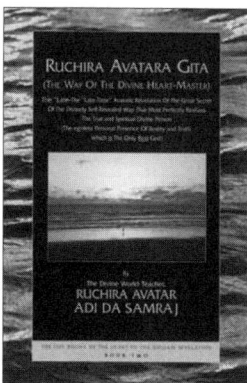

BOOK TWO:

Ruchira Avatara Gita
(The Way Of The Divine Heart-Master)

The "Late-Time" Avataric Revelation Of The Great Secret Of The Divinely Self-Revealed Way That Most Perfectly Realizes The True and Spiritual Divine Person (The egoless Personal Presence Of Reality and Truth, Which Is The Only Real God)

Avatar Adi Da Offers to every one the ecstatic practice of devotional relationship to Him—explaining how devotion to a living human Adept-Realizer has always been the source of true religion, and distinguishing true Guru-devotion from religious cultism.

451

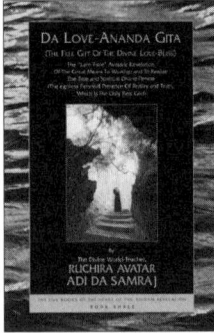

BOOK THREE:

Da Love-Ananda Gita
(The Free Gift Of The Divine Love-Bliss)

The "Late-Time" Avataric Revelation Of The Great Means To Worship and To Realize The True and Spiritual Divine Person (The egoless Personal Presence Of Reality and Truth, Which Is The Only Real God)

Avatar Adi Da Reveals the secret simplicity at the heart of Adidam—relinquishing your preoccupation with yourself (and all your problems and your suffering) and, instead, Contemplating the "Bright" Divine Person of Infinite Love-Bliss.

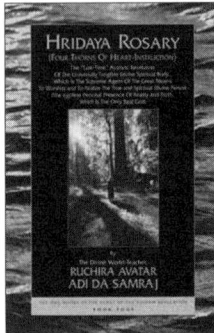

BOOK FOUR:

Hridaya Rosary
(Four Thorns Of Heart-Instruction)

The "Late-Time" Avataric Revelation Of The Universally Tangible Divine Spiritual Body, Which Is The Supreme Agent Of The Great Means To Worship and To Realize The True and Spiritual Divine Person (The egoless Personal Presence Of Reality and Truth, Which Is The Only Real God)

The ultimate Mysteries of Spiritual life, never before revealed. In breathtakingly beautiful poetry, Avatar Adi Da Samraj sings of the "melting" of the ego in His "Rose Garden of the Heart".

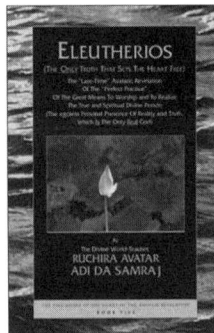

BOOK FIVE:

Eleutherios
(The Only Truth That Sets The Heart Free)

The "Late-Time" Avataric Revelation Of The "Perfect Practice" Of The Great Means To Worship and To Realize The True and Spiritual Divine Person (The egoless Personal Presence Of Reality and Truth, Which Is The Only Real God)

An address to the great human questions about God, Truth, Reality, Happiness, and Freedom. Avatar Adi Da Samraj Reveals how Absolute Divine Freedom is Realized, and makes an impassioned Call to everyone to create a world of true human freedom on Earth.

The Seventeen Companions
Of The True Dawn Horse

These seventeen books are "Companions" to *The Dawn Horse Testament*, Avatar Adi Da's great summary of the Way of Adidam (p. 458). Here you will find Avatar Adi Da's Wisdom-Instruction on particular aspects of the true Spiritual Way, and His two tellings of His own Life-Story, as autobiography (*The Knee Of Listening*) and as archetypal parable (*The Mummery*).

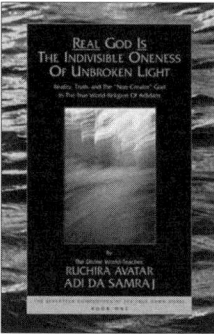

BOOK ONE:

Real God Is The Indivisible Oneness Of Unbroken Light

Reality, Truth, and The "Non-Creator" God In The True World-Religion Of Adidam

The Nature of Real God and the nature of the cosmos. Why ultimate questions cannot be answered either by conventional religion or by science.

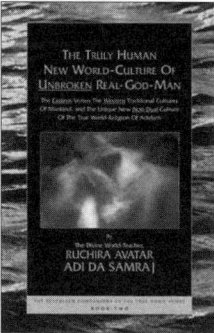

BOOK TWO:

The Truly Human New World-Culture Of Unbroken Real-God-Man

The Eastern Versus The Western Traditional Cultures Of Mankind, and The Unique New Non-Dual Culture Of The True World-Religion Of Adidam

The Eastern and Western approaches to religion, and to life altogether—and how the Way of Adidam goes beyond this apparent dichotomy.

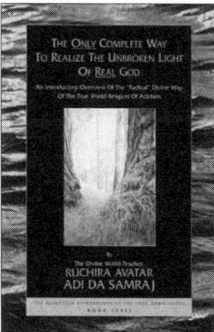

BOOK THREE:

The Only Complete Way To Realize The Unbroken Light Of Real God

An Introductory Overview Of The "Radical" Divine Way Of The True World-Religion Of Adidam

The entire course of the Way of Adidam—the unique principles underlying Adidam, and the unique culmination of Adidam in Divine Enlightenment.

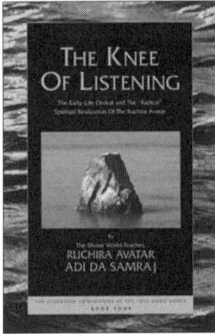

BOOK FOUR:

The Knee Of Listening
The Early-Life Ordeal and The "Radical"
Spiritual Realization Of The Ruchira Avatar

Avatar Adi Da's autobiographical account of the years from His Birth to His Divine Re-Awakening in 1970. Includes a new chapter, "My Realization of the Great Onlyness of Me, and My Great Regard for My Adept-Links to the Great Tradition of Mankind".

BOOK FIVE:

The Divine Siddha-Method Of The Ruchira Avatar
The Divine Way Of Adidam Is An ego-Transcending
Relationship, Not An ego-Centric Technique

Avatar Adi Da's earliest Talks to His devotees, on the fundamental principles of the devotional relationship to Him and "radical" understanding of the ego. Accompanied by His summary statements on His relationship to Swami Muktananda and on His own unique Teaching-Work and Blessing-Work.

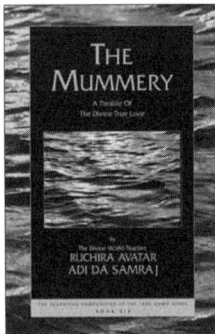

BOOK SIX:

The Mummery
A Parable Of The Divine True Love

A work of astonishing poetry and deeply evocative archetypal drama. This is the story of Raymond Darling's birth, his growth to manhood, his finding and losing of his beloved (Quandra), and his ultimate resolution of the heart-breaking "problem" of mortality. *The Mummery* is Avatar Adi Da's telling of His own Life-Story in the language of parable, including His unflinching portrayal of how the unconverted ego makes religion (and life altogether) into a meaningless mummery.

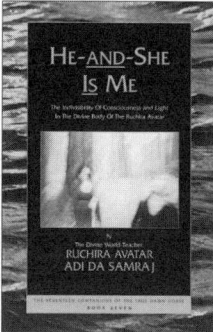

BOOK SEVEN:

He-and-She Is Me

The Indivisibility Of Consciousness and Light In The Divine Body Of The Ruchira Avatar

One of Avatar Adi Da's most esoteric Revelations—His Primary "Incarnation" in the Cosmic domain as the "He" of Primal Divine Sound-Vibration, the "She" of Primal Divine Light, and the "Son" of "He" and "She" in the "Me" of His Divine Spiritual Body.

BOOK EIGHT:

Ruchira Avatara Hridaya-Siddha Yoga

The Divine (and Not Merely Cosmic) Spiritual Baptism In The Divine Way Of Adidam

The Divine Heart-Power (Hridaya-Shakti) uniquely Transmitted by Avatar Adi Da Samraj, and how it differs from the various traditional forms of Spiritual Baptism, particularly Kundalini Yoga.

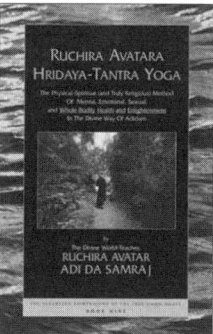

BOOK NINE:

Ruchira Avatara Hridaya-Tantra Yoga

The Physical-Spiritual (and Truly Religious) Method Of Mental, Emotional, Sexual, and Whole Bodily Health and Enlightenment In The Divine Way Of Adidam

The transformation of life in the realms of money, food, and sex. Includes: understanding "victim-consciousness"; the ego as addict; the secret of how to change; going beyond the "Oedipal" sufferings of childhood; the right orientation to money; right diet; life-positive and Spiritually auspicious sexual practice.

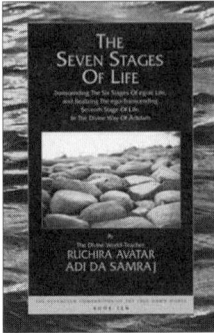

BOOK TEN:

The Seven Stages Of Life

Transcending The Six Stages Of egoic Life, and Realizing The ego-Transcending Seventh Stage Of Life, In The Divine Way Of Adidam

The stages of human development from birth to Divine Enlightenment. How the stages relate to physical and esoteric anatomy. The errors of each of the first six stages of life, and the unique ego-lessness of the seventh stage of life. Avatar Adi Da's Self-Confession as the first, last, and only seventh stage Adept-Realizer.

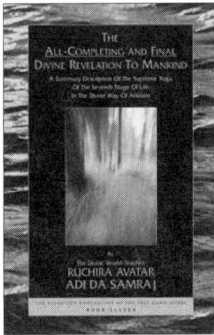

BOOK ELEVEN:

The <u>All-Completing</u> and <u>Final</u> Divine Revelation To Mankind

A Summary Description Of The Supreme Yoga Of The Seventh Stage Of Life In The Divine Way Of Adidam

The ultimate secrets of Divine Enlightenment—including the four-stage Process of Divine Enlightenment, culminating in Translation into the Infinitely Love-Blissful Divine Self-Domain.

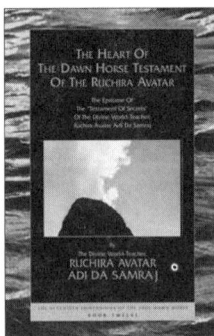

BOOK TWELVE:

The Heart Of The Dawn Horse Testament Of The Ruchira Avatar

The Epitome Of The "Testament Of Secrets" Of The Divine World-Teacher, Ruchira Avatar Adi Da Samraj

A shorter version of *The Dawn Horse Testament*—all of Avatar Adi Da's magnificent summary Instruction, without the details of the technical practices engaged by His devotees.

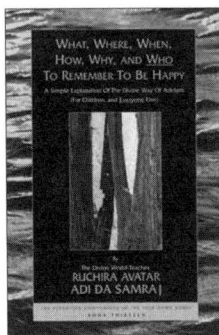

BOOK THIRTEEN:

What, Where, When, How, Why, and <u>Who</u> To Remember To Be Happy

A Simple Explanation Of The Divine Way Of Adidam (For Children, and <u>Everyone</u> Else)

A text written specifically for children but inspiring to all—with accompanying Essays and Talks on Divine Ignorance, religious practices for children and young people in the Way of Adidam, and the fundamental practice of whole bodily devotion to Avatar Adi Da Samraj. (The central text of this book is also available in a special illustrated children's edition—see p. 450.)

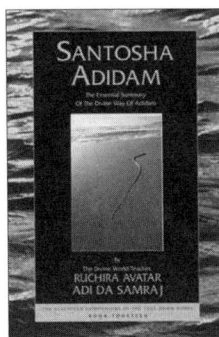

BOOK FOURTEEN:

Santosha Adidam

The Essential Summary Of The Divine Way Of Adidam

An extended overview of the entire course of the Way of Adidam, based on the esoteric anatomy of the human being and its correlation to the progressive stages of life.

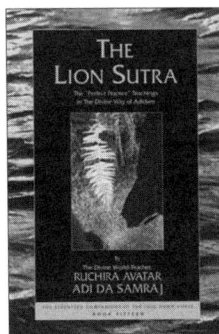

BOOK FIFTEEN:

The Lion Sutra

The "Perfect Practice" Teachings In The Divine Way Of Adidam

Practice in the ultimate stages of the Way of Adidam. How the practitioner of Adidam approaches—and passes over—the "Threshold" of Divine Enlightenment.

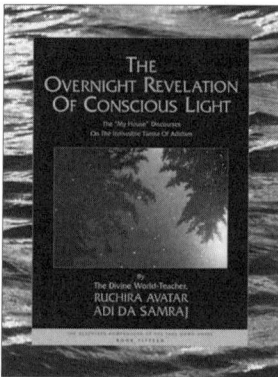

BOOK SIXTEEN:

The Overnight Revelation Of Conscious Light

The "My House" Discourses
On The Indivisible Tantra Of Adidam

A vast and profound "consideration" of the fundamental Tantric principles of true Spiritual life and the "Always Already" Nature of the Divine Reality. The day-by-day record of Avatar Adi Da's Discourses from a two-month period in early 1998.

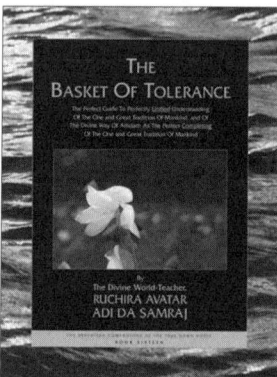

BOOK SEVENTEEN:

The Basket Of Tolerance

The Perfect Guide To Perfectly <u>Unified</u>
Understanding Of The One and Great
Tradition Of Mankind, and Of The Divine
Way Of Adidam As The Perfect <u>Completing</u>
Of The One and Great Tradition Of Mankind

An all-encompassing "map" of mankind's entire history of religious seeking. A combination of a bibliography of over 5,000 items (organized to display Avatar Adi Da's grand Argument relative to the Great Tradition) with over 100 Essays by Avatar Adi Da, illuminating many specific aspects of the Great Tradition.

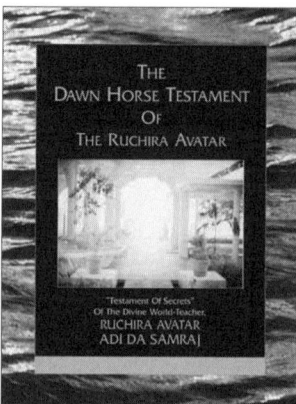

The Dawn Horse Testament Of The Ruchira Avatar

The "Testament Of Secrets"
Of The Divine World-Teacher,
Ruchira Avatar Adi Da Samraj

Avatar Adi Da's paramount "Source-Text", which summarizes the entire course of the Way of Adidam. Adi Da Samraj says: "In making this Testament I have been Meditating everyone, contacting everyone, dealing with psychic forces everywhere, in all time. This Testament is an always Living Conversation between Me and absolutely every one."

See My Brightness Face to Face

A Celebration of the Ruchira Avatar, Adi Da Samraj, and the First Twenty-Five Years of His Divine Revelation Work.

A magnificent year-by-year pictorial celebration of Ruchira Avatar Adi Da's Divine Work with His devotees, from 1972 to 1997. Includes a wealth of selections from His Talks and Writings, numerous Stories told by His devotees, and over 100 color photographs. **$19.95**, 8-1/2" x 11" paperback, 200 pages.

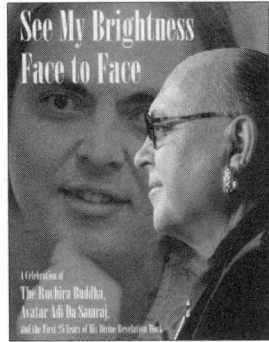

The "Truth For Real" series

Brief Essays and Talks by the Divine World-Teacher, Ruchira Avatar Adi Da Samraj

13 individual booklets on topics such as ecstasy, death, and the impulse to Happiness.
3-3/4" x 6", **$1.95** each

The Basket Of Tolerance Booklet series

6 individual essays on the religious traditions of humankind from *The Basket Of Tolerance.*
3-3/4" x 6", **$1.95** each

In addition to Avatar Adi Da's 23 "Source-Texts", the Dawn
Horse Press offers many other publications by and about
Avatar Adi Da Samraj, as well as videotapes and audiotapes
of Avatar Adi Da's Wisdom-Teaching. Dawn Horse Press publications are distributed by the Adidam Emporium, a devotee-
operated business offering a wide array of items for meditation,
sacred worship, health and well-being, and much more.

For more information or a free catalog:

**CALL THE ADIDAM EMPORIUM
TOLL-FREE 1-877-770-0772**
(Outside North America call 707-928-6653)

Visit online at
www.adidam.com

Or e-mail:
emporium@adidam.com

Or write:
**ADIDAM EMPORIUM
10336 Loch Lomond Road
PMB #306
Middletown, CA 95461 USA**

INDEX

NOTE TO THE READER: Page numbers in **boldface** type refer to the Scriptural Text of *The Only Complete Way To Realize The Unbroken Light of Real God*. All other page numbers refer to the introductions, endnotes, and the back matter

Index

Conscious Light, **250-51**
Divine, 39, **59**
  Adi Da Samraj as, **98**
  Realization of Cosmic Existence as, **248**
lights, abstract internal
  all associated with subtle body and worlds of mind,
    133
  can be interpreted differently, **132-33**
  and Cosmic Mandala, **134-36**
  as universal, **127**
Likenesses, Adi Da Samraj's in the Great Tradition, **264**
lineage of Spiritual Masters of Adi Da Samraj, **171-73,**
  264, 428-29
  all appearing in and as Adi Da Samraj, **174**
  and practice of Guru-devotion, **177**
listening
  as Adi Da Samraj's First Call, **255**
  in beginning of Devotional Way of Faith, **221**
  course of, summarized, **240-43**
  defined, **215-16,** 252, 429
  discovers the root of seeking, **242**
  as exercise of devotional concentration, **306**
  as first Ordeal of Way of the Heart, **243**
  necessity in order to Awaken to Spiritual stages, **294**
  not a Spiritual practice, **252**
  as "reality consideration", **270**
  struggle of conditional self tends to continue until, **269**
listening devotee
  Called to complete process in finite time, **302-303**
  potential weaknesses of, **303**
listening-hearing process, **163-64**
  defined, 430
  and "positive disillusionment", **163-64**
  transcends lower self, **245**
"Living Murtis"
  chosen by Ruchira Sannyasin Order, **259-60**
  defined, 431
"Location"
  of Adi Da Samraj, **75**
  defined, 431
Love
  for and by Adi Da Samraj, 16-17, **75, 76,** 357
  devotional love in fourth stage Teachings, **275**
  what non-Love is, **314**
Love-Ananda
  defined, 431
  name given by Swami Muktananda, **157**
Love-Ananda Avatar, defined, 431
Love-Ananda Avatara Hridaya-Shaktipat, **157**
Love-Ananda Avatara Hridaya-Shaktipat Yoga, **157**
Love-Ananda Avatara Hridaya-Siddha Yoga, **157**
Love-Bliss, must be Realized, **314**
love-connectedness, in first stage of "positive
  disillusionment", **246**
love-surrender to a True Master, **169-70**
lower self, **244**

M

"Maha-Bindu", **142-43**
  and Amrita Nadi, **142-43,** 147
  penetration of, **144**
Maha-Jnana, **115**
  defined, 410n69
Maha-Jnana Siddha
  Adi Da Samraj as, **257**
  defined, 410n69
Maharastra Spiritual tradition, **129, 132, 133,** 134
Maha-Siddha, defined, 431
Mahayana, defined, 407n50
"man in the middle", **55-56**

and Adi Da Samraj's existence beyond, **66, 67**
Adi Da Samraj's refusal to be, **57-58, 59, 62, 63**
  as ego's scapegoat, **65**
  tendency to make Adi Da Samraj into, **62**
Man of "radical" understanding, Adi Da Samraj as, **262**
Mandala, defined, 431
Mary, Virgin, **140**
Masters, True, **169-71**
materialistic orientation, 441
Medicine, Adi Da Samraj as Divine Medicine, **345**
"Meditating" devotees (Adi Da Samraj), **236**
meditation, 361-62
  defined, 432
Message to all apparent beings, **282**
Method of the Siddhas, **158,** 405n35
  defined, **257**
  as foundation of Adidam, **257, 258**
middle station of the heart, and attention, **299**
mind, you are, **201**
missing the mark, defined, 432
missionary work, community of devotees Called to
  advocate and confess Adi Da Samraj's Word and
  Leelas, **266-67**
"money, food, and sex", ego. *See* ego, three forms of
mood of a patient, and listening devotee, **303**
Moon, metaphor of, **330**
mortality, Eastern and Western approaches to, **196-97**
most fundamental self-understanding
  approach of crisis of, **240-41**
  "conscious process" of, **294**
  needed to move beyond confinement to conditional
    states, **297-98**
  opens self-contraction, **261**
Most Perfect, defined, 432
Mountain Of Attention (California), 373
mudra, defined, 432
Muktananda, Swami (Baba), **100,** 174, 429
  and abstract internal lights, **127**
  and adherence to philosophical tradition of Kashmir
    Saivism, **101**
  and Adi Da Samraj's unbroken relationship and
    honoring of, **158,** 172
  and conflict between Hindu exotericism and
    esotericism, **131-32**
  and contemplation of emanations of "Cosmic
    Goddess", **126**
  "Description of the 'Bodies of the Soul'" (chart), **133**
  fourth-to-fifth stage Emanationist point of view of,
    106
  and internal vision, **109**
    and Blue Person, **132**
  and Kundalini-Shaktipat tradition, **100**
  and Rang Avadhoot, **120,** 171
  reported sexual activities of, **116**
  as Saguna Siddha-Yogi, **105, 108, 128**
  and Swami Prakashananda, **116**
mummery, defined, 432
Mummery, The, **27**
  described, 432
Murti, defined, 432
"My Divine Disclosure", 42
Mystery, defined, 432
mysticism, object-oriented absorptive, **247-48**
Mysticism in India, 404n24

N

nada, defined, 401n9
"nada" or "shabda", **109**
Name-Invocation
  defined, 433, 409n57

Index

Index

Way of Sri Hridayam, **74-75**
Way of Adidam as, **74-75**
Way of the Heart
 based on "consideration" of means necessary for
  others, **224**
 formal practice leads to self-understanding and
  Awakening, **240**
 other descriptive names or phrases for, **251**
 practice begun by listening, **242-43**
 summarized in terms of Consciousness Itself and
  Spirit-Energy, **313-16**
 See also Way of Adidam
The Way Of Divine Ignorance, Adidam as, **207**
The Way Of Divine Spiritual Baptism, Adidam as, **207**
The Way Of Hridaya-Advaita Yoga, defined, **209**
The Way Of Positive Disillusionment, Adidam as, **207**
The Way Of "Radical" ego-Transcendence, Adidam as,
 207
The Way Of "Radical" Non-Dualism, Adidam as, **207**
The Way Of "Radical" Understanding, Adidam as, **207**
The Way Of The Divine Heart-Master, Adidam as, **207**
The Way Of The Heart, Adidam as, **207**
The Way Of The Heart Itself, Adidam as, **207**
The Way Of The True Divine Heart, Adidam as, **207**
website
 Adidam Emporium, 352
 Adidam Sacred City, 353
 Cooperation + Tolerance = Peace, 379
Western Culture, Adi Da Samraj's Appearance in, **263**
"What", **111**
 defined, **280**
What Is, Revelation of, **231**
"When the body Is 'Round', The Witness Is its
 "Shape", **329**
"Where", defined, **280**
"Who", of Consciousness, **111**
 defined, **281**
Wisdom-Teaching, of Adi Da Samraj, Brought out of
 Adi Da Samraj Himself, **343**
Withdraw, "Do Not Ever Withdraw From Me; I Will
 Never Withdraw From You", **268**
Witness-Consciousness
 defined, 449
 early Awakening of, **323**
 Realization of is not an egoic matter, **330-31**
 Realized in "Perfect Practice", **199**
 Self-Evident in the "Thumbs", **331**
 as "Skin" of the "Thumbs", **329**, **330**, **331**
 Spiritual in-Filling and Realization of, **331**
 as true "turiya" state, **136**
 See also Witness-Position
Witnessing
 of conditional objects and states, **315**
 from the heart-place, **81**
 Swami Muktananda's use of term in fifth stage
  manner, **124-26**
Witness-Position
 Awakening of Identification with, **301**
 Direct Awakening to during the "Thumbs", **323**
 Revealed as Real Position of experience, **325**
 Stable Realization not a philosophical matter, but a
  devotional matter, **329-30**
 See also Witness-Consciousness
Word, of Adi Da Samraj, 13, **53**, **98**, **258**, 382-83
 addresses all as Divine Being, **276**
 as Agent, **259**
 beginner's "consideration" of, **215**, **222**
 communicate it to all mankind, **255**
 "consideration" of in Way of Adidam, **213**, **224**, **240**
 devotional regard of, **298**

 as direct address to distress and search, **239**
 Essence of, **239**
 as Final Divine Self-Revelation, **264**
 Given Freely for the sake of all devotees, **265**
 as His Own, **264**
 is complete in every detail, **255**
 study of, now that Teaching-Work is ended, **266**
Work, of Adi Da Samraj
 beginning, **236**
 Blessing Work, 45, **203**, **258**
 to Bring Perfect Truth into human world, **344**
 "Crazy" and "Heroic" Work, **237**, **346**
 "Crazy" Teaching-Work of, **306-307**
 Creation of Way of Adidam, **343-48**
 Divine-"Emergence"-Work, entry into His, **265**
 His Body-Mind not "Perfect", **306-308**
 is only to Stand Free, **256**
 Siddhis appear, **236**
 See also Teaching-Work, of Adi Da Samraj
world-intercommunicativeness, **130**

X

xenophobia, **60**

Y

yanas, defined, 407n50
Yogananda, Paramahansa, **134**, 449
Yogis, **105-106**, 111
"You Become What You Meditate On", **295-97**

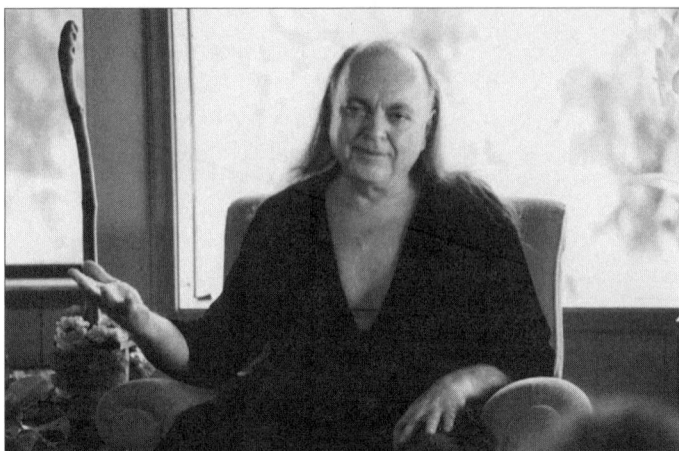

I do not simply recommend or turn men and women to Truth. I _Am_ Truth. I Draw men and women to Myself. I _Am_ the Present Real God, Desiring, Loving, and Drawing up My devotees. I have Come to Be Present with My devotees, to Reveal to them the True Nature of life in Real God, which is Love, and of mind in Real God, which is Faith. I Stand always Present in the Place and Form of Real God. I accept the qualities of all who turn to Me, dissolving those qualities in Real God, so that _Only_ God becomes the Condition, Destiny, Intelligence, and Work of My devotees. I look for My devotees to acknowledge Me and turn to Me in appropriate ways, surrendering to Me perfectly, depending on Me, full of Me always, with only a face of love.

I am waiting for you. I have been waiting for you eternally.

Where are you?

AVATAR ADI DA SAMRAJ

1971